The P.E.O. Founders' Scrapbook

by
Sharon S. Atkins

This photo of the Old Main Building on the campus of Iowa Wesleyan College comes from the Historic American Buildings Survey (HABS), Historic American engineering Record (HAER) or Historic American Landscapes Survey (HALS). These programs of the National Park Service established for the purpose of documenting historic places. Records consist of measured drawings, archival photographs, and written reports.

The P.E.O. Founders' Scrapbook

by
Sharon S. Atkins

Acknowledgements

In addition to the support received from P.E.O. Chapter FH, Prescott Valley, Arizona, this book could not have been put together without the generous contributions of:

Robin Woolson Abrams, Santa Clarita, California

Kae Lynn Durham Caston, P.E.O. Chapter EB, Farmington, Minnesota

Kathy Lee Durham Cobb, P.E.O. Chapter C, Ely, Nevada

Karen Grootemaat Cromey, Tucson, Arizona

Karon R. Durham Dykstra, P.E.O. Chapter ND, Pella, Iowa

Mary Babb Emory, Milwaukee, Wisconsin

Phyllis Nolte Grootemaat, Overland Park, Kansas

Nikki Henderson, Past State President, Arizona P.E.O. and Past President, Chapter FH Arizona, Prescott Valley, Arizona

Evan Jones, Web Master www.scoopsjones.us , Bakersfield, California

Sue Kissel, Board Member, Northern Arizona Genealogical Society, Prescott, Arizona

Lucas County Genealogy Society, Lucas County Iowa

Nancy K. Monk, Greendale, Wisconsin

Joyce Perkins, Director of Communications, P.E.O. International, Des Moines, Iowa

Ellie Babb Pollock, Milwaukee, Wisconsin

Hugh Stafford, President, Tri State Companies, Bettendorf, Iowa and Board of Trustees Iowa Wesleyan College, Mount Pleasant, Iowa

Michelle J. Volk, P.E.O. Chapter EB (Farmington, Minnesota), Lakeville, Minnesota

Fran Waddell, P.E.O. Chapter O, Montana, Helena, Montana

Linda Wheeler, P.E.O. Chapter FH, Prescott Valley, Arizona

John Woolson, Clarinda, Iowa

This book is dedicated with love to
my mother,
Virginia Howland Corwith Staehle Strachan,
Arizona P.E.O. Chapter AQ

Table of Contents

Introduction

Early in 2013, I set out on a journey to understand who were the seven women who founded the P.E.O. Sisterhood? What were the circumstances that brought them together? What did they do with their lives before and after they built the foundation of P.E.O. at such a youthful age? What impact did their lives have beyond the founding of P.E.O.?

To tell the story of the founders of the P.E.O. Sisterhood in a different way and from a different perspective, I decided to research these seven women through finding ephemera associated with them or their families.

For those not familiar with the term "ephemera," it is generally described as an article of memorabilia such as a graduation program, a theater ticket, a newspaper story, a speech, a census record or a photograph; something which is typically designed for short time usage. Locating ephemera is a tactic used by genealogists to help tell the story of an ancestor's life.

This research has been an amazing adventure where I've been able to find and speak with several descendants of these women. To aid my quest, these descendants were gracious enough to share family stories, photos, personal stories and knowledge with me.

What I found out was these seven women were distinctively different from each other, but they found common ground with the desire for a sisterhood. Very representative of how the P.E.O. Sisterhood is today

Of the seven founders, two grew up in homes with fathers who were physicians, Alice Bird and Suela Pearson; and two had fathers who were Methodist clergymen, Hattie Briggs and Ella Stewart. The other three, Mary Allen, Alice Coffin and Franc Roads grew up in homes where over their life spans their fathers participated in a variety of businesses.

Each of the seven P.E.O. founders had ties to Methodism and all were active Methodists when they entered Iowa Wesleyan. Not only were Rev. Elias Briggs and Rev. Isaac Stewart Methodist clergy, but one founder, Mary Allen, married a Methodist clergyman, Rev. Charles Stafford.

The publication "P.E.O. A Society of Our Own, Methodist History," reflects the idea that "Methodists were integrally involved in the promotion of women's higher education during the 1800's. In the denomination's view, the cause of women's education was intertwined with Methodism's evangelistic and social emphases."

When these women entered Iowa Wesleyan University the school was recognized and supported by the Methodist. The emphasis on higher education was especially prominent in the Midwest, which was still considered the frontier. At that time in history, the number of Methodist-related colleges was second only to those supported or affiliated with the Presbyterians.

Mount Pleasant, Iowa, home to Iowa Wesleyan, was also the town where all seven women lived at the time P.E.O. was founded. It provided a perfect local for a college such as Iowa Wesleyan, as it was a pioneer community that followed the spirit of the times by attempting the founding of an academy, and even a college. Mount Pleasant promoted itself as the ideal location for schools, churches and homes of cultured people.

Importantly, three of the founders had fathers, and one a future father-in-law, deeply involved with the university and its establishment. Wellington Bird, Elias L. Briggs and Isaac Stewart all played active roles in the nurturing and formation of Iowa Wesleyan University; which was first known as Mount Pleasant Literary Institute, later changed to Mount Pleasant Collegiate Institute and afterward became known as Iowa Wesleyan University by the time these seven women were students.

Iowa Wesleyan was initially founded in 1842, a few years before any of the founders were born. It also became the first liberal arts college west of the Mississippi to grant a college degree to a woman, Lucy Killpatrick, just six years prior to their entrance into the university. It's noteworthy that Rev. Charles Elliott, Franc Roads future father-in-law, was President of Iowa Wesleyan University when Lucy graduated.

Interestingly, Iowa Wesleyan survived as a college at a time when 81% of chartered colleges across 16 states had failed to thrive. The success of Iowa Wesleyan could be partially attributed to Mount Pleasant being a pioneer community which promoted the idea that the privilege of higher education was seen as an opportunity for the community. In 1841, just prior to the founding of the Institute / University, Mount Pleasant had a population of 300 people; by 1860, just prior to the Civil War, the population reached 3,500 citizens.

Mary Allen, Alice Bird, Hattie Briggs, Alice Coffin and Franc Roads, all whom started at Iowa Wesleyan in 1865, were part of the first post-Civil War class referred to as "The Lifebloods." During those years, campus Literary Societies functioned as the primary means of social interaction. One such Literary Society, the Ruthean Society, was an active part of each the founder's lives long before P.E.O came into being.

Three Literary Societies existed on campus when the founders were students at the university: two for men and one for women. Competition between the societies was very prevalent. Literary Societies are often referred to as "precursors" to sororities and fraternities, and were a common feature of colleges. The societies would meet weekly to discuss, or debate, to read essays and utilize orations to develop thoughts and address topics of the day.

What this all points out is that these women knew each other from multiple facets of their lives; religious, community, school and literary societies. In this light, the formation of P.E.O. appears to have been a natural step for them and merely an "official" recognition of the fact that these women were "sisters" long before P.E.O. was formed.

Most importantly, it can further be reasoned that it was specifically the environment and pioneer spirit of Iowa Wesleyan University which nurtured the opportunity for birth of the P.E.O. Sisterhood.

As we follow the seven founders after college life, we find that Mary Allen's life, and that of her descendants, remained very much centered around her husband's ministry and Iowa Wesleyan; Alice Bird's life was devoted to fulfilling her belief that her most important job was to be a mother and wife who protected family and home; Hattie Briggs married a Civil War veteran and gave birth to a son whose life became one of military service; Alice Coffin, whose mother died when she was nine years old, never married but went on to devote her life after college to helping to raise children through her career in teaching; Suela Pearson, raised to be a prominent socialite and ever the social butterfly, ended her life divorced, caring for her own mother and later being cared for by her daughter, Rose; Franc Roads, a women who believed in the woman's suffrage movement, spent a portion of her life being the primary source of financial support for her family in the aftermath of the economic panic of 1893; and Ella Stewart, the only one not to complete her college studies, was able to become a teacher for eight years until her health declined.

To help set the stage to tell their stories let's delve into their lives, by first placing them in the historical context of their time and place. All seven lived between the years of 1848 and 1927. What happened around them during those years?

Iowa became a state in 1846, just two years before the first of the founders was born, and 23 years before the founding of P.E.O. Early in their lives, and by the time most of them were 10 years old, the California Gold Rush had occurred between the years of 1848-1855, and in 1859, as previously mentioned, Lucy Kilpatrick was the first woman to graduate from Iowa Wesleyan; just six years before they enrolled.

When they were between the ages of 9 and 13, on the national scene, the Civil War was fought between 1861 and 1865. It was the end of the Civil War that brought many men to Iowa Wesleyan, with the promise of a free education for veteran soldiers. Abraham Lincoln was assassinated in April of 1865 – the same year 5 of these 7 young women started college. This was how they lived their teen-aged years. Remember, they ranged in age from 14 to 17 when they started at Iowa Wesleyan, the first liberal arts college west of the Mississippi River to grant a college degree to women.

When they were close to being 20 years old, in 1868, a year before the founding of P.E.O., Susan B. Anthony published a women's rights journal "The Revolution." In June of 1868, the first men's fraternal organization began at Iowa Wesleyan and by December of that same year, the sorority, I.C. Sorosis was organized. So, by January 1869, a month later, the idea of a sisterhood was much in "vogue." While 5 of the 7 graduated from Iowa Wesleyan in June of 1869, elsewhere in Mount Pleasant, Iowa people were preparing for the National Almanac sponsored solar eclipse exposition that was to be held in Mount Pleasant during August that year.

Six months after that graduation, in December of 1869, Wyoming became the first state to grant women the right to vote. Over the next 28 years, between 1869 and 1897, seven other states followed suit. However, between 1897 & 1910 no US state suffrage referendum was successful.

Meanwhile, seven years after these young women graduated, in 1876, Edison was granted a patent for the telephone and in 1877 for the phonograph. In 1881, the French began to dig the Panama Canal, and in 1882 the electric light was invented. The P.E.O. founders were then between 25 and 35 years old.

While these women were between 50 and 70 years of age, the youngest US President, Teddy Roosevelt (who had been governor of New York) was elected in 1901. Wright brothers Kitty Hawk flight was 1903 and in 1904, the US takes on the challenge of the Panama Canal. By 1908, Henry Ford introduces the Model T and from 1914 to 1918 America was submerged in World War I.

Four of them were alive in 1919 to see Iowa become the 10th state to ratify the 19th Amendment to the US Constitution granting women the right to vote. And, they lived to see the Amendment become reality in 1920. This was the world they lived in.

But, what else did they do with their lives? And, what are their personal connections to history?

Taking them one by one, alphabetically, we trace each founder and their descendants through the ephemera they left behind to discover the impact of their pioneering spirit obtained from Iowa Wesleyan, as well as from their foresight in the formation of the P.E.O. Sisterhood.

Historical Background Sources
for Introduction

1. Fran Becque, "The Role of Religion in P.E.O." The P.E.O. Record (May/June 2009).

2. Haselmayer, Louis A. A Sesquicentennial History of Iowa Wesleyan College (1842-1992). Mt. Pleasant, IA: Iowa Wesleyan College, 1992.

3. Kennedy, Charles J. History and Alumni Record of Iowa Wesleyan College 1842-1942. Mt. Pleasant, IA: Iowa Wesleyan College, 1942.

4. Portrait and Biographical Album of Henry County, Iowa. Chicago: Acme Publishing Company, 1888.

5. Moudry, Susan Lyn. "'A Society of Our Own': Methodists, Coeducation and the Founding of P.E.O." Methodist History, 52:1 (October 2013): 33-42.

6. Reeves, Winona Evans. The Story of P.E.O.: Supreme Chapter of P.E.O., 1923.

Chapter 1: Mary Jane Allen

Mary Jane Allen

In December 1848, Mary Jane became the second of five children born to Reuben and Evelyn Caulk Allen. Over the years, Mary's father, Reuben, initially from Ohio, listed his occupation as cabinet making, farming and real estate. Her mother, Evelyn, moved to Iowa from North Carolina with her father, Robert Caulk, sometime between 1830 and 1840.

Mary entered Iowa Wesleyan at the age of 16, in 1865 and help founded P.E.O. at the age of 20. She graduated from Iowa Wesleyan with her A.B. degree in June of 1869.

Her older sister, Cassie Allen, has often been thought to be the first P.E.O. initiated outside of the seven founders.

On the 4th of July in 1871, at the age of 22, Mary married Charles Lewis Stafford, a short time after he had been ordained as a Methodist minister. Their life, and 56 years of marriage, was centered on sharing that ministry. She was said to be a gracious hostess, much like her mother.

Her honorary A.M. degree from Iowa Wesleyan was awarded in June of 1872 when she was 23. And, three months later, on 21 September 1872, her first child, Clarence Allen Stafford was born.

The Stafford's would later have three more children when Mary was between the ages of 29 and 40; a daughter, Eva May (1878), two sons, Charles Ralph (1881) and William Reuben (1889). Sadly, the Stafford's daughter, Eva lived only until she was four years old.

By the time their fourth child was born, Mary's husband, Charles, was Presiding Elder of the Muscatine District of the Methodist Episcopal Church.

Through their married life, Mary and Charles appear to have moved frequently living in a number of locations. They are found living in Keokuk, Iowa with Clarence and Eva in June of 1880, in Muscatine, Iowa in June of 1900, in Grinnell Township, Iowa in May of 1910, back in Muscatine by January 1920 and in that same home in 1925.

From 1891 to 1899, when Mary is between the ages of 43 and 51, her husband Charles, also an Iowa Wesleyan alumnus, was President of Iowa Wesleyan. During his years as President he made it his mission to continue the building of the University. He raised funds, during the difficult economy of 1892-1893, required to build the Chapel and Science Hall. Additionally, he obtained the funds for the construction of Elizabeth Hershey Hall. Dr. Stafford was regarded as an "indomitable worker, a veritable toiler."

Since the days of Mary and Charles the Stafford family has been stanch supporters of the Iowa Wesleyan community. Today, their great-grandson, Hugh Allen Stafford, serves as a Trustee of Iowa Wesleyan.

It was upon her return to Mt. Pleasant in 1891 that Mary became active once more in the sisterhood. Mary lived to participate in the laying of the cornerstone for the P.E.O. Memorial Library at Iowa Wesleyan in 1927. At that ceremony, she paid homage to P.E.O's hometown, "It was here in beautiful Mt. Pleasant that the associations and loving friendship of the seven ripened into our beloved Sisterhood." Her death came just two and a half months later.

Of Mary and Charles's four children, Eva died young and William doesn't appear to have married; Clarence and Charles each married, but the only descendants are from their first son, Clarence.

Clarence married Mary Elizabeth DeLescaille in 1908. Together they had two sons (grandsons to Mary), Charles Joseph (1909-1982) and William Reuben (1914-1999). Clarence began a career with a manufacturer of corrugated and wood boxes, Cloquet Box Company (Rathborne, Hair & Ridgway Co.) in Cloquet, Minnesota. In 1912 he moved his family to Chicago where he continued working for Rathbone, Hair and Ridgway, Company, eventually becoming President of the firm.

Grandson, William Reuben married Katherine Leach and they had Mary's great-grandson, Hugh Allen Stafford, who still lives in Iowa. I spoke with Hugh in August of 2013. He did tell me he has a sister, Mary Catherine Stafford Payne, one son, one daughter and a two and a half-year old grandson, William Stafford, Mary and Charles' 3rd great-grandson.

Hugh related to me the story many of us have heard about Mary losing her P.E.O. pin while gardening one day. Years later, the pin was found by her daughter-in-law in that garden and returned to her. The pin stayed with the family until after Hugh's father, William Reuben, died in 1999, at which time the pin was presented to Iowa Wesleyan for display in the P.E.O. Memorial Room.

Mary's son Charles Ralph Stafford obtained his law degree in 1911 and began practicing law in Muscatine, Iowa. He also served as Muscatine County Attorney for five terms. Charles eventually became District Judge of the seventh Iowa district. He married Lucille Norvis in 1921, but there were no children.

Son William Reuben Stafford also graduated from Iowa Wesleyan in 1911. In 1912 he graduated from Wisconsin. While in college at Iowa Wesleyan, William became a member of Phi Delta Theta Fraternity. According to his obituary, he also was active in athletic activities. At the time of his death he was superintendent of a plant for Rathborne, Hair & Ridgway Co., in Cloquet, Minnesota, the same firm where his brother Clarence was also employed.

Mary had two nieces via her sibling, Elizabeth (Cassie) Fink, Flora Louise, who died after living a few months and Louise, who married Frances Ryan. Louise ultimately divorced Francis and moved to California where she became a secretary to Mrs. William DeMille, sister-in-law to the movie producer Cecil B. DeMille.

Mary also had three nephews; Charles Allen, her brother Robert's son and George William and Reuben Allen Marquardt, sons to her sister, Evelyn Allen Marquardt.

The Iowa Wesleyan connection to Mary, the P.E.O. Sisterhood and the promotion of the pioneering spirit continues to live on today!

Mary Jane Allen Stafford – Life Events

DATE	EVENT	AGE
30 December 1848	Born, Iowa	
August 1850	Residence: Mount Pleasant, Honey, Iowa	1
1856	Residence: Center, Henry, Iowa	8
June 1860	Residence: Mount Pleasant, Henry, Iowa	12
September 1865	Entered Iowa Wesleyan	16
21 January 1869	P.E.O. Founded	20
June 1869	Graduated Iowa Wesleyan A.B. degree	20
June 1870	Residence: Center, Henry, Iowa	21
June 1871	Charles Lewis Stafford ordained Methodist ministry	22
4 July 1871	Married Charles Lewis Stafford	22
1872	Received honorary A.M. degree from Iowa Wesleyan	23
21 September 1872	Son: Clarence Allen Stafford born	23
1878	Daughter: Eva May Stafford born	29
June 1880	Residence: Keokuk, Lee, Iowa	30
6 September 1881	Son: Charles Ralph Stafford born	31
1882	Daughter: Eva May Stafford dies	33
May 1889	Son: William Reuben Stafford born	40
1891-1899	Charles L. Stafford President Iowa Wesleyan	43-51
June 1900	Residence: Muscatine, Muscatine, Iowa	52
11 June 1908	Son: Clarence Allen Stafford marries Mary Elizabeth Delescaille	58
May 1910	Residence: Grinnell, Poweshiek, Iowa	60
19 June 1913	Son: William Reuben Stafford dies	64
January 1920	Residence: Muscatine, Muscatine, Iowa	71
January 1925	Residence: Muscatine, Muscatine, Iowa	76
25 April 1927	Participation in Cornerstone Ceremony P.E.O. Memorial Library	78
12 July 1927	Died: Muscatine, Muscatine, Iowa Buried: Forest Home Cemetery, Mount Pleasant, Iowa	78

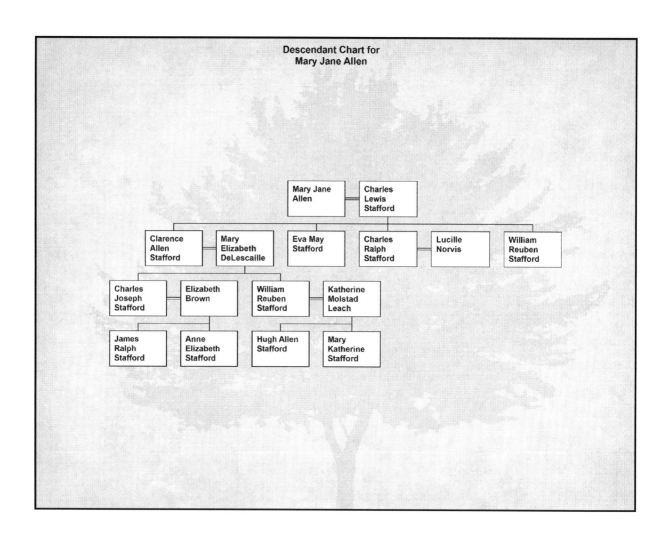

Transcription from:
Oskaloosa Daily Herald, Oskaloosa, Iowa, Monday, October 4, 1909

P.E.O. Sisterhood

The secret sisterhood of P.E.O. widely holds its Supreme Chapter convention in Mt. Pleasant this week. P.E.O. dates it origin from January 21, 1869, in the old chapel of the Iowa Wesleyan University at Mount Pleasant.

The "Original Pleiades" consisted of Alice Bird-Babb, Harriet Briggs Bousquet, Franc Roads-Elliott, Ella Stewart, Mary Allen Stafford, Alice Coffin and Suella Pearson-Penfield. "In the first place," says the P.E.O. history, "the time was ripe for the beginning of women's clubs. Margaret Fuller, not long before had sounded the cry for an uprising of that kind, and not in vain, for it had been proven with women, as with men, that 'In unity there is strength.'"

The seven girls that founded the order had been friends for several years. They were about to be separated by graduation and longed, naturally for a bond that might hold time forever as inseparables and, at the same time, disclose to others the beauty that accrued from their sisterhood.

The beginning was not made in the spirit of a fun-loving group of girls and they had no desire to form the usual college fraternity. They wanted something that should possess the presence of permanency. At the first meeting of the society, however, the earnest young women, despite their fond hopes, had no idea what a sweep their little frame would have later.

So on the morning of January 21 Alice Coffin asked Alice Bird to formulate a constitution that should be submitted to the other six for revision and adoption. It was done and read in the old music room of the university. The records of those first meetings seem to have been lost, but they would cause many smiles, doubtless, should they be found. After the seven were organized Miss Cassie Fink, of Des Moines, was the first to be initiated. The society had pins made, a gold star with P.E.O. engraved on it and enameled in black. At this time also the I.C.'s were organized in Iowa Wesleyan and so strong was the rivalry that the preceptor took away the pins of both societies and stowed them away in the city bank.

Peace being restored between the chapters of P.E.O. and I.C. the pins were returned and P.E.O. went on with more vim than ever before. The next chapters organized were at Mount Pleasant seminary, Jacksonville, Ill, Bloomfield, Ia., Fairfield, Oskaloosa, Centerville and Iowa City. The Iowa State Grand chapter was formed in 1888. Mrs. Nellie Ambler Campbell was a great power at this meeting.

The fame of the sisterly love and character building influence of P.E.O. grew until Iowa consented to relinquish her sole possession and reveal to others her magic secret. Almost every state in the union now knows P.E.O. numbering about 5,000. In all, 130 chapters of which are variously located in Iowa. Among other states prominent in P.E.O.

work are Missouri, Illinois, Nebraska, Colorado, Washington, Oklahoma, Kansas and others. The law permits no town of fewer than 1,000 inhabitants to possess a chapter. The P.E.O. flower is the marguerite and the emblem the five pointed star so often seen. Awe, curiosity and respect follow in the train of the emblem, often imitated, but never excelled. The order, notwithstanding its origin, is non-sectarian. There has been much misunderstanding in regard to this point, by some who thought they knew and had been misinformed.

The conventions are held in response to invitations from the ones who care for the honor. The order shows its spirit in these conventions by the regularity with which they are attended and the work accomplished in so short a session.

A gentleman remarked a few days ago that the most he knew of P.E.O. was the "P.E.O. March," written by Professor Barnhouse, of Oskaloosa, that the P.E.O.'s, all hummed it. Every convention seems to be a better one than the previous ones, more spirited, greater numbers and more work accomplished.

Transcription from:
The Scroll of Phi Delta Theta. Editor Thomas A. Davis. Vol. XXXVIII. Menasha: Collegiate, 1913-1914. Page 503

William Reuben Stafford, Iowa Wesleyan, '11, and Wisconsin, '13

William Reuben Stafford, youngest son of Dr. and Mrs. C.L. Stafford, was born in Muscatine, Iowa, April 15, 1889, and passed away in Duluth, Minnesota, June 19, 1913. At the time of his birth, his father was Presiding Elder of the Muscatine District of the Methodist Episcopal Church. While Reuben was yet an infant, the family removed to Ottumwa, Iowa, and later to Mt. Pleasant, Iowa, in which places the childhood and boyhood of the deceased were spent.

At the close of Doctor Stafford's presidency of Iowa Wesleyan College, the family returned to Muscatine, and during their residence there Reuben enrolled as a student in the Muscatine High School. A later residence in Bloomfield, Iowa, afforded him the opportunity of completing his course of studies in the high school from which he graduated with credit to himself. He then entered the Iowa Wesleyan College where he remained for two years; a year in Grinnell College followed, after which he entered the State University of Wisconsin, from which he graduated a year ago.

While in college at Mt. Pleasant, he became a member of the Phi Delta Theta Fraternity, winning the high personal regard of the boys and endearing himself to all of them in such manner that in his passing away they have experienced a bereavement akin to family loss. During all his college days he was prominent in the athletic activities of the various colleges he attended, and whether at practice or in the swift rush and heated struggle of the game, he was ever the honorable athlete, demanding fair play for his opponents and stimulating his associates with fine athletic enthusiasm.

After graduating from Madison, Wis., he accepted a position with the Rathborne, Hair & Ridgeway Co., at Cloquet, Minn. From the start he threw himself into the business with such perfect abandon, and exhibited such ability that promotion came rapidly. At the time of his death he was superintendent of the plant. During the short period of his service, the officials of the company had discovered in him a young man of exceptional promise, who combined in a large measure fine business ability with the strictest integrity.

Transcription from:
Davenport Democrat and Leader, Davenport, Iowa, 11 July 1927, page 1
Reprinted with permission of Quad City Times

Founder of P.E.O. Dies at Muscatine
Mrs. Mary Allen Stafford, 79, Who Helped Start Famous Society, Called

Muscatine, Ia., July 11

Mrs. Mary Allen Stafford, prominent club and church woman and the last surviving member of the band of seven girls who while attending Iowa Wesleyan College at Mt. Pleasant in 1869, formed the P.E.O. Sisterhood, now a national organization for women, passed away at 11:51 o'clock last night at her home 411 Linn Street.

For the past several months she had been in failing health and during the past week her condition became critical. Death was due to complications due to her advanced age. She was taken seriously ill several weeks ago while on a visit at the home of her son, Clarence Stafford, in Oak Park, Ill., and was brought to her home in Muscatine.

The death of Mrs. Stafford, who was the wife of the Rev. C.L. Stafford, retired Methodist Episcopal minister, comes as a profound shock to the community and to the great host of friends and members of the P.E.O. Sisterhood; in which she was a prominent national figure and leader. Many expressions of sympathy were received today by telegraph to the bereaved family from all parts of the country.

Born in Mt. Pleasant

Mrs. Allen was born Dec. 30, 1848, in Mt. Pleasant, the daughter of Rueben and Evelyn Allen. Her early life was spent in that vicinity, where she attended Iowa Wesleyan College and graduated in 1869. She was united in marriage to C.L. Stafford July 4, 1871.

After her marriage, she lived in various cities of Iowa where her husband held pastorates. During the early years of her married life, Mrs. Stafford lived for five years in Muscatine, when Mr. Stafford served as presiding elder of the First Methodist Episcopal church. She had lived here for the past twenty years, during which time she was active at all times in club work and in the First Methodist Episcopal church circles. She was also a member of the Twentieth Century club.

Despite her advanced age, Mrs. Stafford gave unsparingly of her time in the interest of the P.E.O. Sisterhood. As the last living member of the original group of founders of the organization, she was called upon to take a prominent part in the recent laying of the cornerstone of the new library at Mt. Pleasant.

Dr. and Mrs. Stafford celebrated their golden wedding anniversary on July 4, in a quiet manner at their home in this city.

Besides her husband, Mrs. Stafford is survived by two sons, Clarence A., of Oak Park, Ill., and C. Ralph Stafford, of Muscatine, and one sister, Mrs. G. W. Marquardt of Evanston, Ill., and two grandchildren, Charles Joseph, and William Rueben. One daughter, Eva May died in Washington, Ia., in 1852, and a son William Rueben died at Duluth, Minn., in 1913.

The other founders of the sisterhood, who preceded Mrs. Stafford in death, were: Mrs. Alice Bird Babb, whose death occurred Nov. 21, 1926; Mrs. Frank Rhodes Elliott, who died Aug 9, 1924; Mrs. Suela Pearson Penfield, who died Sept. 22, 1920; Mrs. Hattie Briggs Bousquet, who died in 1877; Ella Stewart, who died in 1895 and Mrs. Alice Virginia Coffin who died in 1895.

Short funeral services will be held at the home here at 10 o'clock Wednesday morning and the body will be taken to Mt. Pleasant where funeral services will be held at 2 o'clock in the afternoon and burial will be in Mt. Pleasant.

Mrs. Stafford had a large circle of acquaintances in Davenport not only thru her activities in the P.E.O. and visits in this city in connection with its work but as a guest of Mrs. H. M. Lescaille. Mississippi Avenue, with whom she had frequently visited. Mrs. Stafford's son, Clarence A., was married to Miss Mary De Lescaille.

Transcription from:
Council Bluffs Iowa Nonpareil, Council Bluffs, Iowa, 7 January 1948, page 2

Judge Stafford Dies After Operation

Cedar Rapids, AP – District Judge C. R. Stafford, 66, of Muscatine, of the seventh Iowa district, died at a hospital here Monday.

Judge Stafford came here about 10 days ago for an operation. He had been reported recovering but suffered a relapse.

Judge Stafford was born in Keokuk Sept 6, 1881, the son of C. L. and Mary Allen Stafford. His father for many years was president of Iowa Wesleyan College at Mt. Pleasant.

He received his Bachelor of Arts degree from Iowa Wesleyan in 1900 and attended the University of Chicago where he was granted a doctor of jurisprudence degree in 1911. He began practicing law in Muscatine that year.

He served as Muscatine county attorney for five terms and as county treasurer for one term.

During World War I Stafford served as a captain in the army and was discharged in February 1919. In 1921 he married Lucille Norvis of Muscatine.

He was a member of the Muscatine county and state bar associations, BPOE and the Masonic order.

C. A. Stafford Dies In California

Word has been received of the death of Clarence Allen Stafford, son of Dr. Charles L. Stafford, former president of Iowa Wesleyan college. Mr. Stafford passed away June 24 at Santa Ana, Calif. He had attended the inauguration services for Dr. J. Raymond Chadwick held recently in Mt. Pleasant.

Services and burial will be in Forest Lawn cemetery, Los Angeles, Calif., June 28.

Mr. Stafford has many friends in Mt. Pleasant who extend sincere sympathy to Mrs. Stafford and their two sons in their bereavement. The Stafford family is held in high esteem in Mt. Pleasant where they have been known from the earliest days. The address of Mrs. Clarence A Stafford is: 2408 Riverside Drive, Santa Ana, Calif.

Clipped By:

ssatkins
Sun, Nov 3, 2013

Transcription from: www.newspapers.com
The Mount Pleasant News, Mount Pleasant, Iowa, 26 June 1950, page 1

C.A. Stafford Dies in California

Word has been received of the death of Clarence Allen Stafford, son of Dr. Charles L. Stafford, former president of Iowa Wesleyan college. Mr. Stafford passed away June 24 at Santa Ana, California. He had attended the inauguration services for Dr. J. Raymond Chadwick held recently in Mt. Pleasant.

Services and burial will be in Forest Lawn cemetery, Los Angeles, Calif. June 28.

Mr. Stafford has many friends in Mt. Pleasant who extend sincere sympathy to Mrs. Stafford and their two sons in their bereavement. The Stafford family is held in high esteem in Mt. Pleasant where they have been known from the earliest days. The address of Mrs. Clarence A. Stafford is; 2408 Riverside Drive, Santa Ana, Calif.

San Diego Union, San Diego, California, Thursday, 16 September 1982

Charles J. "Joe" Stafford

Charles Joseph Stafford, 73, owner of the Village Pet shop in La Jolla for twelve years, died Tuesday in a hospital.

Mr. Stafford, a retired Army major and a native of Chicago, came to La Jolla in 1956. He retired from the General Dynamics in 1967. He and his wife Betty owned the Village Pet Shop from 1965 to 1977.

He was a member of the Lamplighter, a social service organization.

In addition to his wife, he is survived by a son, …Stafford of La Jolla; a daughter, ….of Davis; a brother, ….of Davenport, Iowa and two grandsons.

Cremation and private memorial services are planned. The family suggests contributions to the donor's favorite charity.

Excerpt from: www.findagrave.com
Quad City Times, Quad Cities, Iowa, 10 March 1999
Reprinted with permission of the Quad-City Times

DAVENPORT -- William R. Stafford passed away Wednesday, March 10, at Genesis Medical Center-East Campus. Memorial services will be at 11 a.m. Friday, March 12, at First Presbyterian Church, Davenport. Private burial will be at Oakdale Memorial Gardens, Davenport. Visitation will be 5-7 p.m. today at Weerts Funeral Home. Bill was the son of Clarence A. Stafford and Mary (DeLescaille) Stafford in Oak Park, Ill., the grandson of Mary Allen Stafford, one of the seven founders of PEO. He graduated from Carlton College in 1938. In the years 1937 and 1938, he was a delegate to the Japanese American Conference at Stanford University and in Tokyo, Japan. His trip to Tokyo for the week-long conference evolved into a year-long trip around the world. When he returned home in 1939, he and his brother bought and managed a cattle ranch and his family's Morgan horse ranch in Montana. He married Katherine Leach on Aug. 14, 1943, in Alexandria, Minn., and they spent their first years together in Montana. In 1949, Bill bought the Toro distributorship for the state of Iowa and moved his family to Davenport, where he had spent many happy times as a child with his grandmother, Mrs. Hattie DeLescaille. He was President of Tri-State Toro Co., for 34 years, retiring in 1983, when his son, Hugh, took over the business. During 1983, Bill discovered 180 acres of untamed land in a southwest Wisconsin valley. He and Katherine have spent several months of every year since then at the farm in Seneca, Wis., transforming this land into a beautiful tree farm. Bill leaves 38,000 hard wood trees as his legacy for future generations. Bill was involved with the Boy Scouts all his life and was instrumental in starting of a Boy Scout program to provide a camp experience for underprivileged boys. During his tenure as board member and President of the Buffalo Bill Council (1970-1971), it was joined with the Sac Fox Council in Rock Island to form the Iowa Council. In 1956, he received the Silver Beaver Award, the highest honor a volunteer can receive for service to the Boy Scout organization; He was a 25-year member of Rotary and a long-standing member of the Round Table. Bill served on the boards of the Outing Club and the Associated Employers of the Quad-Cities. He served as President of the latter group in 1959. Bill and Kay received the Wisconsin Forest Management Award in 1986. The family requests that in lieu of flowers memorials be made to the Endowment Fund of the Iowa Council of Boy Scouts of America, Quad-City Symphony or Genesis Foundation. Survivors include his wife, Katherine L.; a daughter and son-in-law, Mary S. and ...; and a son ..., and his grandchildren... . He was preceded by his parents and a brother, Joe Stafford, La Jolla, Calif.

Photo Album for Mary Jane Allen

Mary Jane Allen

Birth:	30 Dec 1848	Father:	Reuben Allen
Death:	10 Jul 1927	Mother:	Evelyn Caulk
Marriage:		Spouse:	Charles Lewis Stafford

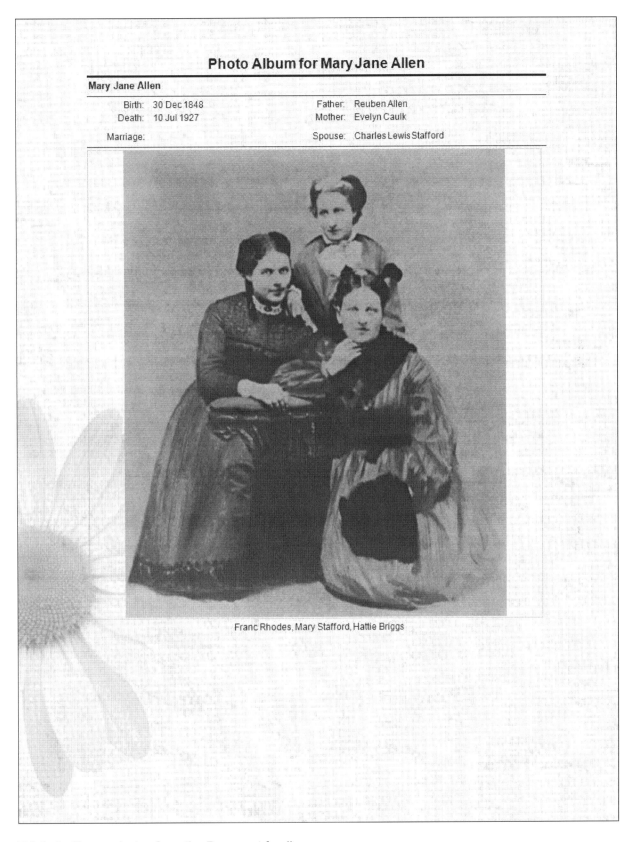

Franc Rhodes, Mary Stafford, Hattie Briggs

Printed with permission from the Bousquet family.

Mary Jane Allen

Birth:	30 Dec 1848	Father:	Reuben Allen
Death:	10 Jul 1927	Mother:	Evelyn Caulk
Marriage:		Spouse:	Charles Lewis Stafford

Mary Allen Stafford 1848-1927

Reproduction of oil portrait by Marion Dunlap Harper,
unveiled in P.E.O. Memorial Hall in Mount Pleasant, Iowa, on 23 September 23 1929.

Photo Album for Mary Elizabeth DeLescaille

Mary Elizabeth DeLescaille

Birth:	29 Apr 1886	Father:	Jules J DeLescaille
Death:	07 Jun 1961	Mother:	Hattie Marie Shaw
Marriage:	11 Jun 1908	Spouse:	Clarence Allen Stafford

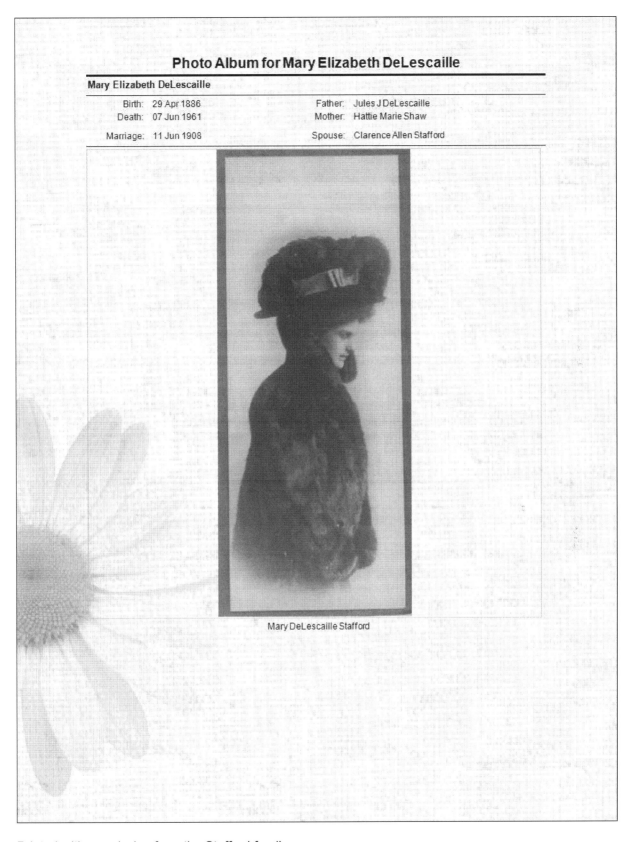

Mary DeLescaille Stafford

Printed with permission from the Stafford family.

Photo Album for William Reuben Stafford

William Reuben Stafford

Birth:	17 Oct 1914	Father:	Clarence Allen Stafford
Death:	10 Mar 1999	Mother:	Mary Elizabeth DeLescaille
Marriage:	14 Aug 1943	Spouse:	Katherine Molstad Leach

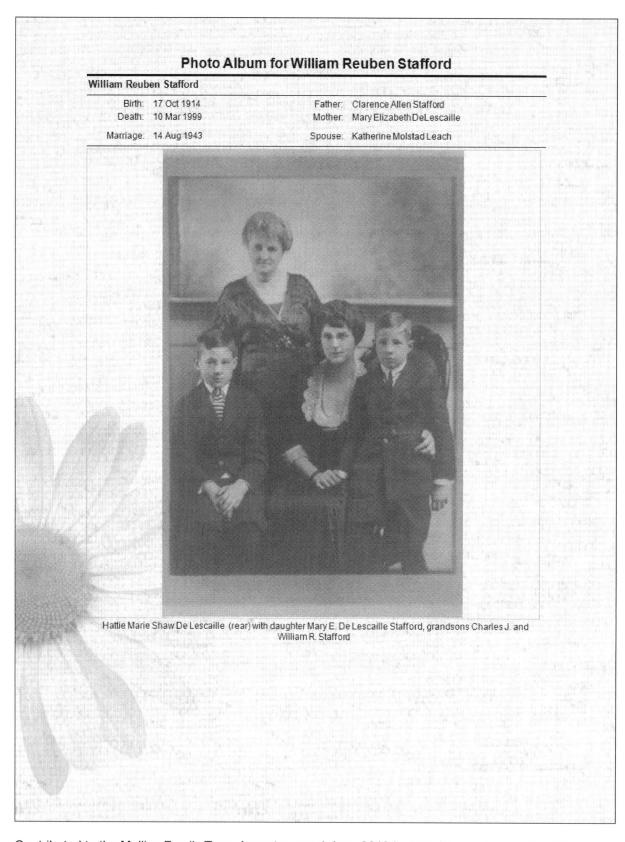

Hattie Marie Shaw De Lescaille (rear) with daughter Mary E. De Lescaille Stafford, grandsons Charles J. and William R. Stafford

Contributed to the Mullins Family Tree, Ancestry.com 1 June 2013 by member suzannemullins52.

Historical Background Sources for
Mary Jane Allen Stafford

1. 1850 United States Federal Census: Census Place: *Mount Pleasant, Henry, Iowa*; Roll:M432_184; Page 180B; Image: 104.

2. 1860 United States Federal Census: Census Place: *Mount Pleasant, Henry, Iowa*; Roll: M653_324; Page: 70; Image 70; Family History Library Film: 803324.

3. 1870 United States Federal Census: Census Place: *Center, Henry, Iowa*; Roll: M593_395; Page: 164A; Image: 332; Family history Library Film: 545894.

4. 1880 United States Federal Census: Census Place: *Keokuk, Lee, Iowa*; Roll: 350; Family history Film: 1254350; Page 261D; Enumeration District: 1=018; Image 0204.

5. 1900 United States Federal Census: Census Place: *Muscatine, Muscatine, Iowa*; Roll: 450; Page: 8B; Enumeration District: 0105; FHL microfilm: 1240450.

6. 1910 United States Federal Census: Census Place: *Grinnell Ward 2, Poweshiek, Iowa*; Roll: T624_421; Page: 20A; Enumeration District: 0114; FHL microfilm: 1374434.

7. 1920 United States Federal Census: Census Place: *Muscatine Ward 1, Muscatine, Iowa*: Roll: T625_504; Page: 9A; Enumeration District: 120; Image 787.

8. 1915 Iowa, State Census Collection, 1836-1925 (database on-line) Provo, UT, USA. Microfilm of *Iowa State Censuses, 1856, 1885, 1895, 1905, 1915, 1925* as well as various special censuses from 1836-1897 obtained from the State Historical Society of Iowa via Heritage Quest..

9. 1925 Iowa, State Census Collection, 1836-1925 (database on-line) Provo, UT, USA. Microfilm of *Iowa State Censuses, 1856, 1885, 1895, 1905, 1915, 1925* as well as various special censuses from 1836-1897 obtained from the State Historical Society of Iowa vs Heritage Quest.

10. "Charles Allen Stafford." *Barrel and Box a Monthly Journal* XIII.4 (June 1908): p27. 2 Nov. 2013.

11. "Charles J. 'Joe' Stafford." *San Diego Union* [San Diego, California] 16 Sept. 1982.

12. Clapp, Stella. *Out of the Heart A Century of P.E.O. 1869-1969.* Des Moines, Iowa: P.E.O. Sisterhood, 1968.

13. "Conversation with Hugh Stafford." Telephone interview conducted by Sharon Atkins. 26 Aug. 2013.

14. "Death Claims Iowa Jurist." *The Telegraph Herald* [Dubuque, Iowa] 06 Jan. 1948.

15. "Founder of P.E.O. Dies at Muscatine." *The Davenport Democrat* [Davenport, Iowa] 11 July 1927.

16. "Iowa Wesleyan College Historical Sketch." *Iowa Wesleyan College Its History and Its Alumni 1842 - 1917.* Ed. Edwin A. Schell, A. M., Ph. D., D. D. (http://archive.org/stream/historicalsketc0iowa/historicalsketc0iowa_djvu.txt.).

17. Johnson, Heidi, *A Society of Our Own,* The P.E.O. Record, Des Moines, Iowa. 1997.

18. "Last Found of P.E.O.Is Dead." *Decatur Review* [Decatur, Illinois] 12 July 1927.

19. Leonard, John W., and Albert N. Marquis, eds. *Stafford, Charles Allen. Who's Who in Chicago and Illinois.* Chicago, IL: A.N. Marquis, 1936. 956. Print.

20. Moudry, Susan Lyn. "'A Society of Our Own'": Methodists, Coeducation and the founding of P.E.O." *Methodist History, 52:1* (2013): pages 33-42.

21. "P.E.O. Sisterhood." *Oskaloosa Daily Herald* [Oskaloosa, Iowa] 04 Oct. 1909: 5.

22. "P.E.O. Founder Is Dead." *Washington Post* [Washington, DC.] 12 July 1927.

23. *The Scroll of Phi Delta Theta*. Ed. Thomas A. Davis. Vol. XXXVIII. Menasha: Collegiate, 1913-1914. p51 and p503. 02 Nov. 2013.

24. "William R. Stafford." *Quad City Times* [Quad Cities, Iowa] 10 Mar. 1999.

Mary Jane Allen Descendant Chart
Source Report

Source Title: **1850 United States Federal Census**
Repository: **Ancestry.com**

Citation: Ancestry.com, 1850 United States Federal Census (Provo, UT, USA, Ancestry.com Operations, Inc., 2009), Ancestry.com, Year: 1850; Census Place: Elizabeth, Miami, Ohio; Roll: M432_711; Page: 6B; Image: 255. [Source citation includes media item(s)]

Citation: Stafford, Charles Lewis Ancestry.com, 1850 United States Federal Census (Provo, UT, USA, Ancestry.com Operations, Inc., 2009), Ancestry.com, Year: 1850; Census Place: Mount Pleasant, Henry, Iowa; Roll: M432_184; Page: 180B; Image: 104. [Source citation includes media item(s)]

Citation: Allen, Elizabeth Catherine Ancestry.com, 1850 United States Federal Census (Provo, UT, USA, Ancestry.com Operations, Inc., 2009), Ancestry.com, Year: 1850; Census Place: Mount Pleasant, Henry, Iowa; Roll: M432_184; Page: 180B; Image: 104. [Source citation includes media item(s)]

Citation: Caulk, Evelyn Ancestry.com, 1850 United States Federal Census (Provo, UT, USA, Ancestry.com Operations, Inc., 2009), Ancestry.com, Year: 1850; Census Place: Mount Pleasant, Henry, Iowa; Roll: M432_184; Page: 180B; Image: 104. [Source citation includes media item(s)] Allen, Mary Jane

Source Title: **1860 United States Federal Census**
Repository: **Ancestry.com**

Citation: Ancestry.com, 1860 United States Federal Census (Provo, UT, USA, Ancestry.com Operations, Inc., 2009), Ancestry.com, Year: 1860; Census Place: Mount Pleasant, Henry, Iowa; Roll: M653_324; Page: 70; Image: 70; Family History Library Film: 803324. [Source citation includes media item(s)]

Citation: Allen, Elizabeth Catherine Ancestry.com, 1860 United States Federal Census (Provo, UT, USA, Ancestry.com Operations, Inc., 2009), Ancestry.com, Year: 1860; Census Place: Mount Pleasant, Henry, Iowa; Roll: M653_324; Page: 70; Image: 70; Family History Library Film: 803324. [Source citation includes media item(s)]

Citation: Allen, Robert E Ancestry.com, 1860 United States Federal Census (Provo, UT, USA, Ancestry.com Operations, Inc., 2009), Ancestry.com, Year: 1860; Census Place: Mount Pleasant, Henry, Iowa; Roll: M653_324; Page: 70; Image: 70; Family History Library Film: 803324. [Source citation includes media item(s)]

Citation: Caulk, Evelyn Ancestry.com, 1860 United States Federal Census (Provo, UT, USA, Ancestry.com Operations, Inc., 2009), Ancestry.com, Year: 1860; Census Place: Mount Pleasant, Henry, Iowa; Roll: M653_324; Page: 70; Image: 70; Family History Library Film: 803324. [Source citation includes media item(s)]

Citation: Allen, Reuben Ancestry.com, 1860 United States Federal Census (Provo, UT, USA, Ancestry.com Operations, Inc., 2009), Ancestry.com, Year: 1860; Census Place: Mount Pleasant, Henry, Iowa; Roll: M653_324; Page: 70; Image: 70; Family History Library Film: 803324. [Source citation includes media item(s)] Allen, Mary Jane

Source Title: **1870 United States Federal Census**
Repository: **Ancestry.com**

Citation: Ancestry.com, 1870 United States Federal Census (Provo, UT, USA, Ancestry.com Operations, Inc., 2009), Ancestry.com, Year: 1870; Census Place: Center, Henry, Iowa; Roll: M593_395; Page: 164A; Image: 332; Family History Library Film: 545894. [Source citation includes media item(s)]

Citation: Ancestry.com, 1870 United States Federal Census (Provo, UT, USA, Ancestry.com Operations, Inc., 2009), Ancestry.com, Year: 1870; Census Place: Center, Henry, Iowa; Roll: M593_395; Page: 164A; Image: 332; Family History Library Film: 545894. [Source citation includes media item(s)]

Citation: Allen, Evalyn Ancestry.com, 1870 United States Federal Census (Provo, UT, USA, Ancestry.com Operations, Inc., 2009), Ancestry.com, Year: 1870; Census Place: Center, Henry, Iowa; Roll: M593_395; Page: 164A; Image: 332; Family History Library Film: 545894. [Source citation includes media item(s)]

Citation: Allen, Elizabeth Catherine Ancestry.com, 1870 United States Federal Census (Provo, UT, USA, Ancestry.com Operations, Inc., 2009), Ancestry.com, Year: 1870; Census Place: Center, Henry, Iowa; Roll: M593_395; Page: 164A; Image: 332; Family History Library Film: 545894. [Source citation includes media item(s)]

Citation: Allen, Robert E Ancestry.com, 1870 United States Federal Census (Provo, UT, USA, Ancestry.com Operations, Inc., 2009), Ancestry.com, Year: 1870; Census Place: Center, Henry, Iowa; Roll: M593_395; Page: 164A; Image: 332; Family History Library Film: 545894. [Source citation includes media item(s)]

Citation: Caulk, Evelyn Ancestry.com, 1870 United States Federal Census (Provo, UT, USA, Ancestry.com Operations, Inc., 2009), Ancestry.com, Year: 1870; Census Place: Center, Henry, Iowa; Roll: M593_395; Page: 164A; Image: 332; Family History Library Film: 545894. [Source citation includes media item(s)]

Citation: Allen, Reuben Ancestry.com, 1870 United States Federal Census (Provo, UT, USA, Ancestry.com Operations, Inc., 2009), Ancestry.com, Year: 1870; Census Place: Center, Henry, Iowa; Roll: M593_395; Page: 164A; Image: 332; Family History Library Film: 545894. [Source citation includes media item(s)] Allen, Mary Jane

Source Title: **1880 United States Federal Census**
Repository: **Ancestry.com**

Citation: Ancestry.com and The Church of Jesus Christ of Latter-day Saints, 1880 United States Federal Census (Provo, UT, USA, Ancestry.com Operations Inc., 2010), Ancestry.com, Year: 1880; Census Place: Keokuk, Lee, Iowa; Roll: 350; Family History Film: 1254350; Page: 261D; Enumeration District: 018; Image: 0204. [Source citation includes media item(s)]

Citation: Allen, Mary Jane Ancestry.com and The Church of Jesus Christ of Latter-day Saints, 1880 United States Federal Census (Provo, UT, USA, Ancestry.com Operations Inc., 2010), Ancestry.com, Year: 1880; Census Place: Keokuk, Lee, Iowa; Roll: 350; Family History Film: 1254350; Page: 261D; Enumeration District: 018; Image: 0204. [Source citation includes media item(s)]

Citation: Stafford, Eva May Ancestry.com and The Church of Jesus Christ of Latter-day Saints, 1880 United States Federal Census (Provo, UT, USA, Ancestry.com Operations Inc., 2010), Ancestry.com, Year: 1880; Census Place: Keokuk, Lee, Iowa; Roll: 350; Family History Film: 1254350; Page: 261D; Enumeration District: 018; Image: 0204. [Source citation includes media item(s)] Stafford, Clarence Allen

Citation: Ancestry.com and The Church of Jesus Christ of Latter-day Saints, 1880 United States Federal Census (Provo, UT, USA, Ancestry.com Operations Inc., 2010), Ancestry.com, Year: 1880; Census Place: Keokuk, Lee, Iowa; Roll: 350; Family History Film: 1254350; Page: 261D; Enumeration District: 018; Image: 0204. [Source citation includes media item(s)]

Citation: Stafford, Charles Lewis Ancestry.com and The Church of Jesus Christ of Latter-day Saints, 1880 United States Federal Census (Provo, UT, USA, Ancestry.com Operations Inc., 2010), Ancestry.com, Year: 1880; Census Place: Omaha, Douglas, Nebraska; Roll: 748; Family History Film: 1254748; Page: 243B; Enumeration District: 020; Image: 0067. [Source citation includes media item(s)]

Citation: Allen, Robert E Ancestry.com and The Church of Jesus Christ of Latter-day Saints, 1880 United States Federal Census (Provo, UT, USA, Ancestry.com Operations Inc., 2010), Ancestry.com, Year: 1880; Census Place: Omaha, Douglas, Nebraska; Roll: 748; Family History Film: 1254748; Page: 289B; Enumeration District: 022; Image: 0159. [Source citation includes media item(s)]

Citation: Allen, Evalyn Ancestry.com and The Church of Jesus Christ of Latter-day Saints, 1880 United States Federal Census (Provo, UT, USA, Ancestry.com Operations Inc., 2010), Ancestry.com, Year: 1880; Census Place: Omaha, Douglas, Nebraska; Roll: 748; Family History Film: 1254748; Page: 289B; Enumeration District: 022; Image: 0159. [Source citation includes media item(s)]

Citation: Caulk, Evelyn Ancestry.com and The Church of Jesus Christ of Latter-day Saints, 1880 United States Federal Census (Provo, UT, USA, Ancestry.com Operations Inc., 2010), Ancestry.com, Year: 1880; Census Place: Omaha, Douglas, Nebraska; Roll: 748; Family History Film: 1254748; Page: 289B; Enumeration District: 022; Image: 0159. [Source citation includes media item(s)]

Citation: Allen, Reuben Ancestry.com and The Church of Jesus Christ of Latter-day Saints, 1880 United States Federal Census (Provo, UT, USA, Ancestry.com Operations Inc., 2010), Ancestry.com, Year: 1880; Census Place: Valley, Polk, Iowa; Roll: 360; Family History Film: 1254360; Page: 535C; Enumeration District: 172; Image: 0590. [Source citation includes media item(s)] Allen, Elizabeth Catherine

Source Title: 1900 United States Federal Census
Repository: Ancestry.com

Citation: Ancestry.com, 1900 United States Federal Census (Provo, UT, USA, Ancestry.com Operations Inc., 2004), Ancestry.com, Year: 1900; Census Place: Des Moines, Polk, Iowa; Roll: 454; Page: 3A; Enumeration District: 0081; FHL microfilm: 1240454. [Source citation includes media item(s)]

Citation: Allen, Elizabeth Catherine Ancestry.com, 1900 United States Federal Census (Provo, UT, USA, Ancestry.com Operations Inc., 2004), Ancestry.com, Year: 1900; Census Place: Des Moines, Polk, Iowa; Roll: 454; Page: 3A; Enumeration District: 0081; FHL microfilm: 1240454. [Source citation includes media item(s)]

Citation: Allen, Elizabeth Catherine Ancestry.com, 1900 United States Federal Census (Provo, UT, USA, Ancestry.com Operations Inc., 2004), Ancestry.com, Year: 1900; Census Place: Des Moines, Polk, Iowa; Roll: 454; Page: 3A; Enumeration District: 0081; FHL microfilm: 1240454. [Source citation includes media item(s)] Allen, Reuben Caulk, Evelyn

Citation: Ancestry.com, 1900 United States Federal Census (Provo, UT, USA, Ancestry.com Operations Inc., 2004), Ancestry.com, Year: 1900; Census Place: Des Moines, Polk, Iowa; Roll: 454; Page: 3A; Enumeration District: 0081; FHL microfilm: 1240454. [Source citation includes media item(s)] Allen, Reuben

Citation: Caulk, Evelyn Ancestry.com, 1900 United States Federal Census (Provo, UT, USA, Ancestry.com Operations Inc., 2004), Ancestry.com, Year: 1900; Census Place: Evanston Ward 3, Cook, Illinois; Roll: 292; Page: 10B; Enumeration District: 1157; FHL microfilm: 1240292. [Source citation includes media item(s)]

Citation: Allen, Evalyn Ancestry.com, 1900 United States Federal Census (Provo, UT, USA, Ancestry.com Operations Inc., 2004), Ancestry.com, Year: 1900; Census Place: Evanston Ward 3, Cook, Illinois; Roll: 292; Page: 10B; Enumeration District: 1157; FHL microfilm: 1240292. [Source citation includes media item(s)]

Citation: Allen, Evalyn Ancestry.com, 1900 United States Federal Census (Provo, UT, USA, Ancestry.com Operations Inc., 2004), Ancestry.com, Year: 1900; Census Place: Muscatine, Muscatine, Iowa; Roll: 450; Page: 8B; Enumeration District: 0105; FHL microfilm: 1240450. [Source citation includes media item(s)]

Citation: Stafford, Charles Ralph Ancestry.com, 1900 United States Federal Census (Provo, UT, USA, Ancestry.com Operations Inc., 2004), Ancestry.com, Year: 1900; Census Place: Muscatine, Muscatine, Iowa; Roll: 450; Page: 8B; Enumeration District: 0105; FHL microfilm: 1240450. [Source citation includes media item(s)]

Citation: Stafford, Clarence Allen Ancestry.com, 1900 United States Federal Census (Provo, UT, USA, Ancestry.com Operations Inc., 2004), Ancestry.com, Year: 1900; Census Place: Muscatine, Muscatine, Iowa; Roll: 450; Page: 8B; Enumeration District: 0105; FHL microfilm: 1240450. [Source citation includes media item(s)]

Citation: Stafford, William Reuben Ancestry.com, 1900 United States Federal Census (Provo, UT, USA, Ancestry.com Operations Inc., 2004), Ancestry.com, Year: 1900; Census Place: Muscatine, Muscatine, Iowa; Roll: 450; Page: 8B; Enumeration District: 0105; FHL microfilm: 1240450. [Source citation includes media item(s)] Allen, Mary Jane

Citation: Stafford, Charles Lewis Ancestry.com, 1900 United States Federal Census (Provo, UT, USA, Ancestry.com Operations Inc., 2004), Ancestry.com, Year: 1900; Census Place: Muscatine, Muscatine, Iowa; Roll: 450; Page: 8B; Enumeration District: 0105; FHL microfilm: 1240450. [Source citation includes media item(s)] Allen, Mary Jane

Citation: Stafford, Charles Lewis Ancestry.com, 1900 United States Federal Census (Provo, UT, USA, Ancestry.com Operations Inc., 2004), Ancestry.com, Year: 1900; Census Place: Omaha Ward 8, Douglas, Nebraska; Roll: 925; Page: 3B; Enumeration District: 0086; FHL microfilm: 1240925. [Source citation includes media item(s)] Allen, Robert E

Source Title: 1910 United States Federal Census
Repository: Ancestry.com

Citation: Ancestry.com, 1910 United States Federal Census (Provo, UT, USA, Ancestry.com Operations Inc., 2006), Ancestry.com, Year: 1910; Census Place: Chicago Ward 7, Cook, Illinois; Roll: T624_247; Page: 8B; Enumeration District: 0392; FHL microfilm: 1374260. [Source citation includes media item(s)]

Citation: Ancestry.com, 1910 United States Federal Census (Provo, UT, USA, Ancestry.com Operations Inc., 2006), Ancestry.com, Year: 1910; Census Place: Chicago Ward 7, Cook, Illinois; Roll: T624_247; Page: 8B; Enumeration District: 0392; FHL microfilm: 1374260. [Source citation includes media item(s)]

Citation: Stafford, Charles Ralph Ancestry.com, 1910 United States Federal Census (Provo, UT, USA, Ancestry.com Operations Inc., 2006), Ancestry.com, Year: 1910; Census Place: Chicago Ward 7, Cook, Illinois; Roll: T624_247; Page: 8B; Enumeration District: 0392; FHL microfilm: 1374260. [Source citation includes media item(s)]

Citation: Stafford, Clarence Allen Ancestry.com, 1910 United States Federal Census (Provo, UT, USA, Ancestry.com Operations Inc., 2006), Ancestry.com, Year: 1910; Census Place: Des Moines Ward 3, Polk, Iowa; Roll: T624_419; Page: 8A; Enumeration District: 0111; FHL microfilm: 1374432. [Source citation includes media item(s)]

Citation: Allen, Elizabeth Catherine Ancestry.com, 1910 United States Federal Census (Provo, UT, USA, Ancestry.com Operations Inc., 2006), Ancestry.com, Year: 1910; Census Place: Des Moines Ward 3, Polk, Iowa; Roll: T624_419; Page: 8A; Enumeration District: 0111; FHL microfilm: 1374432. [Source citation includes media item(s)]

Citation: Caulk, Evelyn Ancestry.com, 1910 United States Federal Census (Provo, UT, USA, Ancestry.com Operations Inc., 2006), Ancestry.com, Year: 1910; Census Place: Evanston Ward 3, Cook, Illinois; Roll: T624_240; Page: 4B; Enumeration District: 0102; FHL microfilm: 1374253. [Source citation includes media item(s)]

Citation: Allen, Evalyn Ancestry.com, 1910 United States Federal Census (Provo, UT, USA, Ancestry.com Operations Inc., 2006), Ancestry.com, Year: 1910; Census Place: Grinnell Ward 2, Poweshiek, Iowa; Roll: T624_421; Page: 20A; Enumeration District: 0114; FHL microfilm: 1374434. [Source citation includes media item(s)]

Citation: Allen, Mary Jane Ancestry.com, 1910 United States Federal Census (Provo, UT, USA, Ancestry.com Operations Inc., 2006), Ancestry.com, Year: 1910; Census Place: Grinnell Ward 2, Poweshiek, Iowa; Roll: T624_421; Page: 20A; Enumeration District: 0114; FHL microfilm: 1374434. [Source citation includes media item(s)]

Citation: Stafford, William Reuben Ancestry.com, 1910 United States Federal Census (Provo, UT, USA, Ancestry.com Operations Inc., 2006), Ancestry.com, Year: 1910; Census Place: Grinnell Ward 2, Poweshiek, Iowa; Roll: T624_421; Page: 20A; Enumeration District: 0114; FHL microfilm: 1374434. [Source citation includes media item(s)] Stafford, Charles Lewis

Source Title: 1920 United States Federal Census
Repository: Ancestry.com

Citation: Ancestry.com, 1920 United States Federal Census (Provo, UT, USA, Ancestry.com Operations Inc., 2010), Ancestry.com, Year: 1920; Census Place: Des Moines Ward 3, Polk, Iowa; Roll: T625_508; Page: 15B; Enumeration District: 122; Image: 448. [Source citation includes media item(s)]

Citation: Allen, Elizabeth Catherine Ancestry.com, 1920 United States Federal Census (Provo, UT, USA, Ancestry.com Operations Inc., 2010), Ancestry.com, Year: 1920; Census Place: Evanston Ward 4, Cook, Illinois; Roll: T625_358; Page: 5B; Enumeration District: 78; Image: 168. [Source citation includes media item(s)] Allen, Evalyn

Citation: Ancestry.com, 1920 United States Federal Census (Provo, UT, USA, Ancestry.com Operations Inc., 2010), Ancestry.com, Year: 1920; Census Place: Muscatine Ward 1, Muscatine, Iowa; Roll: T625_504; Page: 9A; Enumeration District: 120; Image: 787. [Source citation includes media item(s)]

Citation: Allen, Mary Jane Ancestry.com, 1920 United States Federal Census (Provo, UT, USA, Ancestry.com Operations Inc., 2010), Ancestry.com, Year: 1920; Census Place: Muscatine Ward 1, Muscatine, Iowa; Roll: T625_504; Page: 9A; Enumeration District: 120; Image: 787. [Source citation includes media item(s)]

Citation: Stafford, Charles Ralph Ancestry.com, 1920 United States Federal Census (Provo, UT, USA, Ancestry.com Operations Inc., 2010), Ancestry.com, Year: 1920; Census Place: Muscatine Ward 1, Muscatine, Iowa; Roll: T625_504; Page: 9A; Enumeration District: 120; Image: 787. [Source citation includes media item(s)]

Citation:	Stafford, Charles Lewis Ancestry.com, 1920 United States Federal Census (Provo, UT, USA, Ancestry.com Operations Inc., 2010), Ancestry.com, Year: 1920; Census Place: Oak Park Precinct 9, Cook, Illinois; Roll: T625_361; Page: 2A; Enumeration District: 151; Image: 957. [Source citation includes media item(s)] Stafford, Clarence Allen

Source Title: **1930 United States Federal Census**
Repository: **Ancestry.com**

Citation:	Ancestry.com, 1930 United States Federal Census (Provo, UT, USA, Ancestry.com Operations Inc., 2002), Ancestry.com, Year: 1930; Census Place: Evanston, Cook, Illinois; Roll: 500; Page: 19B; Enumeration District: 2135; Image: 783.0; FHL microfilm: 2340235. [Source citation includes media item(s)]
Citation:	Allen, Evalyn Ancestry.com, 1930 United States Federal Census (Provo, UT, USA, Ancestry.com Operations Inc., 2002), Ancestry.com, Year: 1930; Census Place: Muscatine, Muscatine, Iowa; Roll: 670; Page: 16B; Enumeration District: 12; Image: 888.0; FHL microfilm: 2340405. [Source citation includes media item(s)]
Citation:	Stafford, Charles Ralph Ancestry.com, 1930 United States Federal Census (Provo, UT, USA, Ancestry.com Operations Inc., 2002), Ancestry.com, Year: 1930; Census Place: Muscatine, Muscatine, Iowa; Roll: 670; Page: 16B; Enumeration District: 12; Image: 888.0; FHL microfilm: 2340405. [Source citation includes media item(s)]
Citation:	Stafford, Charles Lewis Ancestry.com, 1930 United States Federal Census (Provo, UT, USA, Ancestry.com Operations Inc., 2002), Ancestry.com, Year: 1930; Census Place: Oak Park, Cook, Illinois; Roll: 504; Page: 10B; Enumeration District: 2259; Image: 1039.0; FHL microfilm: 2340239. [Source citation includes media item(s)] Stafford, Clarence Allen

Source Title: **1940 United States Federal Census**
Repository: **Ancestry.com**

Citation:	Ancestry.com, 1940 United States Federal Census (Provo, UT, USA, Ancestry.com Operations, Inc., 2012), Ancestry.com, Year: 1940; Census Place: Limestone, Stillwater, Montana; Roll: T627_2232; Page: 1A; Enumeration District: 48-22. [Source citation includes media item(s)]
Citation:	Stafford, Clarence Allen Ancestry.com, 1940 United States Federal Census (Provo, UT, USA, Ancestry.com Operations, Inc., 2012), Ancestry.com, Year: 1940; Census Place: Muscatine, Muscatine, Iowa; Roll: T627_1186; Page: 8B; Enumeration District: 70-12. [Source citation includes media item(s)]
Citation:	Ancestry.com, 1940 United States Federal Census (Provo, UT, USA, Ancestry.com Operations, Inc., 2012), Ancestry.com, Year: 1940; Census Place: Muscatine, Muscatine, Iowa; Roll: T627_1186; Page: 8B; Enumeration District: 70-12. [Source citation includes media item(s)] Stafford, Charles Ralph

Source Title: **Ancestry Family Trees**
Repository: **Ancestry.com**

Citation:	Ancestry Family Trees (Online publication - Provo, UT, USA: Ancestry.com. Original data: Family Tree files submitted by Ancestry members.), Ancestry.com, Ancestry Family Tree.
Citation:	Allen, Mary Jane Ancestry Family Trees (Online publication - Provo, UT, USA: Ancestry.com. Original data: Family Tree files submitted by Ancestry members.), Ancestry.com, Ancestry Family Tree.
Citation:	Allen, Evalyn Ancestry Family Trees (Online publication - Provo, UT, USA: Ancestry.com. Original data: Family Tree files submitted by Ancestry members.), Ancestry.com, Ancestry Family Tree.

Citation: Allen, Elizabeth Catherine Ancestry Family Trees (Online publication - Provo, UT, USA: Ancestry.com. Original data: Family Tree files submitted by Ancestry members.), Ancestry.com, Ancestry Family Tree.

Citation: Caulk, Evelyn Ancestry Family Trees (Online publication - Provo, UT, USA: Ancestry.com. Original data: Family Tree files submitted by Ancestry members.), Ancestry.com, Ancestry Family Tree.

Citation: Allen, Reuben Ancestry Family Trees (Online publication - Provo, UT, USA: Ancestry.com. Original data: Family Tree files submitted by Ancestry members.), Ancestry.com, Ancestry Family Tree.

Citation: Stafford, Charles Ralph Ancestry Family Trees (Online publication - Provo, UT, USA: Ancestry.com. Original data: Family Tree files submitted by Ancestry members.), Ancestry.com, Ancestry Family Tree.

Citation: Stafford, Eva May Ancestry Family Trees (Online publication - Provo, UT, USA: Ancestry.com. Original data: Family Tree files submitted by Ancestry members.), Ancestry.com, Ancestry Family Tree.

Citation: Stafford, Clarence Allen Ancestry Family Trees (Online publication - Provo, UT, USA: Ancestry.com. Original data: Family Tree files submitted by Ancestry members.), Ancestry.com, Ancestry Family Tree.

Citation: Stafford, William Reuben Ancestry Family Trees (Online publication - Provo, UT, USA: Ancestry.com. Original data: Family Tree files submitted by Ancestry members.), Ancestry.com, Ancestry Family Tree. Stafford, Charles Lewis

Source Title: California, Death Index, 1940-1997
Repository: Ancestry.com

Citation: Ancestry.com, California, Death Index, 1940-1997 (Provo, UT, USA, Ancestry.com Operations Inc., 2000), Ancestry.com, Date: 1950-06-24. Stafford, Clarence Allen

Source Title: Georgia Deaths, 1919-98
Repository: Ancestry.com

Citation: Ancestry.com, Georgia Deaths, 1919-98 (Provo, UT, USA, Ancestry.com Operations Inc., 2001), Ancestry.com, Certificate number: 16959-H. Allen, Elizabeth Catherine

Source Title: Georgia, Deaths Index, 1914-1927
Repository: Ancestry.com

Citation: Ancestry.com, Georgia, Deaths Index, 1914-1927 (Provo, UT, USA, Ancestry.com Operations, Inc., 2011), Ancestry.com. Allen, Elizabeth Catherine

Source Title: Illinois, Deaths and Stillbirths Index, 1916-1947
Repository: Ancestry.com

Citation: Ancestry.com, Illinois, Deaths and Stillbirths Index, 1916-1947 (Provo, UT, USA, Ancestry.com Operations, Inc., 2011), Ancestry.com. Stafford, Charles Lewis

Source Title: Iowa, State Census Collection, 1836-1925
Repository: Ancestry.com

Citation: Ancestry.com, Iowa, State Census Collection, 1836-1925 (Provo, UT, USA, Ancestry.com Operations Inc., 2007), Ancestry.com. [Source citation includes media item(s)]

Citation: Allen, Emma Ancestry.com, Iowa, State Census Collection, 1836-1925 (Provo, UT, USA, Ancestry.com Operations Inc., 2007), Ancestry.com. [Source citation includes media item(s)]

Citation: Allen, Elizabeth Catherine Ancestry.com, Iowa, State Census Collection, 1836-1925 (Provo, UT, USA, Ancestry.com Operations Inc., 2007), Ancestry.com. [Source citation includes media item(s)]

Citation: Allen, Robert E Ancestry.com, Iowa, State Census Collection, 1836-1925 (Provo, UT, USA, Ancestry.com Operations Inc., 2007), Ancestry.com. [Source citation includes media item(s)]

Citation: Caulk, Evelyn Ancestry.com, Iowa, State Census Collection, 1836-1925 (Provo, UT, USA, Ancestry.com Operations Inc., 2007), Ancestry.com. [Source citation includes media item(s)]

Citation: Allen, Reuben Ancestry.com, Iowa, State Census Collection, 1836-1925 (Provo, UT, USA, Ancestry.com Operations Inc., 2007), Ancestry.com. [Source citation includes media item(s)]

Citation: Allen, Mary Jane Ancestry.com, Iowa, State Census Collection, 1836-1925 (Provo, UT, USA, Ancestry.com Operations Inc., 2007), Ancestry.com. [Source citation includes media item(s)]

Citation: Stafford, Charles Ralph Ancestry.com, Iowa, State Census Collection, 1836-1925 (Provo, UT, USA, Ancestry.com Operations Inc., 2007), Ancestry.com. [Source citation includes media item(s)] Stafford, Charles Lewis

Citation: Ancestry.com, Iowa, State Census Collection, 1836-1925 (Provo, UT, USA, Ancestry.com Operations Inc., 2007), Ancestry.com. [Source citation includes media item(s)] Allen, Mary Jane

Source Title: Minnesota, Death Index, 1908-2002
Repository: Ancestry.com

Citation: Ancestry.com, Minnesota, Death Index, 1908-2002 (Provo, UT, USA, Ancestry.com Operations Inc., 2001), Ancestry.com. Stafford, William Reuben

Source Title: Nebraska, State Census Collection, 1860-1885
Repository: Ancestry.com

Citation: Ancestry.com, Nebraska, State Census Collection, 1860-1885 (Provo, UT, USA, Ancestry.com Operations, Inc., 2009), Ancestry.com, National Archives and Records Administration; Nebraska State Census; Year: 1885; Series/Record Group: M352; County: Douglas; Township: Omaha; Page: 25. [Source citation includes media item(s)]

Citation: Allen, Evalyn Ancestry.com, Nebraska, State Census Collection, 1860-1885 (Provo, UT, USA, Ancestry.com Operations, Inc., 2009), Ancestry.com, National Archives and Records Administration; Nebraska State Census; Year: 1885; Series/Record Group: M352; County: Douglas; Township: Omaha; Page: 25. [Source citation includes media item(s)]

Citation: Caulk, Evelyn Ancestry.com, Nebraska, State Census Collection, 1860-1885 (Provo, UT, USA, Ancestry.com Operations, Inc., 2009), Ancestry.com, National Archives and Records Administration; Nebraska State Census; Year: 1885; Series/Record Group: M352; County: Douglas; Township: Omaha; Page: 25. [Source citation includes media item(s)]

Citation: Allen, Reuben Ancestry.com, Nebraska, State Census Collection, 1860-1885 (Provo, UT, USA, Ancestry.com Operations, Inc., 2009), Ancestry.com, National Archives and Records Administration; Nebraska State Census; Year: 1885; Series/Record Group: M352; County: Douglas; Township: Omaha; Page: 28. [Source citation includes media item(s)] Allen, Robert E

Source Title: **U.S. and International Marriage Records, 1560-1900**
Repository: **Ancestry.com**

Citation: Yates Publishing, U.S. and International Marriage Records, 1560-1900 (Provo, UT, USA, Ancestry.com Operations Inc., 2004), Ancestry.com, Source number: 6451.024; Source type: Family group sheet, FGSE, listed as parents; Number of Pages: 1.

Citation: Allen, Elizabeth Catherine Yates Publishing, U.S. and International Marriage Records, 1560-1900 (Provo, UT, USA, Ancestry.com Operations Inc., 2004), Ancestry.com, Source number: 6451.024; Source type: Family group sheet, FGSE, listed as parents; Number of Pages: 1. Allen, Elizabeth Catherine

Source Title: **U.S. City Directories, 1821-1989**
Repository: **Ancestry.com**

Citation: Ancestry.com, U.S. City Directories, 1821-1989 (Provo, UT, USA, Ancestry.com Operations, Inc., 2011), Ancestry.com. [Source citation includes media item(s)]

Citation: Allen, Evalyn Ancestry.com, U.S. City Directories, 1821-1989 (Provo, UT, USA, Ancestry.com Operations, Inc., 2011), Ancestry.com. [Source citation includes media item(s)]

Citation: Allen, Evalyn Ancestry.com, U.S. City Directories, 1821-1989 (Provo, UT, USA, Ancestry.com Operations, Inc., 2011), Ancestry.com. [Source citation includes media item(s)]

Citation: Ancestry.com, U.S. City Directories, 1821-1989 (Provo, UT, USA, Ancestry.com Operations, Inc., 2011), Ancestry.com. [Source citation includes media item(s)]

Citation: Stafford, Charles Ralph Ancestry.com, U.S. City Directories, 1821-1989 (Provo, UT, USA, Ancestry.com Operations, Inc., 2011), Ancestry.com. [Source citation includes media item(s)]

Citation: Stafford, Clarence Allen Ancestry.com, U.S. City Directories, 1821-1989 (Provo, UT, USA, Ancestry.com Operations, Inc., 2011), Ancestry.com. [Source citation includes media item(s)] Stafford, Clarence Allen

Source Title: **U.S., World War I Draft Registration Cards, 1917-1918**
Repository: **Ancestry.com**

Citation: Ancestry.com, U.S., World War I Draft Registration Cards, 1917-1918 (Provo, UT, USA, Ancestry.com Operations Inc., 2005), Ancestry.com, Registration State: Illinois; Registration County: Cook; Roll: 1504116; Draft Board: 5. [Source citation includes media item(s)] Stafford, Clarence Allen

Source Title: **Web: California, Find A Grave Index, 1775-2012**
Repository: **Ancestry.com**

Citation: Ancestry.com, Web: California, Find A Grave Index, 1775-2012 (Provo, UT, USA, Ancestry.com Operations, Inc., 2012), Ancestry.com. Stafford, Clarence Allen

Source Title: **Web: Indiana and Michigan, Michiana Genealogical Cemetery Index, 1800-2010**
Repository: **Ancestry.com**

Citation: Ancestry.com, Web: Indiana and Michigan, Michiana Genealogical Cemetery Index, 1800-2010 (Provo, UT, USA, Ancestry.com Operations, Inc., 2011), Ancestry.com. Allen, Evalyn

Source Title: **Web: Iowa, Find A Grave Index, 1800-2012**
Repository: **Ancestry.com**

Citation: Ancestry.com, Web: Iowa, Find A Grave Index, 1800-2012 (Provo, UT, USA, Ancestry.com Operations, Inc., 2012), Ancestry.com.

Citation: Stafford, Charles Ralph Ancestry.com, Web: Iowa, Find A Grave Index, 1800-2012 (Provo, UT, USA, Ancestry.com Operations, Inc., 2012), Ancestry.com.

Citation: Stafford, Eva May Ancestry.com, Web: Iowa, Find A Grave Index, 1800-2012 (Provo, UT, USA, Ancestry.com Operations, Inc., 2012), Ancestry.com.

Citation: Stafford, William Reuben Ancestry.com, Web: Iowa, Find A Grave Index, 1800-2012 (Provo, UT, USA, Ancestry.com Operations, Inc., 2012), Ancestry.com.

Citation: Stafford, Charles Lewis Ancestry.com, Web: Iowa, Find A Grave Index, 1800-2012 (Provo, UT, USA, Ancestry.com Operations, Inc., 2012), Ancestry.com. Allen, Mary Jane

Source Title: **Web: Michigan, Find A Grave Index, 1805-2012**
Repository: **Ancestry.com**

Citation: Ancestry.com, Web: Michigan, Find A Grave Index, 1805-2012 (Provo, UT, USA, Ancestry.com Operations, Inc., 2012), Ancestry.com. Allen, Evalyn

Source Title: **Web: RootsWeb Marriage Records Index**
Repository: **Ancestry.com**

Citation: Ancestry.com, Web: RootsWeb Marriage Records Index (Provo, UT, USA, Ancestry.com Operations, Inc., 2010), Ancestry.com. Allen, Reuben

Citation: Caulk, Evelyn Ancestry.com, Web: RootsWeb Marriage Records Index (Provo, UT, USA, Ancestry.com Operations, Inc., 2010), Ancestry.com. Allen, Reuben Caulk, Evelyn

Chapter 2: Mary Alice Bird

Mary Alice Bird

Of all the seven founders, the largest volume of information discovered involves the life of Alice Bird. Alice not only lived for 76 years, but she also was a prolific writer and speaker about P.E.O. and her life. Found were a multitude of articles written by her and/or about her; almost enough for a book dedicated to just her!

Mary Alice Bird, or Alice as she was known, came into this world on 8 May of 1850. Alice's parents had moved to Mt. Pleasant from Ohio in 1849. Her father, Dr. Wellington Bird, was the first regularly educated physician to practice in the community.

Alice joined a family which included an older sister, Miranda and an older brother, Hiram Thornton (often referred to as Thornton). Between the time Alice was born and the Civil War started eleven years later, five more siblings would be born into the Bird family. Of the eight children born to Wellington and Sarah Bird, three died at young ages; Caroline at about aged seven, Horace at the age of three due to croup, and Bernetta, who lived only eight months.

When Alice was almost three in February of 1853, her father, Wellington Bird, was appointed to the three man building committee at Iowa Wesleyan. This committee was responsible for constructing what is now known as the Old Main Building. Plans were made, proposals advertised for and the public was invited to view the plans and specifications at Dr. Bird's medical offices. The construction contract was ultimately awarded in 1854 to Alexander Lee.

During the Civil War, from November of 1861 to March 1862, Dr. Bird was an Assistant Surgeon and a commissioned officer of the 4th Iowa Volunteer Calvary. It was during this period in Mt. Pleasant that the Camp Harlan training camp was designated as a cavalry training post for the 4th Iowa Volunteer Calvary. One could surmise that Dr. Bird attended to those volunteers from November of 1861 until they left Mt. Pleasant, by train, in February of 1862 for Benton Barracks, St. Louis, Missouri.

Two years later, in May of 1864, Dr. Bird again mustered into service where he served three months until August of 1864. In addition to being an Assistant Surgeon for the 4th Iowa Volunteer Calvary, he was also a Surgeon for the 17th Iowa Infantry. By the end of the Civil War he had been designated as a Full Captain.

Years later, Alice's granddaughter, Winifred Babb Nolte, recalled in a Founders Day speech, "Grandmother was the daughter of the only doctor in Henry County, (Iowa). As a result, she knew everyone in the area and from childhood was instilled with the ideal of loving and helping people."

Certainly there were many experiences that shaped Alice's life as being one devoted to her family. According to Mary Summers, who wrote the article, "A Look through Alices' Window," for the January 1963 P.E.O. Record; "We know from history and from Alice's own writings, her first and greatest love was home and family."

Much of what is written in this account has been taken from Alice's personal reflections of her life via her own writings and words. She often wrote for the P.E.O. Record in the early years of the publication (founded in January 1889), sometimes using the name "Avis." She also edited the alumni news column for the Iowa Wesleyan magazine.

One reflection was found within the Welcome Address Alice gave in 1909 to P.E.O. Supreme Chapter Convention:

"I am glad that my life began in pioneer Mt. Pleasant, Iowa; that unconsciously I lived the simple life, thus preparing a strong physique, to become a P.E.O. mother. A barefoot girl, a harem sacrum tomboy they called me; I gathered the sweet wild strawberries where now stand the lovely homes of this town. My father gave a portion of each evening to us children, telling us of events happening in a land beyond the borders of Mt. Pleasant, and one evening he said that a real railroad was coming here. Upon asking him what a railroad was, he laid some rods and spools on the table, and showed in a crude way how railroads ran."

The railroad came to Mt. Pleasant in July 1856 when Alice was six years old.

Alice goes on to account, "The day the great event happened, my mother dressed me in my Sunday school clothes, just as other mothers did their children; we held our hymn books and sang 'Joyfully, joyfully, onward we move' as that train entered, at the awful speed of 10 miles an hour, and my father said that only harm could be the result of such speed. As we youngsters gazed upon that engine, with smoke stack like a kitchen stove pipe, and long narrow cars with small cooped-up windows, we felt that "all the world was ours."

In the January 1951 copy of the P.E.O. Record there was a copy of a letter Alice wrote to her brother, Thornton Bird, recalling her memories from during the Civil War; which was occurring while she was in high school. It is interesting to note that Alice's mother's name was Sarah Thornton Bird, thus her son's name – Thornton; actually, Hiram Thornton Bird (1846-1926).

Alice writes, "I stood on the west side of New York Street bridge, because it was a declivity and the soldiers crossing the bridge could be seen to great advantage....I felt that every one of those men was a hero, and that it was a great privilege to be present. When Captain Smith passed, I wanted to take off my hat, and when Washington Irving marched along; I forgave him for all the scolding's he had ever given me and had you been there, my dear brother, memory would have taken such journeys that really I fear I should have made a display of my emotions. As it was I thought of those days of '61 when it seemed to me as a child that there was no more fun in life; and that my playtime was consumed in the everlasting scraping of lint for that box at the Aid Society always waiting to be filled for the soldiers. Even little hands could scrape lint and I never see a nice, old, clean table cloth to this day but I think what good lint that would make."

Alice went on to report how her family had learned of her brother's fate during the war, when he had been taken a prisoner of war on 30 July 1864, and then later released in a prisoner exchange. "We went on Saturday night to a spelling school at Ebenezer school house and as they were choosing sides a man rushed in and screamed, 'Great battle at Franklin and Nashville. John Beeler is killed and lots of our boys are wounded, and Thornton Bird of Mt. Pleasant is missing.' I think our mother was never the care-free creature she was before. In a few days we heard that you were a prisoner at Macon, Georgia, then, carried to Charleston workhouse. Then being in the hospital employ you were exchanged, and in a few months came the telegram from New York City, "Here in butternut clothes. Send me a hundred dollars. "We could not send the money then by telegraph but had to wait until evening before the money could go in a letter. When you came home you were no longer a boy not more than eighteen years old, but a man, an old man in experience." (The term "butternut clothes" was used as a sarcastic nickname for Confederate soldiers' uniforms that faded to resemble butternut-dyed home-made clothing; $100 in 1865 is equal to approximately $1,429 in 2014 dollars.)

Did Thornton's experience, perhaps helping his physician father, ultimately save his life? Perhaps it played a role.

In the P.E.O. Record of November 1894, Alice wrote about her education, "What education I have, was obtained in my early years at Howe's Academy, later at the High School, entering the Iowa Wesleyan University in '66 and graduating in the classical course in '69. I then taught in the High School for three years, then in the College for one year." According to the Founder's Day program given in 1996 by Elizabeth Garrels, P.E.O. Iowa State President, many of Alice's students became her sisters.

Alice explained in the 1909 Welcome Address, "How proud my father was that he could educate his children for, mark you, 50 years ago an educated woman was a scarce article."

Later, Alice would write of a special memory she had of herself and the other founders. "We seven girls were not only together in '69, but during the college years and during select school years, and the first public school years, even farther back than the 'Wide Awake' procession of '69." In 1868 it was predicted that on a certain night in February the stars would fall, just as they had fallen fifty years before and when our young mothers were allowed to stay up all night and stir the apple butter in the great iron kettle in the open.

I have heard my mother say, that every minute she was afraid the stars would fall into the apple butter and spoil it. But bless you, those lovely stars disdained the apple butter more than the apple butter disdained the stars and vanished into pure ether before reaching the earth. Our class, including the seven to be originals, asked Dr. Burns, who taught astronomy, if we could sit up all night and watch for those stars. We told him that for the reputation of the college we should do so. He said we were right and that every one of us could watch from our homes and report the next day what we saw. We told him this was not what we wanted, to stay at home alone, but we wished to come up to the college and be together, and – but we did not have to say this – have a regular old time of it. After a while, to get rid of us, he reluctantly consented. So, we met at Ruthean Hall.

The boys first made a rousing fire in the stove and with wood at $2 a cord; then we ate a substantial lunch which we girls had prepared; then Dillon Payne, suggested that we sing "Weevily Wheat." Of course he did not dare suggest that we dance, that would be wicked, but in those days when one sang "Weevily Wheat" we just had to dance the Virginia reel whether we could dance or not. We sang the old dance tune so long, and saw so many stars in each other's eyes, that to this day, not one of us knows whether the stars fell from heaven or not.

Within the P.E.O. Record of November 1894, Alice recounted, "I was married to W.I. Babb, in October 1873. We have four children, two boys and two girls, Max, Miles, Clarabelle and Alice."

In fact, Alice was 23 years old when she married Washington Irving. An illustration of her mauve silk wedding gown appeared in a Milwaukee newspaper in 1934. And, a photo appears in the January 1936 P.E.O. Record.

Alice's and Washington Irving Babb commitment to Iowa Wesleyan remained very strong over the years; in fact, their marriage ceremony was conducted by Iowa Wesleyan University president Dr. John Wheeler. And, Judge Babb served on the board of trustees at Iowa Wesleyan from 1874 until he died in 1925.

Their son Max was born when Alice was 24, Miles when she was 28, Clarabelle when she was 33 and Alice when she was 37. Over the years both of their sons, Max and Miles were also trustees for Iowa Wesleyan.

Sadly, like Mary, Alice too lost a daughter. Clarabelle died at the age of four, from diphtheria. According to Alice's granddaughter, Winifred, the death of Clarabelle in 1890,"broke Alice's heart. In the months that followed, she suffered as only all mothers can."

In studying the genealogy of Alice, it appears that through the years the Bird and Babb families were quite intertwined.

Washington Irving Babb was six years older than Alice. He became one of the best known lawyers in Iowa and a leader in the Democratic Party. Before their marriage, he was a soldier in the Civil War; he mustered in as a Private and mustered out as a Quartermaster Sargent of the 8th Regiment, Iowa Cavalry; the same Regiment as her brother, Thornton. Washington Irving was slightly wounded in the left arm during the Atlanta campaign – the very campaign that ended with her brother being taken prisoner of war.

As a note of interest, Washington Irving's sister, Belle Aurelia Babb Mansfield, graduated Class Valedictorian from Iowa Wesleyan in 1865. She went on to become the first female lawyer in the country. She was also a charter member of the Iowa Woman Suffrage Society whose convention met in Mt. Pleasant in 1870. A memorial statue dedicated to her memory can be found at Iowa Wesleyan.

In 1894, Alice suffers another loss; Ella Stewart dies and leaves Alice her P.E.O. Emblem. Eight months later, in August of 1895, Alice's mother Sarah died.

Life did have its bright moments for Alice; Max, her oldest son, graduated from Iowa Wesleyan in 1895 and her husband, Washington Irving was the Democratic Party's candidate for Governor of Iowa in 1896. Alice's son, Miles graduates from Iowa Wesleyan in 1897.

In September of 1925, her husband of 51 years, Washington Irving died. Fourteen months later, in November of 1926, Alice died at the age of 76.

Alice's son Max and his wife Vida had three children: Winifred Babb (1905-1998), Irving Thornton (1907-1990) and Max, Jr. (1918-1992). Max, like his father, became an attorney and had a distinguished career. According to an obituary found in the Chicago Tribune, Max ultimately became Chairman of the Board of Directors of the Allis-Chalmers Manufacturing Company, a member on the executive committee of Northwestern Mutual Life Insurance Company as well as a Director of the Federal Reserve Bank of Chicago.

Miles married Lottie Allen in 1904, but no record of children has been found. According to The P.E.O Record, March 1968,"Miles Babb was a man of many interests and a sparkling conversationalist. He was active in political circles and a great student of politics, presidential history, and history in general. He was an authority on the Lincoln family, an interest stimulated by family and Mt. Pleasant association. Robert Lincoln was married to the daughter of Senator Harlan. Senator Harlan, of Mt. Pleasant, was appointed to Lincoln's cabinet shortly before the president was assassinated. He served in Andrew Jackson's cabinet as Secretary of the Interior. The family of Robert Lincoln often visited Mt. Pleasant, and Max Babb, brother of Miles, served as his (Robert Lincoln's) attorney."

Daughter, Alice, married a chemist, Donald K. Ewing in 1917; also no record of children has been found.

To date, Alice and Washington Irving Babb can count 4 children, 3 grandchildren, 9 great-grandchildren, 11 2nd great-grandchildren and 18 3rd great-grandchildren.

Grandchildren: Winifred, Irving Thornton and Max W. Babb

Great-grandchildren: Phyllis W. and Kemble P. Nolte; Irving Taylor, Virginia Alice, Eleanor Vida, and Mary Winifred Babb; Douglas Thurston, Max Wellington III and Harriot Susan Babb.

2nd great-grandchildren: Karen Ann, Derek Pullar and Jana Lynn Grootemaat; Michael Benjamin and Charles Taylor Hanifin; Daniel Lindsay and Cynthia Jean Pollock; John Druse, Jr. and Elizabeth Babb Emory; Alida and Julia Baranowski.

3rd great-grandchildren: Dodge T. and Danielle Grootemaat; Kirth Gerald Cannon; Dalton Thomas Grootemaat; Mark Nathaniel and Benjamin Matthew Cromey; Maxwell

Michael, John Gunther and Wyatt Quinn Hanifin; Sophia Hanifin; Kathryn Lindsay and James Tyson Pollock; Alison Lindsay and Laurel Alexandra Shea; Tyler James and Sarah Josephine Emory; Grace Charlotte and Andrew Benjamin Gabrys.

While doing this research, I learned that Alice's granddaughter, Winifred, lived in Scottsdale, at the same retirement community where my grandmother lived – at the same time! Truly is a small world.

It is evident from the ephemera found that throughout her life Alice continued the pioneer spirit taken from her days as a student at Iowa Wesleyan; in fact, in her speeches she often referred to herself as a "pioneer" woman.

Alice reflected in her own words in the 1909 Welcome Address, "I am not a society lady, nor a suffragette, but I realize daily the great responsibility that is beginning to be placed on women's shoulders."

"I stand before you as a seer, and as a prophet. I stand before you flooded with memories, astonished with results, and most hopeful for our future; for I believe in the germ theory, and because the germ of P.E.O. was so pure God gave it His sanction and has ever smiled at its success."

Nevertheless, while Alice's commitment and devotion to the P.E.O. Sisterhood cannot be questioned, today none of her descendants can be identified as involved in the sisterhood.

Mary Alice Bird Babb – Life Events

DATE	EVENT	AGE
8 May 1850	Born: Mount Pleasant, Henry, Iowa	
August 1850	Residence: Mount Pleasant, Henry, Iowa	0
1856	Residence: Mount Pleasant, Henry, Iowa	6
June 1860	Residence: Mount Pleasant, Henry, Iowa	10
1865	Entered Iowa Wesleyan	15
21 January 1869	P.E.O. Founded	18
June 1869	Graduated from Iowa Wesleyan, A.B. degree	19
After graduation	Taught at the Academy (high school), Mount Pleasant	19
July 1870	Residence: Center, Henry, Iowa	20
1872	Honorary A.M degree awarded	22
1872-1876	Chair of Latin and Greek at Iowa Wesleyan	22-26
9 October 1873	Married Washington Irving Babb	23
28 July 1874	Son: Max Wellington Babb born	24
27 February 1878	Son: Miles Thornton Babb born	28
June 1880	Residence: Mount Pleasant, Henry, Iowa	30
16 February 1883	Daughter: Clara Belle Babb born	33
1884	W. I. Babb member Iowa State house of representatives	34
1885	Residence: Center, Henry, Iowa	35
9 March 1887	Daughter: Alice Lillie Babb born	37
2 January 1890	Daughter: Clara Belle Babb dies due to diphtheria	40
1891-1894	W.I. Babb District Judge in Iowa 2nd District	41-44
1894	Inherited Ella Stewart's P.E.O. emblem	44
1895	Son Max W. Babb graduated from Iowa Wesleyan	45
16 August 1895	Residence: Wart Four, Henry, Iowa	45
12 September 1895	Presentation "Clubs and Homes" at P.E.O. Day at Iowa State Fair	45
1895	W.I. Babb candidate for Governor of Iowa	45
1897	Son Miles T. Babb graduated from Iowa Wesleyan	47
1897	W.I. Babb awarded honorary LL.D	47
June 1900	Residence: Mount Pleasant, Henry, Iowa	50
1902	W.I. Babb nominee of Democratic Party for Governor of Iowa	52
December 1906	Residence: Aurora, Kane, Illinois	56
April 1910	Residence: Aurora, Kane, Illinois	60
April 1918	Daughter Alice Babb married Donald Knox Ewing	68
January 1920	Residence: Aurora, Kane, Illinois	70
4 September 1925	Washington Irving Babb dies	75
21 November 1926	Died Aurora, Kane, Illinois Burial: Forest Home Cemetery, Mount Pleasant, Henry, Iowa	76

Descendant Chart for
Mary Alice Bird

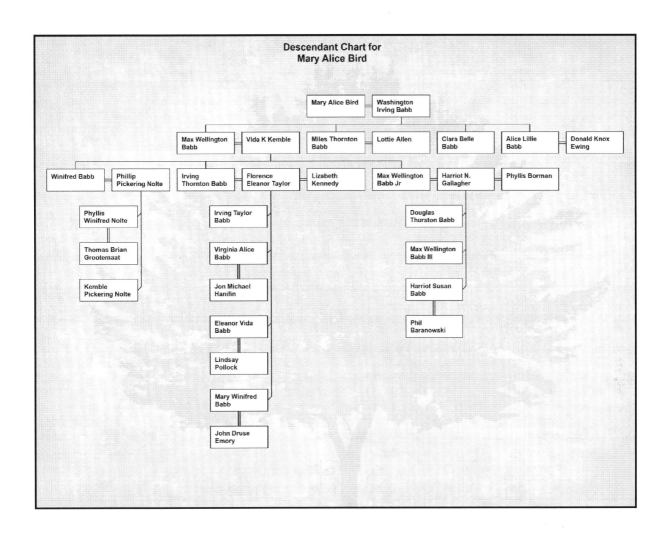

Wellington Bird Civil War Pension

National Archives and Records Administration. *U.S. Civil War Pension Index: General Index to Pension Files,* 1861-1934 (database online) Provo, UT, USA: Ancestry.com Operations Inc. 2000.

Original data: *General Index to Pension Files*, 1861-1934, Washington, D.C. National Archives and Records Administration. T288. 546 rolls.

Excerpt from:
Milwaukee Sentinel, Milwaukee Wisconsin, 21 October 1934, page 4-E

A Wedding Gown of 1874

Transcript: The high note, to point of historic interest as well as of quaint charm, in the Milwaukee P.E.O. grandmothers' style show was the showing of the wedding gown Mrs. Alice Bird Babb wore in 1874, modeled for this picture by Miss Marion Regan, one of the younger members.

Transcription from: www.news.google.com/newspapers
The Clinton Weekly Age, 16 August 1895, page 2

WASHINGTON IRVING BABB

The democratic candidate for Governor was born in the last year of the existence of Iowa as a territory, October 4, 1845, on his father's farm in Des Moines County, near Burlington, Iowa. His parents were Mr. and Mrs. Miles Babb, who came to Iowa from Pennsylvania, and were of Dutch descent. There were but two children in the family, W.I. Babb and his sister, Mrs. Belle Mansfield, now dean of the music and art school of DePauw university, Greencastle, Ind.

Miles Babb died when his son was young. Anxious that her children should have an education, Mrs. Babb sold her farm and moved to Mount Pleasant, that she might enjoy the educational advantage. Young Babb immediately entered the Iowa Wesleyan University and continued until 1863, when at the age of 18, he determined to take a hand in putting down the rebellion, and became a private in company E, Eighth Iowa cavalry, serving until the end of the war. He was all through the memorable "Atlanta to the Sea" campaign and was wounded in the left arm, bearing yet the scars of combat. He was with Thomas at Nashville. His command fought as infantry in nearly all the battles of that campaign. He was also in the Alabama campaign, known as the Wilson raid, and assisted in the capture of Selma. He served with distinction until the close of the war. Then he re-entered college, graduating with distinction in the class of 1866.

Having chosen the law as his profession, he at once entered the office of Ambler & Ambler, and on his admittance to the bar was made a member of the firm under the name of Ambler & Babb. He rapidly rose to the front rank in his profession and after a few years formed a partnership with John S. Woolson, another leading lawyer. The firm of Woolson & Babb at once became recognized as the leading one in southeastern Iowa and enjoyed a large practice. The firm was dissolved four years ago, however, by the election of Mr. Babb to the district bench as a democrat in an overwhelmingly republican district. Shortly after, his partner, Mr. Woolson, was appointed United States judge for the southern district of Iowa. In the Republican landslide of two years ago Judge Babb went down with other Iowa democrats and at once resumed the practice of law becoming a member of the firm of Babb, Withow & Kopp.

Judge Babb has always been a democrat. He has always been a worker and adviser in the party, but repeatedly refused to accept nominations, even with success assured. In 1872 he was elected to the state assembly by this republican county, but aside from this and his term on the bench he has never held office.

He is in no sense a politician, and has never made more than a half dozen political speeches in his life. He is a bimetallist on the national agreement plan, and it is emphatically opposed to the 16 to 1 free silver idea. He is a member of the board of the Iowa Wesleyan University at Mount Pleasant, and is a close personal friend of Senator Harlan, who was defeated in the recent republican convention. Personally he is very popular. He has the faculty of making friends easily, incurs few enmities, is a fair speaker, a good hand shaker and will make a strong and aggressive campaign. Judge Babb finally consented to take the nomination because the committee declared that he was the only man who could harmonize the two monetary wings of the party.

His home life is almost ideal and his handsome residence in East Washington Street is a center where gather the best and brightest in the city. He married in 1873 to Alice Bird, daughter of Dr. Wellington Bird, of this city. Four children blessed this union. Max, 21 years old, who graduated from Iowa Wesleyan last year, is now reading law in his father's office. Miles, 17 years old, is a student in college. The others are Alice, a little miss of 8, and one who they cherish only in memory. Judge Babb and his family belong to the Methodist church in this city and are influential in church as well as in social circles. He has always been identified with educational matters and is now a member of the board of trustees of Iowa Wesleyan University, and for fifteen years has been treasurer of that institution. He also stands high in Masonry and is part eminent grand commander of Iowa Commandery, Knights Templar.

Judge Babb is now in the prime of life. He enjoys perfect health and his life is one round of activity. He has the highest regard of all who know him. He is a man of principle and integrity and endowed with unusual mental and social gifts.

Transcription from:
Biographies and Portraits of the Progressive Men of Iowa, Volume 11, Leaders in Business, Politics and the Professions Together with the Beginners of A Western Commonwealth by Benjamin F. Shambaugh, Ph. D (Des Moines, Conaway & Shaw, 1899)

BABB, WASHINGTON IRVING, of Mount Pleasant, one of the best known lawyers in the state, and a leader in the democratic party.

He was slightly wounded in the left arm during the Atlanta campaign. The day after his return from war he re-entered the university at Mt. Pleasant, graduating in 1866. He immediately began the study of law at Mt. Pleasant in the office of H and R Ambler and was admitted to the bar and commenced practicing with that firm January 1868. In 1873 he formed a partnership with Honorable John S. Woolson, and for years the firm was one of the best known and most widely patronized in that part of the state. Upon his election as judge of the Second judicial district of Iowa, in 1890, Judge Babb retired from the firm, and his partner was soon afterwards appointed judge of the United States District Court, for the Southern Iowa district. Leaving the bench in 1895, Judge Babb resumed the practice of law at Mt. Pleasant.

Judge Babb was brought up in the Republican Party, but soon after the Civil War, not approving its course of reconstruction in the South, he became a democrat and has since remained such. In 1878 his party against his wishes nominated him for representative of the district, which then had over 1,500 republican majority, but he was defeated by only 3. In 1883 he was nominated for the legislature, and though Henry County was considered strongly republican, he was elected, and served in the Twentieth General Assembly, being a member of the judiciary, railroad and other important committees. In 1890 he was again nominated for district judge. This time overcoming the republican majority and serving four years with credit to himself and his party. In 1895, the Democratic Party became divided on the money question. Judge Babb took a firm stand in favor of the existing standard, and was active in securing the adoption of a sound money platform at the Marshalltown convention. He was at this time nominated for governor, and in the legislature of 1896 received the vote of his party for United States Senator. During the campaign of 1896 he was one of the leading democrats of the state who opposed Bryan and the Chicago platform – calling a convention of the sound money democrats of the state, of which convention he was chosen permanent chairman. He represented Iowa as delegate-at-large in the

Indianapolis convention and was the Iowa member on the committee on resolutions and platform. He was also active in the campaign of 1897, but would not again accept the nomination for governor, although he allowed his name to go on the ticket of the national democrats as a candidate for supreme judge.

The judge has always taken an active interest in educational matters and for over twenty years has been a member of the board of trustees and executive committee of the Iowa Wesleyan University, and was in June, 1898, appointed by Governor Shaw as one of the regents of the State University, and is now serving as such having been reelected by the legislature in 1900. He has been a member of the Masonic fraternity since 1870, and was the Grand Commander of the Knight Templars of Iowa in 1893 and 1894.

Judge Babb was married October 9, 1873, Mt. Pleasant to Alice Bird, a daughter of Dr. W. Bird. She is a lady of rare intellectual attainments and very public spirited. She was one of seven young ladies who in 1869 organized the P.E.O. Society, which now number over five thousand members. She is well known as a writer and platform speaker. Four children have been born to Judge and Mrs. Babb: Max Wellington, a graduate of Wesleyan University and the law department of Michigan University, who is now associated with his father in the practice of law, Mile Thornton; Clara Bell, who died in 1890 and Alice.

Judge Babb has a large and one of the best selected private libraries in the state and has been for many years a close and careful student of public affairs. In recognition of his well-known scholarship and abilities in these lines, the Iowa Wesleyan University in 1897 conferred upon him the honorary degree of L.L.D.

Transcription from:
Waterloo Daily Courier, Waterloo, Iowa, 12 September 1895, page 7

P.E.O. – The P.E.O. Register gives the following in regard to the exercises on P.E.O. day at the State Fair Tuesday:

"The exercises opened at 10:30, when Mrs. Walter McHenry, for the P.E.O. Sisterhood, presented Mrs. Alice Bird Babb, of Mt. Pleasant, the first to take the P.E.O. vows. Mrs. Babb has a pleasing personality, and her half-hour address was very happily received. Her subject was 'Clubs and Homes' and she began with the pioneer women, asking if we had really improved on them. We are in a transition period today, the pioneer environments behind us, the coming woman yet to arrive, and the women of today are trying to bridge the chasm. One aid toward this is the formation of women's clubs. A list of prominent women's clubs followed, as well as the history and object of the P.E.O. Sisterhood. Among the advantages arising Mrs. Babb mentioned the respite from household cares, comradeship, harmony of work; in unity as in union there is strength. A prominent object should be the up-building of a better house life; the home life of this state and Nation, it was suggested, was not what it should be."

Transcription from:
Pella Chronicle, Pella, Iowa, 16 December 1926, page 18

Referring to death of Alice Bird Babb (May 8, 1850 - November 21, 1926)

With the recent death of Mrs. Alice Bird Babb at Aurora, Illinois, but one of the founders of the P.E.O. remains, Mrs. C. L. Stafford, of Muscatine. In January, 1869, seven young lady students of Iowa Wesleyan university at Mount Pleasant organized the P.E.O. Sisterhood which through passing years has taken on national prominence. What P.E.O. stands for is a profound secret which the women have been able to keep to themselves for 57 years. Mrs. Babb was born in Mount Pleasant in 1849 and graduated from Iowa Wesleyan in 1869, and soon thereafter became the wife of W.I. Babb, who in after years served on the district bench and was prominent in business and political circles in the First district for many years. He was a large stockholder in the Wheel Scraper manufacturing concern, originally established at Mount Pleasant, but afterwards removed to Aurora, where Judge Babb died a year ago. He was a brother – in-law of the late Judge Woolson, also of Mr. Pleasant, who was on the Federal bench when he died.

Transcription from:
Madison Wisconsin State Journal, 14 March 1943, page 2

Max Babb, Allis Head, Dies at 68

Milwaukee – (UP) – Max Babb, 68, head of Allis-Chalmers Manufacturing Co., died Saturday afternoon.

Babb had been president of the company for 11 years and chairman of the board since January, 1942. Babb started his career in Allis-Chalmers as an attorney for the company in 1904 and was elevated to vice-president in 1913 during a reorganization. Babb was born at Mount Pleasant, Ia., and entered his first law practice there with his father.

P.E.O. REMINISCENCES

Social and Economic Climate of the 1860's:

Colleges were open to women for the first time--the whole world was a challenge to the seven young founders of P.E.O.

"It is easy to see, in retrospect, how these enthusiastic, grateful girls, in the magical days of their youth, set the pattern for P.E.O. The time was right for just such a social awakening among women. The girls were a happy choice for giving those qualities of vigor and hope that were needed, and that have helped lead P.E.O. from brave beginnings into its deserved position of prestige today."

Grandmother, Alice Bird Babb, 1850-1926, was born in Mount Pleasant, Iowa. She was the daughter of the only doctor in Henry County. As a result, she knew everyone in the area and from childhood was instilled with the ideal of loving and helping people. This teaching stayed with her all her life and was part of the founding of P.E.O. She entered college in 1866 and graduated in 1869. In the P.E.O. record of 1894, she writes of herself, "It was my senior year that the idea of originating the P.E.O. sisterhood occurred. Our class had a number of most congenial companions, all residing in Mount Pleasant. We had been friends before entering college, and the outlook was that we would always be near to-gether. We naturally gravitated into this union as hydrogen and oxygen unite. To prove that the union was a foreordained one, the principles which held us are still the same; there has been no desire to change them; the oath is exactly the same, the object as expressed in the Constitution today is worded exactly as then.

"I have sometimes thought, for such giddy girls we showed immense maturity in P.E.O. conception. I take its wonderful growth to rest in the fact that its aims are so unselfish; it seems an organization not so much to advance itself, as to advance the world--to assist in the upward climb toward high and noble ends. I cannot tell the number of calls made upon me in Mount Pleasant from those who want help in some undertaking. 'Can P.E.O. give us an entertainment?' We are known as 'helpers'--certainly more unselfish in our objective than any organization I have met."

Mrs. Babb organized and produced plays. The girls in the chapter were the cast. They were known in all the towns around for helping charities to raise money.

On leaving college, several of the seven stayed in Mount Pleasant and organized original "A" Chapter. Grandmother taught high school for

...cont'd.

three years, then one year in the drama department of the college--still
writing and producing plays for college students. She then married
Washington Irving Babb, a successful young lawyer who became a judge
and active in Iowa politics--also in Washington through the Robert
Lincolns.

By that time they had four children and, to quote Grandmother
again, she writes, "You ask me how my time is spent in these later days.
Entirely in home duties. I take some transitory delight in imagining that
had it not been for this and that, I might have had a 'career'. Whenever I apply myself to study, and I have never ceased taking time for
study in rhetoric or Latin, I often wander into imaginative fields and
think that had it not been for my family, I might possibly have written a
treatise on 'Composition", or made a passable translation of some of the
classics, but that Family has somehow stood in the way of 'plaudits from
the world'--and now I approach my 'hobby'.

"My 'hobby' is the protection which the American woman must give
the American home. And my solution to all the questions which vex the
angry public today is 'a better home life', where principles of anarchy
may be dispelled, where temperance in all things may be preached and
practiced, and where good boys may be sent out into the political field.

"God never made a man who could run a home; the monotonous in
detail of a house, not to mention the soothing of Johnnie's earache, or
Susie's stubbed toe, would drive every man to the insane hospital quick.
But we can attend this successfully. Under our skillful management,
Susie and Johnnie and Tommy may be healthy and happy because we can
mother them. We hope in this country to have the finest civilization the
world has ever known; but neither our form of government, nor system of
schools, nor our proud institutions will advance the American home without
the intelligent, virtuous, absorbing, exclusive devotion of the wife and
mother to its perfection and maintenance. This, weakly expressed, is my
'hobby'. Wish it were better groomed."

A comment from the editor of the Record follows: "The opinion of
Mrs. Babb on the question she has called her hobby is worthy of consideration and will receive the hearty endorsement from the P.E.O. sisterhood.
Of the home life of Mrs. Babb, perhaps it is unnecessary to say anything.
But her friends know of the cordial, kindly welcome always to be found
there. The comfortable home is always open to friends of the family, and
the two sons, Max and Miles, are certainly good examples of the home
training that Mrs. Babb so earnestly urges that mothers ought to give.
They make the evenings melodious, their mother says, with their music and
college meetings--the more the better!"

The death of Claribel, the second youngest, broke Mrs. Babb's
heart. In the months that followed, she suffered as only all mothers can,
and it was during this grief that she wrote the following story of the
little playhouse in her yard. She pictures the tiny housekeepers scouring
and bustling in and out tieing back the curtains with their brothers old
neckties, their sweet happy voices floating up to the porch where the

...cont'd.

mother listened to their prattle about the little cracked dishes and dolls, and the tea party in progress. Something called them out of the play-house and the older one, so soon to be taken away, turn the button on the playhouse door as she ran out and shut it. To go on with Mrs. Babb's own words, "A blight had fallen upon everything."

* * * * *

"As her eyes sadly wandered from object to object, they finally rested on that playhouse door which the precious hands (now folded so quietly under the 'low green tent') had hastily closed weeks before. The form of this 'Rachael' dragged herself to the spot, turned the button and entered. There lay the remains of the tea party, the broken cookie, the dried up apple, the cracked dishes—the dust of weeks upon it all. The dolly, like the sphinx of old whom the Egyptians begged with magician's arts to open its dumb mouth and reveal the secrets it must know, sat dumbly waiting for its little mistress. The curtain on the cupboard was fastened with a ribbon whose history was a poem; pictures decorated the wall colored by her dainty hands with crayons that would get stumpy so quickly; a lace on the window was fastened with a paper rose. The mother stood there stricken and buffeted about as a lonely tree in a winter's blast. Those toys, 'poor dumb mouths' spoke to her in thunder tones of the agony, the sorrow and desolation of human life. The kaleidoscope of memory turned and turned until flesh and blood cried out for a respite. Suddenly, as if borne on the breeze that entered the window, came a balm, like a benediction: 'And they shall hunger no more, neither shall the sun light on them, nor any heat, for the Lamb which is in the midst of the throne shall feed them and shall lead them into living fountains of water. And God shall wipe away all tears from their eyes'. And the mother softly crept out and closed the playhouse door."

Mildred Babb Nolte

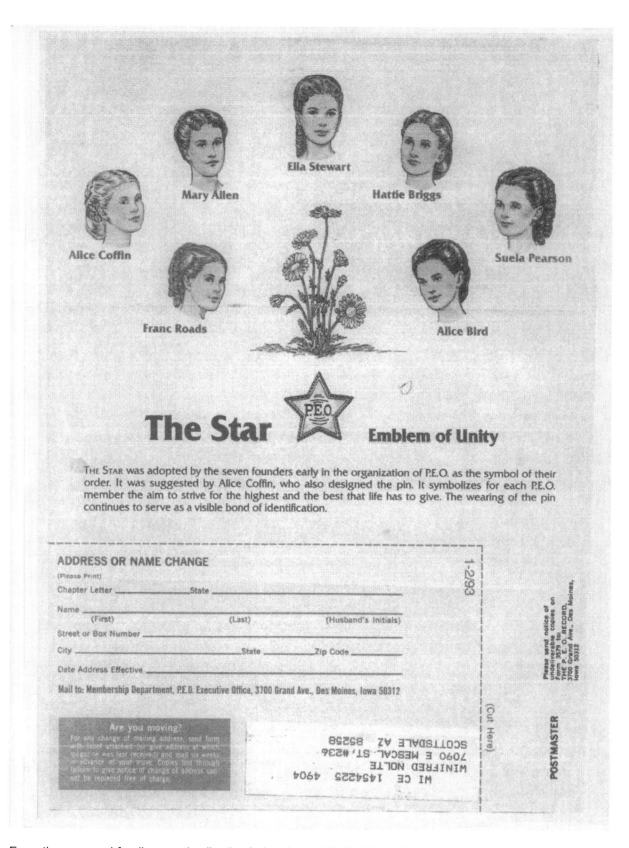

The Star

P.E.O.

Emblem of Unity

THE STAR was adopted by the seven founders early in the organization of P.E.O. as the symbol of their order. It was suggested by Alice Coffin, who also designed the pin. It symbolizes for each P.E.O. member the aim to strive for the highest and the best that life has to give. The wearing of the pin continues to serve as a visible bond of identification.

ADDRESS OR NAME CHANGE

(Please Print)

Chapter Letter _____ State _____

Name _____

    (First)   (Last)   (Husband's Initials)

Street or Box Number _____

City _____ State _____ Zip Code _____

Date Address Effective _____

Mail to: Membership Department, P.E.O. Executive Office, 3700 Grand Ave., Des Moines, Iowa 50312

1-293

Please send notice of undeliverable copies on Form 3579 to:
THE P. E. O. RECORD,
3700 Grand Ave., Des Moines, Iowa 50312

(Cut Here)

POSTMASTER

Are you moving?
For any change of mailing address, send form with label attached (or give address at which copies or mail was last received) and mail six weeks in advance of your move. Copies lost through failure to give notice of change of address can not be replaced free of charge.

WI CE 14545225 4904
WINIFRED NOLTE
7090 E MESCAL ST. #236
SCOTTSDALE AZ 85258

From the personal family record collection belonging to Phyllis Nolte Grootemaat.

The P. E. O. Record.

VOL. VI.   WATERLOO, IOWA, NOVEMBER, 1894.   NO. 11.

Mrs. Alice Bird Babb.

Mrs. Babb kindly furnished the following sketch of her life for THE RECORD at the request of the editor. It is with great satisfaction that we present it in full:

I was born in Mt. Pleasant, Iowa, May 8, 1850. Have always lived here. My early days are so connected with a bas relief of pioneer scenes and the recollection of them has been so distinct that often I have been called upon, along with the "oldest inhabitant," to relate what I remembered of pioneer Iowa. I remember at an old settlers' meeting in Jefferson Co. an old gentleman 104 years old and myself were the speakers. I declare I felt ancient. My maiden name was Alice Bird. What education I have, was obtained in my early years at Howe's Academy, later at the High School, entering the Iowa Wesleyan University in '66 and graduating in the classical course in '69. I then taught in the High School for three years, then in the College for one year, after which I was married to W. I. Babb, in October, 1873. We have had four children, two boys and two girls—Max, Miles, Clarabel and Alice. Max and Miles are attending the same College from which their parents graduated, Max a senior and Miles a freshman. Clarabel has entered a school where she no longer needs our "poor protection," while little Alice is walking literally in her mamma's footsteps, a little girl of seven, but delighting most of all in Hawthorne's fairy stories, and in any subject where the imagination can run riot. I believe that I am a member of the Methodist church, and of course you know, a Democrat in politics. It was in my senior year at College that the idea occurred to me of originating the P. E. O. Sisterhood. Our class had a number of most congenial companions, all residing in Mt. Pleasant. We had been companions before entering College, and the outlook was that we would always be near together. We naturally gravitated into this union just as oxygen and hydrogen unite. To prove that the union was a fore-ordained one, the principles which held us are still the same; there has been no desire to change them; the oath is exactly the same, the object as expressed in the constitution today is worded exactly as then. I have sometimes thought, for such giddy girls, we showed wonderful maturity in P. E. O. conception.

MRS. ALICE BIRD BABB.

I was so full of the plan, that immediately after suggesting the idea, I drafted a constitution, and on the afternoon of the same day, Jan. 20, 1869, I think, we met in the music room of the College and formed the ferment which has "leavened the whole." Ella Stewart first administered the oath to me, then I in turn to the other six, Ella Stewart, Mary Allen, Sue Pearson, Hattie

Briggs, Allie Coffin and Franc Roads. Like the "peach of emerald hue," "it grew," and there is no "tale of woe." to record. For the first three years I was president, and strange, have never been so situated that I could act in this capacity again, but it has needed none of my poor efforts to help the organization more; right onward it has progressed, and from the outlook now, it has a grand future before it. I take its wonderful growth to rest in the fact that its aims are so unselfish; it seems an organization not so much to advance itself, as to advance the world—to assist in the upward climb toward high and noble ends. I can not tell the number of calls made upon me in Mt. Pleasant, from those who want help in some undertaking. "Can the P. E. O.'s give us an entertainment?" We are known as *helpers*—certainly more unselfish in our object than any organization I have met. It may be we will never do greater work than we are doing now, simply assisting wherever our hands find work to do. Still, I feel that some day we will be so completely organized that we can assume some special work, such as Mrs. Briggs, Mrs. Rogers and our loved Miss Pendleton always hoped for, and spoke of in convention, the endowment of some work for children, helpless from some cause. How grand if some day we could construct the "Pendleton Home," to which the helpless and infirm and lonely might come and receive true P. E. O. entertainment. This hope is not at all Quixotic—even greater things may be truthfully foretold.

You ask me how my time is spent in these later days. Entirely in home duties. I take some transitory delight in imagining that had it not been for this, and that, I might have had a "career." Whenever I apply myself to study, and I have never ceased taking time for study, in rhetoric or Latin, I often wander into imagination's fields and think, that had it not been for my family, I might possibly have written a treatise on "Composition," or made a passable translation of some of the classics, but that *family* has somehow stood in the way of "plaudits from the world," and now I approach my hobby. Let me step cautiously and carefully, for I will tread on so many toes,—do my best. My hobby is the protection which the American woman must give the American home. And my solution to all the questions which vex the angry public today is "a better home life,"

where principles of anarchy may be dispelled, where temperance in all things may be preached and practiced, where good boys can be sent out into the political field; good heavens, what work we might save the pulpit, and what a mint of money could be saved which annually goes into useless so-called philanthropic work. And our homes are what the mothers make them. And although the woman question is the vexed one of the day, and likely to win on the side opposite to the stand I take, still, I the more boldly assert that married women have no business with public affairs, and I am sustained in my judgment by the ablest lawyers, the keenest philosophers, the best theologians and the greatest poets. All joking laid aside, the great question of the day is, "is marriage a failure?" and why? Simply because the pitiful fact exists that the question, "how to rear a family," is becoming more and more appalling to the average man, by reason of the aggressive competition of daughters, wives and mothers who, in most instances, led by the spirit of the times, find housework "irksome." The question is not as to woman's ability; of course, she could possibly be a lawyer, or even politician, but who will see to the home while she attends to client or stump? Not man, for while *we* might take the parts of men, God never made a man who could run a home; the monotonous cares in detail of a house, not to mention the soothing Johnnie's earache or Susie's stubbed toe, would drive every man to the insane hospital quick, but we can attend to this successfully. Under our skillful management, Susie and Johnnie and Tommy may be healthy and happy, because we can *mother* them. Oh, the women of ancient Greece were in advance of us; they have descended in history, not as domestic drudges, but as the finest types of noble women the world has ever produced. Just fancy the mother of the Gracchi on a rostrum urging the claims to political preferment of a Roman matron! The American home ought to be the best in the history of the race. We hope in this country to have the finest civilization the world has ever known; but neither our form of government, or system of schools, nor our proud institutions, will advance the American home without the intelligent, virtuous, absorbing, exclusive devotion of the wife and mother to its perfection and maintenance.

This, weakly expressed, is my hobby; wish it were groomed better. And yet so all powerful is the trend toward the so-called emancipation of women, that perhaps often in the future my husband will sit by a dusty, begrimed window, trying in an *un*melodious tone to read a fairy story to little Alice while I will be stumping the State for Mrs. Jessie Thayer for governor of Iowa, and Mrs. Alice Spilman attorney general.

The opinion of Mrs. Babb on the question she has called her hobby is worthy of consideration and will receive hearty endorsement from the P. E. O. Sisterhood. Of the home life of Mrs. Babb, perhaps it is unnecessary to say anything. But her friends know of the cordial, kindly welcome always to be found there. The comfortable home is always open to friends of the family, and the two sons, Max and Miles, are at liberty to make the night melodious, their mother says, with their bums and college meetings, the more the better. These young men are certainly good examples of the home training that Mrs. Babb so earnestly urges that mothers ought to give. Max is a fine looking, scholarly fellow, most reliable wherever placed, and Miles is a rollicking boy of sixteen, rejoicing in athletics and out-door sports.

Mrs. Babb's father, Dr. Wellington Bird, was the first physician in Henry county, Iowa.

Through the Yellowstone.
No. II.

Since our visit a small geyser that we visited and which threw water perhaps 40 feet high while we were there, has taken on greater activity and has thrown water to a great height. It was comparatively a new geyser having blown the hill out, on which it was situated but a few years ago. Here was the Green Pool, its clear depths of the most perfect tint of sea green possible and the shade varying at every change of the spectator's position. The first pool mentioned is the most exquisite robin's egg blue. Then on we go to the Canyon where we are to Sunday, but passing the Mud Pool that some of you may remember Talmage preached about. When in the Park he saw nothing to equal this pool and the Canyon. I agree with him about the Canyon, but felt only utter distaste for this boiling pool coming out from under a rock at the foot of a mountain and looking exactly like a boiling mud hole used by swine for ablutions !

At 5 p. m. we go into camp at the Canyon, all in such haste to see everything that we hardly know where to go first. The roar of the water is deafening; it is like a Niagara, only lacking its volume of water, though perhaps the difference in height makes up for that lack. Near our camp is the upper fall 140 feet high, and a little further away is the lower fall 360 feet high A mile away is the Canyon Hotel and near at hand is the soldiers' camp, and everywhere and at all times is the festive mosquito, so numerous that he makes a hungry man forget his hunger, and, having but one good quality, he gets sleepy and goes to bed early leaving us undisputed possession of the camp-fire after supper. Most of our party go to visit the upper fall and can hardly tear themselves away from the place. The water comes dashing and rushing down the Canyon towards its headlong plunge over the rocks, seemingly master of the place, but there stands a rock like a huge chair out in the center of the rapids that parts the waters and breaks them into white diamonds, but stirs not. We did not break camp the two Sundays we were on the trip, but this Sunday we rode over in the forenoon, through the beautiful pine forests, to a place on the canyon about four miles below the lower falls, called Inspiration Point. Words can never make you see this place as it looked that beautiful July morning; you must see it for yourselves. But from this rib of rock that jutted out into the canyon and gave a magnificent pulpit from which to view the scene, we looked down to the river that still went tumbling on its way 1,500 or 1,800 feet below us; to our left, and across the river, lay the beautifully tinted rocks, in all shades of pink, violet, brown, garnet, lavender, so blended that it was like looking at a beautiful sunset; and up stream, at our right, were the steep banks, with every once in a while a chimney-like rock, left ages ago when this mighty canyon was rent through the solid rock, standing perhaps 200 feet above its base, and carrying its crown of sticks—an eagle's nest. There was no desecration in viewing this scene on a Sabbath morning; if anything could impress the soul of a thoughtless person with the fact that a something there was above us greater than ourselves, such a scene must surely do it.

So much for our start. It would take too

Dec. 1906

Notice.

On the fourth Friday of each month a ta-
will be reserved for P. E. O.'s and their
ilies and friends at the tea room in Coul-
's store at 225-227 S. Broadway, Los An-
es, California. Tourists and visitors espe-
lly urged to bear this in mind.
                              Mrs. Stella Carver.

News From Mrs. Babb.

A LETTER from Mrs. Babb at last! The
E. O. of Illinois will find her at Aurora,
ether it can give her a Chapter there or
t. She writes that a tempting business prop-
ition made to her husband (Judge W. I.
bb) caused their removal. "My heart still
s buried in Caesar's coffin," she writes, but
ere is a note of hope and determination,
o, in her letter. This turning their faces
ew to a rising sun of life will probably be
great good for the pair. Regarding the
t. Pleasant leaving she says, "The P. E. O.'s
ver did themselves so proud as at their
nquet held at our loveliest home, Mrs. See-

ley's, and the entire event was so full of
deep feeling that I cannot describe it. A
long table extending fifty feet or more, with
two crosses, probably one hundred and thirty
ladies, a pansy at each plate done by Edith
Van Cise 'for thoughts' she said. In the center of the table were seven American Beauty
roses, which Mrs. Keeler told me in a most
fitting speech were for 'us seven.'

"As I sat there I felt that one more drop
would overflow the deep ocean of love and
sentiment pervading the scene, and pushing
back the wall of tears that threatened to
overwhelm us, suggested merry thoughts, and
soon the girls were singing, giving yells, and
wit met wit in repartee and joke. Many an
impromptu fine speech was made, and upon
the whole I think this was better than sad-
ness and tears. My heart received a new P.
E. O. baptism and my resolves and hopes
for the order were strengthened.

"I have pressed the petals of the roses for
a cushion of remembrance, and I shall expect to see many a P. E. O. in Aurora. We
are at the hotel yet, waiting for the people
to move out of the home we have bought
here."

CHAPTER LETTERS

Send Chapter letters to reach The Record
, or before, the 15th of the month.
Please observe the uniform style of Chapter
tter dating and closing and make yours so.
Every letter requires the journalist's name to
in The Record.

Riverside, California:

[The following is the report of her Chap-
r's year's work, read by Mrs. Frary M.
hnson at the California convention—Ed. Rec-
d.]

Chapter J still lives and is proud to make
r second bow before Grand convention. We
re like the Irishman—We notice if we live
rough the month of March we generally live
rough the rest of the year. March was a
rying time for several reasons. Those of us
ho wished (?) still to draw down the sal-
ry of our office and keep the glory there-
nto connected with the same pouring down

upon us had to get busy with the wires and
all the appurtenances connected with re-elec-
tion.

About the middle of the month came a note
from the worthy, most high, state organizer,
saying in a polite and deferential way that
if convenient she would inspect our Chapter
the 21st. Convenient or not, we made it so
and polished up our P. E. O. pins, and tried
to steady our nerves for the ordeal. We intended receiving her with P. E. O. colors of
yellow sunshine and white light, out a failure to get in proper touch with the weather
man caused everything to be enveloped in a
stylish shade of grey mist, connected with a
heavy down pour of rain. To the credit of
Chapter J let it be known that all but three
were inspected, and their reasons for not being present were the best. Whether 'twas
their love for P. E. O., curiosity to see the or-

1909 Welcome to Supreme Chapter Convention

By Alice Bird Babb

Alice Bird Babb, 1850-1926
One of the seven P.E.O. founders

The following contains excerpts of a welcome address given to the 19th Biennial Convention of the Supreme Chapter of the P.E.O. Sisterhood in Mt. Pleasant, Iowa.

This is indeed a notable event. The discovery of the North Pole in some respects cannot be compared to it. The onward march of noble womanhood beginning 40 years ago with the feeble tread of seven, with an ever-increasing army until 15,000 are in line, all we hope, actuated by the principles which are supposed to cement, is of more moment to this work-a-day world than the discovery of a barren infield.

I stand before you as a seer, and as a prophet. I stand before you flooded with memories, astonished with results, and most hopeful for our future; for I believe in the germ theory, and because the germ of P.E.O. was so pure God gave it His sanction and has ever smiled at its success.

I am glad that my life began in pioneer Mt. Pleasant, Iowa; that unconsciously I lived the simple life, thus preparing a strong physique, to become a P.E.O. mother. A barefoot girl, a harum scarum tomboy they called me; I gathered the sweet wild strawberries where now stand the lovely homes of this town. I knew, with my brother, where was good fishing in Big Creek, and ran with the boys, shouting in wild glee as the stage horn foretold the daily events . . . the coming of the stage round at Tiffany's corner. My father gave a portion of each evening to us children, telling us of events happening in a land beyond the borders of Mt. Pleasant, and one evening he said that a real railroad was coming here. Upon asking him what a railroad was, he laid some rods and spools on the table, and showed in a crude way how railroads ran.

The day the great event happened, my mother dressed me in my Sunday school clothes, just as other mothers did their children; a green silk shirred bonnet with double bow knot of ribbon under my chin, and white ruching round my face; a buff all-wool delaine cape, pinked all around, a purple delaine dress with impossible green plums all over it, black silk mits, nankeen pantalets, and copper toed shoes. We held our hymn books and sang "joyfully, joyfully, onward we move" as that train entered, at the awful speed of 10 miles an hour, and my father said that only harm could be the result of such speed. As we youngsters gazed upon that engine, with smoke stack like a kitchen stove pipe, and long narrow cars with small cooped-up windows, we felt that "all the world was ours."

And right here, in this town of Mt. Pleasant, a college was building, just so P.E.O. could be born in a suitable environment. How proud my father was that he could educate his children for, mark you, 50 years ago an educated woman was a scarce article.

When the college building in which P.E.O. came to light was raised to the square, a hurricane came and leveled it to the ground. What would P.E.O. have done had not those walls been rebuilt, but they rose again, and in 1860, again the college was threatened. The Civil War robbed it of its best and bravest youths, but the college struggled along nobly, until in 1865-66 when peace was declared, its halls were filled by men wearing the fatigue coat of the soldier. Empty sleeves and stiffened hands were in evidence, but all this made us girls glow with patriotism and humanity. Those soldiers did an amount of mischief; they had learned how to fight and to conquer, and a warfare of hearts began up there that has been going on ever since.

I cannot grow accustomed to the growth of P.E.O. Its growth is one of my individual seven wonders. Without boasting, we can declare that our standing is assured, but have you ever considered what a responsibility is ours simply through the fact that the public commands us? The affection which animated the original seven, even the original Chapter A, cannot permeate through such a large mass. Still, by meeting in Convention and by studying our constitution we find purposes and rules that stimulate to a loving, earnest association. If we cannot know each P.E.O. personally, we love her for the "tie that binds," for the wearing of the star.

In the past 50 years there has been a revolution . . . a bloodless one. When I was a little girl no one dreamed that women could ever learn to speak. On Friday afternoons at school my mother gave me a gingham apron to hem while my brother and other boys spoke pieces. Even then, I recall that the idea came into my head that little girls could not speak worse than the boys did! But today! What does woman not do! I am not a society lady nor a suffragette, but I realize daily the great responsibility that is beginning to be placed on women's shoulders. Whether they want it or not it is coming. The next generation of girls, even the present one, will have to shoulder problems of which the original seven would not have dreamed. I shall always shrink from public life but I cannot check the oncoming current. And as it rolls on I want P.E.O. to be a telling power in all things that help to uplift humanity. ☆

Volume XXII   January 1910   Number 1

The P. E. O. Record

The Official Organ of the Supreme Chapter
of the P. E. O. Sisterhood

THE SEVEN FOUNDERS OF P.E.O.

THE Mt. Pleasant News during the late convention gave reminiscences of the founders with their pictures. The cuts belong to the Record and the majority of P. E. O.'s. of the present day have never seen the pictures made from them, so we decided to give them in this issue copying what Mrs. Babb and Mrs. Stafford have to say about the girls as they were. As Mrs. Babb gives a few items concerning the founding, her story is repeated first.

"Only those who are as old as I, or older, understand the peculiar life and conditions of forty years ago. The pioneer conditions were fast passing, and the end of the Civil war was creating a spirit of unrest everywhere. For almost the first time we awoke to a realization of what our united country meant, and how it became the duty of every man and woman to contribute his or her part to the establishing of new conditions everywhere. That spirit entered our college in '66, and for a time the men who wore the blue—some with empty sleeve, others with stiffened arm or hand—dominated thought. Why I remember listening to the orations of these men as from oracles—they had seen life and knew the needs of our country. The literary societies in I. W. U. took on an impetus never known before. The great political parties were torn to fragments every Friday night in Philo and Hamline Halls.

"Up to '68 secret societies were unknown in western colleges, and this unrest brought forth the first chapter of Beta Theta Pi in that year. I recall the morning when the charter members, wearing pins as large as breast shields, quietly seated themselves in chapel.

"In '69 the first chapter of I. O's. was formed, a couple of girls coming over from Monmouth, I think, to see to its permanency, and the chapter at Iowa Wesleyan now is the oldest chapter of that sorority in existence. I shall always be friendly with that sorority, for I almost became one of them. Only one thing interfered—cliques existed in college then as now and in the passing years seven of us girls were constantly together. Indeed, there were eight, but in '69 Clara Woolson went to Albion college, Michigan, just at the time the ferment took on life. We seven talked the matter over, and decided that it would never do to allow anything to separate us, and the spark was struck by one of us saying, 'Why not form a society ourselves?' It was no sooner said than accomplished. We could scarcely wait till the necessary preliminaries could be arranged. I think Hattie Briggs suggested the name, Alice Coffin the badge, and to me was given the arduous task of the constitution. Fortunately my father liked the idea, and helped me arrange where the 'whereas' and the 'therefore resolved' should enter.

"I recall the hour as yesterday when the wording of the oath occurred to me. I sat in a summer house, wintry day though it was, near our 'Crooked tree-croquet ground.' I was so full of great thoughts that the confusion of the children annoyed me, so I wrapped myself in a shawl and went there to compose that oath. We met in the afternoon of that day, January 20, 1869, and being so anxious to organize and get to work, the little constitution I presented was regarded as 'just splendid.' And as I wrote it, it was suggested that I first take the oath,—the one I wrote in a winter-summer house. We were in the room that is now known as Miss Booth's history room, then the music room. Ella Stewart read the oath to me, then I to the other six. That was our initiation, and for ten years or more the

with little opposition P. E. O. remained as it was born, entering into the larger life of the town and city.

"I could go on indefinitely with tales of these early days, all intensely interesting, but you want to know something about the Original Seven. Hattie Briggs was the daughter of a Methodist preacher; a girl with calm fair brow and sweet blue eyes, winning in manner, never demonstrative,

Mary Allen Stafford.

Alice Coffin.

oath was our initiation ceremony.

"We placed the supervision of our badge, the star, in Mr. Hervey Crane's hands, and in a very short time entered chapel together one morning with the P. E. O. star upon our left shoulder. I would like to tell you of the story of our triumphant entry into the world of mystery, for as I said before, up to '69 secret societies were almost unknown, and to say 'it took' would hardly express it.

"Of course a hot rivalry between the I. C's. and P. E. O.'s was constant, but in the eighties all reason for that was withdrawn as the I. C's. became strictly a college sorority, Pi Beta Phi, and in the convention in Fairfield, where our first grand chapter was formed, came up the important question as to our status,—shall we become a Greek sorority or remain as now. Miss Nellie Ambler warmly championed the former, but

but eager and willing to follow. She had a rather large, commanding figure, and won friends through her inherent personality. She married in 1870, and died a few years after, loving P. E. O. to the last.

"Alice Coffin was a Southern girl, a motherless girl, who came to Mt. Pleasant with her sister for college work. She was exactly the opposite of Hattie in disposition, but like her in appearance. I do not think that anyone of us ever wore the star with more effect—it seemed to scintillate sparks of fire as she enthused and grew vehement. She was quick in anger, quick to forgive. She taught school for several years after graduating, and died at Newton, Iowa, in 1880, I think.

"Ella Stewart was a worker. We always knew when she said, 'now girls,' we had to go to work. She also was the daughter of a

Methodist preacher, and was a most energetic and efficient P. E. O. during her entire life. She lived in Mt. Pleasant and was
a great help in forming the Grand and Supreme chapters, and untangling of early records. She lived with her mother, than
whom P. E. O. never had a stauncher friend,
and died there perhaps twenty years ago.
She is buried in the old city cemetery.

"Mary Allen Stafford you all know. She

has resided for some years in New York City.

"Franc Roads was our wit; just of the
right stature to run instead of walk, and I
recall her as the one always to bring us
news of importance, and suggest remedy for
all our wrongs. She was always using her
pencil by way of illustration, and no wonder that she has become distinguished in the
world of art, teaching with great success
and originality in Aurora and Chicago, and

Ella Stewart.

Alice Bird Babb.

was very much like Hattie Briggs in disposition, more animated and more decided in
opinion, but a most helpful charter P. E. O.
Her home was a little out of the busy part
of town as well as that of Franc Roads, and
formed a fine camping ground for our frequent meetings. She married Dr. C. L.
Stafford, and has filled the place of a Methodist minister's wife with great distinction
and efficiency. She is the mother of four
children, one dead.

"Sue Pearson was our society belle and
our beauty. One does not often see such
rare beauty now—black curls, black sparkling eyes, rosy cheeks, and animation suitable for such folks. She was the beauty
and the pet. She broke the orthodox number of hearts, and finally married a gentleman of great wealth in Cleveland, Ohio. She
is the mother of two children, one dead, and

even to-day giving private instruction. She
has two children of which she is justly
proud. She went abroad a year or two ago
for the purpose of gaining all possible in
her art life, and brought back with her most
valuable information for her class.

"Were I to place these seven in appropriate statues, Alice Coffin would be Juno;
Sue Pearson, Venus; Franc Roads a feminine Mercury; Ella Stewart, Euterpe; Mary
Allen, Vesta; Hattie Briggs, Hygeia, and myself Hecate.

"In 1882 all our girlish and mixed-up con-
stitutions, so-called rituals, etc., went under
the inspection of wise and able eyes, and
P. E. O. began its life of national growth.
State Grand chapters and a Supreme Grand
chapter were formed. The constitution
from which amendments are often now
made, was written in 1893, and I am glad I

was able to prepare that, as I had written the original one. Our first initiation ceremony was prepared principally by Mrs. Nellie Ambler Campbell, at the time the State and Supreme chapters were formed. Our ritual was the work of a committee near the same time.

"Should someone ask what is the seventh chapter member doing, the one I call Hecate I will, like the mother of Gracchi point you

in writing of the past to leave off for the time being the more sober or sedate names of titles of married women and call them as we knew them, who were of them. There were the two (Allies)—Coffin and Bird, and Ella, Franc, Suella, Hattie, and Mary.

"Allie Coffin, tall, graceful, always radiant with sunshine, interested in what we were doing, and interesting and brilliant in her suggestions, "for the good of the order,"

Sue Pearson Penfield.

Franc Roads Elliott.

to my three children and say, 'these are my jewels,' and really I do not believe I do any of us justice without mentioning the fact of which we are most proud. Franc has two grandchildren, I have two (the best ever), and Mary is too stuck up for anything over a little visitor who has lately arrived at the home of her oldest son. So history repeats itself—children, girls, matrons, mothers, grandmothers. Not one of us is old—but constantly renewed to life and vigor by the doings of our large grown up daughter, Miss P. E. O."

The other member, Mrs. Stafford discoursed thus upon the subject.

"To write of the girls who formed the P. E. O. society forty years ago is not to write of girls at all now, but of mature, even matronly women, upon whom time has wrought its inevitable changes. I prefer, however,

but who left us early in our history for the brighter life, or circle, on the other side. One cannot but feel what our sisterhood has lost that would have been added to it had she but tarried with us.

"The other Allie must be recognized now, not as Allie Bird as we knew her then, but as Mrs. Alice Babb, who has always been active in every possible way in the interest of our society. We knew her then as intellectual, resourceful, and always happy in making suggestions or working out some helpful idea for our organization to which she is still so loyal and devoted.

"Ella lived for some years a simple beautiful life, always most happy when she could be ministering to others. She devoted years of faithful service as teacher in one of the state reform schools, and won many a wayward boy or girl to better things by her devotion and kindness. She lived, loved, and served through the years of her life as "Ella Stewart," and was called to be one of "the three of us who in the churchyard lie."

"Franc, always frank by name and in character, with a face full of smiles, eyes sparkling with good cheer, and greeting so cordial that you could not but be happier for meeting her, you know now as Mrs. Elliott, more serious or sedate with added years.

Hattie Briggs Bosquet.

but still always with the spirit of exuberance and gladness, delighting her friends when and wherever she meets them.

"Hattie Briggs-Bosquet, whom we knew as Hattie Briggs, the daughter of a Methodist minister, versatile, hopeful and helpful, always seeking to minister to others and forgetful of herself. She left us too early in her married life, and in our history for many if any, outside the "seven" to remember or know her, but there is much in the character and spirit of our organization that would have been missed but for her faithful ministrations in the early formation of P. E. O.

"'Suella' as we knew her, Mrs. Penfield, was not only the beautiful one and so recognized by all the others of the "seven," but was also a charming, winsome college girl, a joy to know and a delight to have a friend, and one who had much to do with broadening, beautifying, the conception and spirit of friendship always characteristic of the P. E. O. circle wherever found.

"Of the remaining one it is not mine to speak other than merely to say that in the memory of college girlhood days no part brings up sweeter recollections than of the "seven" and our part in the organization of P. E. O.

"Ah! the memories of sweet summer eves,
  Of moonlit wave and willowy way,
Of stars and flowers, and dewy leaves,
  And smiles, and tones, more dear than they."

IOWA CONVENTION PAPERS.

Responsibility of Office—Mrs. Katherine Yeager.

WHEN it was suggested to me that I might choose my own subject for this short talk which I am about to give the first subject that entered my mind was responsibility of office. As this is one of the subjects that has been on my mind ever since I have had the honor of filling an office in the I. G. C. I have felt at times somewhat like the old lady with a large family upon entering a train. The conductor asked her "Be this your family or is it a picnic."

She replied, "Yes this is my family and it is no picnic." I imagine this is the way most of the officers of the P. E. O. sisterhood have felt at some time during their term of office.

But sisters, I have put in a great deal of time searching through old minutes, reading officers' reports, etc., and I believe this is my ninth convention and so far I have failed to find where any of the officers have ever uttered a word of complaint about the great responsibility and work there is attached to carrying on this great sisterhood.

Your past officers have been women of sterling worth, women who have been care-

pears an oasis in the arid desert—a green island in the lonely sea,—"Spinning and Weaving"—"The invention of spinning is ascribed by the ancients to Minerva, Goddess of Wisdom.'

Sisters I progressed still further through steam engines, stenography and stereotyping, through telegraphy and telephones, vaccination, violins and volcanoes; even the X Ray and the Signs of the Zodiac did not escape me but not one lonely, solitary, eenty, teenty word more did I find of the inventions of women and I know that if you could have seen my pathetic figure at the close of the long, weary day as the lengthening shadows fell and I sat there in my desolation and humiliation you would have wept with me as I (so nearly) perished in my pride.

At the close of the above touching paragraph it is a shame not to conclude a paper which might well illustrate the Fourth Dimension as it has neither height breadth nor thickness. But may I add a postcript? One thing that I am sure was invented by women for her own exclusiveness. I rise to inquire the reason of this thusness? And this answer comes to me—who compiled and printed these works excluding our sex from its rightful share in the glory of the race? Man selfish, vainglorious man, while we of the inventive, the ingenious sex, were at home quietly and generously concocting delicious salads and nourishing soups, inventing home-made puddings and cakes, were putting fantastic crimps in our pie crusts and taking them out of our boys; while we were discovering new methods of putting invisible patches in the knees of trowsers, planning trap nests for the hens and devising a fireless brooder out of our best shawls and a market basket behind the kitchen range—they were shamelessly running to the patent office with their measly little contrivances and getting patents upon them so

that they could go down in history as the sex that does things. When we, through days of grinding toil and nights devoid of ease were discovering and suggesting all sorts of worthy devices for making lives easier and homes happier and were generously giving them to the world without money and without price, they were greedily filching these rich ideas of ours and after putting a few hours work upon them were sticking patent marks all over them and claiming all the glory. Well do I remember an incident in my early married life which illustrates all too well the unfair treatment accorded our sex by even the best of men. Many times had my husband upon coming home retired into his study and as I carefully guarded the door I had told the children in bated whispers that their father was writing, was thinking and must not be disturbed; and we had tip-toed about until such time as he should emerge with some burning thoughts transfixed to paper. Now, once upon a time, I, even I, had a thought, a plan, an idea. I intended to do some thinking of my own. So I locked myself within the aforesaid study after affixing upon the door this legend: "Keep out. Be quiet. This is my busy day." Sisters, this is even sadder than the other for do you think I was obeyed? Nay, I say unto you I was not. Did not the wash lady call for her money? Did not the apple and potato men besiege my doorway? Did not the telephone ring forty-seven times in one afternoon? Did not the babies stand in howling concert before that closed room and did not the partner of my joys and sorrows vainly beseech me to unbar the door and at last in a sad and weeping voice did he not tell our offspring that poor mamma must be crazy? So I say that it is plain to me that if we women are not the inventors and discoverers of the race we have no cause to blame ourselves for it. Here endeth the first lesson.

THE PAST IN P. E. O.
Mrs. Alice Babb's Supreme Convention Paper.

 HERE is a law in optics that the farther we go from an object the smaller that object becomes, until confused in the conglomeration of mundane affairs, our original object is lost. Not so with mental and moral optics. The farther

Feb. #912

we recede, the larger the object we love and revere becomes, until our entire present is colored by its influence. Take for instance our Civil War. As the years go by and veterans pass quickly from sight, the memory of their deeds of fifty years ago is encased in magnificent parks and monuments, and it is possible we give 'the "Boys of '60" more than their due, in this bright light of the past, and everyone in her childhood or early youth planted some seed, which the sun of the present protected and fructified, until late in life we see a lovely thought become a thing of wide influence, and we stand in wonder and awe.

Nothing in my life has grown so luxuriously as P. E. O. I have an idea that in the order of our Universe, it was wisely intended for us seven girls to do what we did. A principle, a needed principle, was behind the little gathering on January 20, 1869, when we met in the old music room of J. W. U. and solemnly took the oath, subscribed to by thousands since that day. We hoped the seed was good, and we were anxious to have seven chapters—one chapter for each girl, but the Wise Hand that sees to the growth of an organization, must have pronounced P. E. O. good, else it could not have prospered as it has. It was not because we were seven began P. E. O. It was because the time was ripe for just such an organization; it was needed, and we unsuspecting seven made the ferment. We are proud of our Sisterhood. When we read our "Objects and Aims" we can but feel that true life is the result of such objects and aims, and yet on an occasion of this kind it is well not to be unduly elated by our past, but to examine points along the way where we have made mistakes, and where we can improve them. It has not been my good fortune to be affiliated with P. E. O. as closely as I'd wish since the very early days. I can say the same of each of the seven, so it would not be kind for me to criticise P. E. O. Still I have wondered if it is possible we have grown too fast; have we initiated persons just on account of pleasing presence, or because they were friends of P. E. O's? Then again is our organization becoming more a club than a Sisterhood?

This point I have often tried to impress. The ruling spirit that actuated our birth was pure sisterly love, and I have hoped this might still continue. Of course we cannot expect for the deep rooted affection that animated the seven,—that was unusual,—but let the fact never be forgotten, that affection was the cause of P. E. O. Not th desire for a club. Bear in mind I do not criticise the many noble bands of women that exist in city and town,—our country over. I simply want to impress this thought,—that as we began in deep affection, let us try to cultivate a sisterly spirit as much as possible. With this we can reach forth and delve deeper. It did truly exist in the early days, and the great proof of its existence is the fact, that as I am writing these lines, my heart warms, and my eyes are moist,—just because I love to think of those long ago times. I love the memory of each of the seven, and I live over again our free simple methods of procedure in our meetings. We knew little of Parliamentary ruling,—in fact, if you "count up" you will find that women had not been admitted to the so-called Higher Education, many years previous. Instead of being mature women as we are to-day, we were seven very lively young girls, wanting all the fun that was going, yet loving each other dearly. We wanted to perpetuate P. E. O. because we thought so much of each other.

To-day, a fine method is present in our conventions—a wonderful education is necessary for her who becomes Supreme President and it is well,—but let us remember the early days were marked by a sincere desire to do right, and a simplicity of life which cannot be surpassed, because it was genuine, it was the thing.

A few days ago chapter A of Chicago came out to Aurora to have a "Midsummer social" with one of their number who resides here now. I joined them, and listened to their fine mode of governing the meeting. I noted the lovely gowns, the well poised gestures, and perfect manners, and memory took my hand, and together we flew in our airship back to the days of '69. Can you imagine my dear sisters, the difference between then and now? Take the subject

of dress: Such a thing as a fashion magazine did not exist in Mt. Pleasant. We made
our dresses ourselves according to the cloth.
The time was soon after the war; calico was
75 cents a yard, narrow embroidery $1.00 a
yard. I know this to be true, because after
much discussion my father allowed me to
get five yards for my wedding trousseau,
and gave me a five dollar bill to get it. Oh,
how rich I was! Five whole yards of embroidery an inch wide! Why the cars had
come into our town from Chicago only a few
years; three dresses were an outfit. A de
laine for Sunday, a cheaper material for next
best, then one calico. When we graduated,
we seven P. E. O's. were at our Ruthian
Literary Society open meeting in what we
call mosquito netting to-day; each one of
us a different color, and each one of us made
her own dress, for there were no dress

makers. Mary Allen wore a heliotrope
color, netting; Franc Roads a cream colored,
and I wore a pink, and I imagine Allie Coffin
wore a blue, Ella Stewart a green, and Hattie
Briggs a white, and we looked so pretty. I
spoke "Beautiful Snow"—and when Mary
came to speak she had been suffering from
tooth ache, so that her face was swollen,
and we turned down the wicks in the kero-
sine lamps, so the audience could not see
how her face was swollen.

And as Mrs. Reeves told me only to take
five or six minutes, I'll leave with this lesson from the past of us seven.

Turn down the lights of an undue pub-
licity or criticism on all sister P. E. O's.
until you see whether there are any bumps
there or only gossip.

Be charitable and when you don't know
what to say—keep still.

WHAT DO YE MORE THAN ANOTHER?

Mrs. Kate Darr in Nebraska Convention.

MRS. Babb once said: That the reason
for our existence was because of the
"ferment," the "stir" which seemed
in the air then of the rarely
Women's Clubs. The time was ripe for
something of this kind, and these girls with
a desire to cement their friendship and to
keep each other in tender remembrance
laid the foundation of the first secret
society for women not dependent on, or auxiliary to, one organized by men. In the beginning all ideals and purposes were of the
highest and as this sisterhood has grown
and the influence it radiates reaches out in
every direction like the points of our star,
it means doing more than is possible in a
Woman's Club. In our sisterhood we combine the spiritual and mental and cultivate
a sisterly feeling which makes us a harmonious whole. We are carrying out the
fundamental principles by living for the
best and doing our best and making ourselves a part of this earnest, most beautiful,
most nearly ideal organization of women in
existence.

By being banded together and learning to

depend upon our own resources and constantly struggling to attain our "high
ideals," have we not been made better, our
sympathies quickened, our minds broadened
and o r characters strengthened? It is a
great and noble thing to be an active P. E.
O. in good standing. It is not an honor to
be lightly cast aside, or discarded without
good reasons. Surely P. E. O. like Christi-
anity, is working for the uplift of humanity.
It is progressive and has a mission. We
seek culture not for our own benefit, but
that we may enlarge our sphere of usefulness in the world, and by helping others, receive the benefit which always returns to
one who is helpful to others. Social
pleasures are not our chief aim, yet we
frequently enjoy such recreation and the
pleasure is shared by our friends outside of
P. E. O.

Some of the reasons for our existence are
improvement in manners, mind and morals,
growth in knowledge and mental culture.
Many of us have been occupied with other
duties, and getting down to mental work is
difficult; but the women of our sisterhood

Nov. 1919

by Mrs. June Grable Evans. All the visiting P. E. O.s were called upon for speeches and Miss Durward closed the program with a fore cast of the convention.

On Sunday evening Mr. and Mrs. M. Carl Smith and Miss Virginia Corbett entertained a small company at a beautifully appointed dinner.

Miss Durward's home on South College Avenue was headquarters and her new car was the official bus. Every minute of the visit was enjoyed by all the fortunate P. E. O.s who had belonged to Miss Durward's official family during the biennial.

As a memento of the visit the guests gave Miss Durward for her new car a completely equipped lunch kit.

☆ ☆

CONSIDER THE LILLIES.
By Alice Bird Babb.

As it now seems impossible for me to attend the Supreme convention of P. E. O. I will send to the dear friends through the voice of another, my anniversary message. When Miss Durward first wrote asking me to appear on the program I decided that I should not reminisce. Our summers in the middle west had been so unusually beautiful, that I turned to nature and decided to take for my subject Consider the Lilies, and thus go back not fifty years, but to the time when we seven girls were in the select or private school, before the public schools came into being. Our teachers then gave us such subjects for essays as, "Spring", "Autumn," "Beauties of Nature," so I thought "Consider the Lilies" would be the thing; but in Miss Durward's answer I read between the lines, that she would prefer me at this anniversary meeting to "Consider P. E. O." —and her desire is law.

The reason why I did not care to reminsce is because I have posed as an old settler all my life. I remember Mr. John Palmer's stopping me on the street in Mt. Pleasant forty years ago, and saying to me "Mrs. Babb, you must speak for us on Old Settler's day." I told him that only old settlers should speak on that day. "How long" said he, "have you lived in Henry County?" I told him that I had lived in this world, which amounted to the same thing as living in Iowa, in Henry County, in Mt. Pleasant for thirty years. "Then" said he,

"you are an old settler. It takes just thirty years to make an old settler in Henry County."

Then I asked my mother about the old time bed quilts, the Irish chain, Star of Bethlehem, hit and miss, but when it came to the spinning wheel she said "Oh, Alice, you're older than I am; I never owned a spinning wheel in my life."

And then the commander of McFarland Post, G. A. R., in Mt. Pleasant a little later asked me to tell the school children on Decoration Day, some of my childhood recollections of the Civil War. I told them of the Sanitary commission, which they say today was not sanitary at all, of scraping lint and tearing bandages, not from disinfected cheese cloth, but from well worn muslin. I told them of sitting on the gate post watching for the weekly parade of the fourth Iowa cavalry, which for a few months was camped at Camp Harlan. Then of the incessant music of the fife and drum in the park and how we little girls watched the great spiders of the recruiting officers with their huge epaulets from which dangled gold ropes, enticing what we called "the boys" into their net.

War played the same tricks then as now, it makes a boy a man in a day—in an hour.

Your boy one day comes into your kitchen carrying in mud, and you wish he'd get off to school. He throws corn on the neighbor's windows on hollowe'en—the next day the man is born, of sterner stuff and finer metal, but alas the boy—the dear, dear boy.

All this gave me practice work for the fifty year P. E. O. stunts, and I have been so fortunate as to attend nearly all of them.

I began celebrating our 50th year, two years ago this October, when the bronze P. E. O. tablet was set up in the Iowa Wesleyan College at Mt. Pleasant. Mary and I were there and it was a notable occasion, for tablets are not set up until a society accomplishes something and monuments are not erected the day after a battle.

No, tablets are not placed the day after a society is formed, but after a lapse of years—years that temper the feeling and give a just estimate of what has been done. A notable example of this is the monument set up recently at Saratoga, to commemorate the Revolutionary battle. There are four spaces on that monument for the names of the four great generals who won the battle; three are filled, the fourth will always remain vacant, Benedict Arnold did not make good, he is not remembered.

On that October day in Mt. Pleasant, the notables of Iowa sat on the platform, Miss Bliss was there who originated the thought and Mrs. Jordan who planned its execution. In the audience were P. E. O.s and life long neighbors and friends. The ground seemed consecrated, and the air was filled with harp like echoes from '69. When I returned home I wrote my "Harvest of the Quiet Eye," which I took to the Illinois convention at Chicago when Mrs. Louella Stafford was president and again at the Iowa convention when Mrs. Henely was president.

Now I thought, I've said it all, but as winter approached and the 21st of January, 1919 came around, ushering in the day of our fiftieth anniversary, I received an invitation from Chapter AD Illinois, of which Mrs. Lindsey was president to be present at a luncheon to be given to the twelve Chicago Chapters at the La Salle. On the following day an invitation came from Chapter Original A to be there and I was sorry that one body could not occupy two places at the same time. I went into Chicago and it was a most impressive occasion. My subject was "The Attic and the Living Room—and the stairs between the two became worn and dusty so often did we go up and down. At the close of the meeting the Chapter presented me with a basket of yellow and white blossoms, I took them home and when they were faded I hung the lovely wicker basket in my vestibule and I never pass it today but "the scent of the roses cling to it still."

During the winter I wrote over two hundred letters to chapters celebrating our fiftieth year. And then came the party magnificent. The B. I. Ls of Chicago decided to celebrate and you know when men do attempt to do anything they go over the top every time. Mr. Parks was toast master and that assured the literary success of the evening. Mr. DeMoney was general manager, and these two men were like Don Quixote and Sancho Panza in Cervante's great novel you could not tell "which was tother." I think Mr. De Money asked me three or four times if my room was comfortable until I began to think maybe it was not comfortable.

This party went out in a blaze of glory, and it seemed a most fitting close to the fifty year celebration. As the spring advanced, came the annual conventions and "the lure of the wild" called me to Wisconsin. It seemed fitting since Wisconsin was the youngest P. E. O. daughter that one of the mothers should be there, especially since my daughter, Mrs. Vida Kimble Babb gave the welcome. I took for my subject "Iowa and Wisconsin"—Iowa the Mother, Wisconsin the youngest daughter.

Mr. Parks was there and had a beautiful toast, he also said he had his opinion of a woman who had lived for fifty-seven years in Iowa, when for some good reason had moved to another state, and where did she go, not to Wisconsin but to Illinois and yet she had not a word to say for Illinois. Mr. Williams, one of our best B. I. Ls, was absent from these two meetings and we were all so sorry for the cause of his absence.

Then in June occurred the fiftieth anniversary of our graduating class at Iowa Wesleyan College, not exactly a P. E. O. affair, but I was pleased when Dr. George S. Gassner of the class, who gave the commencement address said to me "Allie, in your alumni speech tonight tell about those bright colored dresses you girls wore at the Ruthean Exhibition." So I could again refer to the rose tarleton and I was glad to remember, that I had tied my little speech written on only one side of the paper with a rose colored ribbon to match the dress. Five of the P. E. O. founders were in his class of 1869.

Recollections crowd, but I will only mention two values the fifty years have brought. One is the value of memory. Cicero in his "De Senectute" gives four reasons why old age is a delightful period, and says it is because of the brightness of memory. In childhood time passes so swiftly, there is no time to recollect. When we are in school and in college we become filled with thoughts of what we are going to do, we take no time to remember. When we leave school we are in the noon time of life, in the heat and in the hurry, we are on our job. But Mother Nature so kind and wise, has stored up a beautiful box for every one of us, and when as Longfellow says "The day is done." "When Evening Shadows Gather," an effulgent radiance is cast up in the west which our enemies, the Germans, are pleased to call "The After Glow," this light is so radiant that all the nooks and crannies of past experiences are exposed and precious and priceless treasures are revealed.

The other value I recommend to younger P. E. O.s is the value of outlook or vision; The Bible says that "Faith without works is dead," and I say that works without faith is dead.

I was talking the other day to a soldier who had camped at Don Ramey where Joan of Arc was born, he had often been at Rheims where she crowned Charles XII, the dauphin, king of France, and he was at Rouan, where she was burned because she saw visions. And I declare to you I'd rather be burned at twenty-one as Joan was, because I saw visions, than to live to be fifty and declare there were no visions.

Booth Tarkington in his "Magnificent Ambursons" asks what writes the lines on a man's face? "Age writes some, work writes, some and worry writes some, but the deepest are carved by the lack of faith." Faith, vision, sentiment, are the windows of life through which we see the truth. Vision is like a lighted candle set in the window of a lonely farm house on a bleak cold night, it lights up the bleak interior, it suggests comfort and companionship. If there be any virtue in the founding of P. E. O. it is not on account of the founders, for we were all ordinary girls, but on account of the time of founding. It was the age of vision, reconstruction not only along national lines, but reconstruction of thought, mind, soul. Woman's Clubs were demanded, they came just at the right time. It was strange soil for them to grow in, our lines were rigid, our paths were straight. Economy was the order of the day, but like Alpine flowers blooming in the snow, they bloom all the more luxuriantly because of the rigidity of the atmos-

phere. P. E. O. thrived, we were not bound by criticism or cynicism. We sang, oh how we sang; every one who had a tongue and a mouth who could keep time, could sing, and there was no talk about trained voices.

Alice Coffin and I would serenade Franc Rhodes and Mary Allen and they'd waken to the strains of "Dream Sweetly, Love" and turn over and go to sleep to the echoes of "In The Starlight." And Sue Pearson and I spoke pieces, I know Franc Rhodes is laughing now, "The Rum Maniac", "Curfew Shall Not Ring Tonight" and we spoke together "Beautiful Snow" while someone threw from above pieces of cotton to accentuate it. And she'll remember how we spoke together Benjamin Taylor's "River of Time;" if we were there we'd speak it. But how little we both thought when we spoke it that in fifty years we'd know all about that "River of Time," its curves, its outlets, its inlets and how it would continue to roll, till it joined that ocean "which rolls round the world and carries us all on its bosom."

May God grant us all a pleasant voyage and safe haven.

☆ ☆

YEAR BOOK SUGGESTIONS.

Chapter A, Denver, Colorado, has for a subject Problems of Today. For every meeting there is a leader to present the topic, and also a discussion leader. In this way everyone has an opportunity to discuss the problems. The topics include world problems, national problems, educational problems, religious problems, P. E. O. problems, civic problems, home problems and personal problems. The program, you see, runs the whole range from world problems to your own personal difficulties. In addition the program includes Mother's Day, a Christmas party, a B. I. L. party, a sewing meeting for charity, and a New Year's reception for all Denver chapters.

Chapter B, Toledo Ohio, has an attractive year book tied with a yellow ribbon in real P. E. O. fashion. For roll call they give current events. At their meetings they will discuss vacation notes, editorials, child welfare, missions and modern American poets.

They take one day each for the Supreme convention report, Educational day, study

The P. E. O. Record

FOUNDED JANUARY, 1889

The Official Organ of the Supreme Chapter of the P. E. O. Sisterhood

Published Monthly by Kable Brothers Company, Mount Morris, Illinois, under the Auspices of the P. E. O. Sisterhood

WINONA EVANS REEVES, Editor, 1039 Hollywood Ave., Chicago, Ill.

Entered as second-class matter at the post-office at Mount Morris, Illinois, June 7, 1921, under the act of August 24, 1912
Acceptance for mailing at special rate of postage provided for in Section 1103, Act of October 3, 1917. Authorized July 29, 1918
Subscription price to P. E. O.'s, 50 cents a year; subscription price to non-P. E. O.'s, $1.00 a year

| Volume XXXVI | October, 1925 | Number 10 |

Judge Washington Irving Babb

OCTOBER 2, 1844-SEPTEMBER 4, 1925

THE RECORD this month carries the sad news of the passing of Judge Babb, the husband of Mrs. Alice Bird Babb, one of the Founders of P. E. O.

Judge Washington I. Babb, President of the Western Wheeled Scraper Company of Aurora and Vice President of the Austin Manufacturing Company of Chicago, died September 4 at 7:30 o'clock at St. Charles Hospital of a general breakdown incident to old age. Judge Babb was for years a prominent figure in the Democratic party of Iowa and the nation. He was elected to the Iowa legislature in 1884 and in 1891 was elected to the bench of the second judicial district of Iowa. In 1895 he was the Democrats' candidate for governor of Iowa and in 1896 received the party's vote in the legislature for United States senator. In the same year Judge Babb was the chairman of the sound money Democratic convention in opposition to the free silver program of the late William Jennings Bryan.

Judge Babb served as a volunteer in the Eighth Iowa Cavalry during the Civil war.

He was born October 2, 1844, on a farm in Des Moines County, Iowa, the son of Miles and Mary B. Babb of Iowa. His boyhood was uneventful enough until in 1860 he moved to Mt. Pleasant, Ia., where he entered Iowa Wesleyan college.

His college career was broken into by the Civil War. He remained in service two years, 1863 to 1865, and was with General Thomas in Sherman's march to the sea. In 1865 he returned to college and received his A. B. degree. For fifty-three years Judge Babb was a member of the Board of Trustees of Iowa Wesleyan College, being a trustee at the time of his death. He was admitted to the bar in 1868 and practiced for 38 years.

In 1907 he went to Aurora to be-

come the legal adviser of the Western Wheeled Scraper Company at Aurora, the largest manufacturer of wheeled scrapers and dump cars in the world, and the Austin Manufacturing Company of Chicago. Upon the death in 1910 of Capt. C. H. Smith, at that time President of the scraper company, Judge Babb was chosen to head the firm. He continued in this capacity ever since. The same year he was elected Vice President of the Austin Manufacturing Company.

Besides being President of the Western Wheeled Scraper Company, and Vice President of the Austin Manufacturing Company, Judge Babb was Vice President of the Old Second National Bank, the Aurora Foundry and the Aurora Cotton mills. He was a member of the Union League clubs of Aurora and of Chicago. He was also a Knight Templar, having been Grand Commander of that Order in Iowa. He

was a member of the McFarland post of G. A. R. of Mt. Pleasant, Ia.

The widow, Mrs. Alice Babb, and three children, Max W. Babb of Milwaukee, Miles T. Babb of Chicago and Mrs. D. K. Ewing of Aurora, survive. One child, Clarabelle, died a number of years ago.

The funeral service was held at the family home, Sunday, September 6, conducted by the Rev. Walter Briggs, pastor of the Galena Boulevard Methodist Episcopal church and was largely attended.

A feature of the brief service was the reading of Wordsworth's "Happy Warrior," by the Hon. James Shaw, City Librarian of Aurora, and a close friend of Judge and Mrs. Babb.

The burial service was held in Mt. Pleasant, Iowa, at Forest Home on September 7.

Mrs. Babb was not able to attend either service, being confined to her bed through illness and grief.

The facts of the life and death of Judge Babb are recorded in "Who's Who in America," in newspapers and journals, and in histories of various sorts, but as is always the case, there is much more untold than is recorded.

Judge Babb was a courtly Christian gentleman, a very scholarly man. Notwithstanding the manifold interests which were his in a business way, his chief interest was in Mrs. Babb. Theirs was a long journey together, more than fifty years of joy and of sorrow.

We like to think that the end of the journey for him was like that of Pilgrim:

"The Pilgrim they laid in a large upper chamber whose window opened toward the sunrising. The name of the chamber was Peace, where he slept till break of day; and then he awoke and sang." A.

Through Memory's Veil

DR. JOHN W. HOLLAND

WHOEVER shows one greatness makes him his debtor. He who looks at a mountain, watches the sea in stormy moods, or gazes long into the wonder of night skies, is sure of enlargement in his soul.

Great as are nature's objects to inspire us, a noble soul surpasses them, by so much as a thinker is greater than an object of thought. The ideas that crowd my brain as I think of the wonderful life of Mrs. Alice Bird Babb are such that language seems too weak to express. If an artist might despair of the inability of colors to portray his fairy images, well may I hesitate to entrust to words the business of carrying the pictures that come to me as I muse on the greatness of the soul of Mrs. Babb.

I was a bashful youth in a freshman class at Iowa Wesleyan College in 1898 at Mount Pleasant, Iowa, when I first saw Mrs. Babb. She was acting as toastmistress at a banquet. I thought how great the distance was between us and how much farther on the roadway of life she was than I. Twenty-five years of acquaintance with her did not seem to lessen the mental distance that I then felt. She simply was made of larger mold than the rest of us.

If it was ever your pleasure to hear her preside at any public function, you well know of the brilliance of her mind. Once I saw her when a great obligation and responsibility was suddenly thrust upon her. She hesitated a moment, and then said, "Well, as Mr. Babb says when he pulls on his shoe in the morning, 'It's a big thing, and I'm into it,' so I will try to make the best of it."

It was my good fortune to be initiated into the fraternity of which her husband, Judge Babb, and her two sons, Max and Miles, were members. This threw me into closer friendship with the family, and many times the pleasure was mine—the keenest pleasure that a boy away from home can know—of eating Sunday dinner in a home such as that over which she presided. Then, occasionally in the evening, the Beta boys were allowed to meet in her parlor, and after the greetings to the boys were over, she sat always with her book or books, by the reading lamp in the living room.

For many years Mrs. Babb coached the plays which the senior classes gave at the commencement season at Iowa Wesleyan. Our class, 1902, gave a dramatization of "The Minister's Wooing" by Harriet Beecher Stowe. My role was that of Candace, the old negro mammy. It seemed to me that I required rather more attention than the remainder of the cast. After the last touches were added to my feminine toilette, Mrs. Babb gave me the final inspection, adding as she did so, "John, you look like a negro, you talk like a negro, but I can't get you quite the right shape."

College over, seminary days completed, I was sent to serve as pastor of the Galena Street Methodist Episcopal Church in Aurora, Ill., in 1909. Imagine my surprise when I looked over the audience to spy Judge and Mrs. W. I. Babb in the congregation. He nodded and she put up one hand a little way and waved at me. It was rather unecclesiastical, but I am sure that it helped warm my heart for that first sermon before a congregation of strangers. For four years I remained as her pastor. I was a frequent visitor in their home, and often I took fragments of poems and sermons over to read to her. Her appreciation was always apparent, but she generally closed her comment with the belief that I could make it better upon another trial. During these years she had grown older, but the brilliancy of her mind increased with the ripening of her soul's experience.

Mrs. Babb was not an easy believer. She wanted to know. Things had to appeal to her sense of justice or she would have nothing of them. Her especial problem was the age-old one of the "why of human suffering." She had literally memorised J. G. Holland's "Bitter Sweet," in the deep hunger of her mind for certainty.

Deaths bothered her, especially the taking away of little children, or the removal of a mother when her children were young. She used to say, in the words of Bitter Sweet,

"I've often thought had I God's power
Or He my love, we'd have a different world."

She used to say, "If I could only trust God as those birds outside the windows do; but then, they haven't the brains to ask why. Sometime I'm going to know." She was not aware that, after all, that is the sublimest faith any of us can have.

A particularly painful affliction came to her in the year 1913. Her nails became affected, and bared to the air the tender nerves under them. She suffered the torments of the lost, whatever they may happen to be. I found her one afternoon, lying on a couch, reading the book of Job. She said, "John, read me some of this. He is the only man who had sense enough to know anything. Read that line which says, 'Though He slay me, yet will I trust Him.' That's my faith."

Like Tennyson, I can say of her, "There was more faith in her honest doubt than in half the creeds."

On visits back to the city of Aurora, we always went to see Judge and Mrs. Babb. She greeted me and my wife, ever with a mother's kiss, and called us by our first names.

I have had frequent letters from her, which I treasure. They are marked with that rare brilliancy and genuineness which was her nature. She was pleased with the growth of P. E. O. though she was always surprised at the love which flowed to her from the thousands of P. E. O. members scattered through forty states. Mrs. Stafford once said to me, "We girls were with her, but we all followed her, for she had an innate sense of leadership that was as certain as it was original."

No finer wish for the future of P. E. O. can I formulate into words than this, that in some real fashion, the loving, genuine devotion of sisters to sisters, which was present in the hearts of your original seven, as they sat out on the campus stile, in Mount Pleasant Iowa, and planned how they might formulate their ideals into an organization that would help them as they looked forward into life, that some way this group, now with one exception, gathered into the unseen world, may guide you in your councils, inspire you in your devotion, and purify your souls.

Of Mrs. Alice Bird Babb, and what her life has meant to me personally, I can truly say with the Scotch poet:

"The monarch may forget the crown
That lately on his head hath been;
The bridegroom may forget the bride
Was made his own but yestere'en;
The mother may forget the babe
Which slept so sweetly at her knee;
But forget thee, will I ne'er, Glencairn,
And all that thou hast done for me."

A Prayer

GRANT us the will to fashion as we feel;
Grant us the strength to labor as we know;
Grant us the purpose, ribbed and edged with steel,
To strike the blow.

Knowledge we ask not; knowledge Thou has lent;
But Lord, the will—there lies our bitter need;
Give us to build above the deep intent
The deed, the deed.

—John Drinkwater.

Our Impressions of Mrs. Babb

MRS. MARY E. GREEN, Chapter BD, Aurora, Ill.

IT IS my privilege to bring to you today a tribute to Mrs. Alice Bird Babb, who was the first P. E. O. and the first President of P. E. O.

To those who have not had the privilege of coming directly in contact with one of the founders it is natural that they would be interested in knowing what that close personal contact might mean to a chapter. While we realized it meant much, as is the case with most blessings we never fully appreciate them until they are taken away. We kept in touch with Mrs. Babb principally through her daughter, Alice Babb Ewing, who is a member of our chapter. As you know, Mrs. Babb's health began to fail about the time the family moved to Aurora. Her ties were so strong in Mt. Pleasant that it literally broke her heart to leave there. In a few years came the loss of Judge Babb, the blow from which she never really recovered. His death was actually more than she could bear with her otherwise failing health, and she followed him the next year.

There were months of anxiety and uncertainty when she saw only her nearest and dearest. The devotion of her children bore testimony to the love and comfort they found in each other, and their quiet courage was a tribute to her. Through all that painful time she preferred to lie on a lovely old couch downstairs rather than take to her bed until the very last weeks.

The first time I met Mrs. Babb was at my own home, three years ago, when she attended the inspection. At that time she related with a flash of her old time fire, the story of the founding of the first chapter. She had pictures of the girls, as they were at that time, and told in her inimitable way the characteristics of the different girls. On another occasion she likened all these girls to different characters from Dickens. It was not hard to picture her in the role she must have taken at that time—someone on the order of Jo in Little Women. One was impressed with the sparkle of those dark eyes, the fun and wealth of wholesome wisdom and philosophy which lay back of them, and her very delicious sense of humor and original way of expressing herself.

As we know, the birthday of P. E. O. was January 21. I couldn't help but note that it was my birthday, too, and thought in connection with that, of how little the seven girls ever dreamed that this act of theirs in their youthful exuberance and need to express just themselves, should have laid the foundations of so large a structure—an act that was to affect the lives of generations yet unborn—as it has done. They loved each other first—the forming of the organization was only the flower of their years of friendship, burst into bloom. Their association was the real thing to them and they tried to crystallize it in the most beautiful form it was in their power to conceive. That spring, which had gushed forth in their lives, that reflected their finest ideals, was destined to bubble up into countless other lives and places long after they were gone. Their only idea at the time was to have a tangible expression of their faith in each other. It was a never ending surprise to her that P. E. O. should have grown so large and she was always touched when remembered so often and so beautifully by P. E. O.'s everywhere.

It is easy to visualize that group trying to "put one over" on the boys, no doubt laughing at themselves for being so serious, and yet in dead earnest. Women's societies in colleges were in their infancy and looked upon as decidedly radical. It was a new departure and one can imagine Mrs. Babb glorying in it all. She was the forceful moving spirit in their project.

Even admitting the toll the years had taken, one could see what a capable and vigorous person she had been; one could not think of her as old—there was that about her which was eternally young and intensely interested in young people and forward movements of any kind. So real and genuine herself, she had no patience with pretense, or superficial insincerity of any kind. In her religious life she took little for granted—not content to "see through a glass darkly" but wished to see face to face.

I feel quite inadequate to the task of making a true picture of a nature so deep and complex as hers was. It is seldom one finds her combination of strength and stability together with such a brilliant and scintillating mentality capable of so many quick changes of mood, though never gloomy moods while she was well and strong. While it is always wrong to try to label and pigeon-hole people, for with most of us, our strengths and weaknesses shade together in a blurred sort of way, in her case it would be impossible, as she was proficient in many ways that were more or less unrelated. Teeming with impulsive and generous impulses she was full of resources and promptly translated her quick thoughts into swift action.

Someone has said that all people may be divided into three groups—those interested in people, those interested in ideas, and those interested in things. Most people are interested in a combination of any two as is the case of a teacher interested in people and ideas, or a craftsman combining an interest in ideas and things but not mingling with people easily. Mrs. Babb really loved people and ideas the most. She loved things too, but they were always the practical things. She loved the new devices for making housekeeping easier and loved to browse around the ten cent store. Someone wishing to make her a nice Christmas present, something she really wanted, asked what they should get and she replied in her jolly way, "Oh a nice new dust pan tied with a red ribbon?" She was a very efficient housekeeper, moved swiftly and could turn off a prodigious amount of work with little apparent effort and when her health was good, parties and wash day often went together. To her homemaking was not filling the house with a lot of furniture and knick-knacks, but filling it with living things like the roses grown in her choice rose garden, a hospitable table around which friends gathered often (for she was a splendid cook), and her best beloved books. With her, the spirit was the thing and the life more than the raiment.

In spite of her poetic and philosophic interpretation of life, we should not think of her as an aesthetic or a dreamy sort of person. There was nothing of the sentimental, the vague or the abstract in her makeup. Aside from her family, literature and the ability to express herself in that medium was her great love and passion in life. No doubt many of you have read that tender and beautiful story she wrote some time ago. I cannot do better than to use it as an illustration of her beautiful diction. This was written some time after the passing away of her little daughter, and because she had touched the depths herself and could articulate all it meant, she was often able to come to others with similar griefs, in just the right and comforting way.

It is the story of the little play house in her yard. She pictures the tiny housekeepers scouring and bustling in and out, tying back the curtains with their brothers' old neckties, their sweet happy voices floating up to the porch where the mother listened to their prattle about the little cracked dishes and dolls and the tea party in progress. Something called them out of the play house, and the older one, so soon to be taken away, turned the button on the play house door as she ran out and shut it. To go on with Mrs. Babb's own words:

"Three months from that time a storm beaten, weary figure stood on that same back porch.

* * * * * *

"A blight had fallen upon everything.

* * * * * * *

"As her eyes sadly wandered from object to object they finally rested on that play house door which the precious hands now folded so quietly under the 'low green tent' had hastily closed weeks before. The form of this 'Rachel' dragged herself to the spot, turned the button and entered.

There lay the remains of the tea party, the broken cooky, the dried up apple, the cracked dishes—the dust of weeks upon it all. The dolly, like the sphinx of old whom the Egyptians begged with magician's arts to open its dumb mouth and reveal the secrets it must know, sat dumb waiting for its little mistress. The curtain on the cupboard was fastened with a ribbon whose history was a poem; pictures decorated the wall, colored by her dainty hands with crayons that *would* get stumpy so quickly; a lace on the window fastened with a paper rose. The mother stood there stricken and buffeted about as a lonely tree in a winter's blast. Those toys, 'poor dumb mouths,' spoke to her in thunder tones of the agony, the sorrow and desolation of human life. The kaleidoscope of memory turned and turned until flesh and blood cried out for a respite. Suddenly as is borne on the breeze that entered the window, came a balm like benediction: 'And they shall hunger no more, neither shall the sun light on them, nor any heat, for the lamb which is in the midst of the throne shall feed them and shall lead them into living fountains of water. And God shall wipe away all tears from their eyes'—and the mother softly crept out and closed the play house door."

What an understanding of the human heart and the appreciation of little children she had! She did not save her wit and engaging conversation for the world but delighted in sharpening the wits of her children with little conundrums and family jokes. Her letters to her children, pretending to be Santa Claus, were classics kept and cherished by them. In one of them she brings in a lot of Grecian mythological characters in a droll way. She says they are friends of hers up in Santa land. In one place speaking of Phineas she calls him "Phin" for short—"but Phin *will* steal all my pet reindeers, this is why this year I shall be compelled to ride on Mercury's back. You know he has wings and he thinks it can be managed all right" * * * I'm afraid a sled would not be a very good present, anyway I have no good ones, maybe another year Mercury will make me some. I am so old and worn out I can't make as many toys as usual. However, the Brownies are here helping me in the doll business, they are very handy because they are small and work at night—the dude though, will not work. Dr. Lamont gave him a dose of medicine the other night and my wife took care of him he got so sick. She made him a bed in a tin pan." How a youngster would love that.

The perfecting of the home life and its atmosphere did not take all of her time. She always found time to be helpful and a real power in the lives of young people around her. The association with her and her family is felt by many to be one of the most prized relationships of life.

Of late years her strength was terribly limited. This was bitter for an ardent nature like hers. Accustomed all her life as she had been to push ahead and give so lavishly of herself to everyone, the fact did not appeal to her. It was more difficult to battle against weakness than to do the many big things she used to put through. Except for a very few times she was unable to be present at the meetings of our chapter though several times she arranged for B. I. L. parties for us and treats of various kinds. Our chapter was organized at her house, although she herself did not send for the charter or anything of the sort. Her daughter was taken in after the original seven charter members took the oath. It was her wish that the First Aurora Chapter should be as near like her own chapter as was possible. In the first place the girls must be congenial; there should be just seven, and all of these must be *new* P. E. O.'s, not former members of other chapters. As it happens nearly all of the chapter were especially fond of literature which pleased her, and she was always interested to know about our programs and what we were doing.

But with such deep strong roots in Mount Pleasant, it was very difficult to transplant such a loyal person. Unable to live an active life here of late years, her thoughts were ever on the "dear and early friends and the few who yet remain"—and she preferred the companionship of her books to new and untried friends. Books are the

life blood of master spirits. She read incessantly and when her eyes failed her, others read to her, sometimes reading the same book again and again. For novels she seldom read any but the English novels of Dickens, Eliot, Thackery, etc., and preferred the American poets. History and biography were her favorites.

Judge and Mrs. Babb never considered giving anything for wedding presents but books elegantly bound, and believed them to be the best inspiration for a strong and useful life. One of our chapter received a magnificent set of Victor Hugo's for *her* wedding present and on the fly leaf of the first volume was Wilbur Nesbit's poem, "Who hath a Book":

"Who hath a book hath friends at hand,
And gold and wealth at his command
And rich estates if he but look—
Are held by him who hath a book."

It was accompanied by a letter in which she said, "Books have been to me an anchor to windward in a weary land. When we were first married we had to look closely to the 'bin and the board.' After all, the life is more than meat and the body than raiment and an elevating influence that raises me into a purer atmosphere away from the cares of daily life should be afforded. I feel today that if I could meet Charles Dickens or Mark Twain I should grasp their hands and burst into tears. I trust both of you will ever find this refuge."

* * * * * *

One young friend said of her—"I don't think Aurora ever really knew Mrs. Babb" (or "Auntie Babb" as she called her). "I used to make it a point to go to see her on all my vacations. Mother and Mrs. Babb were old Mt. Pleasant friends, and she was always so interested in what I was doing she would raise up on her elbow and in that keen way, question me closely—'What are you doing in English—how are they teaching it now?' Always keeping abreast of the times in the technical part of it. She could outstrip me in repeating Virgil's 'Aeneid' although I have had it so recently. She stated more than once that American poets were not appreciated in America as they should be, and every year she presented me with a complete volume of poems by American poets. Her presents were always books and inscribed on the fly leaf was always a thought or quotation. Imagine anyone doing as she did, parsing Greek and Latin sentences for a pastime."

She spent some of the long days and wakeful nights discussing many things with her devoted nurse, who came to love and revere her. It was an education just to be with her. The nurse, who was a Scotch woman and could read Scotch dialect with a rich broad accent, read "The Cotter's Saturday Night" and many other Scottish poems of Bobbie Burns she loved. Bill Hay over the radio (WGN) several times rendered old Scottish songs and many of the Civil War for her benefit. "Beside the Bonnie Brier Bush" was a special favorite and the sermons of Ian MacLaren in their simple earnest heart to heart appeal she loved to have repeated.

You never saw such a memory. Sometimes to while away the time she would name over the characters in plays she had coached back in Mt. Pleasant—and could name the caste and say a good many of the lines. "Thanatopsis," "Crossing the Bar," "The Happy Warrior" and all the sublime poems which expressed the strong and valiant soul meeting the last enemy were dear to her.

Bob Burdette was an *old friend*, and his cheery optimistic things were occasionally much enjoyed. Being such a prolific reader it would take volumes to tell all and tell why she enjoyed hearing them. Eugene Field's "Little Boy Blue" was a favorite, and how well she appreciated all the little dusty toy soldier meant. The Civil War songs were a real part of her life as her father, husband and young brother all took part in the war and she had met and talked with Abraham Lincoln when she was a child. Her father was a surgeon and the sixteen year old brother a prisoner at Andersonville during the War.

Knowing that often she would repeat the whole of Whittier's "Snow Bound," I got the poem to find out if I could see why she had taken the trouble to learn the whole seven hundred and eighty lines. It contains so much that is like her life, it is startling—the young brother in the war, the wise old doctor, the little girl who passed away—her heart was in Mt. Pleasant and the busy happy days gone by. Snow bound *she* was in later years, shut off by her failing strength from the warmth and sunshine of outside contacts—the whole pageant of her busy life passed before her in retrospect. How sweet after the storm and stress of life to be able to bring back so clearly the "Dear and early friends and the few who yet remain," and the little intimate details of the family life and to receive the daily letters from the devoted brother who passed on only a few months before her. To continue in the words of "Snow Bound":

"Shut in from all the world without,
We sat the clean winged hearth about
Content to *let* the North Wind roar—

* * * * * *

"O time, oh change with hair as gray
As was my sires that winter day

How strange it seems with so much
Gone of life and love to still live on

Oh brother, only I and thou are left of all that circle n

The dear home faces where upon
That fitful firelight paled and shone.

* * * * * *

We turn the pages that they read,
Their written words we linger o'er.
No voice is heard, no sign is made.
Yet love will dream, and faith will trust
Since He who knows our needs is just.
That somehow, somewhere, meet we must.
Alas, for him who never sees
The stars shine through his cypress trees.

* * * * * *

Who hath not learned in hours of faith
The truth to flesh and sense unknown
That life is ever lord of death
And love can never lose its own."

Luck

WHAT constitutes the thing called luck?
In it I fancy there is pluck,
And there is faith and there is skill;
It has a part of iron will;
It is born of dreams which brave men hold,
And comes to them if they are bold.
Luck is the joy which men deserve,
The rich reward of those who serve.

Luck lies to help and boost the man
Who bravely does the best he can;
It seldom benefits the base
Or raises high the commonplace.
It often helps the friend in need,
Yet he is helpless here, indeed,
Who has no courage of his own
And must depend on luck alone.

If you have faith and you will work,
If you will go where dangers lurk;
If you possess a dream and cling
To it in spite of everything;
If you are brave and wise and fair,
And have the grit to do and dare;
If you possess your share of pluck,
The chances are that you'll have luck.

                Hammermill Bond.

SEVEN HOMES

ALICE BIRD BABB

WHEN we read the graphic stories of Herbert Quick, Willa Cather, and Hamlin Garland, we are prone to regard the spots they describe, as the most picturesque in Iowa, Nebraska and Wisconsin, but it is simply because the authors lived there in their childhood, heard the tales of pioneers and first settlers, and later placed those points upon the map with the artist's pen. Other places in the same states are as full of romance, tragedy, joy and problems, — but they are waiting for the artist's brush, or the poet's pen; the "bloom of fancy," must destroy the "brier of fact;" plain history must become legend, before the after-glow is produced. We sit by our electric lamp, in furnace heated houses, and read *The Covered Wagon* by Hough. We dismount from a comfortable automobile to see the movie of *The Covered Wagon*, and declare "how interesting, how wonderful," — when the truth is, that *The Covered Wagon* has become a legend; the "bloom of fancy," covers it with a halo, — and the hard lives of those who rode in covered wagons are made pictures of romance. " 'Tis distance lends enchantment to the view."

When I went to Mt. Pleasant the last time, I thought constantly of the white blossoms of *The Orchard Lands of Long Ago.*

And when one evening, — a rare evening in June, — my brother suggested that we walk down to Saunder's Grove, where as little children we had played, I gladly assented; he said he wanted to show me the great improvement there. Saunder's Grove, named after the first settler of Mt. Pleasant, is one of the most beautiful natural groves I ever saw. Magnificent hard mapies, elm, hickory, ash and oak have grown there for a hundred years, and now the town owns it, and has made needed and necessary improvement; t h e

beautiful entrance of graded stone columns, — made from the quarries near by, — the fine hospital, set in the quiet and sheltered grounds, with names on many doors, of those who came to the t o w n in the "covered wagon" and among others, the unusually well equipped room, which Chapter Original A, P. E. O. has furnished.

Then we visited the children's playgrounds — with croquet, tennis, sand piles, and other things which children enjoy, then the extensive golf links, — reaching far over the

Photo from The Story of P. E. O.

Alice Virginia Coffin

Franc Roads (Elliott)

Alice Bird (Babb)

Ella Stewart

Mary Allen (Stafford)

Hattie Briggs (Bousquet)

Suela Pearson (Penfield)

eautiful uplands, — maybe to the iver, — I don't know, — but my houghts went backward, and when ny brother said, "why don't you nthuse more," I touched his arm, nd told him that I wished it would ll vanish for a time, and that the ld rail fence would return, over vhich we climbed in our bare feet, s children, and with pin hooks ished in the small streams, and vhen it rained, ran so gladly to the ld pork house, where we ate the unch, mother had prepared for us. My brother did not reply, — but know history had passed into leg-nd, and that the "bloom of fancy," nveloped old Saunder's G r o v e. Then I told him that I intended to visit the homes, or the spots, where nce we seven girls lived, — even >efore P. E. O. was born, and as we were so near the home of Franc loads, we would walk around it his evening. Franc saw her child-hood visions thru the beautiful trees of this grove. As I walked on the familiar ground, leading to her home, it seemed that I was a girl gain — finding a secret path to attend a P. E. O. meeting — for we used to separate as we approached this place and find ourselves by ac-cident, at the front door, and as Franc lived near what we called "the old grave yard," courage was neces-sary to take the detour.

There stood the house, — once so white, with green shutters, and portico in front, which all houses had in those days. Fifty-six years have told their story, but the house still stands, — sold and rented, and rented and sold; and almost ready to finish its life. In imagination I could hear the jolly laugh of Mr. Roads, welcoming us, and see the placid smile of the mother, always ready to render efficient help; she cut out our aprons, which we wore on the first morning the P. E. O. star was pinned to the left shoulder, and I dared look into one of the windows of that room where we made them. A young niece was one of the family, called, Leone, who is now one of the efficient P. E. O.'s of Mt. Pleasant, married to one of its best men, Mr. Henry Bowman.

I suppose the occupants of the house thought I was pretty fresh walking through the yard, but I did not see them, — I only saw the dear girl who once graced the home, — and even she was not there, but still I saw her, holding a torch, — then I whispered goodbye to old or young Saunder's Grove, and threw

a kiss to the old grave yard where Ella Stewart sleeps by her pioneer father and mother.

Then we walked north to the home where Mary Allen used to live in '69 she had moved north of the college, but this house, was the one filled with "fond recollection." My brother said, — These visits will make you sad Allie." "No," I an-swered, "only glad, glad to think of the splendid girls, who were my playmates in youth; for such asso-ciates, I ought to be a better wom-an." "Well," he said, "you suit me all right." Mary's home was a large, rather aristocratic house, with inner porches, and pagoda like windows. We used to call them "Romeo and Juliet windows." This was a house also situated far from the confusion the turmoil of the city of 4000 in-habitants, and a home to which we seven girls often went, in the early part of a summer evening. I recall how just by accident we'd met there once and began right away to make a l a r g e amount of butterscotch, much more than those seven girls could eat; then, while it cooled, we'd go to the piano and sing, The years creep slowly by, Lorena, or Oh don't you remember sweet, Alice, Ben Bolt.

Then all at once, a noise, a scuffle, and seven tramp students walked right into that room; they made no apology, and Mary received them in her usual gracious manner, — indeed, it almost looked as if she were expecting them, — when ac-cording to college rules, she should have put them out. Now, the way that butterscotch vanished, was a caution—nothing left but the plates. Then began the singing, A i l e e n Aroon, Meet me by moonlight alone, and as I write, I can hear Dil-lon Payne's fine tenor, rising high and strong, in our choice song, In the Starlight. Then a declamation must be given, and Sou Pearson spoke Captain, our Captain, just out, by Walt Whitman. Of course, we seven girls were "Taken up before the faculty," next day — when we told our pitiful story. What could seven weak females do, w h e n charged upon by seven husky men, — some of them just home from the Civil War! Even St. Paul says that "women is the weaker vessel," and there we were. Dr. Holmes told us never to repeat it, — which we did. I am certain the name of one of those young men, was C. L. Stafford, but if he reads this, after his long useful life of Christian ministry, he will say "oh, that's one of Allie

Bird's jokes." I am sure the name of another was W. I. Babb, — but after trying to prove so long in the court room that white is black, he cannot today prove that black is white. The others were Dillon Payne, Robert Burton, Will Pearson, Chester Collins, and Gus Schreiner.

As I looked at the house, with my brother, that June evening, not long ago, it was still in good repair, — made into a stopping place for people traveling along the highway, which passed the house, and my friends told me the meals were ex-cellent, but I did not see the fresh paint, nor the Highway, for I was Tenting on the old camp ground.

My brother urge l me not to pass the grounds where Sou Pearson once lived, — he said I had seen enough for one time, and that a great disap-pointment awaited me; but our path led past her home, and my time was limited. The Pearsons came to Mt. Pleasant about 1858, and built one of the best homes in the town. The large brick house was set back in the yard, perhaps one hundred feet, — and that was the day of flower beds, — in shapes; stars, squares, diamonds, octagons, and fringed round with shells, which w e r e brought by the wagon load from the Mississippi River. Now they are all used in button factories, — and by geodes, which were found at Mud Creek, south of Mt. Pleasant: pyra-mids of rocks piled up, which looked like a heap of cocoanuts, — and when one was cracked open, prisms of beauty appeared. Many geolo-gists from different parts of the country came to examine them, Pro-fessor Winchell among others, and pronounced them rare. As it was the thing then, to border flower beds, the housewives took these geodes and many of Mrs. Pearson's beds were bordered by these rainbow rocks. A side walk led through the center of the hundred flower beds, and on it, I often ran to meet Sou, and her mother would rise from her garden work, and reveal her beauti-ful complexion and liquid brown eyes. Then I readily understood the origin of Sou's beauty. Sou would run to meet me, curls flying, and would remark like this. "Oh Allie, Lord Tennyson has a new piece Charge of the Light Brigade. I tell you, we'll make it hum."

"In that mansion, used to be, royal hospitality."

But changes came! The Pearsons left Mt. Pleasant about '73, — then the house was sold, or rented, —

everything ran down and when the town wished to remove the hitching posts around the square, and fence from the park, the farmers demurred, for it is a farming district, — and finally the town decided to buy the Pearson property and the one next to it, tear everything down, put up sheds for horses and wagons, and thus I saw it, that night with my brother, — now used for auto parking. He looked at me. I looked at him, and felt "All that is bright must fade."

"Now," said he, "You've looked at enough P. E. O. barracks for one day, forget it all, and when you go tomorrow, o the others, 'I'll stay at home, – you take it too hard.'"

The next morning I started for chapel at old Wesleyan. I could not enter the chapel of "Old Main" for it was inhabited by tangible ghosts. I simply held the skeleton key; but I entered the later chapel, which is also full of delightful memories. I sat on the back seat, and was certain I saw the shade of Charles Dickens behind one pillar, and up in the gallery sat Harriet Beecher Stowe, silently applauding, and William Dean Howells looked pleased at the imaginary *Silas Lapham*, upon the stage. Then the fine organ played, and a splendid choir sang, *Faith of our fathers, — holy faith.*

I could stand it no longer, — but went out the door, — passing on the way an imaginary minor author, William Shakespeare, w h o h a d looked in to see how "the boys" acted *Julius Caesar.*

I crossed the campus to the west, where once stood the stile, and hurried up to the home, — so long ago, — of Hattie Briggs. This was a two-story frame house, and it still remained in very good shape. The green shutters were gone, and a broad porch took the place of the old portico, — on it were two hammocks, and I could not be too inquisitive. I saw that the old well and sweep were gone from the rear of the house, from which we girls used to drink from *the old oaken bucket*, and indeed Hattie had been gone from the house so long, that only faint memory remained.

I crossed over to the house where Dr. H. W. Thomas once lived, who had heard all my orations in college, — one of the dearest and best friends we seven P. E. O.'s ever had, — then I walked across what used to be, the fields, and sought the

home of Ella Stewart. This, in college days, was also the home of Allie Coffin, who had come to Mt. Pleasant in '61 with her sister. They were motherless girls, and while in school, Allie boarded, — the most time with Ella Stewart. She was a southern girl, and an inseparable friend of Ella's, — so I place their homes together. There were reasons why Allie Coffin was unusually reserved, and I have always been glad that she and I were great friends, — the "two Allies," they called us.

As I walked over to the old home of our "busy bee," Ella Stewart, I saw that everything was changed. The house still there in an altered shape, but close to it, was a huge canning factory, with puffs of smoke, wheels going around, and belts flying, and it seemed to me, that nothing could be built by Ella's home, more emblematic of her, — than a factory; a bank, or apartment house, would not fill the bill; — *something doing*; she was always planning, always executing, — whenever she came toward us, — we hurriedly took the tatting out of our pockets, and went to work. Ella left college at the close of '68, to assist her widowed mother. She became teacher in the "Boys' Training School" at Eldora, Iowa. She was competent, loved and respected by all, and I think one of the most beautiful things P. E. O. has ever done, is for the Eldora Chapter to place an "Ella Stewart Memorial," in the Library of that "Boys' Training School." Little by little it will become an inspiration and a help to these boys, and I make an appeal to the P. E. O.'s that if you possess among books you have read, some one suitable to boys of twelve to fourteen, send it to this "Memorial." I sent a number of bound Youth's Companions, which my own boys had enjoyed so much, because they contained the continued stories of our best boy writers for boys, in the eighties. The day we laid Ella Stewart in our old cemetery, the P. E. O.'s walked together, as the walk is short, the Sunday School, many, many friends, and along the street men stood with uncovered heads, — for everyone loved and respected her, and regretted that one so useful — so young, should, "perish with the flowers."

Then I turned to *The orchard lands of long age*, on Main Street. I never thought of it before, but I was the only one of the seven who lived on Main Street, and whether

it be a recommendation or a disgrace, I leave it to you and Sinclair Lewis to decide. As I passed by old neighbor's homes, the very windows and walls and trees seemed to nod me a welcome, and as I came to the old yard, the City Library, which stands in place of our rambling house, seemed the most fitting monument, which could be erected to my father. You ask what I looked for first! Why, to see if there were a piece of the old fence back of the Library, where my brother made a wooden step, so that if some student called upon me whom I did not care to see, I could mount the step, jump the fence and run off. Mother would frantically call "Allie, some one's ringing the door bell" and I'd shout, — "I'm not at home, remember, I'm not at home." I asked the Librarian, who had come to the front door when the beautiful Ampleopsis Ivy, which covered half of the building, had been planted. "No one knows," she said, "it comes up everywhere, and we keep cutting it off." Then I knew that the roots of the old Ampleopsis Ivy, were the ones my father planted, perhaps seventy years ago, and I realized as never before, "Oh, a rare old plant is the Ivy Green."

The Librarian walked me to the east side, where stood a huge cut-leaf birch, and she said, that it must soon be cut down, as addition to the building must go that way. I told her, that was well, as an old cut-leaf birch is not a beautiful tree, and no tree more graceful than a young cut-leaf birch. I remember well the time my father planted it. I was a very little girl, and asked him why it was named "cut-leaf," and he told me that at Vick's nurseries in New York, they hired boys and men, to cut the leaves when the trees were small, and as they grew, and to this day, I never see this spliced tree, but I think of the time and expense taken to call it "cutleaf."

Then I walked back to the place, where we once had "the crooked tree croquet ground," but I could not locate it, for buildings set up. Four of us played croquet there, the last time in '72, when Grant and Greely were candidates for president. We played the 38 states, and my father would come out and say, "now if Grant does not win, I'll pull up the stakes." This was pretty hard, when one of the four was a democrat, and thus a Greely man. As I walked away, I did not

(Continued on page 22)

14

95

SEVEN HOMES

(Continued from page 14)

know what direction my feet took. Just unconsciously, as I had walked it so often before, generally wheeling a baby carriage I went straight to the house, where most of my married life had been spent. There were the old tennis court, and croquet-ground. There was the large barn, where the boys cleaned their gun and hunting apparel, and worked on the scroll saw, and dramatized and acted *Uncle Tom's Cabin*, and *Ten Nights in a Bar Room*, and there was the spot where once stood the play-house, where my two little girls had their last banquet, — one balmy day in early winter. The only guest was the doll "Rosy" sitting on a high chair between them. Months after, I opened that door, upon which the elder sister had so carefully turned the button. There sat "Rosy" and faded dead flowers in the cracked vase. "Rosy" sphinx like, seemed to be asking me, where her mistress was, but, "I think she sailed to the heavenly shores, for she never came back to me."

As I walked to the town, certain tunes were running in my head, — the first, "You ask what land I love the best, Iowa, 'tis Iowa." then,

"Wesleyan, — thy honored name, Wesleyan, I love thee."

Then, I was repeating an old piece Sou and I used to speak, and I used her name:

"I've wandered to the village, Sou, I've sat beneath the tree, Upon the village play ground, That sheltered you and me.

But none were left to greet me, Sou, And few were left to know, — *Who* played with us upon the green, Some, — Sixty years ago."

✦

SHE CAN KEEP A SECRET

In a story *But Love the Sinner* by Eve Bennett, which appeared in the *Saturday Evening Post* of Nov. 18, 1939 was this paragraph:

"Of course anyone telling mamma secrets would know that she would tell papa. It was only later, when she joined the P. E. O., that she swayed to utmost secrecy."

✦

Goldenrod lighted the retreating steps of summer across the fields.
—Hamilton W. Mabie.

LOCAL

Chapter

NEWS

CALIFORNIA

PARTY HONORS A HALF CENTURY MEMBER

Chapter AM, San Francisco, on November 3, 1939, celebrated with pride and happiness, the completion of fifty years in P. E. O. of one of its beloved members, Mrs. Sella Russell Cole.

Mrs. Persis S. Harrison was hostess for the day, and the chapter members enjoyed a luncheon at which the crowning feature was a huge yellow and white cake, shaped like a star and lighted with fifty candles.

Mrs. Cole, who looks like a bit of Dresden china, wore the dress in which she was initiated into Chapter Q, Des Moines, fifty years ago. It was her wedding gown, a creation of mull and Princess lace. Its color was the rich cream that only age can give to a fabric. The bustle, the pannier drapes, and the numerous lacy frills might have come right out of a *Godey's Lady's Book*. With the gown she wore a white embroidered shawl that had been a part of her mother's trousseau. On her shoulder was an exquisite orchid, a gift from Chapter AM.

For the program that followed the business meeting, there was first group singing, and then a talk by Mrs. Cole, in which she told most entertainingly, about her P. E. O. experiences from the time she was an initiate until she became a founding member of AM in San Francisco in 1913.

A life membership in the chapter and a memory book in which each AM member had written a personal message were presented to our distinguished sister.—Estelline H. Parcell.

✦

COLORADO

A MISSIONARY, A GUEST SPEAKER

Chapter AJ, Craig, had as speaker on the day on which their mothers were honored guests, a missionary at home on furlough, Mrs. Leona Stukey Tucker, who gave a delightful address.

She has been a missionary for twenty years in Bela Vista, Angola, West Africa. Her talk centered around the home life and customs of the people among whom she has worked so long. She had a

PRAYER FOR A NEW YEAR

Keep me from bravado, God, but make me brave;

Save me from suavity, but give me poise; Silence I ask for, knowing well its splendor, But not that silence harsher than the noise.

Sorrow I would have, but never grieving; Love, but never jealousy or fear; Meeting of friends, God, tempering the leaving . . . Restraint in all Your gifts to me this year!
—Helen E. Murphy

display of lace and other hand work done by native women.

Mrs. Tucker is a member of Chapter X, Steamboat Springs, Colo.—Mary Winder.

✦

LITTLE RED SCHOOL HOUSE PROGRAM

Chapter AP, Idaho Springs, enjoyed a district school session, Nov. 1, at the home of Margaret Carlson with Margaret Keplinger as teacher.

It was educational project night. The teacher had prepared questions and answers concerning our P. E. O. projects; the answers were distributed among the pupils. Members of AP were seated in rows — all facing the teacher, and in the usual school fashion the pupils answered teacher's questions. There was a map of the United States on which one had to bound Missouri, trace its principal rivers, and locate Nevada. Then came a battery of questions concerning Cottey. Nona Harrington was asked to draw on the black board a diagram of the buildings at Cottey. Our educational fund furnished material for the arithmetic class and the story of the library — a history lesson.

When the lessons were finished, teacher gave us time for a Friday afternoon program in which each pupil presented her own contributions. This was real fun. You'll have to try it to know. Many of our chapter members recited the "pieces" which they had actually "spoken" in their school days. Memorable school day experiences retold brought tears — from laughter. One member had never forgotten her program piano piece — and her rendition of it this night we shall never forget.

Then the party. Each pupil was given an arithmetic slate with her name on it. The slates were the serving trays on which each pupil found her school lunch — sandwiches, pickles, candied apples and cookies.—Margaret Shaffer.

✦

COTTEY COLLEGE PROGRAM AND TEA

Mrs. Myra Lewis, member of Chapter AV, Estes Park, was hostess at a Cottey College program and tea on May sixth at her beautiful home in Moraine Park.

Junior and senior high school girls were guests of honor. The Colorado state president Mrs. Louise Darnell, was a special guest as were three past state presidents, Mrs. Mary Keeler Foster of Loveland, Miss Helen Hartford of Berthand and Mrs. Nova Harrington of Idaho Springs. The Colorado emergency chairman for Cottey College Mrs. Maurine T. Herson of Denver and the president of the Loveland chapter Mrs. Florence Hicks were also present. Other guests besides the members of Chapter AV were, Mrs. J. R. Coolidge and daughters Mary Beth, Jane and Patty Lou, of Smith Center, Kansas; Mrs. Wehrli of Longmont, Colorado; Mrs. Estella Snyder of Eaton, Colorado; Mrs. Roland Reed and daughter Virginia and Katherine Green of Estes Park.

All of the visiting officers gave short talks about Cottey College as did Mrs. Rhoda Tallant, president of Chapter AV, and mother of a former Cottey student. Mrs. Foster and Mrs. Harrington have daughters now enrolled at Cottey College.

96

State University of Iowa, is a practising internist and diagnostician in Boston. Their two children Mary Joann and George Lyman are in college.

She takes pride in keeping house and especially enjoys life on her husband's sailboat. Sometime soon she earnestly desires to enroll in a course in music appreciation. Visiting old houses and studying antique furniture afford much delight, but at present her happiest moments are spent in P. E. O. work. So far her most thrilling experiences in P. E. O. took place in 1949 when she organized Chapter N, Worcester and Chapter O, Springfield.

In addition to P. E. O. interests Mrs. Hoyt is a member of the Boston Parliamentary Law Club, the Garden Club of Brookline, The Brookline Historical Society, and Pi Beta Phi. Church affiliation: The First Parish in Brookline (Unitarian).

Home: 50 Fisher Avenue, Brookline, Massachusetts.

Alice Bird Babb in War Times

from a letter to her brother, recalling her experiences during the Civil War.

• I stood on the west side of New York street bridge, because it was a declivity and the soldiers crossing the bridge could be seen to great advantage. As they advanced I thought of the world's great crises, of Xerxes and his conquering hosts, of Alexander, of Caesar, of Napoleon, of the Spanish Armada, of Washington and Lincoln. If every one in the vast crowds felt as elated as I, it is a wonder that then and there we did not ascend. On they came with bands of music, the policemen, the mail carriers, the sons of veterans, the Zouaves, all only as an escort, then they came.

"Many sought truth, and lavished
     Life's best gifts,
Amid the dust of books to find her,
But these our brothers fought for
     her,
In life's dear peril wrought for her;
So loved her, that they died for her,
Tasting the raptured sweetness,
Of divine completeness."

I felt that every one of those men was a hero, and that it was a great privilege to be present.

When Captain Smith passed, I wanted to take off my hat, and when Washington Irving marched along; I forgave him for all the scoldings he had ever given me and had you been there, my dear brother, memory would have taken such journeys that really I fear I should have made a display of my emotions. As it was I thought of those days of '61 when it seemed to me as a child that there was no more fun in life; and that my playtime was consumed in the everlasting scraping of lint for that box at the Aid Society always waiting to be filled for the soldiers. Even little hands could scrape lint and I never see a nice, old, clean table cloth to this day but I think what good lint that would make. My sister's hands were large enough to roll bandages but I could only scrape lint. I thought of how sad our home was with you and father gone to war, and I begged mother to let me go to Uncle Charley Willets over one Saturday. While there we went on Saturday night to a spelling school at Ebenezer school house and as they were choosing sides a man rushed in and screamed, "Great battle at Franklin and Nashville. John Beeler is killed and lots of our boys are wounded, and Thornton Bird of Mt. Pleasant is missing." The next morning Uncle Charlie brought me home and there sat mother and Mira weeping. I think our mother was never the care-free creature she was before. "The poor soldiers" were on her conscience all her life. In a few days we heard that you were a prisoner at Macon, Georgia, then carried to Charleston workhouse. Then being in the hospital employ you were exchanged, and in a few months came the telegram from New York City,

"Here in butter nut clothes. Send me a hundred dollars." We could not send the money then by telegraph but had to wait until evening before the money could go in a letter. When you came home you were no longer a boy not more than eighteen years old, but a man, an old man in experience. Mother had cooked everything in the world she knew you liked but not one of us could eat. I imagine our whole country was full of homes with just such experiences, and today while every mother loves her sons, she would rejoice down in her heart for just such a school in which to teach her boys self-reliance and patriotism. All this was forty-five years ago, and you and I have lived to see this country expand beyond all prophets' dreams. Abraham Lincoln said in '60 that the time would come when Chicago would have 100,000 population. But I must close, for did I begin on the astonishing growth of America, I'd need a new pen. Come over before all the bunting is taken down, but even if that goes the patriotism of Aurora will remain, benefiting it, as could no other invasion. /—*Reprint*

Calling All B. I. L.'s

• From a reliable source, I understand that the sisters are planning another convention. This one is to be in Philadelphia, October 8, 9, 10 and 11, 1951 and we are all not only invited to come, but urged to be there.

I, also, understand that there will be a few meetings behind closed doors where we will be on the outside not even looking in, but there will be a few meetings we can attend if we wish. The Tuesday evening program when Dr. Dow of Cottey College fame will speak and we who heard her in Chicago will be glad of a repeat on that and the Wednesday evening banquet which is the gala occasion.

While the sisters are busy, we can "do" the town. B. I. L. Warren E.

Stanhope of Haverton, Pennsylvania is taking over the local arrangements for our entertainment. He will have the golf courses, big industrial plants, service clubs and the U. S. mint open for us. Just how far Uncle Sam is going to cooperate with the mint is still a question, but we are assured of a tour there. How much we can get away with will be our problem.

Don't fail us — B. I. L.'s of Pennsylvania are going to be looking for a lot of us.

Y.I.T.B.

The meaning of those mystic letters will be revealed for the first time at our luncheon which only B. I. L.'s can attend, Tuesday noon, October 9.

I'll be seeing you — we hope.

          Seaman A. Knapp
          Supreme B. I. L. (for this
          biennium)

tion at Sun Valley in June 1951. Attendance at the convention of Supreme Chapter was another highlight of the year.

Her birthplace was Minnesota but she received most of her schooling in Buffalo, New York, graduating from New York State College for Teachers. Several years were spent in teaching in New York and Idaho, and then she turned to the business world. For many years she has been associated with her brother, Stuart H. Taylor, in his office, handling insurance and bonds.

She has been a life-long member of the Episcopal Church, active in guild and choir work, and music is a major interest.

P. E. O. has been a predominant influence in her life since she became a member of Chapter D, Twin Falls, in May 1921. She joined Chapter AI as a charter member in May 1931. At the recent state convention she was appointed to the Board of Trustees of the P. E. O. Chapter House at Caldwell, and is keenly interested in the development of this new project for Idaho.

To her, P. E. O. has proved to be an investment in friendship — paying rich dividends.

Her home is at 325 Second Street North, Twin Falls, Idaho.

SUPPLY DEPARTMENT

MARION BLAINE was born in Illinois, reared in Indiana and "higher" educated in Michigan. Her father managed glass factories and her husband, Earl C. Blaine, was for years associated with major automobile companies in the midwest. Both connections resulted in so many moves that conservative EASTERNERS were aghast at a recital of the different places Mrs. Blaine had lived.

Happily, the roving seems to be over. For seventeen years Mr. Blaine has been with The Budd Company, and both Mr. and Mrs. Blaine find Philadelphia and Pennsylvania a desirable and beautiful place to live.

Mrs. Blaine was initiated into Chap-

ter E, Philadelphia and is still a member of this group. She served in various local chapter offices and is a past state president of Pennsylvania. The height of her P. E. O. experience was reached when she served as general chairman of the recent convention of Supreme Chapter. The success of this convention brought great joy to her and to all the P. E. O.'s of Pennsylvania.

Mrs. Blaine looks forward to serving on the Board of Trustees, Supply Department, with eagerness. In welcoming her to this board, both Mrs. Clapp and Mrs. Thornton had high words of praise to say for its activities. Mrs. Thornton's recommendation was particularly appreciated. "The work is interesting and doesn't interfere with your home life — that is not much!"

The Blaines have two sons, Lt. James T., attending the infantry officers' school at Ft. Benning, Georgia, and Bob, a junior in high school.

Home: 7501 Boyer Street, Philadelphia 19, Penna.

Mrs. Babb's Old Home

• The old home in Mt. Pleasant, where Mrs. Babb's childhood was spent, being in process of destruction to build on its site a city library, she wrote thus of it in the Free Press:

I prefer not to see the ax and the spade at its destructive work, and will remain away until the funeral of the old home is complete; for why is it, that inanimate objects, which time and association have made dear to us, take upon themselves the rights of living things and demand sighs, tears, love and reverence.

Poetry and romance are full of "old homesteads," "old arm chairs" and "old oaken buckets," worth nothing in money and yet priceless "when fond recollection presents them to view." People are kind, very thoughtful; they speak in sympathetic tones of the old home; they say it is a real landmark in the history of Mt.

Pleasant, especially do they dwell upon the trees which were my father's pride, and some are actually desirous of arranging the library building so that the cut leaf birch at any rate can stand. When my father planted it,—I asked him why the leaves were slashed into so deep. "Why," he said, "did you not know they hire men at the Rochester nuseries, just to cut the leaves of the trees into different shapes, so they will be different trees," and I went away wondering if that were only another of father's jokes, but impressed all the same ever since that the cut leaf birch caused so much work.

I was only five years old when we moved there, but I recall the fact of my father purchasing the property from Dr. Clark, who was my father's partner at an early day. Before the Clarks lived there Mr. Viney resided and I have been told he purchased the

property from a Mr. White who resided in one part of the house and preached in the rooms which afterwards were sitting room and parlor. Shortly after we moved in a gentleman called, and introduced himself as Reverend White, asking to see what we called the guest room. He was in the room a long time and upon coming out, he told us that the room was precious to him for his wife and child had died there. Thus early the old home held dear memories. Every few years that same Mr. White came and was closeted in that room, until we youngsters used to remark, it was time for Mr. White to come. Finally he came for the last time. He was thin and ailing and said he would never come again, which proved true.

When we went into this house my father felt called upon to enter upon extensive decorations, as such a fine,

JANUARY, 1952 ★

3

98

large house called for suitable trimmings. So a long journey to Philadelphia was made, possibly part of the way by stage. We were amazed to see the furniture he bought, actually the first wool carpet, save one, ever in Mt. Pleasant, and a Smith tapestry for the parlor! I can see it now, a jet black background with bouquets of roses here and there such as were never seen on land or sea. People came from all over to see those carpets. I have a piece of one of them yet. And six mahogany chairs with straight backs, and two easy chairs, in exactly equal distances apart stood around the walls of the parlor, and Venetian blinds on the windows. When the piano came then we were fine indeed! I have never seen anything so fine as that parlor. And right among those fine things little children came and went. Laughter, games, music abounded. Out of this house went soldiers to defend their country from '60 to '65.

Then cupid entered, and my father often found that someone had by mistake had taken his hat, and in haste left another, when Judge Woolson, then John Woolson, came to see my sister. Both father and mother wondered if all that gallantry and chivalry were genuine or put on. Father said, "you couldn't tell always about those Yankees." He lived to bless the day that ever introduced that brave, generous dear man to our old home. Well, other ties formed and out of the front door walked brides and grooms and new homes were planted — only to bring into more necessary prominence the old home.

Soon grandchildren crowded, yes, crowded into the house, and Christmas day was not perfect unless spent at grandpapa's. Santa Claus was believed in then, and never failed to give a long, generous visit, after the sumptuous dinner. As time passed and the Smith tapestry carpet became a thing of the past, old age crept apace, the grandparents came oftener to our homes, and the grandchildren were becoming men and women. My father, on account of failing sight could no longer read his Shakespeare, Milton or the large typed family Bible and as the years passed, Dr. Stoddard was called upon during his pastorate here to recount the worthy deeds of the good man and pure woman who had lived together over fifty years. Then the door opened by stranger to stranger, and a kind Providence provides that on the site where this house stood, shall arise an edifice dedicated to books, a most fitting monument.—*Reprint from 1903.*

Formula For Efficiency

By Dr. NORMAN VINCENT PEALE

• This talk is a simple study in that most fascinating subject, human nature. What is it that reduces your efficiency? What is it that adds power?

Riding recently in a New York City taxi, I was impressed by the remarkable cleanliness of the cab. You can tell a good deal about a man or woman by the state in which he keeps his surroundings. This cab was immaculate; the chromium shone; the car was tight without a rattle in it. The driver's hand on the wheel was steady. I was glad of this because he was one of the fastest drivers behind whom I had ever ridden. People jumped out of his way as he rounded corners. Have you ever seen pictures of automobiles rushing through barnyards, hens and roosters flying in all directions? It was like that. But he missed all pedestrians, and strangely enough I had no sense of alarm at his speed; he had transmitted to me a remarkable feeling of control. He stopped when he should, dodged cars successfully. He was that rare creature, a perfect driver.

Finally, having halted at a stoplight, he turned on me a disarming smile, "Mister," he said, "you have seen a demonstration of a perfectly driven car. I do things well. That is my aim in everything."

Conceited? Bumptious? Egotistical? Yes: and yet in a way, admirable. For here was a man responding to one of the deepest drives of human nature, the longing to do a thing well. Personally, I have become convinced that much of the sickness, unhappiness and dissatisfaction of human beings is due to the fact that they have not learned to do anything surpassingly well. Their attitude toward their work is desultory, shoddy, inefficient. They get by with the least effort. They leave loose ends. They never have the incomparable thrill of looking at a piece of work and pronouncing it good.

You know how it is when you hear or see something done superbly; as for example, a singer performing with skill. It is not only the music that charms you; but deep satisfaction comes from having heard an admirable performance.

What we have to master if we want to be happy and healthy, to realize our best selves, is the skill of efficiency. The lives of people are not broken up altogether because they are wicked, bad or sinful; but simply because they are shabby in their reactions.

A few years ago I was visited by a nice looking fellow, a man of good family, good education. But he had had eighteen different jobs. Many employers hired him because of his good looks; but they did not keep him because of his poor performance.

"What is wrong with me?" he asked. "I know I can get another job, but I cannot keep it. I have never in my life done anything well."

I prayed with him, trying to get an answer to his problem. And the Lord gave it in an interesting way. One day when he was visiting me he happened to put his hand on a recently polished table. Rubbing his fingers over the surface, he said," This is an exquisite patina. It is soft and silky to the touch."

"Do you like things like that?" I asked.

"Yes", he replied, "but my father would never let me work with my hands. He always wanted me to be a lawyer as he was."

"Wonderful," I said. "You write to the State University and ask for a pamphlet telling how to refinish furniture. Then go out and buy some old furniture and go to work at it."

I did not see him for a long time, but was reminded of the incident when we met recently. He was an altogether different person. He told me about working with furniture and refinishing a beautiful table that, when he ran his hand over it had a soft, silky touch. "I suddenly realized," he said," that I had made that wood feel like silk. It was the happiest moment of my life." He became a healthy, wholesome person, with no loose ends to his personality. He had focused his achievements. He had learned to do something with excellence.

★ THE P. E. O. RECORD

4

A Look through ALICE'S Window

By MARY SUMMERS, C, Wisconsin

The draperies of time have been drawn back for us today by a small well-worn scrapbook upon whose inside cover is inscribed the following, "Alice Bird Babb, Christmas 1877". This treasure from the past was given to us by a member of our chapter and a granddaughter of Alice Bird, Winifred Nolte.

It has been a very rare privilege, indeed, for me to have gazed through this window into the past. There have been moments when I felt quite like a trespasser, for scrapbooks are in a measure but reflections of ourselves, for behind each item clipped and pasted, a personal feeling is involved.

There are items here that moved me to laughter and there are those deep and poignant, that moved me to tears. I enjoyed quiet pleasure as I sat and contemplated the things I read and mused at length about the character of the woman herein revealed.

Examination of the inside cover reveals this sidelight, "Mark Twain Adhesive Scrapbook, patented June 14, 1873 by Samuel L. Clemens. Directions: Use but a little moisture and only on the gummed lines. Press on the scrap without wetting it." The first clipping in the book is entitled: "Mark Twain's Description of his Invention," with two cartoons — "Before" and "After" said invention.

It is significant that a poem "Home" appears on the first page, significant because as we know from our history and from Alice Bird Babb's own writings, her first and greatest love was home and family. Throughout the book are many, many items that verify this. In 1877 and the immediate years beyond, her family was young and active, and so it is not surprising to find the next clipping, a lengthy poem, "Tired Mothers."

Alice must have been a practical homemaker for there are such items as Recipes for Home Made Candies, Lunches for Travelling, and such household items as "Beeswax and salt will make flatirons as smooth as glass", and "A tablespoon of turpentine boiled with the white clothes will greatly aid the whitening process." The one I enjoyed most was, "The Cares of the Mother and Housekeeper and How They May Be Lightened." I could not help but smile when I came upon a poem, "At Forty," and found in 1890 a woman disliked that birthday as much as we do today.

Clippings Show Wide Interests

But being a mother and a homemaker did not interrupt Alice Babb's interest in history and current events. There are such clippings as these: The Seven Wonders of the World, Inventions and When Introduced, Britain's Rulers, Historic Funerals, The Old Sweethearts of Senator Matt Carpenter and ex Pres. Jefferson Davis, and, believe it or not, the very controversial and recently proposed, Income Tax.

She maintained a lively interest in the arts, too. From newspapers she had clipped the musical scores of The Harps that Once Through Tara's Halls, Believe Me If All Those Endearing Young Charms, and The Last Rose of Summer. The literary figures of the time and some of their yet unpublished (in book form) poems and essays have been included. Appearing are William Cullen Bryant, Mark Twain, Josh Billings, James Whitcomb Riley, and Nathaniel Hawthorne. There is also a poem of Alfred Lord Tennyson's with this byline: "Text of Five Stanzas as They Came Under the Sea Wednesday a.m."

To be found also are lists of words difficult to pronounce and lists difficult to spell.

Many Family Items

I cannot help but wonder if the many clippings included upon the death of relatives and friends are not evidence of her own grief and bereavement. Three of these very flowery eulogies (quite in keeping with the literary style of the times) taken from the Mount Pleasant paper are signed "Aunt Allie." Surely these were written by her.

Her love for and pride of her own family is evidenced by the many items concerning her own children. One item dated 1892 reads, "Max Babb and Clarence Stafford at last reports were climbing Pike's Peak." This was no doubt Mary

4

Allen Stafford's oldest son for the Stafford's lived in Mount Pleasant, too.

Many clippings verify that the Babb home was a gathering place for young and old. This is best explained in the following items dated 1882: "Hon. W. I. Babb and his good wife entertained about one hundred and fifty friends at their pleasant home last Saturday evening, and several hours were passed in social intercourse. The refreshments were of the very best, and all were merry and happy. If their house had been large enough to contain all their friends, several thousand would have been present."

Drama Under P. E. O.

In the clipping "They Played Well" is the only mention of P. E. O. "The histrionic efforts of the amateurs of the city under the auspices of the P. E. O. society Tuesday night at the Grand was in every way a decided success, and warmly applauded by the tremendous audience that assembled in spite of the bitter storm." Two plays had been presented, and the clipping states, "The real credit of the success of the evening should be bestowed on the indefatigable efforts of Mrs. Alice Babb and Mrs. S. C. Howe, who trained and directed the whole thing." It is also interesting to note that the entertainment netted seventy dollars for the organ fund!

On the very last page are three unidentified and faded pictures. One a picture of a young woman with an older woman was, I surmised, Alice and her mother. Of this I am now sure for the dress of the younger woman is the same as the dress worn by Alice Bird in her picture that appears in the book, "A History of P. E. O." A picture I found of Mrs. Babb when she was much, much older so resembles the picture of the older woman in the scrapbook that there is no doubt in my mind but that it was her mother.

Wedding Write-Up

Time does not permit my sharing with you many, many more wonderful items. However, there is one more that I would like to read.

Married.

"On Thursday, October 9, at the residence of Dr. W. Bird, by Rev. John Wheeler, D.D., W. I. Babb, Esq. to Miss Alice Bird. No cards.

"It is seldom that a wedding takes place in our community in which both the parties have so large an acquaintance and so many friends. Both raised here, and graduates of

Mrs. William T. Maynard, C. Milwaukee, right, presents a scrapbook made by Alice Bird Babb, a founder of P. E. O., to Mrs. Uretta A. Hinkhouse, left, first vice president of Supreme Chapter and the honor guest of the convention of Wisconsin State Chapter, 1962. Mrs. Maynard is wearing the mauve silk wedding dress of Mrs. Babb. The wedding dress and the scrapbook will be placed in Memorial Hall in Mount Pleasant. They were given to Chapter C by one of its members, Mrs. Winifred Babb Nolte, Milwaukee, a grand-daughter of Alice Bird Babb. The article on these pages gives a sentimental glimpse of Alice Babb's scrapbook as presented to convention by Mary Summers (Mrs. F.), C.

our University. Mr. Babb, one of the most talented and promising members of our bar, and Miss Bird one of the most brilliant and accomplished ladies in Mount Pleasant society — it is but natural that a deep interest should be felt by all our citizens in the occasion that unites them in marriage, and a warm and hearty Godspeed accord them on the life-journey they have chosen to make together. For ourselves, favored as we are with the friendship of both and knowing as we do their worth, there are no words too strong that we can utter. May their years be many, and useful and happy, crowned with the labors that shall benefit mankind, and the sweet rewards that only such labors can bring."

It is regrettable that the scrapbook does not include a picture of the wedding, but we do have something even better. Chapter C's much beloved Josephine Maynard, wearing Alice Bird's wedding dress. (As the Wedding March was played Mrs. Maynard came down through the auditorium and up onto the platform so that all might see the dress.)

And so through Alice's window these things we've seen — a woman whose interests, whose love and whose loyalties were even as yours and mine.

And now on behalf of Chapter C, I present these treasures from time past to the Supreme Chapter, with the hope they will be put in our Memorial Hall, back to Mount Pleasant from whence they came. ■

5

101

month old child was lost in the high Sierra Nevada mountains.

The famous Sierra Madre Rescue Team was already at the scene, but they needed something from the child's home that could provide a scent for the dogs being used in the search. The necessary materials were obtained and leaving at midnight, I drove five hours over rugged terrain to reach the sight. It was Sunday morning when I arrived. The family had been sheltered at a Boy Scout camp, eight miles from the location of the accident. On that morning, some 250 boys arrived to begin their week at camp; they joined in the hunt. The sheriff's departments from two counties were there. Three search and rescue teams had arrived by mid-day. And on Sunday evening, truckloads of prisoners from a nearby prison camp were brought to the scene. Boy Scouts, law enforcement, professional rescue teams, Marine helicopter units, prisoners, volunteers from nearby areas—some 700 strong searched by water, land, and air for four days. At the end of the fourth day, we were all tired and weary at heart—hot, dirty and badly sunburned. We were depressed, fearful, and anxious. As the sun was going down, I took a short walk to the top of a hill where I sat with my head in my hands, wondering what this was all about. I was sure now that we could not find the child alive; my problem was to find some meaning in all of this. It was a problem of changing from the horizontal dimensions of the past four days to a dimension of depth. To this day I am still awed at what happened there: seven hundred men, women and young people, strangers, from all walks of life,

labored together thoughtfully, devotedly, hopefully. Only these evidences of the dimension of depth—depth of devotion, sacrifice, and love—could possibly give meaning to this tragedy.

Unfortunately there are many such tragedies in the world. But fortunately, there are many more joyful occasions. In every joy and in every sorrow, there are treasures of the heart that lie deep within. Dag Hammerskjold advised well when he said, "Do not then anaesthetize yourself by once again calling up the shouts and horns of the hunt, but gaze steadfastly at the vision until you have plumbed its depths." In doing so we find again some of the joy in the now, some of the peace in the here, some of the love in us and in God which goes to make up the kingdom of heaven on earth.

Dr. Blanche H. Dow, president emeritus of Cottey College, wrote in one of her Meditations for Women, "The deep plays on eternally in strains profound for those who hear; O, may its music evermore be found within my ear!"

In purity, depth is the dimension of simplicity by which we mold life. In justice, depth is the dimension of integrity and conscience. In faith, depth is the dimension of hopefulness and optimism. In truth, depth is the dimension of clear and quiet thought. In love depth is the dimension of the stayed mind wherein dwells peace. It is the dimension of the heart wherein dwells kindness. It is the dimension of the spirit of giving and sharing wherein dwells joy. In all of life depth is the dimension of our intimate and ultimate concern for others.

MILES T. BABB: In Memoriam

MILES THORTON BABB, son of Alice Bird Babb, founder, and Washington Irving Babb, died at the Golden Age Manor, Centerville, Iowa, on December 16, 1967, at the age of 89 years. The sympathy of the sisterhood is extended to his survivors, his wife, Lottie Allen Babb, Centerville; his sister, Alice Babb Ewing (Mrs. D. K.), Aurora, Illinois, now the sole survivor of a founder's immediate family; numerous nephews and nieces, including Mrs. Robert K. Beck, Centerville. Mr. and Mrs. Babb moved to Centerville two years ago from Mt. Pleasant, Iowa, to be near the Becks and Mrs. Will S. Allen, a sister-in-law to Mrs. Babb. Mr. Babb's health had declined in recent years, and his death was attributed to the general attritions of the advancing years. He was preceded in death by his parents; a sister, Clara Belle; and a brother, Max.

Mr. Babb's reminiscences concern-

ing P. E. O. as the son of one of its seven founders have appeared in THE P. E. O. RECORD at various times, and his interesting recall of P. E. O. events made him a sought-after speaker for P. E. O. functions, which he graciously attended when possible. He enjoyed a successful business career specializing in the sale of heavy machinery, starting his career with the Western Wheel Scraper Company in Aurora, Illinois, shortly after his graduation from Iowa Wesleyan College in 1898. At the time of his retirement he was industrial sales manager for Illinois and northern Indiana for the Allis Chalmers Company.

Miles Babb was a man of many interests and a sparkling conversationalist. He was active in political circles and a great student of politics, presidential history, and history in general. He was an authority on the Lincoln family, an interest stimulated by fam-

ily and Mt. Pleasant association. Robert Lincoln was married to the daughter of Senator Harlan, Mt. Pleasant who was appointed to Lincoln's cabinet shortly before the president was assassinated. The family of Robert Lincoln often visited Mt. Pleasant, and Max Babb, a brother of Miles, served as his attorney.

Mr. Babb was a staunch supporter of Iowa Wesleyan and maintained a keen interest in his fraternity, Beta Theta Pi. Several years ago he received a special merit award from Iowa Wesleyan College, which he served as a trustee for 22 years, continuing as an honorary trustee.

Funeral services for Miles Babb were held December 18, 1967, at the Weir Cookes Funeral Home, Mt. Pleasant the Reverend George Sheils, district superintendent of the Methodist Church, officiating. Burial was in the family lot at Forest Home Cemetery Mt. Pleasant. The Sarah Porter Beck with Home, owned by Iowa State Chapter, P. E. O., was named to receive memorials.

also the home of Allie Coffin, who had come to Mt. Pleasant in '61 with her sister. They were motherless girls, and while in school, Allie boarded, — the most time with Ella Stewart. She was a southern girl, and an inseparable friend of Ella's, — so I place their homes together. There were reasons why Allie Coffin was unusually reserved, and I have always been glad that she and I were great friends, — the "two Allies," they called us.

As I walked over to the old home of our "busy bee," Ella Stewart, I saw that everything was changed. The house still there in an altered shape, cut close to it, was a huge canning factory, with puffs of smoke, wheels going around, and belts flying, and it seemed to me, that nothing could be built by Ella's home, more emblematic of her, — than a factory; a bank, or apartment house, would not fill the bill; — *something doing;* she was always planning, always executing, — whenever she came toward us, — we hurriedly took the tatting out of our pockets, and went to work.

Ella left college at the close of '68, to assist her widowed mother. She became teacher in the "Boys' Training School" at Eldora, Iowa. She was competent, loved and respected by all, and I think one of the most beautiful things P. E. O. has ever done, is for the Eldora Chapter to place an "Ella Stewart Memorial," in the Library of that Boys' Training School.

The day we laid Ella Stewart in our old cemetery, the P. E. O.'s walked together, as the walk is short, the Sunday School, many, many friends, and along the street men stood with uncovered heads, — for everyone loved and respected her, and regretted that one so useful — so young, should, "perish with the flowers."

My House was on Main Street

Then I turned to *The orchard lands of long ago* on Main Street. I never thought of it before, but I was the only one of the seven who lived on Main Street, and whether it be a recommendation or a disgrace, I leave it to you and Sinclair Lewis to decide. As I passed by old neighbor's homes, the very windows and walls and trees seemed to nod me a welcome, and as I came to the old yard, the

THIS IS THE BABB FAMILY HOME in Mount Pleasant, the second residence there occupied by Judge and Mrs. Washington Babb.

City Library, which stands in place of our rambling house, seemed the most fitting monument which could be erected to my father.

You ask what I looked for first! Why, to see if there were a piece of the old fence back of the Library, where my brother made a wooden step, so that if some student called upon me whom I did not care to see, I could mount the step, jump the fence and run off. Mother would frantically call "Allie, some one's ringing the door bell" and I'd shout, — "I'm not at home, remember, I'm not at home."

I asked the Librarian, who had come to the front door, when the beautiful Ampleopsis Ivy, which covered half of the building, had been planted. "No ones knows," she said, "it comes up everywhere, and we keep cutting it off." Then I knew that the roots of the old Ampleoposis Ivy were the ones my father planted, perhaps seventy years ago, and I realized as never before, "Oh, a rare old plant is the Ivy Green,"

The Librarian walked with me to the east side, where stood a huge cut-leaf birch, and she said, that it must soon be cut down, as addition to the building must go that way. I told her that was well, as an old cut-leaf birch is not a beautiful tree, yet no tree is more graceful than a young cut-leaf birch. I remember well the time

my father planted it. I was a very little girl, and asked him why it was named "cut-leaf," and he told me that at Vick's nurseries in New York, they hired boys and men, to cut the leaves when the trees were small and as they grew, and to this day, I never see this spliced tree but I think of the time and expense taken to call it "cut-leaf."

Then I walked back to the place, where we once had "the crooked tree croquet ground," but I could not locate it, for buildings set up. Four of us played croquet there, the last time in '72, when Grant and Greeley were candidates for president. We played the 38 states, and my father would come out and say, "now if Grant does not win, I'll pull up the stakes." This was pretty hard, when one of the four was a democrat, and thus a Greeley man. As I walked away, I did not know what direction my feet took.

Then My Own,
My Home Sweet Home

Just unconsciously, as I had walked it so often before, generally wheeling a baby carriage, I went straight to the house where most of my married life had been spent. There were the old tennis court and croquet-ground. There was the large barn, where the boys cleaned their guns and hunting apparel, and worked on the scroll saw, and

Photo Album for Mary Alice Bird

Mary Alice Bird

Birth:	08 May 1850	Father:	Wellington Bird
Death:	21 Nov 1926	Mother:	Sarah Thornton
Marriage:	1873	Spouse:	Washington Irving Babb

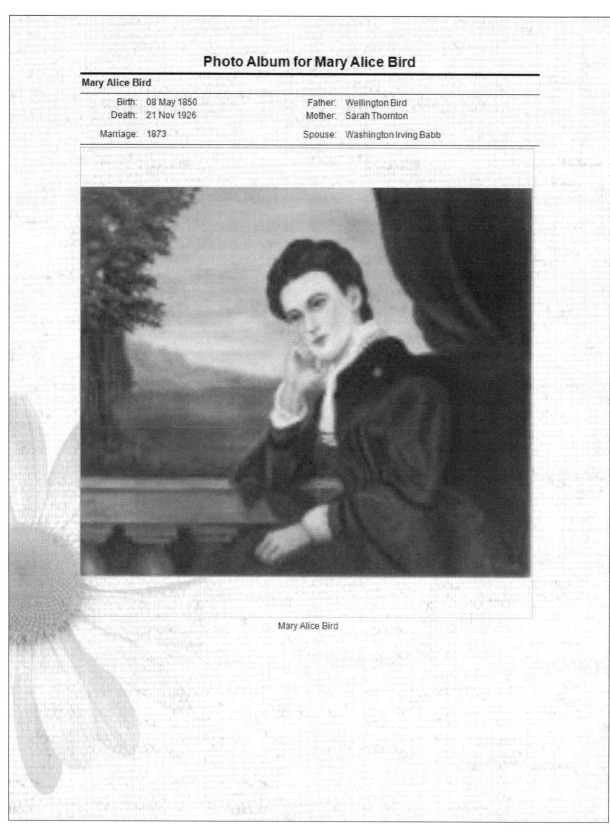

Mary Alice Bird

Reproduction of oil portrait by Marion Dunlap Harper, unveiled in P.E.O. Memorial Hall in Mount Pleasant, Iowa, on September 23, 1929.

Mary Alice Bird

Birth:	08 May 1850	Father:	Wellington Bird
Death:	21 Nov 1926	Mother:	Sarah Thornton
Marriage:	1873	Spouse:	Washington Irving Babb

Washington Irving Babb and Alice Bird Babb 1902

Printed with permission from Evan Jones.

Photo Album for Washington Irving Babb

Washington Irving Babb

Birth:	02 Oct 1844	Father:	Miles Babb
Death:	04 Sep 1925	Mother:	Mary Moyer
Marriage:	1873	Spouse:	Mary Alice Bird

Washington Irving Babb

Printed with permission from the Babb family.

Photo Album for Washington Irving Babb

Washington Irving Babb

Birth:	02 Oct 1844	Father:	Miles Babb
Death:	04 Sep 1925	Mother:	Mary Moyer
Marriage:	1873	Spouse:	Mary Alice Bird

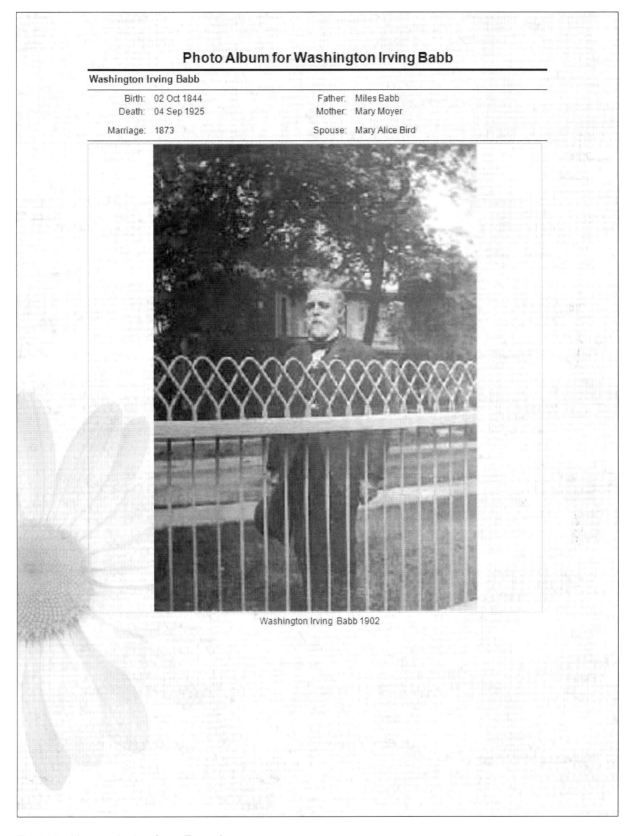

Washington Irving Babb 1902

Printed with permission from Evan Jones.

Photo Album for Max Wellington Babb

Max Wellington Babb

Birth:	28 Jul 1874	Father:	Washington Irving Babb
Death:	14 Mar 1943	Mother:	Mary Alice Bird
Marriage:	1900	Spouse:	Vida K Kemble

Max Wellington Babb

Printed with permission from the Babb family.

Wellington Bird

Birth:	05 May 1817	Father:	William Bird
Death:	18 Aug 1897	Mother:	Margarita Margo Moyer
Marriage:	06 Oct 1841	Spouse:	Sarah Thornton

Wellington Bird

Printed with permission of the Robin Woolson Abrams.

Photo Album for Sarah Thornton

Sarah Thornton

Birth:	01 Nov 1818	Father:	Eli Thornton
Death:	10 Aug 1895	Mother:	Rebecca B Willett
Marriage:	06 Oct 1841	Spouse:	Wellington Bird

Sara Thornton Bird

Printed with permission of the Robin Woolson Abrams.

Photo Album for Miranda Bird

Miranda Bird

Birth:	21 Jul 1844	Father:	Wellington Bird
Death:	23 Nov 1933	Mother:	Sarah Thornton
Marriage:	09 Apr 1867	Spouse:	John Simson Woolson

Miranda Bird

Printed with permission of the Robin Woolson Abrams.

Photo Album for John Simson Woolson

John Simson Woolson

Birth:	06 Dec 1840	Father:	Theron Webb Woolson
Death:	04 Dec 1899	Mother:	Clarissa M Simson
Marriage:	09 Apr 1867	Spouse:	Miranda Bird

John Simson Woolson

Printed with permission of John Woolson.

Historical Background Sources
for Mary Alice Bird Babb

1. 1850 United States Federal Census; Census Place; Mount Pleasant, Henry, Iowa; Roll: M432_184; Page: 183B; Image: 110.

2. 1860 United States Federal Census: Census Place: Mount Pleasant, Henry, Iowa; Roll: M653_324; page: 50; Image: 50; Family History Library Film: 803324.

3. 1870 United States Federal Census; Census Place: Center, Henry, Iowa: Roll: M593_395; Page: 194B: Image: 393: Family History Library Film: 545894.

4. 1870 United States Federal Census; Census Place: Center, Henry, Iowa; Roll: M593_395; Page: 149A; Image: 302; Family History Library Film: 545894.

5. 1880 United States Federal Census; Census Place: Mt. Pleasant, Henry, Iowa; Roll: 344; Family History Film: 1254344; page 317C; Enumeration District: 095; Image: 0196.

6. 1885 Iowa, State Census Collection, 1836-1925 (database on-line) Provo, UT, USA. Microfilm of Iowa State Censuses, 1856, 1885, 1895, 1905, 1915, 1925 as well as various special censuses from 1836-1897 obtained from the State Historical Society of Iowa vs Heritage Quest.

7. 1900 United States Federal Census; Census Place: Mount Pleasant, Henry, Iowa; Roll: 436; Page 12B; Enumeration District: 0031; FHL microfilm: 1240436.

8. 1910 United States Federal Census: Census Place: Aurora Ward 1, Kane, Illinois; Roll: T624_296; Page: 14A; Enumeration District: 0020; FHL microfilm: 1374309.

9. 1920 United States Federal Census: Census place: Aurora Ward 1, Kane, Illinois; Roll: T624_373; page: 1B Enumeration District: 36; Image: 838.

10. "A Wedding Gown of 1874." Milwaukee Sentinel [Milwaukee, Wisconsin] 21 Oct. 1934.

11. "About Iowa's Chapter S." The P.E.O. Record III. No 8 (1902).

12. "Alice Bird Babb in War Times." The P.E.O. Record LII. Number 1 (1951): 9.

13. "Arabella Mansfield." Wikipedia. Wikimedia Foundation, 27 Oct. 2013. Web. 05 Nov. 2013.

14. "Arabella Mansfield – Educator and Administrator." Belle, DePauw, Degree and Iowa. http://law.jrank.org/pages/12255/Mansfield-Arabella-Educator-administrator.html: 07 Nov 2013

15. Babb, Alice B."1909 Welcome to Supreme Chapter Convention." The P.E.O. Record (1909).

16. Babb, Alice B." Abolition of Human Bondage." The P.E.O. Record III. No 10 (1902).

17. Babb, Alice B. "Iowa Grand Chapter Convention." The P.E.O. Record IV. No 6 (1903): 134.

18. "Belle A. Mansfield." Find A Grave. Web. 08 Oct. 2013. <http://www.findagrave.com/cgi-bin/fg.cgi?page=gr&GSln=babb&GSiman=1&GScid=690429&GRid=8593884&>.

19. "Birds and Babbs." Birds and Babbs. Web. 08 Oct. 2013.

20. Clapp, Stella. Out of the Heart A Century of P.E.O. 1869-1969. Des Moines, Iowa: P.E.O. Sisterhood, 1968.

21. "Fold3 Viewer." Fold3 Viewer. Wellington Bird. 30 Aug. 2013. Web. 08 Oct. 2013.

22. Garrels, Elizabeth E. A Dream Come True. Rep. P.E.O. Conference 1996.

23. Green, Mary E. "Our Impressions of Mrs. Babb." The P.E.O. Record XXXVIII. Number 11 (1927).

24. Hull, Druscilla J., ed. Iowa Wesleyan College, Old Main Building. Rep. Washington, DC.: National Parks Service, Print.

25. Illinois, Deaths and Stillbirths Index, 1916-1947 (database on-line). Provo, UT USA: Index. Family Search, Salt Lake City, Utah, 2010. Index entries derived from digital copies of the original records.

26. "Irving Thornton Babb - Retired Lawyer." Milwaukee Journal [Milwaukee, Wisconsin] 29 Jan. 1990: 6b.

27. Johnson, Heidi, ed."A Society of Our Own." The P.E.O. Record (1997).

28. "Judge Washington Irving Babb." The P.E.O. Record XXXVI. Number 10 (1925).

29. "Juglans Cinerea." Wikipedia. Wikimedia Foundation, 22 Dec. 2013. Web. 22 Dec. 2013.

30. "Miles T. Babb: In Memoriam." The P.E.O. Record LXIX. Number 3 (1968): 16.

31. "Mrs. Alice Bird Babb." The P.E.O. Record VL. No 11 (1894).

32. "Mrs. Alice Bird Babb." Pella Chronicle [Pella, Iowa] 16 Dec. 1927: 18.

33. "Mrs. Babb's Old Home." The P.E.O. Record LIII. Number 1 (1952): 3.

34. Nolte, Winifred B."P.E.O. Reminiscences." P.E.O. Reminiscences: 6 Oct. 2013.

35. "P.E.O." Waterloo Daily Courier [Waterloo, Iowa] 12 Sept. 1895: 7.

36. Reeves, Winona E. The Blue Book of Iowa Women. Mexico: Missouri Printing and, Missouri. 1914. <http://www.kinyon.com/iowa/iawomen1914/title.htm>.

37. "Services for Former Iowa District Judge Held on Labor Day." Iowa City Press Citizen [Iowa City, Iowa] 08 Sept. 1925.

38. Shambaugh, Benjamin F., Ph.D. "Washington Irving Babb." Biographies and Portraits of the Progressive Men of Iowa." Vol. 11. Des Moines, Iowa: Conaway & Shaw, 1899. 120.

39. Summers, Mary. "A Look through Alice's Window." The P.E.O. Record LXIV. Number 1 (1963): 4-5.

40. "The Past in P.E.O." The P.E.O. Record XIII. No. 2 (1912): 4-6.

41. "The Seven Founders of P.E.O." The P.E.O. Record XXII. Number 1 (1910): Babb, Alice B. "Seven Homes." The P.E.O. Record XLI (1940): 12-14.

42. "Washington Irving Babb Democratic Candidate for Governor." The Clinton Weekly Age [Clinton, Iowa] 16 Aug. 1895: p2.

43. "Winifred Nolte (Nee Babb)." Milwaukee Sentinel [Milwaukee, Wisconsin] 11 Apr. 1998.

Mary Alice Bird Descendant Chart
Source Report

Source Title: **1850 United States Federal Census**
Repository: **Ancestry.com**

Citation: Ancestry.com, 1850 United States Federal Census (Provo, UT, USA, Ancestry.com Operations, Inc., 2009), Ancestry.com, Year: 1850; Census Place: Mount Pleasant, Henry, Iowa; Roll: M432_184; Page: 183B; Image: 110. [Source citation includes media item(s)]

Citation: Bird, Mary Alice Ancestry.com, 1850 United States Federal Census (Provo, UT, USA, Ancestry.com Operations, Inc., 2009), Ancestry.com, Year: 1850; Census Place: Mount Pleasant, Henry, Iowa; Roll: M432_184; Page: 183B; Image: 110. [Source citation includes media item(s)]

Citation: Thornton, Sarah Ancestry.com, 1850 United States Federal Census (Provo, UT, USA, Ancestry.com Operations, Inc., 2009), Ancestry.com, Year: 1850; Census Place: Mount Pleasant, Henry, Iowa; Roll: M432_184; Page: 183B; Image: 110. [Source citation includes media item(s)]

Citation: Bird, Miranda Ancestry.com, 1850 United States Federal Census (Provo, UT, USA, Ancestry.com Operations, Inc., 2009), Ancestry.com, Year: 1850; Census Place: Mount Pleasant, Henry, Iowa; Roll: M432_184; Page: 183B; Image: 110. [Source citation includes media item(s)]

Citation: Bird, Hiram Thornton Ancestry.com, 1850 United States Federal Census (Provo, UT, USA, Ancestry.com Operations, Inc., 2009), Ancestry.com, Year: 1850; Census Place: Mount Pleasant, Henry, Iowa; Roll: M432_184; Page: 183B; Image: 110. [Source citation includes media item(s)] Bird, Wellington

Source Title: **1860 United States Federal Census**
Repository: **Ancestry.com**

Citation: Ancestry.com, 1860 United States Federal Census (Provo, UT, USA, Ancestry.com Operations, Inc., 2009), Ancestry.com, Year: 1860; Census Place: Franklin, Des Moines, Iowa; Roll: M653_319; Page: 114; Image: 370; Family History Library Film: 803319. [Source citation includes media item(s)]

Citation: Babb, Washington Irving Ancestry.com, 1860 United States Federal Census (Provo, UT, USA, Ancestry.com Operations, Inc., 2009), Ancestry.com, Year: 1860; Census Place: Mount Pleasant, Henry, Iowa; Roll: M653_324; Page: 50; Image: 50; Family History Library Film: 803324. [Source citation includes media item(s)]

Citation: Bird, Mary Alice Ancestry.com, 1860 United States Federal Census (Provo, UT, USA, Ancestry.com Operations, Inc., 2009), Ancestry.com, Year: 1860; Census Place: Mount Pleasant, Henry, Iowa; Roll: M653_324; Page: 50; Image: 50; Family History Library Film: 803324. [Source citation includes media item(s)]

Citation: Thornton, Sarah Ancestry.com, 1860 United States Federal Census (Provo, UT, USA, Ancestry.com Operations, Inc., 2009), Ancestry.com, Year: 1860; Census Place: Mount Pleasant, Henry, Iowa; Roll: M653_324; Page: 50; Image: 50; Family History Library Film: 803324. [Source citation includes media item(s)]

Citation: Bird, Hiram Thornton Ancestry.com, 1860 United States Federal Census (Provo, UT, USA, Ancestry.com Operations, Inc., 2009), Ancestry.com, Year: 1860; Census Place: Mount Pleasant, Henry, Iowa; Roll: M653_324; Page: 50; Image: 50; Family History Library Film: 803324. [Source citation includes media item(s)] Bird, Regina

Citation: Ancestry.com, 1860 United States Federal Census (Provo, UT, USA, Ancestry.com Operations, Inc., 2009), Ancestry.com, Year: 1860; Census Place: Mount Pleasant, Henry, Iowa; Roll: M653_324; Page: 50; Image: 50; Family History Library Film: 803324. [Source citation includes media item(s)]

Citation: Bird, Miranda Ancestry.com, 1860 United States Federal Census (Provo, UT, USA, Ancestry.com Operations, Inc., 2009), Ancestry.com, Year: 1860; Census Place: Mount Pleasant, Henry, Iowa; Roll: M653_324; Page: 50; Image: 50; Family History Library Film: 803324. [Source citation includes media item(s)]

Citation: Bird, Horace Ancestry.com, 1860 United States Federal Census (Provo, UT, USA, Ancestry.com Operations, Inc., 2009), Ancestry.com, Year: 1860; Census Place: Mount Pleasant, Henry, Iowa; Roll: M653_324; Page: 50; Image: 50; Family History Library Film: 803324. [Source citation includes media item(s)] Bird, Wellington

Source Title: 1870 United States Federal Census
Repository: Ancestry.com

Citation: Ancestry.com, 1870 United States Federal Census (Provo, UT, USA, Ancestry.com Operations, Inc., 2009), Ancestry.com, Year: 1870; Census Place: Center, Henry, Iowa; Roll: M593_395; Page: 149A; Image: 302; Family History Library Film: 545894. [Source citation includes media item(s)]

Citation: Babb, Washington Irving Ancestry.com, 1870 United States Federal Census (Provo, UT, USA, Ancestry.com Operations, Inc., 2009), Ancestry.com, Year: 1870; Census Place: Center, Henry, Iowa; Roll: M593_395; Page: 155A; Image: 314; Family History Library Film: 545894. [Source citation includes media item(s)]

Citation: Bird, Hiram Thornton Ancestry.com, 1870 United States Federal Census (Provo, UT, USA, Ancestry.com Operations, Inc., 2009), Ancestry.com, Year: 1870; Census Place: Center, Henry, Iowa; Roll: M593_395; Page: 194B; Image: 393; Family History Library Film: 545894. [Source citation includes media item(s)]

Citation: Bird, Mary Alice Ancestry.com, 1870 United States Federal Census (Provo, UT, USA, Ancestry.com Operations, Inc., 2009), Ancestry.com, Year: 1870; Census Place: Center, Henry, Iowa; Roll: M593_395; Page: 194B; Image: 393; Family History Library Film: 545894. [Source citation includes media item(s)]

Citation: Bird, Leslie L. Ancestry.com, 1870 United States Federal Census (Provo, UT, USA, Ancestry.com Operations, Inc., 2009), Ancestry.com, Year: 1870; Census Place: Center, Henry, Iowa; Roll: M593_395; Page: 194B; Image: 393; Family History Library Film: 545894. [Source citation includes media item(s)]

Citation: Thornton, Sarah Ancestry.com, 1870 United States Federal Census (Provo, UT, USA, Ancestry.com Operations, Inc., 2009), Ancestry.com, Year: 1870; Census Place: Center, Henry, Iowa; Roll: M593_395; Page: 194B; Image: 393; Family History Library Film: 545894. [Source citation includes media item(s)]

Citation: Bird, Regina Ancestry.com, 1870 United States Federal Census (Provo, UT, USA, Ancestry.com Operations, Inc., 2009), Ancestry.com, Year: 1870; Census Place: Center, Henry, Iowa; Roll: M593_395; Page: 194B; Image: 393; Family History Library Film: 545894. [Source citation includes media item(s)] Bird, Wellington

Source Title: 1880 United States Federal Census
Repository: Ancestry.com

Citation: Ancestry.com and The Church of Jesus Christ of Latter-day Saints, 1880 United States Federal Census (Provo, UT, USA, Ancestry.com Operations Inc., 2010), Ancestry.com, Year: 1880; Census Place: MT Pleasant, Henry, Iowa; Roll: 344; Family History Film: 1254344; Page: 314A; Enumeration District: 095; Image: 0190. [Source citation includes media item(s)]

Citation: Bird, Wellington Ancestry.com and The Church of Jesus Christ of Latter-day Saints, 1880 United States Federal Census (Provo, UT, USA, Ancestry.com Operations Inc., 2010), Ancestry.com, Year: 1880; Census Place: MT Pleasant, Henry, Iowa; Roll: 344; Family History Film: 1254344; Page: 314A; Enumeration District: 095; Image: 0190. [Source citation includes media item(s)]

Citation: Thornton, Sarah Ancestry.com and The Church of Jesus Christ of Latter-day Saints, 1880 United States Federal Census (Provo, UT, USA, Ancestry.com Operations Inc., 2010), Ancestry.com, Year: 1880; Census Place: MT Pleasant, Henry, Iowa; Roll: 344; Family History Film: 1254344; Page: 314A; Enumeration District: 095; Image: 0190. [Source citation includes media item(s)]

Citation: Bird, Regina Ancestry.com and The Church of Jesus Christ of Latter-day Saints, 1880 United States Federal Census (Provo, UT, USA, Ancestry.com Operations Inc., 2010), Ancestry.com, Year: 1880; Census Place: MT Pleasant, Henry, Iowa; Roll: 344; Family History Film: 1254344; Page: 314A; Enumeration District: 095; Image: 0190. [Source citation includes media item(s)]

Citation: Bird, Leslie L. Ancestry.com and The Church of Jesus Christ of Latter-day Saints, 1880 United States Federal Census (Provo, UT, USA, Ancestry.com Operations Inc., 2010), Ancestry.com, Year: 1880; Census Place: MT Pleasant, Henry, Iowa; Roll: 344; Family History Film: 1254344; Page: 317C; Enumeration District: 095; Image: 0196. [Source citation includes media item(s)]

Citation: Bird, Mary Alice Ancestry.com and The Church of Jesus Christ of Latter-day Saints, 1880 United States Federal Census (Provo, UT, USA, Ancestry.com Operations Inc., 2010), Ancestry.com, Year: 1880; Census Place: MT Pleasant, Henry, Iowa; Roll: 344; Family History Film: 1254344; Page: 317C; Enumeration District: 095; Image: 0196. [Source citation includes media item(s)]

Citation: Babb, Max Wellington Ancestry.com and The Church of Jesus Christ of Latter-day Saints, 1880 United States Federal Census (Provo, UT, USA, Ancestry.com Operations Inc., 2010), Ancestry.com, Year: 1880; Census Place: MT Pleasant, Henry, Iowa; Roll: 344; Family History Film: 1254344; Page: 317C; Enumeration District: 095; Image: 0196. [Source citation includes media item(s)]

Citation: Babb, Washington Irving Ancestry.com and The Church of Jesus Christ of Latter-day Saints, 1880 United States Federal Census (Provo, UT, USA, Ancestry.com Operations Inc., 2010), Ancestry.com, Year: 1880; Census Place: MT Pleasant, Henry, Iowa; Roll: 344; Family History Film: 1254344; Page: 317C; Enumeration District: 095; Image: 0196. [Source citation includes media item(s)]

Citation: Babb, Miles Thorton Ancestry.com and The Church of Jesus Christ of Latter-day Saints, 1880 United States Federal Census (Provo, UT, USA, Ancestry.com Operations Inc., 2010), Ancestry.com, Year: 1880; Census Place: MT Pleasant, Henry, Iowa; Roll: 344; Family History Film: 1254344; Page: 340A; Enumeration District: 096; Image: 0242. [Source citation includes media item(s)] Bird, Hiram Thornton

Citation: Ancestry.com and The Church of Jesus Christ of Latter-day Saints, 1880 United States Federal Census (Provo, UT, USA, Ancestry.com Operations Inc., 2010), Ancestry.com, Year: 1880; Census Place: MT Pleasant, Henry, Iowa; Roll: 344; Family History Film: 1254344; Page: 348A; Enumeration District: 096; Image: 0258. [Source citation includes media item(s)] Bird, Miranda

Source Title: **1900 United States Federal Census**
Repository: **Ancestry.com**

Citation: Ancestry.com, 1900 United States Federal Census (Provo, UT, USA, Ancestry.com Operations Inc., 2004), Ancestry.com, Year: 1900; Census Place: Center, Henry, Iowa; Roll: 436; Page: 22B; Enumeration District: 0030; FHL microfilm: 1240436. [Source citation includes media item(s)]

Citation: Bird, Leslie L. Ancestry.com, 1900 United States Federal Census (Provo, UT, USA, Ancestry.com Operations Inc., 2004), Ancestry.com, Year: 1900; Census Place: Des Moines, Polk, Iowa; Roll: 454; Page: 2A; Enumeration District: 0088; FHL microfilm: 1240454. [Source citation includes media item(s)]

Citation: Bird, Miranda Ancestry.com, 1900 United States Federal Census (Provo, UT, USA, Ancestry.com Operations Inc., 2004), Ancestry.com, Year: 1900; Census Place: Mount Pleasant, Henry, Iowa; Roll: 436; Page: 12B; Enumeration District: 0031; FHL microfilm: 1240436. [Source citation includes media item(s)] Babb, Washington Irving

Citation: Bird, Mary Alice Ancestry.com, 1900 United States Federal Census (Provo, UT, USA, Ancestry.com Operations Inc., 2004), Ancestry.com, Year: 1900; Census Place: Mount Pleasant, Henry, Iowa; Roll: 436; Page: 12B; Enumeration District: 0031; FHL microfilm: 1240436. [Source citation includes media item(s)]

Citation: Babb, Alice Lillie Ancestry.com, 1900 United States Federal Census (Provo, UT, USA, Ancestry.com Operations Inc., 2004), Ancestry.com, Year: 1900; Census Place: Mount Pleasant, Henry, Iowa; Roll: 436; Page: 12B; Enumeration District: 0031; FHL microfilm: 1240436. [Source citation includes media item(s)]

Citation: Babb, Max Wellington Ancestry.com, 1900 United States Federal Census (Provo, UT, USA, Ancestry.com Operations Inc., 2004), Ancestry.com, Year: 1900; Census Place: Mount Pleasant, Henry, Iowa; Roll: 436; Page: 12B; Enumeration District: 0031; FHL microfilm: 1240436. [Source citation includes media item(s)] Babb, Washington Irving

Citation: Bird, Mary Alice Ancestry.com, 1900 United States Federal Census (Provo, UT, USA, Ancestry.com Operations Inc., 2004), Ancestry.com, Year: 1900; Census Place: Mount Pleasant, Henry, Iowa; Roll: 436; Page: 12B; Enumeration District: 0031; FHL microfilm: 1240436. [Source citation includes media item(s)]

Citation: Babb, Miles Thorton Ancestry.com, 1900 United States Federal Census (Provo, UT, USA, Ancestry.com Operations Inc., 2004), Ancestry.com, Year: 1900; Census Place: Mount Pleasant, Henry, Iowa; Roll: 436; Page: 4A; Enumeration District: 0031; FHL microfilm: 1240436. [Source citation includes media item(s)]

Citation: Bird, Hiram Thornton Ancestry.com, 1900 United States Federal Census (Provo, UT, USA, Ancestry.com Operations Inc., 2004), Ancestry.com, Year: 1900; Census Place: Mount Pleasant, Henry, Iowa; Roll: 436; Page: 4A; Enumeration District: 0031; FHL microfilm: 1240436. [Source citation includes media item(s)]

Citation: Ancestry.com, 1900 United States Federal Census (Provo, UT, USA, Ancestry.com Operations Inc., 2004), Ancestry.com, Year: 1900; Census Place: Mount Pleasant, Henry, Iowa; Roll: 436; Page: 4A; Enumeration District: 0031; FHL microfilm: 1240436. [Source citation includes media item(s)]

Citation: Bird, Hiram Thornton Ancestry.com, 1900 United States Federal Census (Provo, UT, USA, Ancestry.com Operations Inc., 2004), Ancestry.com, Year: 1900; Census Place: Pasadena Precinct 6, Los Angeles, California; Roll: 91; Page: 1A; Enumeration District: 0118; FHL microfilm: 1240091. [Source citation includes media item(s)]

Citation: Bird, Regina Ancestry.com, 1900 United States Federal Census (Provo, UT, USA, Ancestry.com Operations Inc., 2004), Ancestry.com, Year: 1900; Census Place: Pasadena Precinct 6, Los Angeles, California; Roll: 91; Page: 1A; Enumeration District: 0118; FHL microfilm: 1240091. [Source citation includes media item(s)] Bird, Regina

Source Title: **1910 United States Federal Census**
Repository: **Ancestry.com**

Citation: Ancestry.com, 1910 United States Federal Census (Provo, UT, USA, Ancestry.com Operations Inc., 2006), Ancestry.com, Year: 1910; Census Place: Aurora Ward 1, Kane, Illinois; Roll: T624_296; Page: 14A; Enumeration District: 0020; FHL microfilm: 1374309. [Source citation includes media item(s)]

Citation: Bird, Mary Alice Ancestry.com, 1910 United States Federal Census (Provo, UT, USA, Ancestry.com Operations Inc., 2006), Ancestry.com, Year: 1910; Census Place: Aurora Ward 1, Kane, Illinois; Roll: T624_296; Page: 14A; Enumeration District: 0020; FHL microfilm: 1374309. [Source citation includes media item(s)]

Citation: Babb, Alice Lillie Ancestry.com, 1910 United States Federal Census (Provo, UT, USA, Ancestry.com Operations Inc., 2006), Ancestry.com, Year: 1910; Census Place: Aurora Ward 1, Kane, Illinois; Roll: T624_296; Page: 14A; Enumeration District: 0020; FHL microfilm: 1374309. [Source citation includes media item(s)]

Citation: Babb, Washington Irving Ancestry.com, 1910 United States Federal Census (Provo, UT, USA, Ancestry.com Operations Inc., 2006), Ancestry.com, Year: 1910; Census Place: Center, Henry, Iowa; Roll: T624_405; Page: 13A; Enumeration District: 0033; FHL microfilm: 1374418. [Source citation includes media item(s)]

Citation: Bird, Hiram Thornton Ancestry.com, 1910 United States Federal Census (Provo, UT, USA, Ancestry.com Operations Inc., 2006), Ancestry.com, Year: 1910; Census Place: Chicago Ward 25, Cook, Illinois; Roll: T624_268; Page: 15A; Enumeration District: 1058; FHL microfilm: 1374281. [Source citation includes media item(s)]

Citation: Babb, Miles Thorton Ancestry.com, 1910 United States Federal Census (Provo, UT, USA, Ancestry.com Operations Inc., 2006), Ancestry.com, Year: 1910; Census Place: Milwaukee Ward 18, Milwaukee, Wisconsin; Roll: T624_1727; Page: 2A; Enumeration District: 0201; FHL microfilm: 1375740. [Source citation includes media item(s)]

Citation: Babb, Max Wellington Ancestry.com, 1910 United States Federal Census (Provo, UT, USA, Ancestry.com Operations Inc., 2006), Ancestry.com, Year: 1910; Census Place: Montclair Ward 1, Essex, New Jersey; Roll: T624_883; Page: 13A; Enumeration District: 0193; FHL microfilm: 1374896. [Source citation includes media item(s)] Bird, Miranda

Citation: Ancestry.com, 1910 United States Federal Census (Provo, UT, USA, Ancestry.com Operations Inc., 2006), Ancestry.com, Year: 1910; Census Place: Pasadena Ward 4, Los Angeles, California; Roll: T624_86; Page: 1B; Enumeration District: 0296; FHL microfilm: 1374099. [Source citation includes media item(s)] Bird, Regina

Source Title: **1920 United States Federal Census**
Repository: **Ancestry.com**

Citation: Ancestry.com, 1920 United States Federal Census (Provo, UT, USA, Ancestry.com Operations Inc., 2010), Ancestry.com, Year: 1920; Census Place: Aurora Ward 1, Kane, Illinois; Roll: T625_373; Page: 1B; Enumeration District: 36; Image: 838. [Source citation includes media item(s)]

Citation: Bird, Mary Alice Ancestry.com, 1920 United States Federal Census (Provo, UT, USA, Ancestry.com Operations Inc., 2010), Ancestry.com, Year: 1920; Census Place: Aurora Ward 1, Kane, Illinois; Roll: T625_373; Page: 1B; Enumeration District: 36; Image: 838. [Source citation includes media item(s)]

Citation: Babb, Washington Irving Ancestry.com, 1920 United States Federal Census (Provo, UT, USA, Ancestry.com Operations Inc., 2010), Ancestry.com, Year: 1920; Census Place: Aurora Ward 2, Kane, Illinois; Roll: T625_373; Page: 3A; Enumeration District: 38; Image: 889. [Source citation includes media item(s)]

Citation: Babb, Alice Lillie Ancestry.com, 1920 United States Federal Census (Provo, UT, USA, Ancestry.com Operations Inc., 2010), Ancestry.com, Year: 1920; Census Place: Chicago Ward 25, Cook (Chicago), Illinois; Roll: T625_342; Page: 10A; Enumeration District: 1480; Image: 1122. [Source citation includes media item(s)]

Citation: Babb, Miles Thorton Ancestry.com, 1920 United States Federal Census (Provo, UT, USA, Ancestry.com Operations Inc., 2010), Ancestry.com, Year: 1920; Census Place: Milwaukee Ward 18, Milwaukee, Wisconsin; Roll: T625_2003; Page: 9A; Enumeration District: 211; Image: 23. [Source citation includes media item(s)]

Citation: Babb, Max Wellington Ancestry.com, 1920 United States Federal Census (Provo, UT, USA, Ancestry.com Operations Inc., 2010), Ancestry.com, Year: 1920; Census Place: Mount Pleasant, Henry, Iowa; Roll: T625_493; Page: 10A; Enumeration District: 38; Image: 733. [Source citation includes media item(s)]

Citation: Bird, Hiram Thornton Ancestry.com, 1920 United States Federal Census (Provo, UT, USA, Ancestry.com Operations Inc., 2010), Ancestry.com, Year: 1920; Census Place: Newton Ward 5, Middlesex, Massachusetts; Roll: T625_717; Page: 3A; Enumeration District: 378; Image: 160. [Source citation includes media item(s)]

Citation: Bird, Miranda Ancestry.com, 1920 United States Federal Census (Provo, UT, USA, Ancestry.com Operations Inc., 2010), Ancestry.com, Year: 1920; Census Place: Pasadena, Los Angeles, California; Roll: T625_117; Page: 16B; Enumeration District: 532; Image: 1167. [Source citation includes media item(s)] Bird, Regina

Source Title: 1930 United States Federal Census
Repository: Ancestry.com

Citation: Ancestry.com, 1930 United States Federal Census (Provo, UT, USA, Ancestry.com Operations Inc., 2002), Ancestry.com, Year: 1930; Census Place: Aurora, Kane, Illinois; Roll: 523; Page: 1A; Enumeration District: 1; Image: 567.0; FHL microfilm: 2340258. [Source citation includes media item(s)]

Citation: Ancestry.com, 1930 United States Federal Census (Provo, UT, USA, Ancestry.com Operations Inc., 2002), Ancestry.com, Year: 1930; Census Place: Aurora, Kane, Illinois; Roll: 523; Page: 1A; Enumeration District: 1; Image: 567.0; FHL microfilm: 2340258. [Source citation includes media item(s)]

Citation: Babb, Alice Lillie Ancestry.com, 1930 United States Federal Census (Provo, UT, USA, Ancestry.com Operations Inc., 2002), Ancestry.com, Year: 1930; Census Place: Milwaukee, Milwaukee, Wisconsin; Roll: 2593; Page: 20A; Enumeration District: 223; Image: 332.0; FHL microfilm: 2342327. [Source citation includes media item(s)]

Citation: Babb, Max Wellington Ancestry.com, 1930 United States Federal Census (Provo, UT, USA, Ancestry.com Operations Inc., 2002), Ancestry.com, Year: 1930; Census Place: Montclair, Essex, New Jersey; Roll: 1332; Page: 5A; Enumeration District: 542; Image: 935.0; FHL microfilm: 2341067. [Source citation includes media item(s)]

Citation: Bird, Miranda Ancestry.com, 1930 United States Federal Census (Provo, UT, USA, Ancestry.com Operations Inc., 2002), Ancestry.com, Year: 1930; Census Place: New Trier, Cook, Illinois; Roll: 503; Page: 1B; Enumeration District: 2224; Image: 516.0; FHL microfilm: 2340238. [Source citation includes media item(s)]

Citation: Babb, Miles Thorton Ancestry.com, 1930 United States Federal Census (Provo, UT, USA, Ancestry.com Operations Inc., 2002), Ancestry.com, Year: 1930; Census Place: Pasadena, Los Angeles, California; Roll: 169; Page: 7B; Enumeration District: 1246; Image: 227.0; FHL microfilm: 2339904. [Source citation includes media item(s)] Bird, Regina

Source Title: **Ancestry Family Trees**
Repository: **Ancestry.com**

Citation: Ancestry Family Trees (Online publication - Provo, UT, USA: Ancestry.com. Original data: Family Tree files submitted by Ancestry members.), Ancestry.com, Ancestry Family Tree.

Citation: Bird, Wellington Ancestry Family Trees (Online publication - Provo, UT, USA: Ancestry.com. Original data: Family Tree files submitted by Ancestry members.), Ancestry.com, Ancestry Family Tree.

Citation: Bird, Mary Alice Ancestry Family Trees (Online publication - Provo, UT, USA: Ancestry.com. Original data: Family Tree files submitted by Ancestry members.), Ancestry.com, Ancestry Family Tree.

Citation: Thornton, Sarah Ancestry Family Trees (Online publication - Provo, UT, USA: Ancestry.com. Original data: Family Tree files submitted by Ancestry members.), Ancestry.com, Ancestry Family Tree.

Citation: Babb, Miles Thorton Ancestry Family Trees (Online publication - Provo, UT, USA: Ancestry.com. Original data: Family Tree files submitted by Ancestry members.), Ancestry.com, Ancestry Family Tree.

Citation: Babb, Alice Lillie Ancestry Family Trees (Online publication - Provo, UT, USA: Ancestry.com. Original data: Family Tree files submitted by Ancestry members.), Ancestry.com, Ancestry Family Tree. Bird, Regina

Citation: Ancestry Family Trees (Online publication - Provo, UT, USA: Ancestry.com. Original data: Family Tree files submitted by Ancestry members.), Ancestry.com, Ancestry Family Tree.

Citation: Bird, Miranda Ancestry Family Trees (Online publication - Provo, UT, USA: Ancestry.com. Original data: Family Tree files submitted by Ancestry members.), Ancestry.com, Ancestry Family Tree.

Citation: Babb, Max Wellington Ancestry Family Trees (Online publication - Provo, UT, USA: Ancestry.com. Original data: Family Tree files submitted by Ancestry members.), Ancestry.com, Ancestry Family Tree.

Citation: Babb, Clara Belle Ancestry Family Trees (Online publication - Provo, UT, USA: Ancestry.com. Original data: Family Tree files submitted by Ancestry members.), Ancestry.com, Ancestry Family Tree.

Citation: Bird, Bernetta Ancestry Family Trees (Online publication - Provo, UT, USA: Ancestry.com. Original data: Family Tree files submitted by Ancestry members.), Ancestry.com, Ancestry Family Tree.

Citation: Bird, William N Ancestry Family Trees (Online publication - Provo, UT, USA: Ancestry.com. Original data: Family Tree files submitted by Ancestry members.), Ancestry.com, Ancestry Family Tree.

Citation: Bird, Leslie L. Ancestry Family Trees (Online publication - Provo, UT, USA: Ancestry.com. Original data: Family Tree files submitted by Ancestry members.), Ancestry.com, Ancestry Family Tree.

Citation: Bird, Caroline Ancestry Family Trees (Online publication - Provo, UT, USA: Ancestry.com. Original data: Family Tree files submitted by Ancestry members.), Ancestry.com, Ancestry Family Tree.

Citation: Babb, Washington Irving Ancestry Family Trees (Online publication - Provo, UT, USA: Ancestry.com. Original data: Family Tree files submitted by Ancestry members.), Ancestry.com, Ancestry Family Tree.

Citation: Bird, Hiram Thornton Ancestry Family Trees (Online publication - Provo, UT, USA: Ancestry.com. Original data: Family Tree files submitted by Ancestry members.), Ancestry.com, Ancestry Family Tree. Bird, Horace

Source Title: California, Death Index, 1905-1939
Repository: Ancestry.com

Citation: Ancestry.com, California, Death Index, 1905-1939 (Provo, UT, USA, Ancestry.com Operations, Inc., 2013), Ancestry.com. Bird, Regina

Source Title: Family Data Collection - Individual Records
Repository: Ancestry.com

Citation: Edmund West, comp., Family Data Collection - Individual Records (Provo, UT, USA, Ancestry.com Operations Inc., 2000), Ancestry.com, Birth year: 1818; Birth city: Columbia; Birth state: PA. Bird, Wellington Thornton, Sarah

Source Title: Illinois, Deaths and Stillbirths Index, 1916-1947
Repository: Ancestry.com

Citation: Ancestry.com, Illinois, Deaths and Stillbirths Index, 1916-1947 (Provo, UT, USA, Ancestry.com Operations, Inc., 2011), Ancestry.com.

Citation: Bird, Mary Alice Ancestry.com, Illinois, Deaths and Stillbirths Index, 1916-1947 (Provo, UT, USA, Ancestry.com Operations, Inc., 2011), Ancestry.com. Babb, Washington Irving

Source Title: Iowa, Births and Christenings Index, 1857-1947
Repository: Ancestry.com

Citation: Ancestry.com, Iowa, Births and Christenings Index, 1857-1947 (Provo, UT, USA, Ancestry.com Operations, Inc., 2011), Ancestry.com. Babb, Clara Belle

Source Title: Iowa, State Census Collection, 1836-1925
Repository: Ancestry.com

Citation: Ancestry.com, Iowa, State Census Collection, 1836-1925 (Provo, UT, USA, Ancestry.com Operations Inc., 2007), Ancestry.com. [Source citation includes media item(s)]

Citation: Bird, Wellington Ancestry.com, Iowa, State Census Collection, 1836-1925 (Provo, UT, USA, Ancestry.com Operations Inc., 2007), Ancestry.com. [Source citation includes media item(s)]

Citation: Bird, Mary Alice Ancestry.com, Iowa, State Census Collection, 1836-1925 (Provo, UT, USA, Ancestry.com Operations Inc., 2007), Ancestry.com. [Source citation includes media item(s)]

Citation: Bird, Hiram Thornton Ancestry.com, Iowa, State Census Collection, 1836-1925 (Provo, UT, USA, Ancestry.com Operations Inc., 2007), Ancestry.com. [Source citation includes media item(s)]

Citation: Bird, Wellington Ancestry.com, Iowa, State Census Collection, 1836-1925 (Provo, UT, USA, Ancestry.com Operations Inc., 2007), Ancestry.com. [Source citation includes media item(s)]

Citation: Thornton, Sarah Ancestry.com, Iowa, State Census Collection, 1836-1925 (Provo, UT, USA, Ancestry.com Operations Inc., 2007), Ancestry.com. [Source citation includes media item(s)]

Citation: Thornton, Sarah Ancestry.com, Iowa, State Census Collection, 1836-1925 (Provo, UT, USA, Ancestry.com Operations Inc., 2007), Ancestry.com. [Source citation includes media item(s)]

Citation: Bird, Leslie L. Ancestry.com, Iowa, State Census Collection, 1836-1925 (Provo, UT, USA, Ancestry.com Operations Inc., 2007), Ancestry.com. [Source citation includes media item(s)]

Citation: Bird, Miranda Ancestry.com, Iowa, State Census Collection, 1836-1925 (Provo, UT, USA, Ancestry.com Operations Inc., 2007), Ancestry.com. [Source citation includes media item(s)] Bird, Hiram Thornton

Citation: Ancestry.com, Iowa, State Census Collection, 1836-1925 (Provo, UT, USA, Ancestry.com Operations Inc., 2007), Ancestry.com. [Source citation includes media item(s)]

Citation: Bird, Horace Ancestry.com, Iowa, State Census Collection, 1836-1925 (Provo, UT, USA, Ancestry.com Operations Inc., 2007), Ancestry.com. [Source citation includes media item(s)]

Citation: Babb, Miles Thorton Ancestry.com, Iowa, State Census Collection, 1836-1925 (Provo, UT, USA, Ancestry.com Operations Inc., 2007), Ancestry.com. [Source citation includes media item(s)]

Citation: Bird, Mary Alice Ancestry.com, Iowa, State Census Collection, 1836-1925 (Provo, UT, USA, Ancestry.com Operations Inc., 2007), Ancestry.com. [Source citation includes media item(s)]

Citation: Babb, Max Wellington Ancestry.com, Iowa, State Census Collection, 1836-1925 (Provo, UT, USA, Ancestry.com Operations Inc., 2007), Ancestry.com. [Source citation includes media item(s)]

Citation: Babb, Clara Belle Ancestry.com, Iowa, State Census Collection, 1836-1925 (Provo, UT, USA, Ancestry.com Operations Inc., 2007), Ancestry.com. [Source citation includes media item(s)] Babb, Washington Irving

Source Title: Iowa, State Census, 1895
Repository: Ancestry.com

Citation: Ancestry.com, Iowa, State Census, 1895 (Provo, UT, USA, Ancestry.com Operations Inc, 2003), Ancestry.com.

Citation: Bird, Mary Alice Ancestry.com, Iowa, State Census, 1895 (Provo, UT, USA, Ancestry.com Operations Inc, 2003), Ancestry.com.

Citation: Bird, Hiram Thornton Ancestry.com, Iowa, State Census, 1895 (Provo, UT, USA, Ancestry.com Operations Inc, 2003), Ancestry.com.

Citation: Babb, Max Wellington Ancestry.com, Iowa, State Census, 1895 (Provo, UT, USA, Ancestry.com Operations Inc, 2003), Ancestry.com.

Citation: Babb, Alice Lillie Ancestry.com, Iowa, State Census, 1895 (Provo, UT, USA, Ancestry.com Operations Inc, 2003), Ancestry.com.

Citation: Babb, Washington Irving Ancestry.com, Iowa, State Census, 1895 (Provo, UT, USA, Ancestry.com Operations Inc, 2003), Ancestry.com. Babb, Miles Thorton

Source Title: Kansas State Census Collection, 1855-1925
Repository: Ancestry.com

Citation: Ancestry.com., Kansas State Census Collection, 1855-1925 (Provo, UT, USA, Ancestry.com Operations Inc., 2009), Ancestry.com. [Source citation includes media item(s)] Bird, Regina

Source Title: **Navy Widows' Certificates at Fold3**
Repository: **www.fold3.com**

Citation: Navy Widows' Certificates at Fold3, www.fold3.com, Navy Widows Civil War Pension Application. http://www.fold3.com/image/29003434/.

Citation: Bird, Miranda Navy Widows' Certificates at Fold3, www.fold3.com, Page 4 - Navy Widows' Certificates. http://www.fold3.com/image/29003434/. Bird, Miranda

Source Title: New York, Passenger Lists, 1820-1957
Repository: Ancestry.com

Citation: Ancestry.com, New York, Passenger Lists, 1820-1957 (Provo, UT, USA, Ancestry.com Operations, Inc., 2010), Ancestry.com, Year: 1936. [Source citation includes media item(s)] Babb, Max Wellington

Source Title: **U.S. City Directories, 1821-1989**
Repository: **Ancestry.com**

Citation: Ancestry.com, U.S. City Directories, 1821-1989 (Provo, UT, USA, Ancestry.com Operations, Inc., 2011), Ancestry.com. [Source citation includes media item(s)]

Citation: Bird, Mary Alice Ancestry.com, U.S. City Directories, 1821-1989 (Provo, UT, USA, Ancestry.com Operations, Inc., 2011), Ancestry.com. [Source citation includes media item(s)]

Citation: Bird, Regina Ancestry.com, U.S. City Directories, 1821-1989 (Provo, UT, USA, Ancestry.com Operations, Inc., 2011), Ancestry.com. [Source citation includes media item(s)]

Citation: Bird, Regina Ancestry.com, U.S. City Directories, 1821 1989 (Provo, UT, USA, Ancestry.com Operations, Inc., 2011), Ancestry.com. [Source citation includes media item(s)]

Citation: Bird, Regina Ancestry.com, U.S. City Directories, 1821-1989 (Provo, UT, USA, Ancestry.com Operations, Inc., 2011), Ancestry.com. [Source citation includes media item(s)]

Citation: Bird, Miranda Ancestry.com, U.S. City Directories, 1821-1989 (Provo, UT, USA, Ancestry.com Operations, Inc., 2011), Ancestry.com. [Source citation includes media item(s)]

Citation: Babb, Max Wellington Ancestry.com, U.S. City Directories, 1821-1989 (Provo, UT, USA, Ancestry.com Operations, Inc., 2011), Ancestry.com. [Source citation includes media item(s)]

Citation: Babb, Alice Lillie Ancestry.com, U.S. City Directories, 1821-1989 (Provo, UT, USA, Ancestry.com Operations, Inc., 2011), Ancestry.com. [Source citation includes media item(s)]

Citation: Babb, Alice Lillie Ancestry.com, U.S. City Directories, 1821-1989 (Provo, UT, USA, Ancestry.com Operations, Inc., 2011), Ancestry.com. [Source citation includes media item(s)]

Citation: Babb, Alice Lillie Ancestry.com, U.S. City Directories, 1821-1989 (Provo, UT, USA, Ancestry.com Operations, Inc., 2011), Ancestry.com. [Source citation includes media item(s)]

Citation: Babb, Alice Lillie Ancestry.com, U.S. City Directories, 1821-1989 (Provo, UT, USA, Ancestry.com Operations, Inc., 2011), Ancestry.com. [Source citation includes media item(s)]

Citation: Babb, Miles Thorton Ancestry.com, U.S. City Directories, 1821-1989 (Provo, UT, USA, Ancestry.com Operations, Inc., 2011), Ancestry.com. [Source citation includes media item(s)] Babb, Washington Irving

Source Title: U.S. Civil War Soldiers, 1861-1865
Repository: Ancestry.com

Citation: National Park Service, U.S. Civil War Soldiers, 1861-1865 (Provo, UT, USA, Ancestry.com Operations Inc., 2007), Ancestry.com. Bird, Hiram Thornton

Source Title: U.S. Federal Census Mortality Schedules, 1850-1885
          Repository: Ancestry.com

Citation: Ancestry.com, U.S. Federal Census Mortality Schedules, 1850-1885 (Provo, UT, USA, Ancestry.com Operations, Inc., 2010), Ancestry.com, Census Year: 1859. [Source citation includes media item(s)] Bird, Horace

Source Title: U.S. Passport Applications, 1795-1925
Repository: Ancestry.com

Citation: Ancestry.com, U.S. Passport Applications, 1795-1925 (Provo, UT, USA, Ancestry.com Operations, Inc., 2007), Ancestry.com, National Archives and Records Administration (NARA); Washington D.C.; Passport Applications, January 2, 1906 - March 31, 1925; Collection Number: ARC Identifier 583830 / MLR Number A1 534; NARA Series: M1490; Roll #: 130. [Source citation includes media item(s)] Babb, Alice Lillie

Source Title: U.S., Adjutant General Military Records, 1631-1976
Repository: Ancestry.com

Citation: Ancestry.com, U.S., Adjutant General Military Records, 1631-1976 (Provo, UT, USA, Ancestry.com Operations, Inc., 2011), Ancestry.com, California State Library; Sacramento; Report of the Adjutant General of the State of Iowa. [Source citation includes media item(s)] Bird, Wellington

Source Title: U.S., Civil War Pension Index: General Index to Pension Files, 1861-1934
Repository: Ancestry.com

Citation: National Archives and Records Administration, U.S., Civil War Pension Index: General Index to Pension Files, 1861-1934 (Provo, UT, USA, Ancestry.com Operations Inc., 2000), Ancestry.com. [Source citation includes media item(s)] Bird, Wellington

Source Title: U.S., Civil War Soldier Records and Profiles, 1861-1865
Repository: Ancestry.com

Citation: Historical Data Systems, comp, U.S., Civil War Soldier Records and Profiles, 1861-1865 (Provo, UT, USA, Ancestry.com Operations Inc., 2009), Ancestry.com.

Citation: Bird, Wellington Historical Data Systems, comp, U.S., Civil War Soldier Records and Profiles, 1861-1865 (Provo, UT, USA, Ancestry.com Operations Inc., 2009), Ancestry.com. Babb, Washington Irving

Source Title: U.S., Social Security Death Index, 1935-Current
Repository: Ancestry.com

Citation: Ancestry.com, U.S., Social Security Death Index, 1935-Current (Provo, UT, USA, Ancestry.com Operations Inc., 2011), Ancestry.com, Number: 333-42-7269; Issue State: Illinois; Issue Date: 1964-1965.

Citation: Babb, Alice Lillie Ancestry.com, U.S., Social Security Death Index, 1935-Current (Provo, UT, USA, Ancestry.com Operations Inc., 2011), Ancestry.com, Number: 398-09-6525; Issue State: Wisconsin; Issue Date: Before 1951. Babb, Miles Thorton

Source Title: U.S., World War I Draft Registration Cards, 1917-1918
Repository: Ancestry.com

Citation: Ancestry.com, U.S., World War I Draft Registration Cards, 1917-1918 (Provo, UT, USA, Ancestry.com Operations Inc., 2005), Ancestry.com, Registration State: Missouri; Registration County: Jackson; Roll: 1683385; Draft Board: 12. [Source citation includes media item(s)]

Citation: Babb, Miles Thorton Ancestry.com, U.S., World War I Draft Registration Cards, 1917-1918 (Provo, UT, USA, Ancestry.com Operations Inc., 2005), Ancestry.com, Registration State: Wisconsin; Registration County: Milwaukee; Roll: 1674815; Draft Board: 13. [Source citation includes media item(s)] Babb, Max Wellington

Source Title: U.S., World War II Draft Registration Cards, 1942
Repository: Ancestry.com

Citation: Ancestry.com, U.S., World War II Draft Registration Cards, 1942 (Provo, UT, USA, Ancestry.com Operations, Inc., 2010), Ancestry.com, National Archives and Records Administration (NARA); Washington, D.C.; State Headquarters: Illinois; Microfilm Series: M2097; Microfilm Roll: 10. [Source citation includes media item(s)] Babb, Miles Thorton

Source Title: Web: California, Find A Grave Index, 1775-2012
Repository: Ancestry.com

Citation: Ancestry.com, Web: California, Find A Grave Index, 1775-2012 (Provo, UT, USA, Ancestry.com Operations, Inc., 2012), Ancestry.com. Bird, Regina

Source Title: Web: Illinois, Find A Grave Index, 1809-2012
Repository: Ancestry.com

Citation: Ancestry.com, Web: Illinois, Find A Grave Index, 1809-2012 (Provo, UT, USA, Ancestry.com Operations, Inc., 2012), Ancestry.com. Babb, Alice Lillie

Source Title: Web: Iowa, Find A Grave Index, 1800-2012
Repository: Ancestry.com

Citation: Ancestry.com, Web: Iowa, Find A Grave Index, 1800-2012 (Provo, UT, USA, Ancestry.com Operations, Inc., 2012), Ancestry.com.

Citation: Bird, Mary Alice Ancestry.com, Web: Iowa, Find A Grave Index, 1800-2012 (Provo, UT, USA, Ancestry.com Operations, Inc., 2012), Ancestry.com.

Citation: Bird, Hiram Thornton Ancestry.com, Web: Iowa, Find A Grave Index, 1800-2012 (Provo, UT, USA, Ancestry.com Operations, Inc., 2012), Ancestry.com.

Citation: Bird, Wellington Ancestry.com, Web: Iowa, Find A Grave Index, 1800-2012 (Provo, UT, USA, Ancestry.com Operations, Inc., 2012), Ancestry.com.

Citation: Thornton, Sarah Ancestry.com, Web: Iowa, Find A Grave Index, 1800-2012 (Provo, UT, USA, Ancestry.com Operations, Inc., 2012), Ancestry.com.

Citation: Bird, Miranda Ancestry.com, Web: Iowa, Find A Grave Index, 1800-2012 (Provo, UT, USA, Ancestry.com Operations, Inc., 2012), Ancestry.com.

Citation: Babb, Clara Belle Ancestry.com, Web: Iowa, Find A Grave Index, 1800-2012 (Provo, UT, USA, Ancestry.com Operations, Inc., 2012), Ancestry.com. Bird, Bernetta

Citation: Ancestry.com, Web: Iowa, Find A Grave Index, 1800-2012 (Provo, UT, USA, Ancestry.com Operations, Inc., 2012), Ancestry.com.

Citation: Bird, Leslie L. Ancestry.com, Web: Iowa, Find A Grave Index, 1800-2012 (Provo, UT, USA, Ancestry.com Operations, Inc., 2012), Ancestry.com.

Citation: Bird, Horace Ancestry.com, Web: Iowa, Find A Grave Index, 1800-2012 (Provo, UT, USA, Ancestry.com Operations, Inc., 2012), Ancestry.com.

Citation: Babb, Miles Thorton Ancestry.com, Web: Iowa, Find A Grave Index, 1800-2012 (Provo, UT, USA, Ancestry.com Operations, Inc., 2012), Ancestry.com. Babb, Washington Irving

Source Title: Web: Wisconsin, Find A Grave Index, 1836-2012
Repository: Ancestry.com

Citation: Ancestry.com, Web: Wisconsin, Find A Grave Index, 1836-2012 (Provo, UT, USA, Ancestry.com Operations, Inc., 2012), Ancestry.com. Babb, Max Wellington

Chapter 3: Harriet Jane Briggs

Harriet Jane Briggs

According to research done by Francis C. Briggs Waddell, in her book "The Briggs Family History 1621-1921," the first Briggs in Hattie's family to arrive in America was Clement Briggs, who arrived in Plymouth Colony in November 1621. Francis Briggs Waddell is a past president of P.E.O Chapter O, Helena, Montana.

Clement was Hattie's 5th great-grandfather. Clement's grandson, Thomas, while Hattie's 3rd great-grandfather, was a brother to Francis Briggs Waddell's 7th great-grandfather, David. So, they share a 4th/8th great-grandfather. Consequently, Francis and Hattie are first cousins, several times removed.

Most biographies about Harriet (Hattie) mention that she was the daughter of Reverend Elias Lyman and Jane Johnson Briggs. However, Elias didn't become a Reverend until about the time of Hattie's fourth birthday. If one goes back to the 1850 Census, taken shortly after Hattie was born, her father Elias lists himself, at the age of 28, as a carpenter. By delving back a bit, it appears that Elias actually became a minister in the Methodist Episcopal Church in 1853, four years after Hattie was born. Records indicate that in 1854-55, Rev. Briggs was pastor at the First Methodist Church, Knoxville, Iowa. Rev. Briggs would return to the First Methodist Church in Knoxville to serve as pastor again from 1871-1873.

Due to his vocation, the Briggs family moved a bit. Evidenced by the fact that in 1849, Hattie was born in Troy, Iowa; in 1850 they were 150 miles away in Union, Iowa; by 1860 they were in Jefferson, Iowa – 85 miles from Union – and, in the early 1860's the family moved to Mount Pleasant, a little over 200 miles from Jefferson, where Hattie attended Iowa Wesleyan.

Hattie was the second of five children. She had one older brother, Abington, two younger brothers and a younger sister. One of her younger brothers, James Ancil Briggs, entered Iowa Wesleyan in 1869, just after Hattie graduated.

A few months prior to the founding of the P.E.O. Sisterhood, on 17 March 1869, a photo was taken of Franc, Mary and Hattie. This photo is often seen in with the collection of historical P.E.O. photos. Initially, the photo was donated in July 1905 to Mrs. Maude Gilson Mentzer, first president of the Wyoming state chapter by Hattie's husband, Henri Bousquet. Mrs. Mentzer later contributed the photo to the collection in the P.E.O. Memorial Room in "Old Main" at Iowa Wesleyan.

By 1870 Census we find the Briggs family in Ottumwa, Iowa, 50 miles west of Mt. Pleasant; and, by 1873 the family was living in Knoxville, Iowa. This is where Hattie met her husband Henry Bousquet.

Henry Louis Bousquet had been born in Amsterdam in 1840. He emigrated to America with his family in 1849 when he was nine years old, possibly aboard the ship *Jacob Kats,* which reflects passenger records for his father, Abraham and sons, Herman and

John. Many from the Netherlands pioneer settlers who arrived in the 1840's emigrated to central Iowa to escape religious tyranny.

Henry was the third of four boys born to Abraham and Henrietta Bousquet. Pierre Henri, the oldest, often referred to as P.H., became a prominent attorney in Marion County and established what was to become Pella National Bank. John, Abraham's second son, spent his life's work in business, mostly in the produce business. He also became deaf. And, Henry's younger brother, Herman, was said to be the first graduate from the old Central University of Iowa, established in 1853 by the Baptist church in Pella.

Henry was a student at Central University in Pella, Iowa when he left to enlist in the Civil War on 4 September 1862. He served in Company G, Iowa 33rd Infantry Regiment until he was commissioned an officer in Company S, Arkansas 4th Calvary Regiment on 30 December 1864. Three years later he mustered out on 30 June 1865. At the close of the war, Henry returned to Pella, Iowa and was elected county clerk of Marion County and he later became the Supreme Court clerk for Marion County, Iowa from 1908-1912.

After Hattie and Henry were married they settled in Pella, Iowa, a mere 14 miles from Knoxville. During their four and a half years of marriage, Hattie and Henry had two sons; Cutts Briggs Bousquet, born in October 1873 and Henry Lyman Bousquet in 1875. During their marriage Henry was an assistant cashier in the Pella National Bank, founded by his brother Pierre.

Hattie and her brother, Henry Lyman Briggs, must have been close siblings as evidenced by the naming of their respective children. Hattie's and Henry's second son was named Henry Lyman Bousquet. Additionally, we learn that in 1875, Henry married Virginia Seevers, daughter of William H. Seevers, Sr., who ultimately became a respected Judge of the Supreme Court of Iowa. Henry and Virginia named their only child, a daughter born in 1878, Hattie. Virginia herself dies in 1881.

It is interesting to note that prior to Judge Seevers appointment to the court, he was at one time a law partner with Mr. Marsena Edgar Cutts. Within a historical account of Mahaska County, Iowa, Mr. Cutts is referred to as a "distinguished citizen" who was very active in state politics. During his career he served in the Iowa House of Representatives, the Iowa Senate and as Attorney General of Iowa. Family conjecture is that the Seevers, Cutts, Briggs and Bousquet families were intertwined socially, and Marsena Cutts may have been the motivation for Hattie's first born son's name to be Cutts.

Hattie's great-granddaughter, Kae Lynn Durham Caston, shared a copy of an article from the January-February 2002 P.E.O. Record. This article contained a letter, found by Juli Wilson, Chapter AA, Nevada, written by P.E.O. founder Hattie Bousquet, in January 1877, five months before her death. The letter was addressed to her husband Henry's Uncle, John (Jan) Bousquet. Juli is the great-great granddaughter of Pierre H. Bousquet, a brother to John (Jean), Henry and Herman Bousquet.

In this letter Hattie writes, "We were married four years the 12th of this month, and Cutts was three years old the 26th of October; and Lyman was one year old the 4th of December. Of myself I can say very little, only that since our marriage, my health has been very bad, until this winter; I think I am regaining some of my former strength." She continues, showing her desire to continue learning with ….. "As my children grow older, I hope to have more leisure; and then I am going to try to learn Holland – not anticipating that I can acquaint myself with the language sufficiently to speak it correctly, but rather so I can more readily understand it. Would it be asking too much of you to send me a Holland primmer (sic) sometime, as I wish to begin at the very foundation."

Five months after writing that letter Hattie died at the age of 27 in June of 1877. She left behind Henry, her son Cutts, not quite four years old, and her young son Henry, only 18 months old.

This was a year before her mother and just three years before her brother, James, died. Both James and Hattie died young; James at age 26 and Hattie at age 27. Hattie's father, Elias, outlived them all, along with his second wife, Maria Herr Reed Briggs.

After Hattie's death it appears Cutts and his brother are taken in to be nurtured and raised by Hattie's brother, Abington. For in 1880, we find both Cutts and his brother, Henry Lyman, living with their uncle Abington and his wife Alice Briggs, their son, their cousin George, and Hattie's sister, Clara. Henry Bousquet seems to be living in a separate residence; although they are all living in Knoxville, Iowa. Sadly, Hattie's son Henry died in 1881, four years after his mother, just shy of his 6th birthday.

The 1885 Iowa State Census for Henry Bousquet lists him as living without his son Cutts. And, Cutts is noted in the 1885 Nebraska State Census, age 11, still living with his Uncle Abington and Aunt Alice Briggs – and their son, George. According to *Out of the Heart* book about P.E.O. published in 1969, Cutts attended Iowa Wesleyan for a time; most likely sometime between 1890 and 1895. It is difficult to tell what the relationship was between father and son.

Henry Bousquet marries his second wife, May Bain, in May of 1891. In 1895, Cutts is 21 years old and living with his father, Henry, his step-mother May and their two year old son, John Bousquet. Regrettably, John dies in July of 1897 at the age of five. The second son of Henry's to die at a young age. Henry and May do have another son, Pierre Henri Bousquet, born two months after John's death in September 1897.

Cutts joined the military in September of 1895 in time for the Spanish-American War and remained in military service off and on until 1910. He is reported to have been with Troop D of the First U.S. Cavalry and to have ridden in the charge at San Juan Hill with Teddy Roosevelt.

Cutts's military records list him as also having served in the A, E & H Signal Corp. The A, E & H Signal Corp had roles in the Spanish American War of 1898 and in the subsequent Philippine Insurrection. In addition to visual signaling, including heliograph, the Corp supplied telephone and telegraph wire lines and cable communications, fostered the use of telephones in combat and employed combat photography. During the time of Cutts's service, the Signal Corp constructed the Washington-Alaska Military Cable and Telegraph System (WAMCATS) also known as the Alaskan Communication System introducing the first wireless telegraph in the Western Hemisphere.

The 1904 Des Moines, Iowa City Directory shows both Henry and Cutts. However, they are living in separate residences. Cutts occupation is listed as an Assistant Engineer, CRI&P (Chicago, Rock Island and Pacific Railroad), while Henry's occupation is listed as a Deputy Clerk of the State Supreme Court.

Newspaper reports, dated in 1906, are written by Cutts about his experience with the railroad surveying crew in Canada. In his reports he recounts his impressions of the countryside and the locations of his journey.

Cutts is found in November 1913 to be an "organizer" for the National Highways association. He was one of two hundred organizers employed by the association to work for legislation by Congress for an appropriation of $500,000,000 for a system of trunk roads covering all states. The proposal was for the Federal Government to fund the unification of the various roads and state highways within the country.

In 1916 Cutts was 42 and married Hattie Clara Degenaar, daughter of another immigrant from Holland. He presented his wife Hattie with the same wedding ring his father Henry had given his mother, Hattie. This wedding ring was later worn by Hattie's granddaughter, Cutts's only child, Geraldine, when she was initiated into P.E.O. Chapter M, in Knoxville, Iowa. That wedding ring was eventually given by Geraldine and two of Hattie's great-granddaughters, Kathy Lee Durham Cobb and Karen Rae Durham Dykstra to P.E.O. The ring can be viewed today at P.E.O. International Headquarters in Des Moines, Iowa.

Geraldine, Cutts's daughter, was born in October of 1918, just a couple of weeks before Cutts turned 45. Geraldine's daughter, Kae, shared, "Mother was an only child, born as she said, to parents old enough to be her grandparents."

Cutts's life must not have been an easy one as we find him listed in 1919 as a patient in a U.S. National Home for Disabled Volunteer Soldiers, Hot Springs, South Dakota and in the 1920 Census living in a National Soldiers Home in Tennessee. Cutts is also shown from 1919 thru 1932 as in and out of the U.S. National Home for Disabled Volunteer Soldiers, in Sawtelle, California.

By the end of 1922, Cutts has applied for a military pension. The 1930 Census shows Cutts living with his wife Hattie and daughter Geraldine in Knoxville, Iowa. However, by the time of the 1940 Census, Cutts is back to being listed as a patient in the Knoxville Veterans Hospital. Cutts died at the age of 83 while a patient in the Veterans Hospital in Des Moines, Iowa in June of 1957.

His daughter, Geraldine married Kenneth Durham in 1936 and lived in Nevada until her death at age 76 in 1994. Geraldine was active in the American Red Cross, the Daughters of Union Veterans of the Civil War and was a P.E.O. member of Chapter M,

Knoxville, Iowa. Geraldine and Kenneth retired to Ely, Nevada, which is where both of them are buried.

During the course of this research communication and input was contributed by Hattie's great-granddaughters; Kae Lynn Durham Caston of Farmington, MN; Karon Rae Durham Dykstra, Pella, IA and Kathy Lee Durham Cobb, Ely, NV. Additionally, Hattie's great-great granddaughter, Michelle Volk provided insight into Hattie's family and descendants.

Thus far there have been four generations of P.E.O. sisters descended from Hattie!

Grand-Daughter: Geraldine, Chapter M, Knoxville

Great-granddaughters: Kae is a member of Chapter EB, Farmington, Minnesota; Karen a member of Chapter ND, Pella, Iowa; and Kathy is a member of Chapter C, Ely, Nevada.

Great-Great Granddaughters: Michelle Caston Volk and Andrea Caston Meyer, Chapter EB, Farmington, MN; Tammy L. Dykstra, Chapter DZ, Dodge City, KS; and Christy Dykstra, Chapter ND, Pella, IA.

3rd Great-Granddaughters: Jacqueline Surish Caston, Carrie Volk Hoffman, Janee Volk Luikens and Tanya Volk all in Chapter EB, Farmington MN

What a wonderful impact, even in her short life, Hattie had by fostering her pioneering spirit!

Harriett Jane Briggs Bousquet – Life Events

DATE	EVENT	AGE
10 October 1849	Born: Troy, Davis Iowa	
1849	Future husband Henry Bousquet emigrates from Holland	
August 1850	Residence: Union, Davis, Iowa	0
July 1860	Residence: Round Prairie, Jefferson, Iowa	10
1863	Family moved to Mount Pleasant, Henry, Iowa	13
September 1865	Entered Iowa Wesleyan	15
21 January 1869	P.E.O. Founded	19
June 1869	Graduated Iowa Wesleyan with B.S. degree	19
1869-1873	Taught music and art: Ottumwa, Iowa and Knoxville, Iowa	19-23
July 1870	Residence: Ottumwa, Wapello, Iowa	20
June 1872	Honorary degree M.S. from Iowa Wesleyan	22
12 January 1873	Married Henry Louis Bousquet	23
26 October 1873	Son: Cutts Briggs Bousquet born	24
4 December 1875	Son: Henry Lyman Bousquet born	26
22 June 1877	Died Pella, Marion, Iowa Buried: Oakwood Cemetery, Pella, Marion, Iowa	27

Descendant Chart for
Harriet Jane Briggs

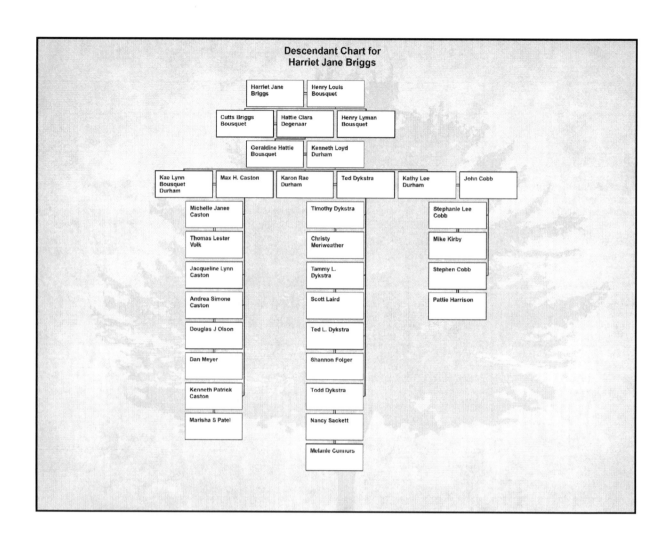

Harriet Jane Briggs	Henry Louis Bousquet

Cutts Briggs Bousquet	Hattie Clara Degenaar	Henry Lyman Bousquet

Geraldine Hattie Bousquet	Kenneth Loyd Durham

Kae Lynn Bousquet Durham	Max H. Caston	Karon Rae Durham	Ted Dykstra	Kathy Lee Durham	John Cobb

Kae Lynn Bousquet Durham / Max H. Caston line:
- Michelle Janee Caston
- Thomas Lester Volk
- Jacqueline Lynn Caston
- Andrea Simone Caston
- Douglas J Olson
- Dan Meyer
- Kenneth Patrick Caston
- Marisha S Patel

Karon Rae Durham / Ted Dykstra line:
- Timothy Dykstra
- Christy Meriweather
- Tammy L. Dykstra
- Scott Laird
- Ted L. Dykstra
- Shannon Folger
- Todd Dykstra
- Nancy Sackett
- Melanie Connors

Kathy Lee Durham / John Cobb line:
- Stephanie Lee Cobb
- Mike Kirby
- Stephen Cobb
- Pattie Harrison

136

Copy of newspaper clipping of

Wedding of

Hattie Briggs to
Mr. Henri L. Bousquet,

January 12, 1873

"Married — On Sabbath Day, the 12th Inst., at the Methodist Episcopal Church, in this city, by the Rev. E. L. Briggs, Mr. Henri L. Bousquet to Miss Hattie J., daughter of the officiating clergyman. A very large congregation consisting of friends of both parties, witnessed the celebration of the nuptials of the above happy couple. The pleasure of both were reflected in the hearts of every one who heard the solemn promises and all joined fully in the prayer of the Reverend father for the faithfulness of the wedded pair, and for the happiness and prosperity which all felt will be their reward. May they as they grow older, never look back upon the scene of last Sabbath with regret; but when they advance upon the scene in which we all must be actors, may they welcome the rising of death's curtain with the same fervor and pleasure they have exhibited when they began their hand-in-hand travel through life. Mr. Bousquet and his bride, accompanied by a large retinue of friends from Pella, departed for that city soon after the conclusion of the ceremony. Mr. Bousquet will, we understand, at once enter into business in the city of his, almost nativity and we of Knoxville will not, for some time at least, as of yore, daily see his pleasant face and welcome his hearty greeting."

*   *   *   *

Two sons were born to this couple. Henri Lyman who died in infancy and Cutts Dudock who died July 12, 1937 at Des Moines, Iowa. He is buried at Knoxville, Iowa, beside his wife.   *

★ THE P E. O. RECORD

Briggs

From the personal family records belonging to Kae Lynn Bousquet Dunham Caston.

Family Ties

Founders' Relatives Keep in Touch

Editor's Note: From time to time, THE P.E.O. RECORD hears from P.E.O.s who are related to the Sisterhood's Founders. Following are two such examples. If you have a connection to any of P.E.O.'s seven Founders and wish to share your story or information, please contact THE RECORD at the address printed inside the front cover of this issue.

An Update on Hattie Briggs

Thank you to Juli Wilson, AA, Nevada, for discovering a letter written by Hattie Briggs Bousquet, excerpts from which are printed at the right, along with a photograph also discovered by Juli. The great-granddaughter of P. H. Bousquet, Juli was looking through boxes of family history when she came across photographs of P. H.'s brother, Henry Louis Bousquet, and his wife, Founder Hattie Briggs Bousquet.*

Juli contacted the P.E.O. Executive Office in search of Hattie's descendants and was put in touch with Karon Dykstra, JO, Iowa, one of Hattie's great-granddaughters. Karon then shared the news with her sisters, Kae Lynn Caston, EB, Minnesota, and Kathy Cobb, C, Nevada.

Kae Lynn, who notified THE RECORD, comments, "I love the letter, as Hattie mentions her health, although not what her illness was. She did die just months later. I'd like to think this letter conveys the feeling of the very caring, loving person that all her friends said she was."

*The photograph of Hattie was taken around the time of her marriage to Henry in 1873. The letter, written in January 1877, five months before her death, is to Henry's uncle, John (Jan) Bousquet, who was living in Holland at the time.

Great-granddaughters of Founder Hattie Briggs Bousquet include, top photo, from the left: sisters Karon Dykstra, JO, Iowa; Kathy Cobb, C, Nevada; and Kae Lynn Caston, EB, Minnesota.

Bottom photo, from the left: Kae Lynn's daughter, Michelle Volk, and her daughters, Janeé and Carrie, also belong to Chapter EB. Janeé and Carrie are fifth-generation members of the Sisterhood.

Karon's daughter and daughter-in-law are P.E.O.s as well: Tammy Laird, FL, Kansas; and Christy Dykstra, JO, Iowa.

...And now I come to our own family. Henry, the husband and father is sitting by me tonight as usual, working away in some of his banking books. And when I look up at him, I can see that he has grown thinner and paler, since he entered the bank, and has been so closely confined with much hard, tiresome work. But for all this, I am truly thankful he is no idler, and I am proud that I have such a good, kind husband as Henry makes me. Our two sons, Cutts and Lyman, we think are the most wonderful of all boys; but when you come to consider the matter seriously, you find they are not superior to other children as far as smartness is concerned. They are doubtless healthy in both mind and body now, and I hope sincerely to see them grown up into strong, industrious, good men someday. We were married four years the 12th of this month, and Cutts was three years old the 26th of October; and Lyman was one year old the 4th of December. Of myself I can say very little, only that since our marriage, my health has been very bad, until this winter, I think I am regaining some of my former strength. With the help of one little servant girl, I do all my work and take care of the children. So you can imagine that my time is very nearly, if not quite all occupied. As my children grow older, I hope to have more leisure, and then I am going to try to learn Holland—not anticipating that I can acquaint myself with the language sufficiently to speak it correctly, but rather so I can more readily understand it. Would it be asking too much of you to send me a Holland primmer [sic] sometime, as I wish to begin at the very foundation.

...But it is growing late and I must retire; beside[s] I have told you all I can think of, and I earnestly hope such as it is may prove interesting to you. Please give my kindest regards to aunt Herminia; Henry, too, joins me in sending love to you. And now Uncle, I shall be amply repaid, if at your earliest convenience you see fit to answer this. Wishing you a kind good night! I close: remaining your affectionate niece,

Hattie Bousquet "nee" Briggs

From the personal family records belonging to Kae Lynn Bousquet Dunham Caston.

Home in Superior, NB where Cutts lived with his aunt & uncle

From the personal family records belonging to Kae Lynn Bousquet Dunham Caston

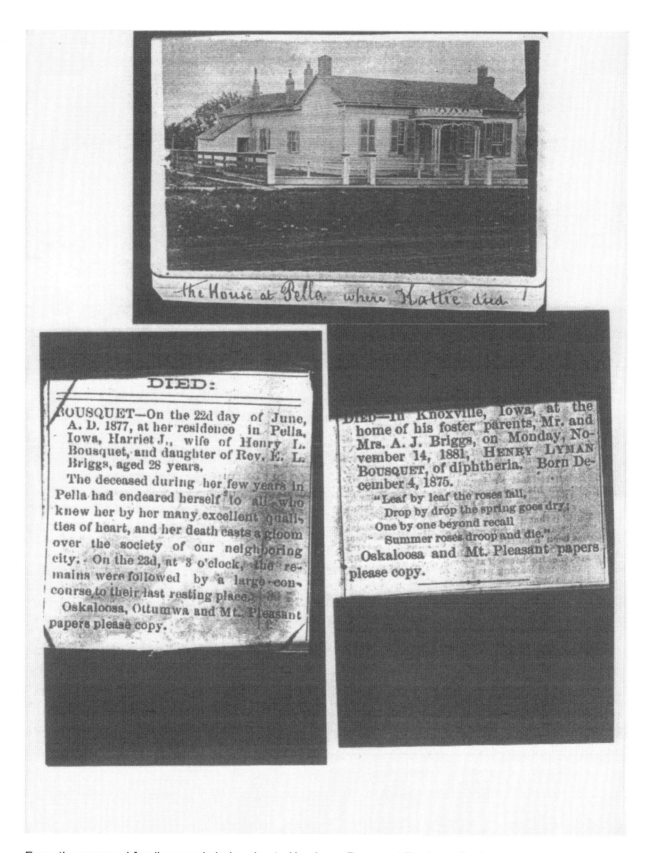

the House at Pella where Hattie died

DIED:

BOUSQUET—On the 22d day of June, A. D. 1877, at her residence in Pella, Iowa, Harriet J., wife of Henry L. Bousquet, and daughter of Rev. E. L. Briggs, aged 28 years.

The deceased during her few years in Pella had endeared herself to all who knew her by her many excellent qualities of heart, and her death casts a gloom over the society of our neighboring city. On the 23d, at 3 o'clock, the remains were followed by a large concourse to their last resting place.

Oskaloosa, Ottumwa and Mt. Pleasant papers please copy.

DIED—In Knoxville, Iowa, at the home of his foster parents, Mr. and Mrs. A. J. Briggs, on Monday, November 14, 1881, HENRY LYMAN BOUSQUET, of diphtheria, Born December 4, 1875.

"Leaf by leaf the roses fall,
Drop by drop the spring goes dry,
One by one beyond recall
Summer roses droop and die."

Oskaloosa and Mt. Pleasant papers please copy.

From the personal family records belonging to Kae Lynn Bousquet Dunham Caston.

Home in Superior, NB where Cutts lived with his aunt & uncle

From the personal family records belonging to Kae Lynn Bousquet Dunham Caston.

Letter from Cutts Bousquet to his friend Fred Woodruff
From the personal family records belonging to Kae Lynn Bousquet Dunham Caston.

Aug 5th 1884

Dear friend Fred,

I think that song is a fine one. How do you like it down there. Do you think you will come up here again before you return home. Yesterday Harry McHugh and I caught thirty-four fish. I went down to pick grapes (they are ripe) and couldn't get very many so I seen the Race was going down so I went fishing. One of our fish weighed one pound half. Give Love to your mother. I am your friend,

Cutts

Fred we are lonely without you come back again.

"Cutts Bousquet" (My Grandfather)
Picture taken when he was attending
"Iowa Wesleyan College" Mt Pleasant, Iowa

From the personal family records belonging to Kae Lynn Bousquet Dunham Caston.

Cutts Bousquet Military Medals
From the personal family records belonging to Kae Lynn Bousquet Dunham Caston.

Transcription from:
The Pella Chronicle, 20 February 1908, page 1

Pierre Henri Bousquet Dead After a Brief Illness Passes to the Great Beyond on Friday, February 14, 1908

Mr. Pierre Henri Bousquet after an illness of but a short time, died at his home February 14, and was buried from the First Reformed Church, on the 17th. The remains were laid to rest in the Oakwood Cemetery. Mr. Bousquet was taken sick while attending court in Knoxville. He came home and grew no better. The outward indications were like quinsy, but it was found after a consultation of the best physicians on throat trouble and an operation that it was phlegm nous erysipelas and not curable. The angel of death soon called and Mr. Bousquet answered the summons.

The funeral was held at the First Reformed Church at 2 o'clock Monday afternoon. Rev. Pietenpol read the Scripture in Holland and offered prayer. Rev. S. Vander Werf spoke in Holland in regard to how Mr. Bousquet would be missed as a citizen. Court being in session at Knoxville still, it adjourned and judge and attorneys came to attend the funeral, and Judge Crozier spoke of the high esteem in which Mr. Bousquet was held by the Marion County Bar. Then Rev. W.J. Van Kersen spoke briefly some very encouraging words, linking this world with the next in interest, from the words of the apostle brought to mind by a conversation with Mr. Bouquet a few days before his death,"but we know, that when He shall appear we shall be like Him."

Pierre Henri Bousquet was born on the 23rd of December 1835, at Zalt Bommel, province of Gelderland, Kingdom of the Netherlands, where his father, A.E.D. Bousquet, a man of considerable wealth, of Huguenot descent, was interested in extensive brickyards. After he had enjoyed a careful education in the excellent schools of the Netherlands, he was destined for the merchants marine and sent to the naval academy of Amsterdam. Before he finished his course at that institution his parents, who had joined the religious movement that was initiated by Rev. H.P. Scholte, followed that divine to the United States in America with their four sons arriving in Pella in 1849.

In Pella P.H. Bousquet first worked as a clerk in the store of Bousquet & Smeenk. He subsequently studied law under the guidance of Rev. H.P. Scholte and became one of the leading Lawyers in Iowa. At the time of his death he was the senior attorney of the Marion County Bar. In 1857 he engaged with John Nollen in the banking business, establishing the Pella Savings Institution, of which he acted as president, while John Nollen took the office of cashier. In 1872 this institution was converted into the Pella National Bank, which, he assisted in conducting first as Vice–President and later as President until the time of his death.

On December 6th, 1864, he was married to Sara Maria, Rev. H.P. Scholte's daughter, who died in 1876. From this union there remain two daughters. On August 27th 1879, he was united in marriage to Emma, daughter of Judge Joseph Thompson of New Jersey. She, with her daughters, Emma Josephine, Anna Caroline now Mrs. LaForce and Sara Maria survive him.

P.H. Bousquet was a very successful business man, having been engaged in a number of prosperous enterprises, some of them of considerable magnitude, and is entitled to the credit of being one of the founders of what is now the oldest banking institution in the State. He was liberal and public spirited, always contributing largely to whatever could promote the welfare of the community, Central College especially, being the beneficiary of his magnificence. Many therefore will pay a well merited tribute to his memory and regret the cessation of his useful life.

Colonel Bousquet Passes Away.

Henry L. Bousquet, aged 73, formerly clerk of the Iowa supreme court and for seven years a clerk in the office of the clerk of that body, died Wednesday at the Methodist hospital. Last week he underwent an operation for ulcer of the stomach, and pneumonia set in, resulting in his death.

Owing to his long service in the office of the supreme court, Mr. Bousquet was well known in Des Moines and over the state. His parents came to Pella in 1849 from Holland, and the deceased spent many years of his life in southeastern Iowa, where he was most prominently known.

He served throughout the war in the Thirty-third Iowa, and following the war was elected clerk of the Marion county courts. Later he was assistant cashier in a bank at Pella. Following his banking experience, Colonel Bousquet engaged in the dry goods business at Pella. Then he came to Des Moines to enter the office of the clerk of the supreme court.

Henry L. Bousquet The Humeston New Era 30 July 1915

Clipped By:

ssatkins
Tue, Oct 8, 2013

Transcription from: www.newspapers.com
The Humeston New Era, Humeston, Iowa, 30 July 1913, page 3

Colonel Bousquet Passes Away

Henry L. Bousquet, aged 73, formerly clerk of the Iowa supreme court and for seven years a clerk in the office of the clerk of that body, died Wednesday at the Methodist hospital. Last week he underwent an operation for ulcer of the stomach, and pneumonia set in, resulting in his death.

Owing to his long service in the office of the supreme court, Mr. Bousquet was well known in Des Moines and over the state. His parents came to Pella in 1849 from Holland, and the deceased spent many years of his life in southeastern Iowa, where he was most prominently known.

He served throughout the war in the Thirty-third Iowa, and following the war was elected clerk of the Marion county courts. Later he was assistant cashier in a bank at Pella. Following his banking experience, Colonel Bousquet engaged in the dry goods business at Pella. Then he came to Des Moines to enter the office of the clerk of the supreme court.

Miss Bess Rousquet, a graduate of Grinnell college in the class of 1905, and afterwards teacher in several high schools in Iowa, but who in recent years has been employed as secretary to the educational representative of the Siamese government at Boston will sail on the S. S. Nile from San Francisco to Bankok, Siam about April 1st with a young woman of high rank in that country whose interpreter she is to be on the journey. This Siamese lady is titled a princess after the custom of her country. The princess has been traveling and studying in the United States and is now returning to Siam to be married to a brother of the king of Siam. Miss Bousquet will remain for the royal wedding as a guest and will return via Europe. Miss Bousquet is the daughter of Herman L. Bousquet, for many years a hardware dealer at Pella, Marion county. He was a soldier in the war of the rebellion and was the first graduate from the old Central University of Iowa, established by the Baptist denomination at Pella in 1853, but now known as Central college and belonging to the Dutch Reformed church.

Clipped By:

ssatkins
Sun, Nov 17, 2013

Miss Bess Bousquet, a graduate of Grinnell college in the class of 1905, and afterwards teacher in several high schools in Iowa, but who in recent years has been employed as secretary to the educational representative of the Siamese government at Boston will sail on the S.S, Nile from San Francisco to Bangkok, Siam about April 1st with a young woman of high rank in that country whose interpreter she is to be on the journey. This Siamese lady is titled a princess after the custom of her country. The princess has been traveling and studying in the United States and is now returning to Siam to be married to a brother of the king of Siam. Miss Bousquet will remain for the royal wedding as a guest and will return via Europe. Miss Bousquet is the daughter of Herman L. Bousquet, for many years a hardware dealer at Pella, Marion county. He was a soldier in the war of the rebellion and was the first graduate from the old Central University of Iowa, established by the Baptist denomination at Pella in 1853, but now known as Central college and belonging to the Dutch Reformed church.

Pella Chronicle, Pella, Iowa, 3 June 1920

Herman F. Bousquet

Relatives in Pella received word this week of the death on Wednesday, June 2, 1920, of Herman F. Bousquet at the National Soldiers Home at Leavenworth, Kansas, at the age of 78 years.

Mr. Bousquet was long a prominent business man in Pella, engaged in the hardware business. Mr. Bousquet was a soldier in the civil war, a member of Co. B. 3rd Iowa Infantry.

At the time of his death he was the oldest alumnus of Central College. His last visit to Pella was at commencement time just a year ago, when he spent a month renewing acquaintances at the college and in town, greatly enjoying his visit.

Since discontinuing his business in Pella, a considerable part of his time has been spent in Soldiers Homes, although he spent several winters traveling in the south.

His wife died some years ago. He is survived by three sons and two daughters. One of the sons, Arthur, lives at Kansas City and was with his father in his last illness. One daughter, Mrs. C.D. Woods, lives at Alpine, Texas, and another, Miss Bess Bousquet is now traveling in the Orient. J.J. Bousquet of Pella is a brother,

The time of the funeral will depend upon Mrs. Wood's arrival, and at the time it can only be said that burial will be at Pella.

Pella Chronicle, Pella, Iowa, August 4, 1921

John Joseph Bousquet was born in the Netherlands, March 23, 1837. When twelve years of age he came to this country with his parents and three brothers, all of whom preceded him in death. They settled in Pella, founded just two years before, in the development of which the father took a great interest and honorable part.

In 1861, when the country's call came, John Bousquet enlisted in the Union Army, Co. B. 3rd Iowa Infantry, serving first as private and later as lieutenant. His marriage to Miss Anna Vander Linden took place in Pella in 1868. For several years they made their home in Ames, Iowa. Here were born to them four children, one of whom died in infancy. In 1880 they returned to Pella which has been their home since then. Here he engaged in the produce business, retiring some ten years ago.

Although on account of deafness he was cut off gradually from social intercourse, he retained a vivid interest in church life and activities. He was church treasurer for many years. Appreciation of his faithful service as elder was shown when, on resigning his office, he was chosen elder emeritus.

During the last year his physical powers waned gradually and death came without any long drawn out suffering or painful struggle. Sunday morning, July 31, 1921, just as the church bells, whose summons he had always so gladly welcomed, were ringing out their call to worship, he passed into the "Great Beyond," to the glorious company of the redeemed, into the presence of his Lord and Savior. With him at death were his wife and his children, Mrs. Hattie Eagan of Burlington, Mr. Louis and Miss Agnes Bousquet of Pella. Funeral services were held at the Second Reformed church, Rev. H.M. Bruins, the pastor preaching the sermon Tuesday afternoon.

The thought which he emphasized is found in 1 Cor. 4-2 –"Faithfulness." Faithful to family, country, business, community, church and God. This same thought has come to many others.

As a former citizen expressed it –"He was absolutely stable, no lightness of character there: firm in conviction, loyal in service." From the far west, too, came a message of sympathy containing the same sentiment in a quotation from 2 Tim. 4:7, 8: A quiet, unassuming gentleman, a prince in faithfulness. May it be ours to meditate and seek to insulate.

"And when the stream
Which overflowed the soul was passed
A consciousness remained that it had left,
Deposited upon the silent shore
Of memory, images and precious thoughts
That shall not die, and cannot be destroyed."

The Granddaughter of a Founder Initiated

Geraldine Bousquet Durham

* A special meeting of Chapter M, P. E. O., Knoxville, Iowa, was held in the home of Bernice Job (Mrs. E. L.) January 21, 1950. The spacious living room formed a perfect setting for the initiation of Geraldine Bousquet Durham, the only granddaughter of Hattie Briggs Bousquet. Mrs. Durham is the second granddaughter of a founder, a real granddaughter, to be initiated.

Since it was Hattie Briggs who suggested that the seven girls form a Sisterhood, it is particularly appropriate that this initiation was held on the eighty-first anniversary of the organization of the Sisterhood.

Hattie Briggs' father was the Methodist minister in Knoxville, Iowa at the time of his daughter's marriage to Henri Bousquet of Pella, Iowa, and performed the marriage ceremony, January 12, 1873. Geraldine wore her grandmother's wedding ring during her initiation.

A short program, arranged by the program chairman, Betty Galvin (Mrs. C. R.) was given following the initiation. Miss Eleanor Miller, accompanied by her mother, Esther Miller, sang "Kind Hearts and Gentle People" and "The Sunshine of Your Smile" dedicating the latter to Geraldine. Miss Marcia May, a niece of the chapter president, played two piano solos, "Impromptu" by Schubert and "The Hunting Song" by Mendelssohn.

A chart giving the names of descendents of the Founders had been prepared and was read by the president, Beneti Bridgeman.

CHRISTIANITY'S OPEN DOOR

* If ever the world was groping in the dark for an open door, we find it doing so now. The front page of any newspaper would raise hackles on a dove! Strikes, explosions, accidents, atrocities and murders are everyday fare. I read the papers and so do you. You and I can't go and individually right those wrongs, much as we might like to. I wonder if you have asked the question as often as I have—"What can *I* do about it?"

May I humbly venture to open just three doors—open them wide and turn on the light. Three doors that are as new as the flowers you will have in your garden this spring and as old as the stable in Bethlehem.

I. *I will have a personal righteousness.* (Light first candle)

Jesus shook the conscience of the centuries with these simple and direct words: "Seek ye first His king-

P.E.O. Record May 1950
From the personal family records belonging to Kae Lynn Bousquet Dunham Caston.

The initiation of Geraldine Bousquet Durham
↓

Chapter M, P.E.O.
Knoxville, Iowa   Jan 21, 1950

From the personal family records belonging to Kae Lynn Bousquet Dunham Caston.

CENTENNIAL ALBUM
1869 - 1969

Descendants of the founders served as honorary pages during convention. From left are Karen Rae Bousquet Dykstra, great granddaughter of Hattie Briggs Bousquet; Geraldine Bousquet Dunham, granddaughter of Hattie Briggs Bousquet; Kae Bousquet Gordon, great granddaughter of Hattie Briggs; Rosslyn Fennekohl Crawford, great, great niece of Alice Coffin; Verna Ross Ornduff, great niece of Alice Coffin; Diane Ross Fennekohl, great niece of Alice Coffin; Alice Coffin Ornduff Gordon, great, great niece of Alice Coffin, Blanche Skiff Ross, niece of Alice Coffin, was present at convention and was introduced. Alice Babb Ewing, daughter of Alice Bird Babb, could not attend.

✻ Supreme Convention in Des Moines — 1969

P.E.O. Record 1969
From the personal family records belonging to Kae Lynn Bousquet Dunham Caston.

156

Glendale News Press, February 13, 1965 and P.E.O. Record, February 1985
From the personal family records belonging to Kae Lynn Bousquet Dunham Caston.

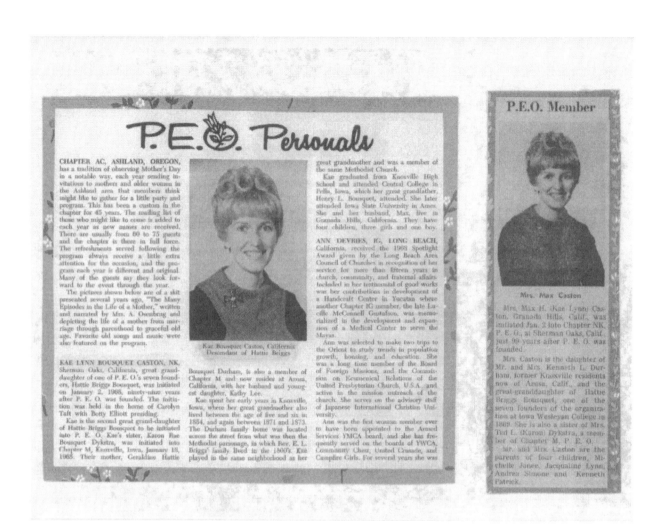

P.E.O. Record – 1968
From the personal family records belonging to Kae Lynn Bousquet Dunham Caston.

Excerpt from: www.knoxvillealumniassoc.com

Knoxville Alumni Association

Supporting our Knoxville Panthers with "Generations of Black & Gold pride!"

Home

Upcoming Events

Reunion News

Albums

Class Albums

Save Our Stadium

Links

Join

Guestbook

Meeting Minutes

Contact Us

ShareThis

Geraldine (Bousquet) Durham

Geraldine B. Durham, 76, Ely, Nev., and formerly of Knoxville, died November 26, at the William Bree Ririe Hospital in Ely, Nev. During funeral services, John Cobb, Stephen Cobb, Loyde Cobb, Mike Kirby, Fook Queong, George Carnes and Ted Dykstra served as pallbearers.

Geraldine was born October 3, 1918, in Cedar Rapids, the daughter of Cutts and Hattie Degenaar Bousquet. She attended school in Knoxville.

On December 22, 1936, she was united in marriage to Kenneth L. Burham in Pella. The couple moved to Ely, Nev. from Los Angeles in 1972. Geraldine worked as a medical assistant for more than 35 years, retiring in 1975. She was a member of the P.E.O. Sisterhood, Chapter M. of Knoxville.

Survivors include her husband, Kenneth of Ely, Nev.; three daughters, Kae Caston of Farmington, Minn., Karon Dykstra of Knoxville and Kathy Cobb of Ely, Nev.; 10 grandchildren and 10 great-grandchildren.

Home   Reunion News   Guestbook   Links Contact Us

Printed with permission of Knoxville Alumni Association.

Excerpt from: www.knoxvillealumniassoc.com

Knoxville Alumni Association

Supporting our Knoxville Panthers with "Generations of Black & Gold pride!"

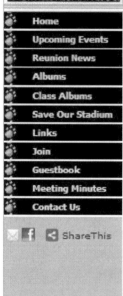

Home
Upcoming Events
Reunion News
Albums
Class Albums
Save Our Stadium
Links
Join
Guestbook
Meeting Minutes
Contact Us

ShareThis

Kenneth Durham

Graveside services for Kenneth L. Durham, 81, of Ely, Nevada, who died May 3, at the White Pine Care Center, were held May 6, 1997, at the Ely City Cemetery in Ely, Nevada.

Pallbearers were John Cobb, Stephen Cobb, Loyde Cobb, Mike Kirby, George Carnes, and Fook Quong.

Kenneth was born September 18, 1915, in Knoxville, the son of Arza and Nancy Durham. He was united in marriage to Geraldine Bousquet.

He was the manager of the Gamble's Store in Des Moines, Lawrence, Kan., and Knoxville. He was also the advertising manager at the Knoxville Journal for a few years. He managed Western Auto Stores in Glendale, Calif., Azusa, Calif., Montebello, Calif., and Ely, Nevada. He retired in Ely in 1980.

He was preceded in death by his parents; his wife, Geraldine; and two sisters, Dorothy Durham and Lorraine Van Gorp.

He is survived by three daughters, Kae Lynn Caston of Farmington, Minn., Karon R. Dykstra of Knoxville, and Kathy Lee Cobb of Ely, Nevada; 10 grandchildren, and 13 great-grandchildren.

Printed with permission of Knoxville Alumni Association.

My sisters L- Karon Rae Dykstra and R- Kae Lynn Caston
They visited the head quarters of P.E.O. Sisterhood, Des Moines, Iowa
July 1999 " Kae is wearing Hattie's wedding ring"

Left - Hattie Briggs Bousquet wedding Ring
Right - Child's gloves worn by Cutts Briggs Bousquet, son of Hattie

From the personal family records belonging to Kae Lynn Bousquet Durham Caston.

Harriet Jane Briggs

Birth:	10 Oct 1849	Father:	Elias Lyman Briggs Rev.
Death:	22 Jun 1877	Mother:	Jane Johnson
Marriage:	12 Jan 1873	Spouse:	Henry Louis Bousquet

Franc Roads, Mary Allen and Hattie Briggs

Printed with permission of the Bousquet family.

Harriet Jane Briggs

Birth:	10 Oct 1849	Father:	Elias Lyman Briggs Rev.
Death:	22 Jun 1877	Mother:	Jane Johnson
Marriage:	12 Jan 1873	Spouse:	Henry Louis Bousquet

Harriet Briggs

Reproduction of oil portrait by Marion Dunlap Harper, unveiled in P.E.O. Memorial Hall in Mount Pleasant, Iowa, on September 23, 1929.

Harriet Jane Briggs

Birth:	10 Oct 1849	Father:	Elias Lyman Briggs Rev.
Death:	22 Jun 1877	Mother:	Jane Johnson
Marriage:	12 Jan 1873	Spouse:	Henry Louis Bousquet

Hattie Jane Briggs

Printed with permission of the Bousquet family.

Abraham Everardus Dudok Bousquet

Birth:	06 Sep 1803	Father:	Pierre Henri Dudok Bousquet
Death:	08 Sep 1856	Mother:	Anna Carolina De Wit
Marriage:	26 Nov 1834	Spouse:	Henriette Marthe Chabot

A. E. D. BOUSQUET, SR.

A.E.D. Bousquet

Printed with permission of Nancy K. Monk.

Photo Album for Henry Louis Bousquet

Henry Louis Bousquet

Birth:	14 Feb 1840	Father:	Abraham Everardus Dudok Bousquet
Death:	23 Jan 1913	Mother:	Henriette Marthe Chabot
Marriage:	12 Jan 1873	Spouse:	May Bain

Cutts_Pierre and Henry Bousquet

HBousquet

Henry Bousquet

Henry Bousquet and Brothers - Pierre, Jean and Herman

Printed with permission of the Bousquet family and Nancy K. Monk.

Photo Album for Cutts Briggs Bousquet

Cutts Briggs Bousquet

Birth:	26 Oct 1873	Father:	Henry Louis Bousquet
Death:	10 Jul 1957	Mother:	Harriet Jane Briggs
Marriage:	10 Sep 1916	Spouse:	Hattie Clara Degenaar

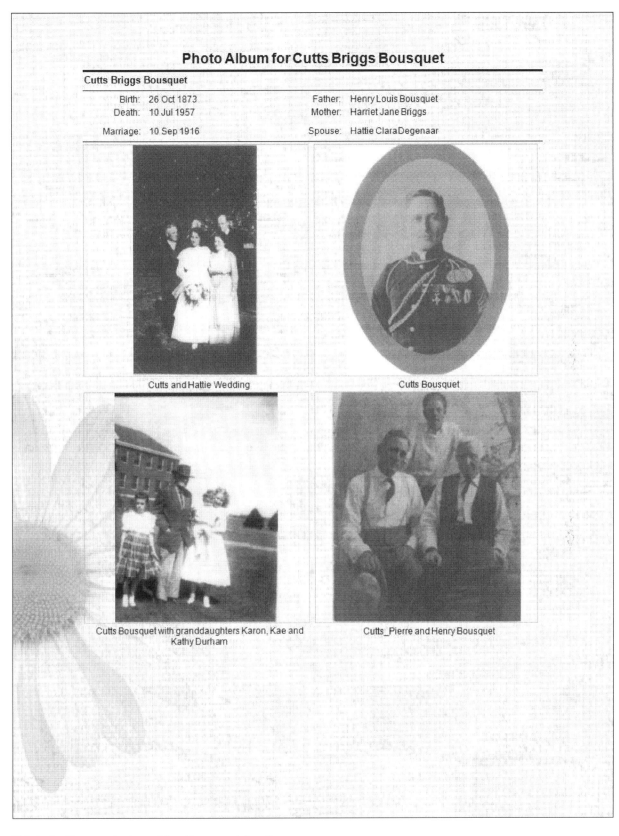

Cutts and Hattie Wedding

Cutts Bousquet

Cutts Bousquet with granddaughters Karon, Kae and Kathy Durham

Cutts_Pierre and Henry Bousquet

Printed with permission of the Bousquet family.

Photo Album for Geraldine Hattie Bousquet

Geraldine Hattie Bousquet

Birth:	03 Oct 1918	Father:	Cutts Briggs Bousquet
Death:	26 Nov 1994	Mother:	Hattie Clara Degenaar
Marriage:	22 Dec 1936	Spouse:	Kenneth Loyd Durham

Geraldine Bousquet

Geraldine Bousquet

Hattie and Geraldine Bousquet

Hattie and Geraldine Bousquet

Printed with permission of the Bousquet family.

Historical Background Sources
for Harriet Jane Briggs Bousquet

1. Ancestry.com. *U.S. Army, Register of Enlistments, 1798-1914* [database on-line]. Provo, UT, USA: Ancestry.com Operations Inc., 2007. Original data: Register of Enlistments in the U.S. Army, 1798-1914; (National Archives Microfilm Publication M233, 81 rolls); Records of the Adjutant General's Office, 1780's-1917, Record Group 94; National Archives, Washington, D.C.

2. Ancestry.com: *U.S. City Directories, 1821-1989* (database on-line), Provo, UT, USA: Ancestry.com Operations, Inc., 2011.

3. Ancestry.com. *U.S. National Homes for Disabled Volunteer Soldiers, 1866-1938*[database on-line]. Provo, UT, USA: Ancestry.com Operations Inc., 2007. Original data: Historical Register of National Homes for Disabled Volunteer Soldiers, 1866-1938; (National Archives Microfilm Publication M1749, 282 rolls); Records of the Department of Veterans Affairs, Record Group 15; National Archives, Washington, D.C.

4. 1850 United States Federal Census, Census Place: *Union, Davis, Iowa;* Roll: M432_182; Page 243A, Image 470.

5. 1850 United States Federal Census; Census Place; *Lake Prairie, Marion, Iowa*; Roll; M432_187; Page: 286A; image 438.

6. 1856 Iowa, State Census Collection, 1836-1925 (database on-line) Provo, UT, USA. Microfilm of *Iowa State Censuses, 1856, 1885, 1895, 1905, 1915, 1925* as well as various special censuses from 1836-1897 obtained from the State Historical Society of Iowa via Heritage Quest.

7. 1860 United States Federal Census, Census Place: *Round Prairie, Jefferson, Iowa*; Roll M653_328, Page 168; Image 163 Family History Library Film 803328.

8. 1860 United States Federal Census: Census Place: *Pella, Marion, Iowa*; Roll: M653_335; Page: 248; Image: 252; Family History Library Film: 803335.

9. 1870 United States Federal Census; Census Place: *Ottumwa Ward 1, Wapello, Iowa*; Roll M593_422. Page 175B; Image 354. Family History Library Film:54592.

10. 1870 United States Federal Census: Census Place: *Knoxville, Marion, Iowa*; Roll: M593_409; Page: 110A; Image: 224; Family History Library Film: 545908.

11. 1880 United States Federal Census: Census Place: *Pella, Marion, Iowa*; Roll: 354; Family History Film: 1254354; Page: 703A; Enumeration district: 126; Image: 0688.

12. 1900 United States Federal Census: Census Place: *Knoxville, Marion, Iowa*; Roll 447; Page: 12A; Enumeration district: 0045; FHL microfilm: 124044.

13. 1900 United States Federal Census: Census Place: *Fort D A Russell, Laramie, Wyoming*; Roll: 1827; Enumeration District: 0074; FHL microfilm: 1241827.

14. 1910 United States Federal Census: Census Place: *Knoxville Ward 2, Marion, Iowa*: Roll: T624_412; Page; 5A.

15. 1920 United States Federal Census: Census Place: *National Home for Disabled Volunteer Soldiers, Washington, Tennessee*: Roll: T625_1770; Page 6B; Enumeration District: 202; Image: 52.

16. 1920 United States Federal Census: Census Place: *National Home for Disabled Volunteer Soldiers, Washington, Tennessee*: Roll: T625_1770; Page 6B; Enumeration District: 202; Image: 52.

17. 1930 United States Federal Census: Census Place: *Knoxville, Marion, Iowa*: Roll: 668; Page: 2A; Enumeration District: 9; Image: 195.0; FHL microfilm: 2340403.

18. 1930 United States Federal Census: Census Place: *Knoxville, Marion, Iowa*: Roll: 668; Page: 2A; Enumeration District: 9; Image: 195.0; FHL microfilm: 2340403.

19. 1940 United States Federal Census: Census Place: *Knoxville, Marion, Iowa*; Roll: T627_1181; page: 2A; Enumeration District; 63-11.

20. 1940 United States Federal Census: Census Place: *Knoxville, Marion, Iowa*; Roll: T627_1181; page: 2A; Enumeration District; 63-11.

21. "About Central." *Central College.* Web. 16 Nov. 2013.

22. Babcock, Betty Lee. Letter to Becky Frazier, Editor. 2 Dec. 2011. MS. Helena, Montana.

23. Briggs, Francis C. "Pedigree Chart Hattie J. Briggs." Chart. *Founder Briggs Descendant Pedigree.* Print.

24. Clapp, Stella. *Out of the Heart A Century of P.E.O. 1869-1969.* Des Moines, Iowa: P.E.O. Sisterhood, 1968.

25. Clark, Fannie Hunter. "Historical Sketch of First Methodist Church 1845-1946." *Centennial of the First Methodist Church, Knoxville, Iowa* (1946): Print.

26. "Cutts Bousquet Military Pension File."*Fold3 Viewer.* Web. 29 Aug. 2013.

27. "Down Memory Lane." *A History of the First United Methodist Church Knoxville, Iowa 1843-1976* (1976): p3. Print.

28. "Find A Grave - Millions of Cemetery Records and Online Memorials." *Find A Grave - Millions of Cemetery Records and Online Memorials.* Henry Louis Bousquet Web. 17 Nov. 2013.

29. "Find A Grave - Millions of Cemetery Records and Online Memorials." *Find A Grave - Millions of Cemetery Records and Online Memorials.* Herman F. Bousquet Web. 17 Nov. 2013.

30. "Find A Grave - Millions of Cemetery Records and Online Memorials." *Find A Grave - Millions of Cemetery Records and Online Memorials.* John Joseph Bousquet Web. 17 Nov. 2013.

31. "Find A Grave - Millions of Cemetery Records and Online Memorials. *Find A Grave - Millions of Cemetery Records and Online Memorials.* Pierre H. Bousquet, Web. 17 Nov. 2013.

32. "Find A Grave - Millions of Cemetery Records and Online Memorials." *Find A Grave - Millions of Cemetery Records and Online Memorials.* Marsena E. Cutts Web. 12 Dec. 2013.

33. Historical Data Systems, comp. U.S., Civil War Soldier Records and Profiles, 1861-1865 (database on-line). Provo, UT, USA: Ancestry.com Operations Inc., 2009. Original data: Data compiled by historical Data Systems of Kingston, Massachusetts.

34. Iowa, County Marriages, 1838-1934,"Index, *FamilySearch* (https://familysearch.org/pal:/MM9.1.1/XJHH-DZD: accessed 23 October 2013), Henri Louis Bousquet and May Bain, 1891.

35. Iowa, Marriages, 1809-1992, index, *FamilySearch* (https://familysearch.org/pal:/MM9.1.1/XJGZ-MZ9 : accessed 09 Oct 2013), Henri L. Bousquet and Harriet J. Briggs, 12 Jan 1873.

36. "Iowa State Census, 1885,"index and images, *FamilySearch* (https;//familysearch.org/pal:/mM9.11/HD4D-M6Z: accessed 23 October) Henry L. Bousquet in entry for Joseph Oppenheimer, 1885.

37. Johnson, Heidi, ed."A Society of Our Own." *The P.E.O. Record* (1997).

38. "Lake Prairie Township." *The History of Marion County Iowa.* Des Moines, Iowa: Union Historical, 1881. 644-45. Print.

39. Marion County Genealogical Society. *History of Marion County, Iowa 1915.* Vol. II. Walsworth,1983.

40. "Marsena E. Cutts." *Wikipedia.* Wikimedia Foundation, 19 Oct. 2013. Web. 12 Dec. 2013.

41. "Miss Bess Bousquet." *Adams County Free Press* [Corning, Iowa] 6 Mar. 1920: 8. Print.

42. National Archives and Records Administration: *Nebraska State Census*: year; 1885: Series/Record Group: M352: County: Nuckolls; Township: Beaver; Page 9

43. National Archives Publication T289, Index to Pension Files of Veterans Who Served Between 1861 and 1900, Record Group 15, Engineers, Regiment 3, Company K, Bousquet, Cutts B.

44. National Archives Publication T289, Index to Pension Files of Veterans Who Served Between 1861 and 1900, complied 1949-1949, Record Group 15, Calvary, Regiment 1, Company D, Bousquet, Cutts B.

45. National Archives Publication T289, Index to Pension Files of Veterans Who Served Between 1861 and 1900, grouped according to the units in which they served, Record Group 15, Calvary, Regiment 1, Company B, Bousquet, Cutts B., Date 27-Dec-1922. Roll No 690.

46. Reeves, Winona E."From the Editor's Desk." Editorial. *P.E.O. Record* Jan. 1938: Print.

47. Sperry, Andrew F. *History of the 33rd Iowa Infantry Volunteer Regiment 1863-66.*: University of Arkansas, 1999. Web.

48. "The Founders." *P.E.O. Record* Feb. 1986: 5. Print.

49. Waddell, Francis B. *The Briggs Family History 1621-1991*, 1991. Print.

Harriet Jane Briggs Descendant Chart
Source Report

Source Title: **1850 United States Federal Census**
Repository: **Ancestry.com**

Citation: Ancestry.com, 1850 United States Federal Census (Provo, UT, USA, Ancestry.com Operations, Inc., 2009),. Ancestry.com, Year: 1850; Census Place: Lake Prairie, Marion, Iowa; Roll: M432_187; Page: 286A; Image: 438. [Source citation includes media item(s)].

Citation: Bousquet, Henry Louis. Ancestry.com, 1850 United States Federal Census (Provo, UT, USA, Ancestry.com Operations, Inc., 2009),. Ancestry.com, Year: 1850; Census Place: Union, Davis, Iowa; Roll: M432_182; Page: 243A; Image:. Name: Abington H Briggs Birth: abt 1846 in Iowa Death:. http://search.ancestry.com/cgi-bin/sse.dll?db=1850usfedcenancestry&h=1412622&ti=0&i ndiv=try&gss=pt. [Source citation includes media item(s)].

Citation: Briggs, Abington Johnson. Ancestry.com, 1850 United States Federal Census (Provo, UT, USA, Ancestry.com Operations, Inc., 2009),. Ancestry.com, Year: 1850; Census Place: Union, Davis, Iowa; Roll: M432_182; Page: 243A; Image: 470. [Source citation includes media item(s)]

Citation: Briggs, Harriet Jane. Ancestry.com, 1850 United States Federal Census (Provo, UT, USA, Ancestry.com Operations, Inc., 2009),. Ancestry.com, Year: 1850; Census Place: Union, Davis, Iowa; Roll: M432_182; Page: 243A; Image: 470. [Source citation includes media item(s)]

Citation: Johnson, Jane. Ancestry.com, 1850 United States Federal Census (Provo, UT, USA, Ancestry.com Operations, Inc., 2009),. Ancestry.com, Year: 1850; Census Place: Union, Davis, Iowa; Roll: M432_182; Page: 243A; Image: 470. [Source citation includes media item(s)]

Citation: Briggs, Elias Lyman Rev. Ancestry.com, 1850 United States Federal Census (Provo, UT, USA, Ancestry.com Operations, Inc., 2009),. Ancestry.com, Year: 1850; Census Place: Union, Davis, Iowa; Roll: M432_182; Page: 243A; Image: 470. [Source citation includes media item(s)]

Source Title: **1860 United States Federal Census**
Repository: **Ancestry.com**

Citation: Ancestry.com, 1860 United States Federal Census (Provo, UT, USA, Ancestry.com Operations, Inc., 2009),. Ancestry.com, Year: 1860; Census Place: Pella, Marion, Iowa; Roll: M653_335; Page: 248; Image: 252; Family History Library Film: 803335. [Source citation includes media item(s)]

Citation: Bousquet, Henry Louis. Ancestry.com, 1860 United States Federal Census (Provo, UT, USA, Ancestry.com Operations, Inc., 2009),. Ancestry.com, Year: 1860; Census Place: Round Prairie, Jefferson, Iowa; Roll: ; Page: 168; Image: 163. Name: Carria M Briggs Birth: abt 1856 in Iowa Death:. http://search.ancestry.com/cgi-bin/sse.dll?db=1860usfedcenancestry&h=5546428&ti=0&i ndiv=try&gss=pt. [Source citation includes media item(s)]

Citation: Briggs, Clara Margaret. Ancestry.com, 1860 United States Federal Census (Provo, UT, USA, Ancestry.com Operations, Inc., 2009),. Ancestry.com, Year: 1860; Census Place: Round Prairie, Jefferson, Iowa; Roll: ; Page: 168; Image: 163. Name: Heny L Briggs Birth: abt 1851 in Iowa Death:. http://search.ancestry.com/cgi-bin/sse.dll?db=1860usfedcenancestry&h=5546426&ti=0&i ndiv=try&gss=pt. [Source citation includes media item(s)]

Citation: Briggs, Henry Lyman. Ancestry.com, 1860 United States Federal Census (Provo, UT, USA, Ancestry.com Operations, Inc., 2009),. Ancestry.com, Year: 1860; Census Place: Round Prairie, Jefferson, Iowa; Roll: ; Page: 168; Image: 163. Name: James A Briggs Birth: abt 1854 in Iowa Death:. http://search.ancestry.com/cgi-bin/sse.dll?db=1860usfedcenancestry&h=5546427&ti=0&i ndiv=try&gss=pt. [Source citation includes media item(s)]

Citation: Briggs, James Ancil. Ancestry.com, 1860 United States Federal Census (Provo, UT, USA, Ancestry.com Operations, Inc., 2009),. Ancestry.com, Year: 1860; Census Place: Round Prairie, Jefferson, Iowa; Roll: M653_328; Page: 168; Image: 163; Family History Library Film: 803328. [Source citation includes media item(s)]

Citation: Briggs, Harriet Jane. Ancestry.com, 1860 United States Federal Census (Provo, UT, USA, Ancestry.com Operations, Inc., 2009),. Ancestry.com, Year: 1860; Census Place: Round Prairie, Jefferson, Iowa; Roll: M653_328; Page: 168; Image: 163; Family History Library Film: 803328. [Source citation includes media item(s)]

Citation: Briggs, Abington Johnson. Ancestry.com, 1860 United States Federal Census (Provo, UT, USA, Ancestry.com Operations, Inc., 2009),. Ancestry.com, Year: 1860; Census Place: Round Prairie, Jefferson, Iowa; Roll: M653_328; Page: 168; Image: 163; Family History Library Film: 803328. [Source citation includes media item(s)]

Citation: Johnson, Jane. Ancestry.com, 1860 United States Federal Census (Provo, UT, USA, Ancestry.com Operations, Inc., 2009),. Ancestry.com, Year: 1860; Census Place: Round Prairie, Jefferson, Iowa; Roll: M653_328; Page: 168; Image: 163; Family History Library Film: 803328. [Source citation includes media item(s)]

Source Title: **1870 United States Federal Census**
Repository: **Ancestry.com**

Citation: Briggs, Elias Lyman Rev. Ancestry.com, 1870 United States Federal Census (Provo, UT, USA, Ancestry.com Operations, Inc., 2009),. Ancestry.com, Year: 1870; Census Place: Oskaloosa Ward 3, Mahaska, Iowa; Roll: M593_408; Page: 376B; Image: 399; Family History Library Film: 545907. [Source citation includes media item(s)]

Citation: Briggs, Henry Lyman. Ancestry.com, 1870 United States Federal Census (Provo, UT, USA, Ancestry.com Operations, Inc., 2009),. Ancestry.com, Year: 1870; Census Place: Ottumwa Ward 1, Wapello, Iowa; Roll: M593_422; Page: 175B; Image: 354; Family History Library Film: 545921. [Source citation includes media item(s)]

Citation: Briggs, Henry Lyman. Ancestry.com, 1870 United States Federal Census (Provo, UT, USA, Ancestry.com Operations, Inc., 2009),. Ancestry.com, Year: 1870; Census Place: Ottumwa Ward 1, Wapello, Iowa; Roll: M593_422; Page: 175B; Image: 354; Family History Library Film: 545921. [Source citation includes media item(s)]

Citation: Briggs, Elias Lyman Rev. Ancestry.com, 1870 United States Federal Census (Provo, UT, USA, Ancestry.com Operations, Inc., 2009),. Ancestry.com, Year: 1870; Census Place: Ottumwa Ward 1, Wapello, Iowa; Roll: M593_422; Page: 175B; Image: 354; Family History Library Film: 545921. [Source citation includes media item(s)]

Citation: Briggs, Harriet Jane. Ancestry.com, 1870 United States Federal Census (Provo, UT, USA, Ancestry.com Operations, Inc., 2009),. Ancestry.com, Year: 1870; Census Place: Ottumwa Ward 1, Wapello, Iowa; Roll: M593_422; Page: 175B; Image: 354; Family History Library Film: 545921. [Source citation includes media item(s)]

Citation: Ancestry.com, 1870 United States Federal Census (Provo, UT, USA, Ancestry.com Operations, Inc., 2009),. Ancestry.com, Year: 1870; Census Place: Ottumwa Ward 1, Wapello, Iowa; Roll: M593_422; Page: 175B; Image: 354; Family History Library Film: 545921. [Source citation includes media item(s)]

Citation:	Briggs, James Ancil. Ancestry.com, 1870 United States Federal Census (Provo, UT, USA, Ancestry.com Operations, Inc., 2009),. Ancestry.com, Year: 1870; Census Place: Ottumwa Ward 1, Wapello, Iowa; Roll: M593_422; Page: 175B; Image: 354; Family History Library Film: 545921. [Source citation includes media item(s)]
Citation:	Briggs, Clara Margaret. Ancestry.com, 1870 United States Federal Census (Provo, UT, USA, Ancestry.com Operations, Inc., 2009),. Ancestry.com, Year: 1870; Census Place: Ottumwa Ward 1, Wapello, Iowa; Roll: M593_422; Page: 175B; Image: 354; Family History Library Film: 545921. [Source citation includes media item(s)]
Citation:	Johnson, Jane . Ancestry.com, 1870 United States Federal Census (Provo, UT, USA, Ancestry.com Operations, Inc., 2009),. Ancestry.com, Year: 1870; Census Place: St Louis Ward 11, St Louis, Missouri; Roll: M593_821; Page: 298A; Image: 79; Family History Library Film: 552320. [Source citation includes media item(s)]

Source Title: **1880 United States Federal Census**
Repository: **Ancestry.com**

Citation:	Briggs, Abington Johnson. Ancestry.com and The Church of Jesus Christ of Latter-day Saints, 1880 United States Federal Census (Provo, UT, USA, Ancestry.com Operations Inc., 2010),. Ancestry.com, Source Citation: Year: 1880; Census Place: Knoxville, Marion, Iowa; Roll: 354; Family History Film: 1254354; Page: 685A; Enumeration District: 125; Image: 0652. birth date: abt 1856 birth place: Iowa Name: Clara Margaret Kramer residence date: 1880 residence place: Knoxville, Marion, Iowa, United States. http://search.ancestry.com/cgi-bin/sse.dll?db=1880usfedcen&h=47807945&ti=0&indiv=try&gss=pt. [Source citation includes media item(s)]
Citation:	Briggs, Clara Margaret Ancestry.com and The Church of Jesus Christ of Latter-day Saints, 1880 United States Federal Census (Provo, UT, USA, Ancestry.com Operations Inc., 2010),. Ancestry.com, Year: 1880; Census Place: Knoxville, Marion, Iowa; Roll: 354; Family History Film: 1254354; Page: 685A; Enumeration District: 125; Image: 0652. [Source citation includes media item(s)]
Citation:	Bousquet, Henry Lyman Ancestry.com and The Church of Jesus Christ of Latter-day Saints, 1880 United States Federal Census (Provo, UT, USA, Ancestry.com Operations Inc., 2010),. Ancestry.com, Year: 1880; Census Place: Knoxville, Marion, Iowa; Roll: 354; Family History Film: 1254354; Page: 685A; Enumeration District: 125; Image: 0652. [Source citation includes media item(s)]
Citation:	Bousquet, Cutts Briggs Ancestry.com and The Church of Jesus Christ of Latter-day Saints, 1880 United States Federal Census (Provo, UT, USA, Ancestry.com Operations Inc., 2010),. Ancestry.com, Year: 1880; Census Place: Knoxville, Marion, Iowa; Roll: 354; Family History Film: 1254354; Page: 685A; Enumeration District: 125; Image: 0652. [Source citation includes media item(s)]
Citation:	Briggs, Henry Lyman. Ancestry.com and The Church of Jesus Christ of Latter-day Saints, 1880 United States Federal Census (Provo, UT, USA, Ancestry.com Operations Inc., 2010),. Ancestry.com, Year: 1880; Census Place: Knoxville, Marion, Iowa; Roll: 354; Family History Film: 1254354; Page: 685A; Enumeration District: 125; Image: 0652. [Source citation includes media item(s)]
Citation:	Briggs, Abington Johnson Ancestry.com and The Church of Jesus Christ of Latter-day Saints, 1880 United States Federal Census (Provo, UT, USA, Ancestry.com Operations Inc., 2010),. Ancestry.com, Year: 1880; Census Place: Oskaloosa, Mahaska, Iowa; Roll: 353; Family History Film: 1254353; Page: 330A; Enumeration District: 174; Image: 0666. [Source citation includes media item(s)]

Citation: Briggs, Henry Lyman Ancestry.com and The Church of Jesus Christ of Latter-day Saints, 1880 United States Federal Census (Provo, UT, USA, Ancestry.com Operations Inc., 2010),. Ancestry.com, Year: 1880; Census Place: Pella, Marion, Iowa; Roll: 354; Family History Film: 1254354; Page: 703A; Enumeration District: 126; Image: 0688. [Source citation includes media item(s)]

Citation: Bousquet, Henry Louis Ancestry.com and The Church of Jesus Christ of Latter-day Saints, 1880 United States Federal Census (Provo, UT, USA, Ancestry.com Operations Inc., 2010),. Ancestry.com, Year: 1880; Census Place: Wilton, Muscatine, Iowa; Roll: 358; Family History Film: 1254358; Page: 70A; Enumeration District: 241; Image: 0142. [Source citation includes media item(s)]

Source Title: **1900 United States Federal Census**
Repository: **Ancestry.com**

Citation: Briggs, Elias Lyman Rev. Ancestry.com, 1900 United States Federal Census (Provo, UT, USA, Ancestry.com Operations Inc., 2004),. Ancestry.com, Year: 1900; Census Place: Chicago Ward 11, Cook, Illinois; Roll: 257; Page: 15B; Enumeration District: 0312; FHL microfilm: 1240257. [Source citation includes media item(s)]

Citation: Briggs, Abington Johnson. Ancestry.com, 1900 United States Federal Census (Provo, UT, USA, Ancestry.com Operations Inc., 2004),. Ancestry.com, Year: 1900; Census Place: Chicago Ward 11, Cook, Illinois; Roll: 257; Page: 15B; Enumeration District: 0312; FHL microfilm: 1240257. [Source citation includes media item(s)]

Citation: Briggs, Abington Johnson. Ancestry.com, 1900 United States Federal Census (Provo, UT, USA, Ancestry.com Operations Inc., 2004),. Ancestry.com, Year: 1900; Census Place: Chicago Ward 32, Cook, Illinois; Roll: 287; Page: 13A; Enumeration District: 1039; FHL microfilm: 1240287. [Source citation includes media item(s)]

Citation: Briggs, Henry Lyman. Ancestry.com, 1900 United States Federal Census (Provo, UT, USA, Ancestry.com Operations Inc., 2004),. Ancestry.com, Year: 1900; Census Place: Chicago Ward 32, Cook, Illinois; Roll: 287; Page: 13A; Enumeration District: 1039; FHL microfilm: 1240287. [Source citation includes media item(s)]

Citation: Briggs, Henry Lyman. Ancestry.com, 1900 United States Federal Census (Provo, UT, USA, Ancestry.com Operations Inc., 2004),. Ancestry.com, Year: 1900; Census Place: Des Moines, Jasper, Iowa; Roll: 439; Page: 5B; Enumeration District: 0018; FHL microfilm: 1240439. [Source citation includes media item(s)] Briggs, Clara Margaret

Citation: Ancestry.com, 1900 United States Federal Census (Provo, UT, USA, Ancestry.com Operations Inc., 2004),. Ancestry.com, Year: 1900; Census Place: Des Moines, Jasper, Iowa; Roll: 439; Page: 5B; Enumeration District: 0018; FHL microfilm: 1240439. [Source citation includes media item(s)]

Citation: Briggs, Clara Margaret. Ancestry.com, 1900 United States Federal Census (Provo, UT, USA, Ancestry.com Operations Inc., 2004),. Ancestry.com, Year: 1900; Census Place: Fort D A Russell, Laramie, Wyoming; Roll: 1827; Enumeration District: 0074; FHL microfilm: 1241827. [Source citation includes media item(s)]

Citation: Bousquet, Cutts Briggs. Ancestry.com, 1900 United States Federal Census (Provo, UT, USA, Ancestry.com Operations Inc., 2004),. Ancestry.com, Year: 1900; Census Place: Knoxville, Marion, Iowa; Roll: 447; Page: 12A; Enumeration District: 0045; FHL microfilm: 1240447. [Source citation includes media item(s)]

Citation: Bousquet, Henry Louis. Ancestry.com, 1900 United States Federal Census (Provo, UT, USA, Ancestry.com Operations Inc., 2004),. Ancestry.com, Year: 1900; Census Place: Knoxville, Marion, Iowa; Roll: 447; Page: 12A; Enumeration District: 0045; FHL microfilm: 1240447. [Source citation includes media item(s)]

Source Title: **1910 United States Federal Census**
Repository: **Ancestry.com**

Citation: Bousquet, Henry Louis. Ancestry.com, 1910 United States Federal Census (Provo, UT, USA, Ancestry.com Operations Inc., 2006),. Ancestry.com, Year: 1910; Census Place: Big Rock, Pulaski, Arkansas; Roll: T624_62; Page: 2B; Enumeration District: 0103; FHL microfilm: 1374075. [Source citation includes media item(s)]

Citation: Briggs, Henry Lyman. Ancestry.com, 1910 United States Federal Census (Provo, UT, USA, Ancestry.com Operations Inc., 2006),. Ancestry.com, Year: 1910; Census Place: Knoxville Ward 2, Marion, Iowa; Roll: T624_412; Page: 5A; Enumeration District: 0046; FHL microfilm: 1374425. [Source citation includes media item(s)]

Citation: Bousquet, Henry Louis. Ancestry.com, 1910 United States Federal Census (Provo, UT, USA, Ancestry.com Operations Inc., 2006),. Ancestry.com, Year: 1910; Census Place: Los Angeles Assembly District 72, Los Angeles, California; Roll: T624_82; Page: 12B; Enumeration District: 0203; FHL microfilm: 1374095. [Source citation includes media item(s)]

Citation: Briggs, Abington Johnson. Ancestry.com, 1910 United States Federal Census (Provo, UT, USA, Ancestry.com Operations Inc., 2006),. Ancestry.com, Year: 1910; Census Place: Searchlight, Clark, Nevada; Roll: T624_858; Page: 8B; Enumeration District: 0008; FHL microfilm: 1374871. [Source citation includes media item(s)]

Source Title: **1920 United States Federal Census**
Repository: **Ancestry.com**

Citation: Briggs, Abington Johnson. Ancestry.com, 1920 United States Federal Census (Provo, UT, USA, Ancestry.com Operations Inc., 2010),. Ancestry.com, Source Citation: Year: 1920; Census Place: Los Angeles Assembly District 75, Los Angeles, California; Roll: T625_116; Page: 12B; Enumeration District: 467; Image: 182. birth date: abt 1846 birth place: Iowa Name: Abington Johnson Briggs residence date: 1920 residence place: Los Angeles Assembly District 75, Los Angeles, California, USA. http://search.ancestry.com/cgi-bin/sse.dll?db=1920usfedcen&h=730565&ti=0&indiv=try&gss=pt. [Source citation includes media item(s)]

Citation: Briggs, Abington Johnson. Ancestry.com, 1920 United States Federal Census (Provo, UT, USA, Ancestry.com Operations Inc., 2010),. Ancestry.com, Year: 1920; Census Place: Knoxville Ward 2, Marion, Iowa; Roll: T625_501; Page: 3A; Enumeration District: 48; Image: -789. [Source citation includes media item(s)]

Citation: Bousquet, Cutts Briggs. Ancestry.com, 1920 United States Federal Census (Provo, UT, USA, Ancestry.com Operations Inc., 2010),. Ancestry.com, Year: 1920; Census Place: Little Rock Ward 8, Pulaski, Arkansas; Roll: T625_79; Page: 16B; Enumeration District: 143; Image: 757. [Source citation includes media item(s)]

Citation: Briggs, Henry Lyman. Ancestry.com, 1920 United States Federal Census (Provo, UT, USA, Ancestry.com Operations Inc., 2010),. Ancestry.com, Year: 1920; Census Place: National Home for Disabled Volunteer Soldiers, Washington, Tennessee; Roll: T625_1770; Page: 6B; Enumeration District: 202; Image: 52. [Source citation includes media item(s)]

Source Title: **1930 United States Federal Census**
Repository: **Ancestry.com**

Citation: Bousquet, Cutts Briggs. Ancestry.com, 1930 United States Federal Census (Provo, UT, USA, Ancestry.com Operations Inc., 2002),. Ancestry.com, Year: 1930; Census Place: Knoxville, Marion, Iowa; Roll: 668; Page: 2A; Enumeration District: 0009; Image: 195.0; FHL microfilm: 2340403. [Source citation includes media item(s)]

Citation: Bousquet, Cutts Briggs. Ancestry.com, 1930 United States Federal Census (Provo, UT, USA, Ancestry.com Operations Inc., 2002),. Ancestry.com, Year: 1930; Census Place: Los Angeles, Los Angeles, California; Roll: 149; Page: 15A; Enumeration District: 0439; Image: 243.0; FHL microfilm: 2339884. [Source citation includes media item(s)]

Citation: Briggs, James Ancil. Ancestry.com, 1930 United States Federal Census (Provo, UT, USA, Ancestry.com Operations Inc., 2002),. Ancestry.com, Year: 1930; Census Place: Los Angeles, Los Angeles, California; Roll: 149; Page: 15A; Enumeration District: 0439; Image: 243.0; FHL microfilm: 2339884. [Source citation includes media item(s)]

Source Title: Ancestry Family Trees
Repository: Ancestry.com

Citation: Briggs, Abington Johnson. Ancestry Family Trees (Online publication - Provo, UT, USA: Ancestry.com. Original data: Family Tree files submitted by Ancestry members.),. Ancestry.com, Ancestry Family Tree.

Citation: Bousquet, Henry Lyman Ancestry Family Trees (Online publication - Provo, UT, USA: Ancestry.com. Original data: Family Tree files submitted by Ancestry members.),. Ancestry.com, Ancestry Family Tree.

Citation: Bousquet, Henry Louis. Ancestry Family Trees (Online publication - Provo, UT, USA: Ancestry.com. Original data: Family Tree files submitted by Ancestry members.),. Ancestry.com, Ancestry Family Tree.

Citation: Bousquet, Cutts Briggs Ancestry Family Trees (Online publication - Provo, UT, USA: Ancestry.com. Original data: Family Tree files submitted by Ancestry members.),. Ancestry.com, Ancestry Family Tree.

Citation: Briggs, Henry Lyman Ancestry Family Trees (Online publication - Provo, UT, USA: Ancestry.com. Original data: Family Tree files submitted by Ancestry members.),. Ancestry.com, Ancestry Family Tree.

Citation: Johnson, Jane Ancestry Family Trees (Online publication - Provo, UT, USA: Ancestry.com. Original data: Family Tree files submitted by Ancestry members.),. Ancestry.com, Ancestry Family Tree.

Citation: Briggs, Elias Lyman Rev. Ancestry Family Trees (Online publication - Provo, UT, USA: Ancestry.com. Original data: Family Tree files submitted by Ancestry members.),. Ancestry.com, Ancestry Family Tree.

Citation: Briggs, Harriet Jane Ancestry Family Trees (Online publication - Provo, UT, USA: Ancestry.com. Original data: Family Tree files submitted by Ancestry members.),. Ancestry.com, Ancestry Family Tree.

Citation: Briggs, James Ancil Ancestry Family Trees (Online publication - Provo, UT, USA: Ancestry.com. Original data: Family Tree files submitted by Ancestry members.),. Ancestry.com, Ancestry Family Tree.

Citation: Briggs, Abington Johnson Ancestry Family Trees (Online publication - Provo, UT, USA: Ancestry.com. Original data: Family Tree files submitted by Ancestry members.),. Ancestry.com, Ancestry Family Tree.

Source Title: California, Death Index, 1905-1939
Repository: Ancestry.com

Citation: Briggs, Clara Margaret. Ancestry.com, California, Death Index, 1905-1939 (Provo, UT, USA, Ancestry.com Operations, Inc., 2013), Ancestry.com. [Source citation includes media item(s)]

Source Title: **Iowa, Cemetery Records, 1662-1999**
Repository: **Ancestry.com**

Citation: Briggs, Abington Johnson. Ancestry.com, Iowa, Cemetery Records, 1662-1999 (Provo, UT, USA, Ancestry.com Operations Inc., 2000), Ancestry.com.

Source Title: **Iowa, Marriages, 1851-1900**
Repository: **Ancestry.com**

Citation: Bousquet, Henry Louis. Dodd, Jordan, Liahona Research, comp., Iowa, Marriages, 1851-1900 (Provo, UT, USA, Ancestry.com Operations Inc., 2000), Ancestry.com.

Citation: Briggs, Clara Margaret Dodd, Jordan, Liahona Research, comp., Iowa, Marriages, 1851-1900 (Provo, UT, USA, Ancestry.com Operations Inc., 2000), Ancestry.com. Briggs, Clara Margaret

Citation: Dodd, Jordan, Liahona Research, comp., Iowa, Marriages, 1851-1900 (Provo, UT, USA, Ancestry.com Operations Inc., 2000), Ancestry.com.

Citation: Bousquet, Henry Louis Dodd, Jordan, Liahona Research, comp., Iowa, Marriages, 1851-1900 (Provo, UT, USA, Ancestry.com Operations Inc., 2000), Ancestry.com.

Source Title: **Iowa, State Census Collection, 1836-1925**
Repository: **Ancestry.com**

Citation: Bousquet, Henry Louis. Ancestry.com, Iowa, State Census Collection, 1836-1925 (Provo, UT, USA, Ancestry.com Operations Inc., 2007), Ancestry.com. [Source citation includes media item(s)]

Citation: Briggs, Harriet Jane. Ancestry.com, Iowa, State Census Collection, 1836-1925 (Provo, UT, USA, Ancestry.com Operations Inc., 2007), Ancestry.com. [Source citation includes media item(s)]

Citation: Briggs, Clara Margaret. Ancestry.com, Iowa, State Census Collection, 1836-1925 (Provo, UT, USA, Ancestry.com Operations Inc., 2007), Ancestry.com. [Source citation includes media item(s)]

Citation: Bousquet, Henry Louis. Ancestry.com, Iowa, State Census Collection, 1836-1925 (Provo, UT, USA, Ancestry.com Operations Inc., 2007), Ancestry.com. [Source citation includes media item(s)]

Citation: Bousquet, Cutts Briggs. Ancestry.com, Iowa, State Census Collection, 1836-1925 (Provo, UT, USA, Ancestry.com Operations Inc., 2007), Ancestry.com. [Source citation includes media item(s)]

Citation: Bousquet, Cutts Briggs. Ancestry.com, Iowa, State Census Collection, 1836-1925 (Provo, UT, USA, Ancestry.com Operations Inc., 2007), Ancestry.com. [Source citation includes media item(s)]

Citation: Briggs, Elias Lyman Rev. Ancestry.com, Iowa, State Census Collection, 1836-1925 (Provo, UT, USA, Ancestry.com Operations Inc., 2007), Ancestry.com. [Source citation includes media item(s)]

Citation: Briggs, Henry Lyman. Ancestry.com, Iowa, State Census Collection, 1836-1925 (Provo, UT, USA, Ancestry.com Operations Inc., 2007), Ancestry.com. [Source citation includes media item(s)]

Citation: Johnson, Jane. Ancestry.com, Iowa, State Census Collection, 1836-1925 (Provo, UT, USA, Ancestry.com Operations Inc., 2007), Ancestry.com. [Source citation includes media item(s)]

Citation: Briggs, Elias Lyman Rev. Ancestry.com, Iowa, State Census Collection, 1836-1925 (Provo, UT, USA, Ancestry.com Operations Inc., 2007), Ancestry.com. [Source citation includes media item(s)]

Citation: Briggs, James Ancil. Ancestry.com, Iowa, State Census Collection, 1836-1925 (Provo, UT, USA, Ancestry.com Operations Inc., 2007), Ancestry.com. [Source citation includes media item(s)]

Source Title: Iowa, State Census, 1895
Repository: Ancestry.com

Citation: Briggs, Abington Johnson. Ancestry.com, Iowa, State Census, 1895 (Provo, UT, USA, Ancestry.com Operations Inc., 2003), Ancestry.com.

Citation: Briggs, Clara Margaret. Ancestry.com, Iowa, State Census, 1895 (Provo, UT, USA, Ancestry.com Operations Inc., 2003), Ancestry.com.

Citation: Bousquet, Henry Louis. Ancestry.com, Iowa, State Census, 1895 (Provo, UT, USA, Ancestry.com Operations Inc., 2003), Ancestry.com.

Source Title: Nebraska, State Census Collection, 1860-1885
Repository: Ancestry.com

Citation: Bousquet, Cutts Briggs. Ancestry.com, Nebraska, State Census Collection, 1860-1885 (Provo, UT, USA, Ancestry.com Operations, Inc., 2009),. Ancestry.com, National Archives and Records Administration; Nebraska State Census; Year: 1885; Series/Record Group: M352; County: Nuckolls; Township: Beaver; Page: 9. [Source citation includes media item(s)]

Citation: Bousquet, Cutts Briggs. Ancestry.com, Nebraska, State Census Collection, 1860-1885 (Provo, UT, USA, Ancestry.com Operations, Inc., 2009),. Ancestry.com, National Archives and Records Administration; Nebraska State Census; Year: 1885; Series/Record Group: M352; County: Nuckolls; Township: Beaver; Page: 9. [Source citation includes media item(s)]

Source Title: Nebraska, State Census, 1885
Repository: Ancestry.com

Citation: Briggs, Abington Johnson. Ancestry.com, Nebraska, State Census, 1885 (Online publication - Provo, UT, USA: Ancestry.com Operations Inc., 2002.Original data - National Archives and Records Administration. Schedules of the Nebraska State Census of 1885. M352. RG 29. 56 rolls. National Archives and Records Administration, Washington),. Ancestry.com, birth date: abt 1846 birth place: Iowa residence date: 02 Jun 1885 residence place: Beaver, Nuckolls, Nebraska Name: Abington Johnson Briggs. http://search.ancestry.com/cgi-bin/sse.dll?db=nebstatecen1885&h=711195&ti=0&indiv=try&gss=pt.

Source Title: The Greene Recorder at Newspapers.com
Repository: www.newspapers.com

Citation: Briggs, Abington Johnson. The Greene Recorder at Newspapers.com, www.newspapers.com, : Found in The Greene Recorder. http://www.newspapers.com/clip/187473/the_greene_recorder/.

Source Title: The Humeston New Era at Newspapers.com
Repository: www.newspapers.com

Citation: Bousquet, Henry Louis. The Humeston New Era at Newspapers.com, www.newspapers.com, : Found in The Humeston New Era. http://www.newspapers.com/clip/187488/the_humeston_new_era/.

Source Title: **U.S. Army, Register of Enlistments, 1798-1914**
Repository: **Ancestry.com**

Citation: Bousquet, Henry Louis. Ancestry.com, U.S. Army, Register of Enlistments, 1798-1914 (Provo, UT, USA, Ancestry.com Operations Inc., 2007), Ancestry.com. [Source citation includes media item(s)].

Citation: Ancestry.com, U.S. Army, Register of Enlistments, 1798-1914 (Provo, UT, USA, Ancestry.com Operations Inc., 2007), Ancestry.com. [Source citation includes media item(s)]

Source Title: **U.S. City Directories, 1821-1989**
Repository: **Ancestry.com**

Citation: Bousquet, Cutts Briggs. Ancestry.com, U.S. City Directories, 1821-1989 (Provo, UT, USA, Ancestry.com Operations, Inc., 2011),. Ancestry.com, Name: Abington Johnson Briggs residence date: 1922 residence place: Elkhart, Indiana, USA. http://search.ancestry.com/cgi-bin/sse.dll?db=usdirectories&h=652550555&ti=0&indiv=try&gss=pt. [Source citation includes media item(s)].

Citation: Briggs, Abington Johnson. Ancestry.com, U.S. City Directories, 1821-1989 (Provo, UT, USA, Ancestry.com Operations, Inc., 2011), Ancestry.com. [Source citation includes media item(s)]

Source Title: **U.S. Federal Census Mortality Schedules, 1850-1885**
Repository: **Ancestry.com**

Citation: Bousquet, Henry Louis. Ancestry.com, U.S. Federal Census Mortality Schedules, 1850-1885 (Provo, UT, USA, Ancestry.com Operations, Inc., 2010),. Ancestry.com, Census Year: 1880. [Source citation includes media item(s)]

Source Title: **U.S. National Homes for Disabled Volunteer Soldiers, 1866-1938**
Repository: **Ancestry.com**

Citation: Briggs, James Ancil. Ancestry.com, U.S. National Homes for Disabled Volunteer Soldiers, 1866-1938 (Provo, UT, USA, Ancestry.com Operations Inc., 2007), Ancestry.com. [Source citation includes media item(s)]

Source Title: **U.S., Civil War Pension Index: General Index to Pension Files, 1861-1934**
Repository: **Ancestry.com**

Citation: Bousquet, Cutts Briggs. National Archives and Records Administration, U.S., Civil War Pension Index: General Index to Pension Files, 1861-1934 (Provo, UT, USA, Ancestry.com Operations Inc., 2000), Ancestry.com. [Source citation includes media item(s)].

Citation: Bousquet, Henry Louis National Archives and Records Administration, U.S., Civil War Pension Index: General Index to Pension Files, 1861-1934 (Provo, UT, USA, Ancestry.com Operations Inc., 2000), Ancestry.com. [Source citation includes media item(s)]

Source Title: **U.S., Civil War Soldier Records and Profiles, 1861-1865**
Repository: **Ancestry.com**

Citation: Bousquet, Cutts Briggs. Historical Data Systems, comp, U.S., Civil War Soldier Records and Profiles, 1861-1865 (Provo, UT, USA, Ancestry.com Operations Inc., 2009),. Ancestry.com, residence place: Columbus City, Iowa Name: Abington Johnson Briggs birth date: abt 1846 birth place: Iowa military date: 15 Feb 1864 military place: Iowa. http://search.ancestry.com/cgi-bin/sse.dll?db=civilwar_histdatasys&h=1173782&ti=0&indiv=try&gss=pt.

Citation: Historical Data Systems, comp, U.S., Civil War Soldier Records and Profiles, 1861-1865 (Provo, UT, USA, Ancestry.com Operations Inc., 2009),. Ancestry.com, residence place: Columbus City, Iowa Name: Abington Johnson Briggs birth date: abt 1846 birth place: Iowa military date: 15 Feb 1864 military place: Iowa. http://search.ancestry.com/cgi-bin/sse.dll?db=civilwar_histdatasys&h=1173782&ti=0&ind iv=try&gss=pt.

Citation: Briggs, Abington Johnson Historical Data Systems, comp, U.S., Civil War Soldier Records and Profiles, 1861-1865 (Provo, UT, USA, Ancestry.com Operations Inc., 2009), Ancestry.com.

Source Title: U.S., World War I Draft Registration Cards, 1917-1918
Repository: Ancestry.com

Citation: Bousquet, Henry Louis. Ancestry.com, U.S., World War I Draft Registration Cards, 1917-1918 (Provo, UT, USA, Ancestry.com Operations Inc., 2005),. Ancestry.com, Registration State: Iowa; Registration County: Marion; Roll: 1643152. [Source citation includes media item(s)]

Source Title: Web: Iowa, Find A Grave Index, 1800-2012
Repository: Ancestry.com

Citation: Bousquet, Cutts Briggs. Ancestry.com, Web: Iowa, Find A Grave Index, 1800-2012 (Provo, UT, USA, Ancestry.com Operations, Inc., 2012), Ancestry.com.

Citation: Bousquet, Cutts Briggs. Ancestry.com, Web: Iowa, Find A Grave Index, 1800-2012 (Provo, UT, USA, Ancestry.com Operations, Inc., 2012), Ancestry.com.

Citation: Briggs, Harriet Jane. Ancestry.com, Web: Iowa, Find A Grave Index, 1800-2012 (Provo, UT, USA, Ancestry.com Operations, Inc., 2012), Ancestry.com.

Citation: Johnson, Jane. Ancestry.com, Web: Iowa, Find A Grave Index, 1800-2012 (Provo, UT, USA, Ancestry.com Operations, Inc., 2012), Ancestry.com.

Citation: Briggs, Elias Lyman Rev. Ancestry.com, Web: Iowa, Find A Grave Index, 1800-2012 (Provo, UT, USA, Ancestry.com Operations, Inc., 2012), Ancestry.com.

Citation: Bousquet, Henry Lyman. Ancestry.com, Web: Iowa, Find A Grave Index, 1800-2012 (Provo, UT, USA, Ancestry.com Operations, Inc., 2012), Ancestry.com.

Citation: Bousquet, Henry Louis. Ancestry.com, Web: Iowa, Find A Grave Index, 1800-2012 (Provo, UT, USA, Ancestry.com Operations, Inc., 2012), Ancestry.com.

Chapter 4: Alice Virginia Coffin

Alice Virginia Coffin

Alice Virginia Coffin has often been referred to as a "southern belle." However, she actually only lived in Kentucky, or the "south" as it was known in post-Civil War times, for one year. The Kentucky Historical Highway Program has placed *Marker 1715,* a marker dedicated to Alice, on Jefferson Street, between Preston & Floyd Streets, in Louisville, honoring the street where Alice was born in 1848.

Alice's parents were Matthew Starbuck Coffin and Martha Thompson Coffin. Martha's father was Judge John Handley Thompson, who served Indiana as a senator, secretary of state and as lieutenant governor.

Her friend Alice Bird once described Alice as, "a blonde of the animated type, which is more striking than a brunette."

According to a niece of Alice's, Stella Skiff Jannotta, author of the biographical sketch of Alice, *Alice Virginia Coffin, One of the Seven Founders of the P.E.O. Sisterhood*, "Alice Coffin family's came from a long line of Quaker ancestors. Her 5th great-grandfather, Tristam Coffin, was one of the ten men to buy and settle on the island of Nantucket in 1660." Tristam's daughter, Mary Coffin Starbuck (a sister to Alice's 4th great-grandfather), was responsible for the establishment of the Society of Friends in Nantucket, where she was a Quaker preacher known for her sound judgment.

Perhaps a Quaker heritage of having a peace-loving mentality found its way into Alice's personality. It was certainly characteristic of many Coffins. For example, in the mid-1800's the Coffin families were known to be very much for freedom for slaves. It was written in Alice's biographical sketch that "there was not a Coffin man who would not assist a runaway slave." In fact, one of Alice's father Matthew Coffin's cousins, Levi Coffin, was one of the founders and President of the Underground Railway. In Harriet Beecher Stowe's book "Uncle Tom's Cabin," the kindly Quaker couple who assisted Eliza and her little boy after crossing the Ohio was in reality Levi Coffin and his wife.

When Alice's mother died in 1857, she left a two week old son, George, a four year old son, Matthew, a fourteen year old daughter, Mary Francis and Alice who was but 9 years old. Alice's brother, George would die four months later. Alice's niece, Stella, laments in the biographical sketch she wrote, that "if the proper medical care had been available in that pioneer village where Martha Coffin gave birth to a son, she might have lived a much longer life."

At the beginning of the Civil War in 1861, Alice's father, Matthew was appointed Superintendent of Transportation of the Troops and Supplies on the Mississippi and Ohio Rivers. Not much is known about specifically where Alice lived during those years; was she with family or boarding elsewhere?

It was recounted that Matthew moved his family to Mount Pleasant so that they could have the "privilege" of attending Iowa Wesleyan University. He apparently was determined that if he should leave them, if nothing else, he explained, "They should have a good education. For of that, nobody can rob you."

It is known that by 1865 Alice was a boarder in Mrs. Stewart's home, living with Ella Stewart, another one of the P.E.O. seven founders.

Although Alice never married, while she was a student at Iowa Wesleyan she was often paired socially with Will Pearson, P.E.O. founder Suela Pearson's brother. According to her niece, Stella, Alice did have her heart broken while she was a student at Iowa Wesleyan and in her later years she did receive an offer of marriage. When queried by her sister Mary Francis as to why she didn't accept this offer, Alice replied smiling, "But I cannot, it is impossible for me to marry a home where my inclination does not lead me. It has always been that way. So, I am resigned to my fate."

After graduation from Iowa Wesleyan, Alice taught a short time in Des Moines, Iowa; several years in the public schools of Chariton, Iowa and then in Newton where she taught during the last years of her life...and where she lived near her father her sister, Mary Francis Skiff.

While a teacher in Chariton, Iowa, Alice appears on the 1880 census records as a boarder with the Hatcher family. Mr. William Hatcher owned the local foundry and was an employer in the area. Unfortunately, in December of 1886 the foundry was destroyed by fire and was uninsured. After the fire, the foundry closed.

Memories recalled by her many students often reflect of her as though she were a very maternal figure in their lives. One such memory comes from the daughter of a widow who recounted, "I said to Miss Coffin, 'Miss Coffin, it is impossible for me to go on to my graduation. Mother cannot buy clothes, and she needs my help.' Alice responded, 'Go on with your graduation, I will see that you look just as well as the other girls." Alice went on to make all the garments for that student, and at her graduation Alice was said to adorn the girl with flowers.

In Chariton the Library Association often gave plays to help finance the library. Alice often played the lead heroine role. One of her students, Ethel Bartholomew recounted, "We thrilled at the finished way she 'wiped the earth' with the villain of the play...she looked the part of the heroine, having a fine physique, with wonderful hair falling far below her waist, and just a glint of gold in it to make it more glorious."

Alice, or "Allie" as she was known to her friends, was a friend of Ella Gardner Van Dyke. Ella mentions Allie in her personal journal, as being the person to plan the P.E.O. pin (emblem). According to Melody Wilson, a member of the Lucas County Genealogical Society, Ella Gardner Van Dyke was the daughter of Chariton's mayor, Capt. Nelson Gardner. And, probably the first woman to run a business in Chariton, she owned and operated Chariton's Hotel Bates.

To her niece, Stella, she was always "Aunt Alice" whom she remembered as a woman who loved to act and read. In her biographical sketch of Alice, Stella remembers that Alice spent a great deal of time in the library, or Reading Room, as it was known. She quotes Alice as saying, "One may tire of society, but never of books. "She also remembers her Aunt Alice telling her, "Hitch your wagon to a star. Never mind if you never attain your star, the effort will be a development." Remember, it was Alice who suggested the star as the P.E.O. emblem.

Apparently, Alice was also very good at playing the role of the heroine in community plays while she lived in Newton. There she trained students for the Newton High School Oratorical Contest; coaching many of the town and state contest winners. Reports are that Alice also really enjoyed music and dancing, so much so, that it is thought her love of dance was a reason why she stopped attending the Methodist church and started attending the Episcopal church while teaching in Chariton.

Ella Vaughan Eberhart, a lifelong friend, was quoted in Stella's biographical sketch of Alice, "Whatever was to be done, Alice was in favor of doing promptly. My memories of her are many and vivid. She was tall and stately, fine looking and always tastily gowned. I recall her genial companionship with pleasure and can hear her voice, even now, as she recounted many interesting occurrences of the past. She was of a cheerful nature, bright, witty, high-minded, well educated, and anxious to be helpful to her friends or pupils or in the betterment of humanity in any way possible."

In 1887, at the P.E.O. Convention of Grand Chapter held in Alvia, Iowa, Alice Coffin communicated this message, "I greet you as true sisters; may you raise the standard of true womanhood, elevate the fallen, help the weak, give smiles, scatter rose blossoms, making light the burdens of the oppressed, and may our badge of sincerity and friendship, our star, be emblematic of the star of Bethlehem, a guide of our Sisterhood to holier, purer and better things than earth can give—guide to heaven. May we, indeed be stars among women in whatever vocation we fill." Such beautiful words speak to us today as strongly as they spoke to the women of 1887.

While Alice did not ever have any children of her own, her sister Mary Francis, who married Vernon W. Skiff , had three children to whom Alice was very close; Stella (1867-1954), author of the book *Alice Virginia Coffin*, Frank Vernon Skiff (1869-1933), who in 1899 founded of the origins of Jewel Tea Company, later to become Jewel Grocery Store chain; and Blanche Alice Skiff (1873-1969), who married Franklin P. Ross, a partner in Jewel Tea Company with her brother Frank.

Stella was the family historian and was instrumental in creating and collecting what is today known as the Jannotta Family Paper Collection, part of the collections held by Chronicling Illinois, Abraham Lincoln Presidential Library & Museum. This collection includes, among other items, copies of letters written by both Alice's parents; Matthew and Martha Coffin.

Stella, once a student at the Chicago Conservatory, met her future husband, an Italian maestro, Alfredo Antonio Jannotta, while studying vocal music. During their 20 years of marriage they had three sons; Alfred, Francis and Joseph. Stella was an active participant in women's suffrage movement and in rationalist religious organizations. Amazingly, four years after her husband died, and at the age of 41, Stella arranged to adopt three foster sisters of Italian descent who were ages ten, four and two. Stella brought them to America, raised these three girls on her own and provided them all with private school educations.

Frank Vernon Skiff, the Jewel Tea Company founder, and his wife Ida did not have children.

Blanche and Franklin Ross were married in 1899 and had two daughters, Verna Mary Ross and Mildred Blanche Ross. Oddly enough, Verna and Mary share the same birthday, February 7th; Verna being born in 1901 and Mary five years later in 1906.

Alice also had three other nieces, Francis, Alice and Grace Coffin, daughters of her brother, Charles Thompson Coffin and his wife, Lillie Marcks Coffin.

Alice, as well as other descendants of Matthew and Martha Coffin certainly demonstrated by their actions a life driven by an overwhelming pioneering spirit.

Alice's cause of death was listed as Bright's disease, which today is described as a broad category of kidney disease that could be referred to as chronic nephritis. She was buried next to her parents, at sunset, per her request.

Stella ended her biography of Alice saying, "She radiated upon her world a love always loyal, an enrichment of the cultural life of her community, a hopeful courage, a tender and helpful sympathy for distress, and an abiding confidence in the nobility of human destiny."

Alice Virginia Coffin – Life Events

DATE	EVENT	AGE
29 March 1848	Born: Louisville, Kentucky	
1849	Coffin family moved to Salem, Indiana to family farm	1
September 1850	Residence: Washington township, Washington, Indiana	2
Fall 1854	Matthew coffin sold farm/household goods at auction Moved family to home of Judge John Handley Thompson	6
May 1855	Family moved from Indianapolis, Indiana to Newton, Iowa	7
1856	Residence: Newton, Jasper, Iowa	8
30 July 1857	Mother, Martha Thompson Coffin dies	9
July 1860	Residence: Newton, Jasper, Iowa	12
1861-1865	Alice father worked for government Family settles in Mount Pleasant with her sister; also said to have boarded with Ella Stewart's family	13-17
September 1865	Entered Iowa Wesleyan	17
21 January 1869	P.E.O. Founded	20
June 1869	Graduated Iowa Wesleyan with B.S. degree	21
June 1870	Residence: Center, Henry, Iowa	22
1872	Honorary M.S. degree awarded from Iowa Wesleyan	24
June 1880	Residence: Charlton, Lucas, Iowa (Teacher)	29
1885	Residence: Newton, Jasper, Iowa	36
1888	Teacher Newton, Jasper, Iowa	39
28 July 1888	Died: Charlton, Tama, Iowa due to Bright's disease Buried: Newton Cemetery, Newton, Iowa	39

Descendant Chart for
Coffin Family

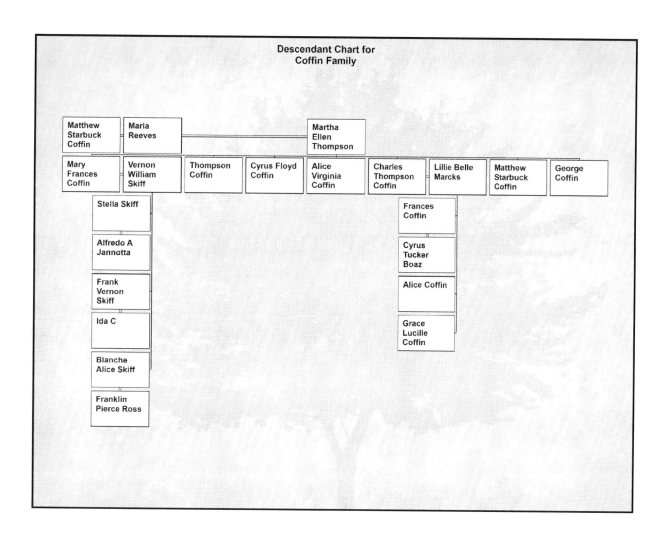

- Matthew Starbuck Coffin
- Maria Reeves
- Martha Ellen Thompson
  - Mary Frances Coffin
  - Vernon William Skiff
    - Stella Skiff
    - Alfredo A Jannotta
    - Frank Vernon Skiff
    - Ida C
    - Blanche Alice Skiff
    - Franklin Pierce Ross
  - Thompson Coffin
  - Cyrus Floyd Coffin
  - Alice Virginia Coffin
  - Charles Thompson Coffin
  - Lillie Belle Marcks
    - Frances Coffin
    - Cyrus Tucker Boaz
    - Alice Coffin
    - Grace Lucille Coffin
  - Matthew Starbuck Coffin
  - George Coffin

Transcribed from:
Alice Virginia Coffin, a Biographical Sketch, 3rd Edition, 1940, Stella Skiff Jannotta

Excerpts from a letter, dated May 11, 1853 from Martha Thompson Coffin to her husband Matthew Coffin:

"On this lovely afternoon, after a refreshing shower, which seems to have enlivened and invigorated all nature, the merry little warblers are chanting their songs of joy amongst the trees. With the air freshly fragrant with perfumes from the orchard, making it a moment truly befitting the month of May, my heart naturally turns to you, responding to your hope that we may hereafter be permitted to spend the lovely month of May, and all other months, together, with our little band of pledges to cheer us with their happy sports and glee….Never was a mother blessed with a more interesting family than our little group. Although my duties have been of too pressing a nature to admit of my devoting great time and care to the cultivation of their vigorous and inquiring intellects which is a source of deep regret to me, yet I derive great comfort from the thought that they are endowed with the capacity of receiving instruction, which, when directed by a father more competent to impart than their mother, will make them interesting and happy ornaments of our home and society."

Amid extended comments and eulogies concerning all of her children, she speaks of Alice as follows:

"Little joyous Alice is of a confiding, affectionate nature, which greatly endears her to us, despite the little waywardness to which she is occasionally addicted; for like her mother, her joys as well as her crosses partake of the nature of her affections, too deeply they sink into her heart and too ardently to be easily removed.

From a journal compiled about 1920 by Ella Gardner Van Dyke reflecting her memories.
Reprinted with permission of the Lucas County Genealogical Society.

1869

My Sister Mary died Aug 4th 1869.

Total eclipse of the Sun Aug 7th 1869.

B R VanDyke came to Chariton
July 12th 1869

Prof Hamlin Freer came to Chariton
Aug 11th 1869. He was a graduate of
Cornell College. He was to be Principal of
our schools. My Class finished our
School days with Prof Freer & Prof Stevens
both fine teachers. as soon as School was out
Maggie Reed Minnie Stanton. Mary Larimer
and myself decided we would teach school
next year.
Before this term We had Prof Homer
and Miss Amanda Shelton of
Mt Pleasant. She was fine in History
During the War She was a Nurse
in the South

The P E O chapter was organized
Jan 20 1869 in Mt Pleasant.
My friend Allie Coffin planed the
P E O pin. Sue Pearson was a school mate
of mine in Mt Pleasant and Allie & Meira Bird
Allie married Judge Babb.

Transcription from:
Journal belonging to Ella Gardner Van Dyke, created about 1920 by Ella reflecting her memories
Reprinted with the permission of Lucas County Genealogical Society

1869

My sister Mary died Aug 4th 1869

Total eclipse of the sun Aug 7th 1869

B.R. Van Dyke came to Chariton July 12 1869

Prof Hamlin Freer came to Chariton Aug 11th 1869. He was a graduate of Cornell College. He was to be Principal of our school. My Class finished our school days with Prof Freer and Prof Stevens both fine teachers as soon as school was out Maggie Reed Minnie Stanton Mary Larimer and myself decided we would teach school next year.

Before this term we had Prof Horner and Miss Amanda Shelton of Mt. Pleasant. She was a fine in History.

During the war she was a Nurse in the South.

The P.E.O chapter was organized Jan 20, 1869 in Mt. Pleasant. My friend Allie Coffin planed the P.E.O. pin. Sue Pearson was a school mate of mine in Mt. Pleasant and Allie and Mira Bird. Allie married Judge Babb.

Transcription from:
Muscatine Journal and News Tribune, 11 May 1929, page 5

P.E.O. Sisterhood to Meet

Newton Ia., May 11 – (AP) More than 300 out-of-town delegates are expected here May 14, 15 and 16 for the state convention of the P.E.O. Sisterhood. During the convention, tribute will be paid to Miss Alice Virginia Coffin, one of the founders of the order, whose body lies in the Newton cemetery. A pageant will be presented Wednesday evening. A banquet will close the convention on Thursday evening.

Tea Merchant Dead; Famed For Premiums

NEW YORK, June 3—(UP)— Frank Vernon Skiff, 63, the tea merchant who introduced the distribution of household articles as premiums and built up his business from $2000 to $18,000,000 annually, died yesterday after an illness of three months.

Clipped By:

ssatkins
Tue, Jan 28, 2014

Transcription from: www.newspapers.com
The Ogden Standard Examiner, Ogden City, Utah, 3 June 1933, page 1

Tea Merchant Dead; Famed for Premiums

New York, June 1 – (UP) – Frank Vernon Skiff, 63, the tea merchant who introduced the distribution of household articles of premiums and built up his business from $2200 to $18,000,000 annually, died yesterday after an illness of three months.

History of Jewel Supermarket

Jewel-Osco is a supermarket chain headquartered in Itasca, Illinois, a Chicago suburb. Jewel-Osco has 176 stores across northern, central, and western Illinois; eastern Iowa; and portions of northwest Indiana. Jewel-Osco and Jewel are currently wholly owned subsidiaries of Boise, Idaho-based Albertsons.

In 1899, Frank Vernon Skiff founded Jewel in Chicago, Illinois, as a door-to-door coffee delivery service. In 1902, Skiff partnered with Frank P. Ross, renaming the venture the Jewel Tea Company. In 1929, the company built a new office, warehouse, and coffee roasting facility in suburban Barrington, Illinois, creating hundreds of local jobs despite the Great Depression. Area residents nicknamed the new, five-story headquarters the "Gray Lady" due to its sophisticated art deco style.

The company's expansion continued throughout the mid-20th century. In 1932, Jewel acquired the Chicago unit of Loblaw Groceterias, Inc., and then a chain of 72 self-service stores, as well as four Chicago grocery stores operated by the Middle West Stores Company, and began operating them under the name Jewel Food Stores in 1934, Jewel Food Stores merged with Jewel Tea Company. In 1957, Jewel acquired Eisner Food Stores, located in downstate Illinois and west central Indiana (Lafayette, West Lafayette, Indiana), and in 1981, the Eisner stores were converted to the Jewel name. Also in 1981, Jewel sold its home shopping service, which now operates under the name "J.T.'s General Store."

Today

Jewel-Osco employs more than 45,000 associates. Its customer base gives it a 45 percent share of the grocery market in Chicago, trailed by the Safeway Inc. owned Dominick's chain (ranking second at 15 percent). Consumers from 80 percent of all households in the Chicago metropolitan area visit a Jewel-Osco store at least once a month.

On January 10, 2013, SuperValue announced the sale of Jewel food stores to Cerberus Capital Management in a $3.3 billion deal. The deal closed on March 21, 2013.

Photo Album for Alice Virginia Coffin

Alice Virginia Coffin

Birth:	29 Mar 1848	Father:	Matthew Starbuck Coffin
Death:	28 Jul 1888	Mother:	Martha Ellen Thompson
Marriage:		Spouse:	

Alice Coffin abt. 1885

From: Jannotta, Stella S. *Alice Virginia Coffin a Biographical Sketch*, 3rd ed. 70 pages. Privately Printed, 1940.

Alice Virginia Coffin

Birth: 29 Mar 1848	Father: Matthew Starbuck Coffin
Death: 28 Jul 1888	Mother: Martha Ellen Thompson
Marriage:	Spouse:

Alice teaching school in Chariton, Iowa.

Alice Coffin as a teacher in Chariton Iowa

From: Jannotta, Stella S. *Alice Virginia Coffin a Biographical Sketch*, 3rd ed. 70 pages. Privately Printed, 1940.

Alice Virginia Coffin

Birth:	29 Mar 1848	Father:	Matthew Starbuck Coffin
Death:	28 Jul 1888	Mother:	Martha Ellen Thompson
Marriage:		Spouse:	

Alice Virginia Coffin
Young school girl in Mount
Pleasant, Iowa

Alice Coffin as school girl in Mt. Pleasant, Iowa

From: Jannotta, Stella S. *Alice Virginia Coffin a Biographical Sketch*, 3rd ed. 70 pages. Privately Printed, 1940.

Alice Virginia Coffin

Birth:	29 Mar 1848	Father:	Matthew Starbuck Coffin
Death:	28 Jul 1888	Mother:	Martha Ellen Thompson
Marriage:		Spouse:	

Alice, all in white at graduation. Her friends say she looked beautiful and delivered an interesting oration.

Alice Coffin in white for graduation

From: Jannotta, Stella S. *Alice Virginia Coffin a Biographical Sketch*, 3rd ed. 70 pages. Privately Printed, 1940.

Photo Album for Alice Virginia Coffin

Alice Virginia Coffin

Birth: 29 Mar 1848	Father: Matthew Starbuck Coffin
Death: 28 Jul 1888	Mother: Martha Ellen Thompson
Marriage:	Spouse:

Alice Coffin

Reproduction of oil portrait by Marion Dunlap Harper, unveiled in P.E.O. Memorial Hall in Mount Pleasant, Iowa, on September 23, 1929.

Alice Virginia Coffin

Birth:	29 Mar 1848		Father:	Matthew Starbuck Coffin
Death:	28 Jul 1888		Mother:	Martha Ellen Thompson
Marriage:			Spouse:	

Mary Frances, Alice Virginia and Charles Thomas Coffin abt 1853

From: Jannotta, Stella S. *Alice Virginia Coffin a Biographical Sketch*, 3rd ed. 70 pages. Privately Printed, 1940.

Photo Album for John Handley Thompson

John Handley Thompson

Birth:	28 Jan 1782	Father:	Anthony Thompson
Death:	26 Mar 1870	Mother:	Rachel Handley
Marriage:	29 Jun 1813	Spouse:	Margaret McLoney

Judge John H Thompson

Contributed to Semple Family Tree Ancestry.com 11 March 2007 by BrianSemple.

Photo Album for Matthew Starbuck Coffin

Matthew Starbuck Coffin

Birth:	25 Mar 1811	Father:	James Coffin
Death:	10 Mar 1884	Mother:	Sarah Sally Starbuck
Marriage:	07 Nov 1841	Spouse:	Maria Reeves

Matthew Starbuck Coffin

From: Jannotta, Stella S. *Alice Virginia Coffin a Biographical Sketch*, 3rd ed. 70 pages. Privately Printed, 1940.

Photo Album for Martha Ellen Thompson

Martha Ellen Thompson

Birth:	20 May 1819		Father:	John Handley Thompson
Death:	30 Jul 1857		Mother:	Margaret McLoney
Marriage:	07 Nov 1841		Spouse:	Matthew Starbuck Coffin

Martha Ellen Thompson Coffin abt 1854

From: Jannotta, Stella S. *Alice Virginia Coffin a Biographical Sketch*, 3rd ed. 70 pages. Privately Printed, 1940.

Photo Album for Mary Frances Coffin

Mary Frances Coffin

Birth:	25 Oct 1842	Father:	Matthew Starbuck Coffin
Death:	30 Dec 1918	Mother:	Martha Ellen Thompson
Marriage:	23 Jan 1867	Spouse:	Vernon William Skiff

"Mollie" Mary Frances Coffin

Contributed to Semple Family Tree Ancestry.com 11 March 2007 by Brian Semple.

Photo Album for Vernon William Skiff

Vernon William Skiff

Birth:	23 Jan 1841	Father:	William Robinson Skiff
Death:	29 Apr 1926	Mother:	Abigail Whitcomb Axtell
Marriage:	23 Jan 1867	Spouse:	Mary Frances Coffin

Vernon William Skiff

Photo Album for Stella Skiff

Stella Skiff

Birth: 29 Oct 1867	Father: Vernon William Skiff
Death: 01 Oct 1954	Mother: Mary Frances Coffin
Marriage: 25 Jul 1893	Spouse: Alfredo A Jannotta

Stella Skiff

Photo Album for Frank Vernon Skiff

Frank Vernon Skiff

Birth:	03 Jul 1869	Father:	Vernon William Skiff
Death:	03 Jun 1933	Mother:	Mary Frances Coffin
Marriage:	1898	Spouse:	Ida C

Frank Vernon and Ida C. Skiff

Ancestry.com. *U.S. Passport Applications, 1795-1925* [database on-line]. Provo, UT, USA: Ancestry.com Operations, Inc., 2007.National Archives and Records Administration (NARA); Washington D.C.; *Passport Applications, January 2, 1906 - March 31, 1925*; Collection Number: *ARC Identifier 583830 / MLR Number A1 534*; NARA Series: *M1490*; Roll #: *1526*.

Photo Album for Blanche Alice Skiff

Blanche Alice Skiff

Birth:	Abt. 1873	Father:	Vernon William Skiff
Death:	24 Nov 1969	Mother:	Mary Frances Coffin
Marriage:	08 Feb 1899	Spouse:	Franklin Pierce Ross

Blanche Skiff Ross and Franklin Pierce Ross

Photo Album for Charles Thompson Coffin

Charles Thompson Coffin

Birth:	25 Sep 1850	Father:	Matthew Starbuck Coffin
Death:	31 May 1928	Mother:	Martha Ellen Thompson
Marriage:	Abt. 1881	Spouse:	Lillie Belle Marcks

Charles Thompson Coffin Abt 1879 Age 29

Contributed to Semple Family Tree Ancestry.com 11 March 2007 by Brian Semple.

Photo Album for Lillie Belle Marcks

Lillie Belle Marcks

Birth: 07 Jul 1862	Father:	Willoughby Mandes Marcks
Death: 14 Feb 1937	Mother:	Sarah Anne Hittell
Marriage: Abt. 1881	Spouse:	Charles Thompson Coffin

Lillie Belle Marcks Abt 1880 Age 18

Contributed to Semple Family Tree Ancestry.com 11 March 2007 by BrianSemple.

Historical Background Sources
for Alice Virginia Coffin

1. 1850 United States Federal Census. Census Place: Washington, Washington, Indiana; Roll: M432_179. Page: 320A; Image 468.

2. 1860 United States Federal Census. Census Place: Newton, Jasper, Iowa, Roll: M653_325; Page: 131; Image 459; Family History Library Film: 803325.

3. 1880 United States Federal Census. Census Place: Chariton, Lucas, Iowa; Roll: 352: Family History Film: 1254352. Page 467C; Enumeration District: 104: Image: 0095.

4. 1885 Iowa, State Census Collection, 1836-1925 (database on-line) Provo, UT, USA. Microfilm of Iowa State Censuses, 1856, 1885, 1895, 1905, 1915, 1925 as well as various special censuses from 1836-1897 obtained from the State Historical Society of Iowa vs Heritage Quest.

5. "Chariton, Iowa." Wikipedia. Wikimedia Foundation, 09 Nov. 2013. Web. 10 Oct. 2013. <http://en.wikipedia.org/wiki/Chariton%2C_Iowa>.

6. Clapp, Stella. Out of the Heart A Century of P.E.O. 1869-1969. Des Moines, Iowa: P.E.O. Sisterhood, 1968.

7. Jannotta Family Papers, 1809-1972. Web. 12 Nov. 2013. Chronicling Illinois, Abraham Lincoln Presidential Library & Museum.

8. Jannotta, Stella S. Alice Virginia Coffin a Biographical Sketch, 3rd ed. 70 pages. Privately Printed, 1940. Print.

9. Jannotta, Stella S. Alice Virginia Coffin a Biographical Sketch. 3rd ed. 70 pages. Privately Printed, 1940. eBook http://ia600409.us.archive.org/31/items/alicevirginiacof00jann/alicevirginiacof00jann.pdf.

10. "Jewel (supermarket)." Wikipedia. Wikimedia Foundation, 11 May 2013. Web. 10 Nov. 2013.

11. Johnson, Heidi, ed. "A Society of Our Own." The P.E.O. Record (1997).

12. P.E.O. Historian. From Our History 2000. Rep. Vol. Prg F-77. Print.

13. Prior, Frederick J. Professional - Music, Alfredo A. Jannotta. "Columbian Exposition Dedication Ceremonies Memorial, October 1892." Chicago, IL: Metropolitan Art Engraving &, 1893. 577. Print.

14. "Tea Merchant Dead; Famed For Premiums." The Ogden Standard Examiner [Ogden City, Utah] 3 June 1933: 1. Print.

15. Van Dyke, Ella Gardner. "Personal Journal." 1920. Lucas County Genealogy Society, Charlton, Iowa.

16. "William F. Hatcher." A Memorial and Biographical Record of Iowa. Chicago: Lewis, 1896. 372. Print.

Coffin Family Descendant Chart
Source Report

Source Title: **1850 United States Federal Census**
Repository: **Ancestry.com**

Citation: Ancestry.com, 1850 United States Federal Census (Provo, UT, USA, Ancestry.com Operations, Inc., 2009), Ancestry.com, Year: 1850; Census Place: Hume, Allegany, New York; Roll: M432_476; Page: 308B; Image: 213. [Source citation includes media item(s)]
Skiff, Vernon William
Birth: 23 Jan 1841 in Hume, Allegany, New York, USA
Name: Skiff, Vernon William
Res: 1850 in Hume, Allegany, New York; Age: 9

Citation: Ancestry.com, 1850 United States Federal Census (Provo, UT, USA, Ancestry.com Operations, Inc., 2009), Ancestry.com, Year: 1850; Census Place: Washington, Washington, Indiana; Roll: M432_179; Page: 320A; Image: 468. [Source citation includes media item(s)]
Coffin, Alice Virginia
Birth: 29 Mar 1848 in Louisville, Kentucky
Name: Coffin, Alice Virginia
Res: 1850 in Washington, Washington, Indiana; Age: 2

Citation: Ancestry.com, 1850 United States Federal Census (Provo, UT, USA, Ancestry.com Operations, Inc., 2009), Ancestry.com, Year: 1850; Census Place: Washington, Washington, Indiana; Roll: M432_179; Page: 320A; Image: 468. [Source citation includes media item(s)]
Thompson, Martha Ellen
Birth: 20 May 1819 in Charleston, Clark, IN
Name: Thompson, Martha Ellen
Res: 1850 in Washington, Washington, Indiana; Age: 31

Citation: Ancestry.com, 1850 United States Federal Census (Provo, UT, USA, Ancestry.com Operations, Inc., 2009), Ancestry.com, Year: 1850; Census Place: Washington, Washington, Indiana; Roll: M432_179; Page: 320A; Image: 468. [Source citation includes media item(s)]
Coffin, Mary Frances
Birth: 25 Oct 1842 in Salem, Washington, Indiana, USA
Name: Coffin, Mary Frances
Res: 1850 in Washington, Washington, Indiana; Age: 8

Citation: Ancestry.com, 1850 United States Federal Census (Provo, UT, USA, Ancestry.com Operations, Inc., 2009), Ancestry.com, Year: 1850; Census Place: Washington, Washington, Indiana; Roll: M432_179; Page: 320A; Image: 468. [Source citation includes media item(s)]
Coffin, Matthew Starbuck
Birth: 25 Mar 1811 in Deep River, Guilford, NC
Name: Coffin, Matthew Starbuck
Res: 1850 in Washington, Washington, Indiana; Age: 39

Source Title: **1860 United States Federal Census**
Repository: **Ancestry.com**

Citation:
Ancestry.com, 1860 United States Federal Census (Provo, UT, USA, Ancestry.com Operations, Inc., 2009), Ancestry.com, Year: 1860; Census Place: Newton, Jasper, Iowa; Roll: M653_325; Page: 128; Image: 456; Family History Library Film: 803325. [Source citation includes media item(s)]
Skiff, Vernon William
Birth: 23 Jan 1841 in Hume, Allegany, New York, USA
Name: Skiff, Vernon William
Res: 1860 in Newton, Jasper, Iowa, United States; Age: 19

Citation:
Ancestry.com, 1860 United States Federal Census (Provo, UT, USA, Ancestry.com Operations, Inc., 2009), Ancestry.com, Year: 1860; Census Place: Newton, Jasper, Iowa; Roll: M653_325; Page: 131; Image: 459; Family History Library Film: 803325. [Source citation includes media item(s)]
Coffin, Matthew Starbuck
Birth: 25 Mar 1811 in Deep River, Guilford, NC
Name: Coffin, Matthew Starbuck
Res: 1860 in Newton, Jasper, Iowa, United States; Age: 49

Citation:
Ancestry.com, 1860 United States Federal Census (Provo, UT, USA, Ancestry.com Operations, Inc., 2009), Ancestry.com, Year: 1860; Census Place: Newton, Jasper, Iowa; Roll: M653_325; Page: 131; Image: 459; Family History Library Film: 803325.] Source citation includes media item(s)]
Coffin, Alice Virginia
Birth: 29 Mar 1848 in Louisville, Kentucky
Name: Coffin, Alice Virginia
Res: 1860 in Newton, Jasper, Iowa, United States; Age: 12

Citation:
Ancestry.com, 1860 United States Federal Census (Provo, UT, USA, Ancestry.com Operations, Inc., 2009), Ancestry.com, Year: 1860; Census Place: Newton, Jasper, Iowa; Roll: M653_325; Page: 131; Image: 459; Family History Library Film: 803325.] Source citation includes media item(s)]
Coffin, Mary Frances
Birth: 25 Oct 1842 in Salem, Washington, Indiana, USA
Name: Coffin, Mary Frances
Res: 1860 in Newton, Jasper, Iowa, United States; Age: 17

Citation:
Ancestry.com, 1860 United States Federal Census (Provo, UT, USA, Ancestry.com Operations, Inc., 2009), Ancestry.com, Year: 1860; Census Place: Newton, Jasper, Iowa; Roll: M653_325; Page: 131; Image: 459; Family History Library Film: 803325.] Source citation includes media item(s)]
Coffin, Charles Thompson
Birth: 25 Sep 1850 in Salem, Washington, Indiana, USA
Name: Coffin, Charles Thompson
Res: 1860 in Newton, Jasper, Iowa, United States; Age: 9

Citation:
Ancestry.com, 1860 United States Federal Census (Provo, UT, USA, Ancestry.com Operations, Inc., 2009), Ancestry.com, Year: 1860; Census Place: Newton, Jasper, Iowa; Roll: M653_325; Page: 131; Image: 459; Family History Library Film: 803325.] Source citation includes media item(s)]
Coffin, Matthew Starbuck
Birth: 30 Mar 1853 in Salem, Washington, Indiana, USA
Name: Coffin, Matthew Starbuck
Res: 1860 in Newton, Jasper, Iowa, United States; Age: 7

Source Title: **1870 United States Federal Census**
Repository: **Ancestry.com**

Citation: Ancestry.com, 1870 United States Federal Census (Provo, UT, USA, Ancestry.com Operations, Inc., 2009), Ancestry.com, Year: 1870; Census Place: Newton, Jasper, Iowa; Roll: M593_398; Page: 386B; Image: 413; Family History Library Film: 545897.] Source citation includes media item(s)]
Skiff, Vernon William
Birth: 23 Jan 1841 in Hume, Allegany, New York, USA
Name: Skiff, Vernon William
Res: 1870 in Newton, Jasper, Iowa, United States
Age: 29; Census Post Office: Newton

Citation: Ancestry.com, 1870 United States Federal Census (Provo, UT, USA, Ancestry.com Operations, Inc., 2009), Ancestry.com, Year: 1870; Census Place: Newton, Jasper, Iowa; Roll: M593_398; Page: 386B; Image: 413; Family History Library Film: 545897.] Source citation includes media item(s)]
Coffin, Mary Frances
Birth: 25 Oct 1842 in Salem, Washington, Indiana, USA
Name: Coffin, Mary Frances
Res: 1870 in Newton, Jasper, Iowa, United States
Age: 26; Census Post Office: Newton

Citation: Ancestry.com, 1870 United States Federal Census (Provo, UT, USA, Ancestry.com Operations, Inc., 2009), Ancestry.com, Year: 1870; Census Place: Newton, Jasper, Iowa; Roll: M593_398; Page: 386B; Image: 413; Family History Library Film: 545897.] Source citation includes media item(s)]
Skiff, Frank Vernon
Birth: 03 Jul 1869 in Newton, Jasper, Iowa, USA
Name: Skiff, Frank Vernon
Res: 1870 in Newton, Jasper, Iowa, United States
Age: 1; Census Post Office: Newton

Citation: Ancestry.com, 1870 United States Federal Census (Provo, UT, USA, Ancestry.com Operations, Inc., 2009), Ancestry.com, Year: 1870; Census Place: Newton, Jasper, Iowa; Roll: M593_398; Page: 386B; Image: 413; Family History Library Film: 545897.] Source citation includes media item(s)]
Skiff, Stella
Birth: 29 Oct 1867 in Newton, Jasper, Iowa, USA
Name: Skiff, Stella
Res: 1870 in Newton, Jasper, Iowa, United States
Age: 2; Census Post Office: Newton

Source Title: **1880 United States Federal Census**
Repository: **Ancestry.com**

Citation: Ancestry.com and The Church of Jesus Christ of Latter-day Saints, 1880 United States Federal Census (Provo, UT, USA, Ancestry.com Operations Inc., 2010), Ancestry.com, Year: 1880; Census Place: Chariton, Lucas, Iowa; Roll: 352; Family History Film: 1254352; Page: 467C; Enumeration District: 104; Image: 0095. [Source citation includes media item(s)]
Coffin, Alice Virginia
Birth: 29 Mar 1848 in Louisville, Kentucky
Name: Coffin, Alice Virginia
Res: 1880 in Chariton, Lucas, Iowa, United States
Age: 29; Marital Status: Single

Citation: Ancestry.com and The Church of Jesus Christ of Latter-day Saints, 1880 United States Federal Census (Provo, UT, USA, Ancestry.com Operations Inc., 2010), Ancestry.com, Year: 1880; Census Place: De Soto, Johnson, Kansas; Roll: 384; Family History Film: 1254384; Page: 41C; Enumeration District: 095; Image: 0285. [Source citation includes media item(s)]
Marcks, Lillie Belle
Birth: 07 Jul 1862 in Ohio
Name: Marcks, Lillie Belle
Res: 1880 in De Soto, Johnson, Kansas, United States
Age: 17; Marital Status: Single
Relation to Head of House: Daughter

Citation: Ancestry.com and The Church of Jesus Christ of Latter-day Saints, 1880 United States Federal Census (Provo, UT, USA, Ancestry.com Operations Inc., 2010), Ancestry.com, Year: 1880; Census Place: Newton, Jasper, Iowa; Roll: 346; Family History Film: 1254346; Page: 94D; Enumeration District: 094; Image: 0413. [Source citation include media item(s)]
Skiff, Blanche Alice
Birth: Abt. 1873 in Newton, Jasper, Iowa, USA
Name: Skiff, Blanche Alice
Res: 1880 in Newton, Jasper, Iowa, United States
Age: 7;
Marital Status: Single
Relation to Head of House: Daughter

Citation: Ancestry.com and The Church of Jesus Christ of Latter-day Saints, 1880 United States Federal Census (Provo, UT, USA, Ancestry.com Operations Inc., 2010), Ancestry.com, Year: 1880; Census Place: Newton, Jasper, Iowa; Roll: 346; Family History Film: 1254346; Page: 94D; Enumeration District: 094; Image: 0413. [Source citation includes media item(s)]
Coffin, Matthew Starbuck
Birth: 25 Mar 1811 in Deep River, Guilford, NC
Name: Coffin, Matthew Starbuck
Res: 1880 in Newton, Jasper, Iowa, United States
Age: 69
Marital Status: Widower

Citation: Ancestry.com and The Church of Jesus Christ of Latter-day Saints, 1880 United States Federal Census (Provo, UT, USA, Ancestry.com Operations Inc., 2010), Ancestry.com Year: 1880; Census Place: Newton, Jasper, Iowa; Roll: 346; Family History Film: 1254346; Page: 94D; Enumeration District: 094; Image: 0413. [Source citation includes media item(s)]
Skiff, Vernon William
Birth: 23 Jan 1841 in Hume, Allegany, New York, USA
Name: Skiff, Vernon William
Res: 1880 in Newton, Jasper, Iowa, United States
Age: 39
Marital Status: Married
Relation to Head of House: Self

Citation: Ancestry.com and The Church of Jesus Christ of Latter-day Saints, 1880 United States
Federal Census (Provo, UT, USA, Ancestry.com Operations Inc., 2010), Ancestry.com
Year: 1880; Census Place: Newton, Jasper, Iowa; Roll: 346; Family History Film:
1254346; Page: 94D; Enumeration District: 094; Image: 0413. [Source citation includes
media item(s)]
Coffin, Mary Frances
Birth: 25 Oct 1842 in Salem, Washington, Indiana, USA
Name: Coffin, Mary Frances
Res: 1880 in Newton, Jasper, Iowa, United States
Age: 37
Marital Status: Married
Relation to Head of House: Wife

Citation: Ancestry.com and The Church of Jesus Christ of Latter-day Saints, 1880 United States
Federal Census (Provo, UT, USA, Ancestry.com Operations Inc., 2010), Ancestry.com
Year: 1880; Census Place: Newton, Jasper, Iowa; Roll: 346; Family History Film:
1254346; Page: 94D; Enumeration District: 094; Image: 0413. [Source citation includes
media item(s)]
Skiff, Frank Vernon
Birth: 03 Jul 1869 in Newton, Jasper, Iowa, USA
Name: Skiff, Frank Vernon
Res: 1880 in Newton, Jasper, Iowa, United States
Age: 10
Marital Status: Single
Relation to Head of House: Son

Citation: Ancestry.com and The Church of Jesus Christ of Latter-day Saints, 1880 United States
Federal Census (Provo, UT, USA, Ancestry.com Operations Inc., 2010), Ancestry.com,
Year: 1880; Census Place: Newton, Jasper, Iowa; Roll: 346; Family History Film:
1254346; Page: 94D; Enumeration District: 094; Image: 0413. [Source citation includes
media item(s)]
Skiff, Stella
Birth: 29 Oct 1867 in Newton, Jasper, Iowa, USA
Name: Skiff, Stella
Res: 1880 in Newton, Jasper, Iowa, United States
Age: 12;
Marital Status: Single
Relation to Head of House: Daughter

Citation: Ancestry.com and The Church of Jesus Christ of Latter-day Saints, 1880 United States
Federal Census (Provo, UT, USA, Ancestry.com Operations Inc., 2010), Ancestry.com,
Year: 1880; Census Place: Richhill, Greene, Pennsylvania; Roll: 1133; Family History
Film: 1255133; Page: 355D; Enumeration District: 082; Image: 0720. [Source citation
includes media item(s)]
Ross, Franklin Pierce
Birth: 22 Jul 1869 in Wind Ridge, Greene, Pennsylvania, USA
Res: 1880 in Richhill, Greene, Pennsylvania, United States
Age: 10
Marital Status: Single
Relation to Head of House: Son

Source Title: **1900 United States Federal Census**
Repository: **Ancestry.com**

Citation: Ancestry.com, 1900 United States Federal Census (Provo, UT, USA, Ancestry.com
Operations Inc., 2004), Ancestry.com, Year: 1900; Census Place: Chicago Ward 2, Cook,
Illinois; Roll: 246; Page: 6B; Enumeration District: 0046; FHL microfilm: 1240246.] Source
citation includes media item(s)]
Ida C
Birth: Abt. 1871 in Pennsylvania
Name: Ida C
Res: 1900 in Chicago Ward 2, Cook, Illinois, USA
Age: 26; Marital Status: Married
Relation to Head of House: Wife
Marr: 1898
Skiff, Frank Vernon
Marr: 1898

Citation: Ancestry.com, 1900 United States Federal Census (Provo, UT, USA, Ancestry.com
Operations Inc., 2004), Ancestry.com, Year: 1900; Census Place: Chicago Ward 2, Cook,
Illinois; Roll: 246; Page: 6B; Enumeration District: 0046; FHL microfilm: 1240246.] Source
citation includes media item(s)]
Ida C
Marr: 1898
Skiff, Frank Vernon
Birth: 03 Jul 1869 in Newton, Jasper, Iowa, USA
Name: Skiff, Frank Vernon
Res: 1900 in Chicago Ward 2, Cook, Illinois, USA
Age: 29
Marital Status: Married
Relation to Head of House: Head
Marr: 1898

Citation: Ancestry.com, 1900 United States Federal Census (Provo, UT, USA, Ancestry.com
Operations Inc., 2004), Ancestry.com, Year: 1900; Census Place: Cicero, Cook, Illinois;
Roll: 292; Page: 3A; Enumeration District: 1145; FHL microfilm: 1240292. [Source citation
includes media item(s)]
Jannotta, Alfredo A
Birth: 20 Dec 1843 in Capua, Caserta, Campania, Italy
Name: Jannotta, Alfredo A

Citation: Ancestry.com, 1900 United States Federal Census (Provo, UT, USA, Ancestry.com
Operations Inc., 2004), Ancestry.com, Year: 1900; Census Place: Cicero, Cook, Illinois;
Roll: 292; Page: 3A; Enumeration District: 1145; FHL microfilm: 1240292. [Source citation
includes media item(s)]
Jannotta, Alfredo A
Arrive: 1867
Age: 21
Res: 1900 in Cicero, Cook, Illinois, USA
Age: 53
Marital Status: Married
Relation to Head of House: Head
Marr: 25 Jul 1893 in Chicago, Cook, Illinois, USA
Skiff, Stella
Marr: 25 Jul 1893 in Chicago, Cook, Illinois, USA

Citation:	Ancestry.com, 1900 United States Federal Census (Provo, UT, USA, Ancestry.com
	Operations Inc., 2004), Ancestry.com, Year: 1900; Census Place: Cicero, Cook, Illinois;
	Roll: 292; Page: 3A; Enumeration District: 1145; FHL microfilm: 1240292. [Source citation
	includes media item(s)]
	Jannotta, Alfredo A
	Marr: 25 Jul 1893 in Chicago, Cook, Illinois, USA
	Skiff, Stella
	Birth: 29 Oct 1867 in Newton, Jasper, Iowa, USA
	Name: Skiff, Stella
	Res: 1900 in Cicero, Cook, Illinois, USA
	Age: 22
	Marital Status: Married
	Relation to Head of House: Wife
	Marr: 25 Jul 1893 in Chicago, Cook, Illinois, USA

Citation:	Ancestry.com, 1900 United States Federal Census (Provo, UT, USA, Ancestry.com
	Operations Inc., 2004), Ancestry.com, Year: 1900; Census Place: Monmouth, Warren,
	Illinois; Roll: 350; Page: 12B; Enumeration District: 0091; FHL microfilm: 1240350.]
	Source citation includes media item(s)]
	Ross, Franklin Pierce
	Marr: 08 Feb 1899 in Newton, IA
	Skiff, Blanche Alice
	Birth: Abt. 1873 in Newton, Jasper, Iowa, USA
	Name: Skiff, Blanche Alice
	Res: 1900 in Monmouth, Warren, Illinois, USA
	Age: 27
	Marital Status: Married
	Relation to Head of House: Wife
	Marr: 08 Feb 1899 in Newton, IA

Citation:	Ancestry.com, 1900 United States Federal Census (Provo, UT, USA, Ancestry.com
	Operations Inc., 2004), Ancestry.com, Year: 1900; Census Place: Monmouth, Warren,
	Illinois; Roll: 350; Page: 12B; Enumeration District: 0091; FHL microfilm: 1240350.]
	Source citation includes media item(s)]
	Ross, Franklin Pierce
	Birth: 22 Jul 1869 in Wind Ridge, Greene, Pennsylvania, USA
	Name: Ross, Franklin Pierce
	Res: 1900 in Monmouth, Warren, Illinois, USA
	Age: 30
	Marital Status: Married
	Relation to Head of House: Head
	Marr: 08 Feb 1899 in Newton, IA
	Skiff, Blanche Alice
	Marr: 08 Feb 1899 in Newton, IA

Citation:	Ancestry.com, 1900 United States Federal Census (Provo, UT, USA, Ancestry.com
	Operations Inc., 2004), Ancestry.com, Year: 1900; Census Place: Newton, Jasper, Iowa;
	Roll: 439; Page: 1A; Enumeration District: 0029; FHL microfilm: 1240439. [Source citation
	includes media item(s)]
	Coffin, Mary Frances
	Marr: 23 Jan 1867 in Newton, Jasper, Iowa, USA

Citation: Ancestry.com, 1900 United States Federal Census (Provo, UT, USA, Ancestry.com
            Operations Inc., 2004), Ancestry.com, Year: 1900; Census Place: Newton, Jasper, Iowa;
            Roll: 439; Page: 1A; Enumeration District: 0029; FHL microfilm: 1240439. [Source citation
            includes media item(s)]
            Skiff, Vernon William
            Birth: 23 Jan 1841 in Hume, Allegany, New York, USA
            Name: Skiff, Vernon William
            Res: 1900 in Newton, Jasper, Iowa, USA
            Age: 59
            Marital Status: Married
            Relation to Head of House: Head
            Marr: 23 Jan 1867 in Newton, Jasper, Iowa, USA

Citation: Ancestry.com, 1900 United States Federal Census (Provo, UT, USA, Ancestry.com
            Operations Inc., 2004), Ancestry.com, Year: 1900; Census Place: Newton, Jasper, Iowa;
            Roll: 439; Page: 1A; Enumeration District: 0029; FHL microfilm: 1240439. [Source citation
            includes media item(s)]
            Coffin, Mary Frances
            Birth: 25 Oct 1842 in Salem, Washington, Indiana, USA
            Name: Coffin, Mary Frances
            Res: 1900 in Newton, Jasper, Iowa, USA
            Age: 57; Marital Status: Married;
            Relation to Head of House: Wife
            Marr: 23 Jan 1867 in Newton, Jasper, Iowa, USA
            Skiff, Vernon William
            Marr: 23 Jan 1867 in Newton, Jasper, Iowa, USA

Citation: Ancestry.com, 1900 United States Federal Census (Provo, UT, USA, Ancestry.com
            Operations Inc., 2004), Ancestry.com, Year: 1900; Census Place: Topeka Ward 2,
            Shawnee, Kansas; Roll: 500; Page: 5A; Enumeration District: 0152; FHL microfilm:
            1240500. [Source citation includes media item(s)]
            Coffin, Grace Lucille
            Birth: 09 Sep 1889 in Topeka, KA
            Name: Coffin, Grace Lucille
            Res: 1900 in Topeka Ward 2, Shawnee, Kansas, USA
            Age: 10
            Marital Status: Single
            Relation to Head of House: Daughter

Citation: Ancestry.com, 1900 United States Federal Census (Provo, UT, USA, Ancestry.com
            Operations Inc., 2004), Ancestry.com, Year: 1900; Census Place: Topeka Ward 2,
            Shawnee, Kansas; Roll: 500; Page: 5A; Enumeration District: 0152; FHL microfilm:
            1240500. [Source citation includes media item(s)]
            Coffin, Alice
            Birth: 1885 in Kansas
            Name: Coffin, Alice
            Res: 1900 in Topeka Ward 2, Shawnee, Kansas, USA
            Age: 16
            Marital Status: Single
            Relation to Head of House: Daughter

Citation: Ancestry.com, 1900 United States Federal Census (Provo, UT, USA, Ancestry.com
               Operations Inc., 2004), Ancestry.com, Year: 1900; Census Place: Topeka Ward 2,
               Shawnee, Kansas; Roll: 500; Page: 5A; Enumeration District: 0152; FHL microfilm:
               1240500. [Source citation includes media item(s)]
               Coffin, Frances
               Birth: 31 May 1882 in Kansas, United States
               Name: Coffin, Frances
               Res: 1900 in Topeka Ward 2, Shawnee, Kansas, USA
               Age: 18
               Marital Status: Single
               Relation to Head of House: Daughter

Citation: Ancestry.com, 1900 United States Federal Census (Provo, UT, USA, Ancestry.com
               Operations Inc., 2004), Ancestry.com, Year: 1900; Census Place: Topeka Ward 2,
               Shawnee, Kansas; Roll: 500; Page: 5A; Enumeration District: 0152; FHL microfilm:
               1240500. [Source citation includes media item(s)]
               Coffin, Charles Thompson

Citation: Ancestry.com, 1900 United States Federal Census (Provo, UT, USA, Ancestry.com
               Operations Inc., 2004), Ancestry.com, Year: 1900; Census Place: Topeka Ward 2,
               Shawnee, Kansas; Roll: 500; Page: 5A; Enumeration District: 0152; FHL microfilm:
               1240500. [Source citation includes media item(s)]
               Coffin, Charles Thompson
               Birth: 25 Sep 1850 in Salem, Washington, Indiana, USA
               Name: Coffin, Charles Thompson
               Marr: Abt. 1881 in , , , USA
               Res: 1900 in Topeka Ward 2, Shawnee, Kansas, USA
               Age: 46
               Marital Status: Married
               Relation to Head of House: Head
               Marcks, Lillie Belle
               Marr: Abt. 1881 in , , , USA

Citation: Ancestry.com, 1900 United States Federal Census (Provo, UT, USA, Ancestry.com
               Operations Inc., 2004), Ancestry.com, Year: 1900; Census Place: Topeka Ward 2,
               Shawnee, Kansas; Roll: 500; Page: 5A; Enumeration District: 0152; FHL microfilm:
               1240500. [Source citation includes media item(s)]
               Coffin, Charles Thompson
               Marr: Abt. 1881 in , , , USA
               Marcks, Lillie Belle
               Birth: 07 Jul 1862 in Ohio
               Name: Marcks, Lillie Belle
               Marr: Abt. 1881 in , , , USA
               Res: 1900 in Topeka Ward 2, Shawnee, Kansas, USA
               Age: 37
               Marital Status: Married
               Relation to Head of House: Wife

Source Title: **1910 United States Federal Census**
Repository: **Ancestry.com**

Citation: Ancestry.com, 1910 United States Federal Census (Provo, UT, USA, Ancestry.com Operations Inc., 2006), Ancestry.com, Year: 1910; Census Place: Kansas Ward 4, Jackson, Missouri; Roll: T624_785; Page: 5A; Enumeration District: 0053; FHL microfilm: 1374798. [Source citation includes media item(s)]
Coffin, Grace Lucille
Birth: 09 Sep 1889 in Topeka, KA
Name: Coffin, Grace Lucille
Res: 1910 in Kansas Ward 4, Jackson, Missouri, USA
Age: 19
Marital Status: Single
Relation to Head of House: Daughter

Citation: Ancestry.com, 1910 United States Federal Census (Provo, UT, USA, Ancestry.com Operations Inc., 2006), Ancestry.com, Year: 1910; Census Place: Kansas Ward 4, Jackson, Missouri; Roll: T624_785; Page: 5A; Enumeration District: 0053; FHL microfilm: 1374798. [Source citation includes media item(s)]
Coffin, Alice
Birth: 1885 in Kansas
Name: Coffin, Alice
Res: 1910 in Kansas Ward 4, Jackson, Missouri, USA
Age: 25
Marital Status: Single
Relation to Head of House: Daughter

Citation: Ancestry.com, 1910 United States Federal Census (Provo, UT, USA, Ancestry.com Operations Inc., 2006), Ancestry.com, Year: 1910; Census Place: Kansas Ward 4, Jackson, Missouri; Roll: T624_785; Page: 5A; Enumeration District: 0053; FHL microfilm: 1374798. [Source citation includes media item(s)]
Coffin, Frances
Birth: 31 May 1882 in Kansas, United States
Name: Coffin, Frances
Res: 1910 in Kansas Ward 4, Jackson, Missouri, USA
Age: 27
Marital Status: Single
Relation to Head of House: Daughter

Citation: Ancestry.com, 1910 United States Federal Census (Provo, UT, USA, Ancestry.com Operations Inc., 2006), Ancestry.com, Year: 1910; Census Place: Kansas Ward 4, Jackson, Missouri; Roll: T624_785; Page: 5A; Enumeration District: 0053; FHL microfilm: 1374798. [Source citation includes media item(s)]
Coffin, Charles Thompson
Birth: 25 Sep 1850 in Salem, Washington, Indiana, USA
Name: Coffin, Charles Thompson
Res: 1910 in Kansas Ward 4, Jackson, Missouri, USA
Age: 49
Marital Status: Married
Relation to Head of House: Head

Citation: Ancestry.com, 1910 United States Federal Census (Provo, UT, USA, Ancestry.com Operations Inc., 2006), Ancestry.com, Year: 1910; Census Place: Kansas Ward 4, Jackson, Missouri; Roll: T624_785; Page: 5A; Enumeration District: 0053; FHL microfilm: 1374798. [Source citation includes media item(s)]
Marcks, Lillie Belle
Birth: 07 Jul 1862 in Ohio
Name: Marcks, Lillie Belle
Res: 1910 in Kansas Ward 4, Jackson, Missouri, USA
Age: 48
Marital Status: Married
Relation to Head of House: Wife

Citation: Ancestry.com, 1910 United States Federal Census (Provo, UT, USA, Ancestry.com Operations Inc., 2006), Ancestry.com, Year: 1910; Census Place: Oak Park, Cook, Illinois; Roll: T624_239; Page: 11B; Enumeration District: 0075; FHL microfilm: 1374252.] Source citation includes media item(s)]
Jannotta, Alfredo A
Birth: 20 Dec 1843 in Capua, Caserta, Campania, Italy
Name: Jannotta, Alfredo A
Res: 1910 in Oak Park, Cook, Illinois, USA
Age: 66
Marital Status: Married
Relation to Head of House: Head
Arrive: 1866
Age: 22

Citation: Ancestry.com, 1910 United States Federal Census (Provo, UT, USA, Ancestry.com Operations Inc., 2006), Ancestry.com, Year: 1910; Census Place: Oak Park, Cook, Illinois; Roll: T624_239; Page: 11B; Enumeration District: 0075; FHL microfilm: 1374252.] Source citation includes media item(s)]
Skiff, Stella
Birth: 29 Oct 1867 in Newton, Jasper, Iowa, USA
Name: Skiff, Stella
Res: 1910 in Oak Park, Cook, Illinois, USA
Age: 42
Marital Status: Married
Relation to Head of House: Wife

Citation: Ancestry.com, 1910 United States Federal Census (Provo, UT, USA, Ancestry.com Operations Inc., 2006), Ancestry.com, Year: 1910; Census Place: Oak Park, Cook, Illinois; Roll: T624_239; Page: 1A; Enumeration District: 0070; FHL microfilm: 1374252.] Source citation includes media item(s)]
Skiff, Blanche Alice
Birth: Abt. 1873 in Newton, Jasper, Iowa, USA
Name: Skiff, Blanche Alice
Res: 1910 in Oak Park, Cook, Illinois, USA
Age: 36
Marital Status: Married
Relation to Head of House: Wife

Citation: Ancestry.com, 1910 United States Federal Census (Provo, UT, USA, Ancestry.com Operations Inc., 2006), Ancestry.com, Year: 1910; Census Place: Oak Park, Cook, Illinois; Roll: T624_239; Page: 1A; Enumeration District: 0070; FHL microfilm: 1374252.] Source citation includes media item(s)]
Ross, Franklin Pierce
Birth: 22 Jul 1869 in Wind Ridge, Greene, Pennsylvania, USA
Name: Ross, Franklin Pierce

Citation: Ancestry.com, 1910 United States Federal Census (Provo, UT, USA, Ancestry.com
Operations Inc., 2006), Ancestry.com, Year: 1910; Census Place: Oak Park, Cook,
Illinois; Roll: T624_239; Page: 1A; Enumeration District: 0070; FHL microfilm: 1374252.]
Source citation includes media item(s)]
Ross, Franklin Pierce
Res: 1910 in Oak Park, Cook, Illinois, USA
Age: 40
Marital Status: Married
Relation to Head of House: Head

Citation: Ancestry.com, 1910 United States Federal Census (Provo, UT, USA, Ancestry.com
Operations Inc., 2006), Ancestry.com, Year: 1910; Census Place: Oak Park, Cook,
Illinois; Roll: T624_239; Page: 1A; Enumeration District: 0070; FHL microfilm: 1374252.]
Source citation includes media item(s)]
Skiff, Vernon William
Birth: 23 Jan 1841 in Hume, Allegany, New York, USA
Name: Skiff, Vernon William
Res: 1910 in Oak Park, Cook, Illinois, USA
Age: 69
Marital Status: Married
Relation to Head of House: Father

Citation: Ancestry.com, 1910 United States Federal Census (Provo, UT, USA, Ancestry.com
Operations Inc., 2006), Ancestry.com, Year: 1910; Census Place: Oak Park, Cook,
Illinois; Roll: T624_239; Page: 1A; Enumeration District: 0070; FHL microfilm: 1374252.]
Source citation includes media item(s)]
Coffin, Mary Frances
Birth: 25 Oct 1842 in Salem, Washington, Indiana, USA
Name: Coffin, Mary Frances
Res: 1910 in Oak Park, Cook, Illinois, USA
Age: 67
Marital Status: Married
Relation to Head of House: Mother

Citation: Ancestry.com, 1910 United States Federal Census (Provo, UT, USA, Ancestry.com
Operations Inc., 2006), Ancestry.com, Year: 1910; Census Place: Oak Park, Cook,
Illinois; Roll: T624_239; Page: 1A; Enumeration District: 0070; FHL microfilm: 1374252.]
Source citation includes media item(s)]
Ida C
Birth: Abt. 1871 in Pennsylvania
Name: Ida C
Res: 1910 in Oak Park, Cook, Illinois, USA
Age: 39
Marital Status: Married
Relation to Head of House: Wife

Citation: Ancestry.com, 1910 United States Federal Census (Provo, UT, USA, Ancestry.com
Operations Inc., 2006), Ancestry.com, Year: 1910; Census Place: Oak Park, Cook,
Illinois; Roll: T624_239; Page: 1A; Enumeration District: 0070; FHL microfilm: 1374252.]
Source citation includes media item(s)]
Skiff, Frank Vernon
Birth: 03 Jul 1869 in Newton, Jasper, Iowa, USA
Name: Skiff, Frank Vernon
Res: 1910 in Oak Park, Cook, Illinois, USA
Age: 40
Marital Status: Married
Relation to Head of House: Head

Source Title: **1920 United States Federal Census**
Repository: **Ancestry.com**

Citation: Ancestry.com, 1920 United States Federal Census (Provo, UT, USA, Ancestry.com Operations Inc., 2010), Ancestry.com, Year: 1920; Census Place: Oak Park Precinct 19, Cook, Illinois; Roll: T625_361; Page: 1A; Enumeration District: 152; Image: 979. [Source citation includes media item(s)]
Skiff, Stella
Birth: 29 Oct 1867 in Newton, Jasper, Iowa, USA
Name: Skiff, Stella

Citation: Ancestry.com, 1920 United States Federal Census (Provo, UT, USA, Ancestry.com Operations Inc., 2010), Ancestry.com, Year: 1920; Census Place: Oak Park Precinct 19, Cook, Illinois; Roll: T625_361; Page: 1A; Enumeration District: 152; Image: 979. [Source citation includes media item(s)]
Skiff, Stella
Res: 1920 in Oak Park Precinct 19, Cook, Illinois, USA
Age: 52
Marital Status: Widowed; Marital Status: Widow
Relation to Head of House: Head

Citation: Ancestry.com, 1920 United States Federal Census (Provo, UT, USA, Ancestry.com Operations Inc., 2010), Ancestry.com, Year: 1920; Census Place: Oak Park Precinct 3, Cook, Illinois; Roll: T625_361; Page: 11B; Enumeration District: 144; Image: 796.] Source citation includes media item(s)]
Skiff, Blanche Alice
Birth: Abt. 1873 in Newton, Jasper, Iowa, USA
Name: Skiff, Blanche Alice
Res. 1920 in Oak Park Precinct 3, Cook, Illinois, USA
Age: 47
Marital Status: Married
Relation to Head of House: Wife

Citation: Ancestry.com, 1920 United States Federal Census (Provo, UT, USA, Ancestry.com Operations Inc., 2010), Ancestry.com, Year: 1920; Census Place: Oak Park Precinct 3, Cook, Illinois; Roll: T625_361; Page: 11B; Enumeration District: 144; Image: 796.] Source citation includes media item(s)]
Ross, Franklin Pierce
Birth: 22 Jul 1869 in Wind Ridge, Greene, Pennsylvania, USA
Name: Ross, Franklin Pierce
Res: 1920 in Oak Park Precinct 3, Cook, Illinois, USA
Age: 50
Marital Status: Married
Relation to Head of House: Head

Source Title: **1930 United States Federal Census**
Repository: **Ancestry.com**

Citation: Ancestry.com, 1930 United States Federal Census (Provo, UT, USA, Ancestry.com Operations Inc., 2002), Ancestry.com, Year: 1930; Census Place: De Soto, Johnson, Kansas; Roll: 706; Page: 2B; Enumeration District: 4; Image: 515.0; FHL microfilm: 2340441. [Source citation includes media item(s)]
Marcks, Lillie Belle
Birth: 07 Jul 1862 in Ohio
Name: Marcks, Lillie Belle
Res: 1930 in De Soto, Johnson, Kansas
Age: 67; Marital Status: Widowed;
Relation to Head of House: Head

Citation: Ancestry.com, 1930 United States Federal Census (Provo, UT, USA, Ancestry.com Operations Inc., 2002), Ancestry.com, Year: 1930; Census Place: Millburn, Essex, New Jersey; Roll: 1332; Page: 2A; Enumeration District: 506; Image: 27.0; FHL microfilm: 2341067. [Source citation includes media item(s)]
Ida C
Birth: Abt. 1871 in Pennsylvania
Name: Ida C
Res: 1930 in Millburn, Essex, New Jersey
Age: 59; Marital Status: Married;
Relation to Head of House: Wife

Citation: Ancestry.com, 1930 United States Federal Census (Provo, UT, USA, Ancestry.com Operations Inc., 2002), Ancestry.com, Year: 1930; Census Place: Millburn, Essex, New Jersey; Roll: 1332; Page: 2A; Enumeration District: 506; Image: 27.0; FHL microfilm: 2341067. [Source citation includes media item(s)]
Skiff, Frank Vernon
Birth: 03 Jul 1869 in Newton, Jasper, Iowa, USA
Name: Skiff, Frank Vernon

Citation: Ancestry.com, 1930 United States Federal Census (Provo, UT, USA, Ancestry.com Operations Inc., 2002), Ancestry.com, Year: 1930; Census Place: Millburn, Essex, New Jersey; Roll: 1332; Page: 2A; Enumeration District: 506; Image: 27.0; FHL microfilm: 2341067. [Source citation includes media item(s)]
Skiff, Frank Vernon
Res: 1930 in Millburn, Essex, New Jersey
Age: 60; Marital Status: Married;
Relation to Head of House: Head

Citation: Ancestry.com, 1930 United States Federal Census (Provo, UT, USA, Ancestry.com Operations Inc., 2002), Ancestry.com, Year: 1930; Census Place: Oak Park, Cook, Illinois; Roll: 504; Page: 2B; Enumeration District: 2251; Image: 789.0; FHL microfilm: 2340239. [Source citation includes media item(s)]
Skiff, Blanche Alice
Birth: Abt. 1873 in Newton, Jasper, Iowa, USA
Name: Skiff, Blanche Alice
Res: 1930 in Oak Park, Cook, Illinois
Age: 56; Marital Status: Married;
Relation to Head of House: Wife

Citation: Ancestry.com, 1930 United States Federal Census (Provo, UT, USA, Ancestry.com Operations Inc., 2002), Ancestry.com, Year: 1930; Census Place: Oak Park, Cook, Illinois; Roll: 504; Page: 2B; Enumeration District: 2251; Image: 789.0; FHL microfilm: 2340239. [Source citation includes media item(s)]
Ross, Franklin Pierce
Birth: 22 Jul 1869 in Wind Ridge, Greene, Pennsylvania, USA
Name: Ross, Franklin Pierce
Res: 1930 in Oak Park, Cook, Illinois
Age: 60; Marital Status: Married;
Relation to Head of House: Head

Citation: Ancestry.com, 1930 United States Federal Census (Provo, UT, USA, Ancestry.com
             Operations Inc., 2002), Ancestry.com, Year: 1930; Census Place: Starr Lake, Polk,
             Florida; Roll: 331; Page: 5B; Enumeration District: 62; Image: 637.0; FHL microfilm:
             2340066. [Source citation includes media item(s)]
             Skiff, Stella
             Birth: 29 Oct 1867 in Newton, Jasper, Iowa, USA
             Name: Skiff, Stella
             Res: 1930 in Starr Lake, Polk, Florida
             Age: 65; Marital Status: Widowed;
             Relation to Head of House: Head

Source Title: **1940 United States Federal Census**
Repository: **Ancestry.com**

Citation: Ancestry.com, 1940 United States Federal Census (Provo, UT, USA, Ancestry.com
             Operations, Inc., 2012), Ancestry.com, Year: 1940; Census Place: Chicago, Cook,
             Illinois; Roll: T627_1021; Page: 6B; Enumeration District: 103-3181. [Source citation
             includes media item(s)]
             Skiff, Stella
             Birth: 29 Oct 1867 in Newton, Jasper, Iowa, USA
             Name: Skiff, Stella
             Res: 1935 in Precinct 32, Polk, Florida
             Age: 67
             Relation to Head of House: Head
             Relation to Head of House: Mother
             Res: 01 Apr 1940 in Chicago, Cook, Illinois, United States
             Age: 72
             Marital Status: Widowed
             Relation to Head of House: Head

Citation: Ancestry.com, 1940 United States Federal Census (Provo, UT, USA, Ancestry.com
             Operations, Inc., 2012), Ancestry.com, Year: 1940; Census Place: Oak Park, Cook,
             Illinois; Roll: T627_784; Page: 68B; Enumeration District: 16-353. [Source citation
             includes media item(s)]
             Skiff, Blanche Alice
             Birth: Abt. 1873 in Newton, Jasper, Iowa, USA

Citation: Ancestry.com, 1940 United States Federal Census (Provo, UT, USA, Ancestry.com
             Operations, Inc., 2012), Ancestry.com, Year: 1940; Census Place: Oak Park, Cook,
             Illinois; Roll: T627_784; Page: 68B; Enumeration District: 16-353. [Source citation
             includes media item(s)]
             Skiff, Blanche Alice
             Name: Skiff, Blanche Alice
             Res: 1935 in Oak Park, Cook, Illinois
             Res: 01 Apr 1940 in Oak Park, Cook, Illinois, United States
             Age: 67
             Marital Status: Married
             Relation to Head of House: Wife

Citation: Ancestry.com, 1940 United States Federal Census (Provo, UT, USA, Ancestry.com
             Operations, Inc., 2012), Ancestry.com, Year: 1940; Census Place: Oak Park, Cook,
             Illinois; Roll: T627_784; Page: 68B; Enumeration District: 16-353. [Source citation
             includes media item(s)]
             Ross, Franklin Pierce
             Birth: 22 Jul 1869 in Wind Ridge, Greene, Pennsylvania, USA
             Name: Ross, Franklin Pierce
             Res: 1935 in Oak Park, Cook, Illinois
             Res: 01 Apr 1940 in Oak Park, Cook, Illinois, United States
             Age: 70
             Marital Status: Married
             Relation to Head of House: Head

Source Title: Ancestry Family Trees
Repository: Ancestry.com

Citation: Ancestry Family Trees (Online publication - Provo, UT, USA: Ancestry.com. Original
             data: Family Tree files submitted by Ancestry members.), Ancestry.com, Ancestry Family
             Tree. Skiff, Blanche Alice
             Name: Skiff, Blanche Alice

Citation: Ancestry Family Trees (Online publication - Provo, UT, USA: Ancestry.com. Original
             data: Family Tree files submitted by Ancestry members.), Ancestry.com, Ancestry Family
             Tree. Coffin, Matthew Starbuck
             Name: Coffin, Matthew Starbuck

Citation: Ancestry Family Trees (Online publication - Provo, UT, USA: Ancestry.com. Original
             data: Family Tree files submitted by Ancestry members.), Ancestry.com, Ancestry Family
             Tree. Ross, Franklin Pierce
             Name: Ross, Franklin Pierce

Citation: Ancestry Family Trees (Online publication - Provo, UT, USA: Ancestry.com. Original
             data: Family Tree files submitted by Ancestry members.), Ancestry.com, Ancestry Family
             Tree. Boaz, Cyrus Tucker
             Name: Boaz, Cyrus Tucker

Citation: Ancestry Family Trees (Online publication - Provo, UT, USA: Ancestry.com. Original
             data: Family Tree files submitted by Ancestry members.), Ancestry.com, Ancestry Family
             Tree. Jannotta, Alfredo A
             Name: Jannotta, Alfredo A

Citation: Ancestry Family Trees (Online publication - Provo, UT, USA: Ancestry.com. Original
             data: Family Tree files submitted by Ancestry members.), Ancestry.com, Ancestry Family
             Tree. Coffin, Alice Virginia
             Name: Coffin, Alice Virginia

Citation: Ancestry Family Trees (Online publication - Provo, UT, USA: Ancestry.com. Original
             data: Family Tree files submitted by Ancestry members.), Ancestry.com, Ancestry Family
             Tree. Skiff, Vernon William.
             Name: Skiff, Vernon William

Citation: Ancestry Family Trees (Online publication - Provo, UT, USA: Ancestry.com. Original
             data: Family Tree files submitted by Ancestry members.), Ancestry.com, Ancestry Family
             Tree. Coffin, James.
             Name: Coffin, James.

Citation: Ancestry Family Trees (Online publication - Provo, UT, USA: Ancestry.com. Original
             data: Family Tree files submitted by Ancestry members.), Ancestry.com, Ancestry Family
             Tree. Starbuck, Sarah Sally.
             Name: Starbuck, Sarah Sally.

Citation: Ancestry Family Trees (Online publication - Provo, UT, USA: Ancestry.com. Original data: Family Tree files submitted by Ancestry members.), Ancestry.com, Ancestry Family Tree. Thompson, William Finley

Citation: Name: Thompson, William Finley
              Ancestry Family Trees (Online publication - Provo, UT, USA: Ancestry.com. Original data: Family Tree files submitted by Ancestry members.), Ancestry.com, Ancestry Family Tree. Thompson, John Handley
              Name: Thompson, John Handley

Citation: Ancestry Family Trees (Online publication - Provo, UT, USA: Ancestry.com. Original data: Family Tree files submitted by Ancestry members.), Ancestry.com, Ancestry Family Tree. McLoney, Margaret
              Name: McLoney, Margaret

Citation: Ancestry Family Trees (Online publication - Provo, UT, USA: Ancestry.com. Original data: Family Tree files submitted by Ancestry members.), Ancestry.com, Ancestry Family Tree. Reeves, Maria
              Name: Reeves, Maria

Citation: Ancestry Family Trees (Online publication - Provo, UT, USA: Ancestry.com. Original data: Family Tree files submitted by Ancestry members.), Ancestry.com, Ancestry Family Tree. Coffin, Grace Lucille
              Name: Coffin, Grace Lucille

Citation: Ancestry Family Trees (Online publication - Provo, UT, USA: Ancestry.com. Original data: Family Tree files submitted by Ancestry members.), Ancestry.com, Ancestry Family Tree. Coffin, Alice
              Name: Coffin, Alice

Citation: Ancestry Family Trees (Online publication - Provo, UT, USA: Ancestry.com. Original data: Family Tree files submitted by Ancestry members.), Ancestry.com, Ancestry Family Tree. Coffin, Frances
              Name: Coffin, Frances

Citation: Ancestry Family Trees (Online publication - Provo, UT, USA: Ancestry.com. Original data: Family Tree files submitted by Ancestry members.), Ancestry.com, Ancestry Family Tree.

Citation: Ancestry Family Trees (Online publication - Provo, UT, USA: Ancestry.com. Original data: Family Tree files submitted by Ancestry members.), Ancestry.com, Ancestry Family Tree. Thompson, Martha Ellen
              Name: Thompson, Martha Ellen

Citation: Ancestry Family Trees (Online publication - Provo, UT, USA: Ancestry.com. Original data: Family Tree files submitted by Ancestry members.), Ancestry.com, Ancestry Family Tree. Coffin, Jabez Hunt
              Name: Coffin, Jabez Hunt

Citation: Ancestry Family Trees (Online publication - Provo, UT, USA: Ancestry.com. Original data: Family Tree files submitted by Ancestry members.), Ancestry.com, Ancestry Family Tree. Coffin, Cyrus Floyd

Citation: Name: Coffin, Cyrus Floyd
              Ancestry Family Trees (Online publication - Provo, UT, USA: Ancestry.com. Original data: Family Tree files submitted by Ancestry members.), Ancestry.com, Ancestry Family Tree. Coffin, Mary Frances
              Name: Coffin, Mary Frances

Citation: Ancestry Family Trees (Online publication - Provo, UT, USA: Ancestry.com. Original data: Family Tree files submitted by Ancestry members.), Ancestry.com, Ancestry Family Tree. Coffin, Charles Thompson
Name: Coffin, Charles Thompson

Citation: Ancestry Family Trees (Online publication - Provo, UT, USA: Ancestry.com. Original data: Family Tree files submitted by Ancestry members.), Ancestry.com, Ancestry Family Tree. Coffin, Matthew Starbuck
Name: Coffin, Matthew Starbuck

Citation: Ancestry Family Trees (Online publication - Provo, UT, USA: Ancestry.com. Original data: Family Tree files submitted by Ancestry members.), Ancestry.com, Ancestry Family Tree. Coffin, Thompson
Name: Coffin, Thompson

Citation: Ancestry Family Trees (Online publication - Provo, UT, USA: Ancestry.com. Original data: Family Tree files submitted by Ancestry members.), Ancestry.com, Ancestry Family Tree. Coffin, George
Name: Coffin, George

Citation: Ancestry Family Trees (Online publication - Provo, UT, USA: Ancestry.com. Original data: Family Tree files submitted by Ancestry members.), Ancestry.com, Ancestry Family Tree. Marcks, Lillie Belle
Name: Marcks, Lillie Belle

Citation: Ancestry Family Trees (Online publication - Provo, UT, USA: Ancestry.com. Original data: Family Tree files submitted by Ancestry members.), Ancestry.com, Ancestry Family Tree. Coffin, William Barney
Name: Coffin, William Barney

Citation: Ancestry Family Trees (Online publication - Provo, UT, USA: Ancestry.com. Original data: Family Tree files submitted by Ancestry members.), Ancestry.com, Ancestry Family Tree.

Citation: Ancestry Family Trees (Online publication - Provo, UT, USA: Ancestry.com. Original data: Family Tree files submitted by Ancestry members.), Ancestry.com, Ancestry Family Tree. Coffin, Cyrus Sitkirk
Name: Coffin, Cyrus Sitkirk

Citation: Ancestry Family Trees (Online publication - Provo, UT, USA: Ancestry.com. Original data: Family Tree files submitted by Ancestry members.), Ancestry.com, Ancestry Family Tree. Coffin, Eunice
Name: Coffin, Eunice

Citation: Ancestry Family Trees (Online publication - Provo, UT, USA: Ancestry.com. Original data: Family Tree files submitted by Ancestry members.), Ancestry.com, Ancestry Family Tree. Coffin, Priscilla
Name: Coffin, Priscilla

Citation: Ancestry Family Trees (Online publication - Provo, UT, USA: Ancestry.com. Original data: Family Tree files submitted by Ancestry members.), Ancestry.com, Ancestry Family Tree. Coffin, Charlotte
Name: Coffin, Charlotte

Citation: Ancestry Family Trees (Online publication - Provo, UT, USA: Ancestry.com. Original data: Family Tree files submitted by Ancestry members.), Ancestry.com, Ancestry Family Tree. Starbuck, Lydia
Name: Starbuck, Lydia

Citation: Ancestry Family Trees (Online publication - Provo, UT, USA: Ancestry.com. Original data: Family Tree files submitted by Ancestry members.), Ancestry.com, Ancestry Family Tree. Ida C
Name: Ida C

Citation: Ancestry Family Trees (Online publication - Provo, UT, USA: Ancestry.com. Original data: Family Tree files submitted by Ancestry members.), Ancestry.com, Ancestry Family Tree. Skiff, Frank Vernon
Name: Skiff, Frank Vernon

Citation: Ancestry Family Trees (Online publication - Provo, UT, USA: Ancestry.com. Original data: Family Tree files submitted by Ancestry members.), Ancestry.com, Ancestry Family Tree. Skiff, Stella
Name: Skiff, Stella

Source Title: Army Register of Enlistments, 1798-1914 at Fold3
Repository: www.fold3.com

Citation: Army Register of Enlistments, 1798-1914 at Fold3, www.fold3.com, Page 99 – Army Register of Enlistments, 1798-1914. http://www.fold3.com/image/310950936/.
Boaz, Cyrus Tucker
Name: Boaz, Cyrus Tucker

Source Title: California, Death Index, 1905-1939
Repository: Ancestry.com

Citation: Ancestry.com, California, Death Index, 1905-1939 (Provo, UT, USA, Ancestry.com Operations, Inc., 2013), Ancestry.com. [Source citation includes media item(s)] Jannotta, Alfredo A

Citation: Ancestry.com, California, Death Index, 1905-1939 (Provo, UT, USA, Ancestry.com Operations, Inc., 2013), Ancestry.com. [Source citation includes media item(s)] Jannotta, Alfredo A
Birth: 20 Dec 1843 in Capua, Caserta, Campania, Italy
Death: 11 Apr 1913 in Los Angeles, Los Angeles, California
Age: 76
Name: Jannotta, Alfredo A

Source Title: City Directories - Los Angeles at Fold3
Repository: www.fold3.com

Citation: City Directories - Los Angeles at Fold3, www.fold3.com, Janes, Luther F (p. 739) – City Directories - Los Angeles. http://www.fold3.com/image/228902412/. Jannotta, Alfredo A
Name: Jannotta, Alfredo A

Source Title: Cook County, Illinois, Deaths Index, 1878-1922
Repository: Ancestry.com

Citation: Ancestry.com, Cook County, Illinois, Deaths Index, 1878-1922 (Provo, UT, USA, Ancestry.com Operations, Inc., 2011), Ancestry.com. Coffin, Mary Frances
Death: 30 Dec 1918 in Oak Park, , Illinois, USA
Age: 76
Birth: 25 Oct 1842 in Salem, Washington, Indiana, USA
Name: Coffin, Mary Frances
Burial: 01 Jan 1919 in Newton, Jasper County, Iowa, USA
Age: 76
Res: 633 N. East Ave.; Marital Status: Married

Source Title:	Cook County, Illinois, Marriages Index, 1871-1920
Repository:	Ancestry.com

Citation: Ancestry.com, Cook County, Illinois, Marriages Index, 1871-1920 (Provo, UT, USA, Ancestry.com Operations, Inc., 2011), Ancestry.com. Jannotta, Alfredo A
Birth: 20 Dec 1843 in Capua, Caserta, Campania, Italy
Name: Jannotta, Alfredo A
Marr: 25 Jul 1893 in Chicago, Cook, Illinois, USA
Skiff, Stella
Marr: 25 Jul 1893 in Chicago, Cook, Illinois, USA

Citation: Ancestry.com, Cook County, Illinois, Marriages Index, 1871-1920 (Provo, UT, USA, Ancestry.com Operations, Inc., 2011), Ancestry.com.
Jannotta, Alfredo A
Marr: 25 Jul 1893 in Chicago, Cook, Illinois, USA
Skiff, Stella
Birth: 29 Oct 1867 in Newton, Jasper, Iowa, USA
Name: Skiff, Stella
Marr: 25 Jul 1893 in Chicago, Cook, Illinois, USA

Source Title:	Florida, State Census, 1867-1945
Repository:	Ancestry.com

Citation: Ancestry.com, Florida, State Census, 1867-1945 (Provo, UT, USA, Ancestry.com Operations Inc., 2008), Ancestry.com. [Source citation includes media item(s)]
Skiff, Stella
Birth: 29 Oct 1867 in Newton, Jasper, Iowa, USA
Name: Skiff, Stella
Res: 1935 in Precinct 32, Polk, Florida
Age: 67
Relation to Head of House: Head
Relation to Head of House: Mother

Source Title:	Honolulu, Hawaii, Passenger and Crew Lists, 1900-1959
Repository:	Ancestry.com

Citation: Ancestry.com, Honolulu, Hawaii, Passenger and Crew Lists, 1900-1959 (Provo, UT, USA, Ancestry.com Operations, Inc., 2009), Ancestry.com, Repository Name: National Archives and Records Administration (NARA). [Source citation includes media item(s)]
Ross, Franklin Pierce
Birth: 22 Jul 1869 in Wind Ridge, Greene, Pennsylvania, USA
Name: Ross, Franklin Pierce
Orig: Illinois
Depart: 24 Jan 1931 in San Francisco, California
Age: 62
Arrive: 28 Jan 1931 in Honolulu, Hawaii
Age: 62

Source Title: **Illinois, Deaths and Stillbirths Index, 1916-1947**
Repository: **Ancestry.com**

Citation: Ancestry.com, Illinois, Deaths and Stillbirths Index, 1916-1947 (Provo, UT, USA,
Ancestry.com Operations, Inc., 2011), Ancestry.com.
Skiff, Vernon William
Birth: 23 Jan 1841 in Hume, Allegany, New York, USA
Death: 29 Apr 1926 in Oak Park, , Illinois, USA
Age: 85
Name: Skiff, Vernon William
Burial: 30 Apr 1926 in Newton, Iowa
Age: 85

Citation: Ancestry.com, Illinois, Deaths and Stillbirths Index, 1916-1947 (Provo, UT, USA,
Ancestry.com Operations, Inc., 2011), Ancestry.com.
Coffin, Mary Frances
Death: 30 Dec 1918 in Oak Park, , Illinois, USA
Age: 76
Birth: 25 Oct 1842 in Salem, Washington, Indiana, USA
Name: Coffin, Mary Frances
Res: Oak Park, Cook, Illinois; Marital Status: M
Burial: 01 Jan 1919 in Newton, Jasper County, Iowa, USA
Age: 76

Source Title: **Indiana, Marriage Collection, 1800-1941**
Repository: **Ancestry.com**

Citation: Ancestry.com, Indiana, Marriage Collection, 1800-1941 (Provo, UT, USA, Ancestry.com
Operations Inc., 2005), Ancestry.com, Book: Family History Library, Salt Lake City, UT;
Page: 1306388.
Coffin, Matthew Starbuck
Marr: 07 Nov 1841 in Newton, Buchanan, Iowa, USA
Thompson, Martha Ellen
Name: Thompson, Martha Ellen
Marr: 07 Nov 1841 in Newton, Buchanan, Iowa, USA

Citation: Ancestry.com, Indiana, Marriage Collection, 1800-1941 (Provo, UT, USA, Ancestry.com
Operations Inc., 2005), Ancestry.com, Book: Family History Library, Salt Lake City, UT;
Page: 1306388.
Coffin, Matthew Starbuck
Marr: 13 Mar 1832 in Washington Reeves, Maria
Name: Reeves, Maria
Marr: 13 Mar 1832 in Washington

Citation: Ancestry.com, Indiana, Marriage Collection, 1800-1941 (Provo, UT, USA, Ancestry.com
Operations Inc., 2005), Ancestry.com, Book: Family History Library, Salt Lake City, UT;
Page: 1306388.
Coffin, Matthew Starbuck
Name: Coffin, Matthew Starbuck Marr: 13 Mar 1832 in Washington
Reeves, Maria

Citation: Ancestry.com, Indiana, Marriage Collection, 1800-1941 (Provo, UT, USA, Ancestry.com
Operations Inc., 2005), Ancestry.com, Book: Family History Library, Salt Lake City, UT;
Page: 1306388.
Reeves, Maria
Marr: 13 Mar 1832 in Washington

Citation: Ancestry.com, Indiana, Marriage Collection, 1800-1941 (Provo, UT, USA, Ancestry.com
Operations Inc., 2005), Ancestry.com, Book: Family History Library, Salt Lake City, UT;
Page: 1306388.
Coffin, Matthew Starbuck
Name: Coffin, Matthew Starbuck
Marr: 07 Nov 1841 in Newton, Buchanan, Iowa, USA
Thompson, Martha Ellen
Marr: 07 Nov 1841 in Newton, Buchanan, Iowa, USA

Source Title: Iowa, State Census Collection, 1836-1925
Repository: Ancestry.com

Citation: Ancestry.com, Iowa, State Census Collection, 1836-1925 (Provo, UT, USA,
Ancestry.com Operations Inc., 2007), Ancestry.com. [Source citation includes media
item(s)]
Thompson, Martha Ellen
Birth: 20 May 1819 in Charleston, Clark, IN
Name: Thompson, Martha Ellen
Res: 1856 in Jasper, Iowa
Age: 37
Marital Status: Married

Citation: Ancestry.com, Iowa, State Census Collection, 1836-1925 (Provo, UT, USA,
Ancestry.com Operations Inc., 2007), Ancestry.com. [Source citation includes media
item(s)]
Skiff, Stella
Birth: 29 Oct 1867 in Newton, Jasper, Iowa, USA
Name: Skiff, Stella
Res: 1885 in Jasper, Iowa
Age: 17

Citation: Ancestry.com, Iowa, State Census Collection, 1836-1925 (Provo, UT, USA,
Ancestry.com Operations Inc., 2007), Ancestry.com. [Source citation includes media
item(s)]
Coffin, Matthew Starbuck
Birth: 25 Mar 1811 in Deep River, Guilford, NC
Name: Coffin, Matthew Starbuck
Res: 1856 in Jasper, Iowa
Age: 45
Marital Status: Married

Citation:
Ancestry.com, Iowa, State Census Collection, 1836-1925 (Provo, UT, USA,
Ancestry.com Operations Inc., 2007), Ancestry.com. [Source citation includes media
item(s)]
Skiff, Blanche Alice
Birth: Abt. 1873 in Newton, Jasper, Iowa, USA
Name: Skiff, Blanche Alice
Res: 1885 in Jasper, Iowa
Age: 12

Citation: Ancestry.com, Iowa, State Census Collection, 1836-1925 (Provo, UT, USA, Ancestry.com Operations Inc., 2007), Ancestry.com. [Source citation includes media item(s)]
Coffin, Alice Virginia
Birth: 29 Mar 1848 in Louisville, Kentucky
Name: Coffin, Alice Virginia
Res: 1885 in Jasper, Iowa
Age: 36; Marital Status: Single

Citation: Ancestry.com, Iowa, State Census Collection, 1836-1925 (Provo, UT, USA, Ancestry.com Operations Inc., 2007), Ancestry.com. [Source citation includes media item(s)]
Coffin, Alice Virginia
Birth: 29 Mar 1848 in Louisville, Kentucky
Name: Coffin, Alice Virginia
Res: 1856 in Jasper, Iowa
Age: 8

Citation: Ancestry.com, Iowa, State Census Collection, 1836-1925 (Provo, UT, USA, Ancestry.com Operations Inc., 2007), Ancestry.com. [Source citation includes media item(s)]
Skiff, Vernon William
Birth: 23 Jan 1841 in Hume, Allegany, New York, USA
Name: Skiff, Vernon William
Res: 1885 in Jasper, Iowa
Age: 44
Marital Status: Married

Citation: Ancestry.com, Iowa, State Census Collection, 1836-1925 (Provo, UT, USA, Ancestry.com Operations Inc., 2007), Ancestry.com. [Source citation includes media item(s)]
Coffin, Mary Frances
Birth: 25 Oct 1842 in Salem, Washington, Indiana, USA
Name: Coffin, Mary Frances
Res: 1856 in Jasper, Iowa
Age: 13

Citation: Ancestry.com, Iowa, State Census Collection, 1836-1925 (Provo, UT, USA, Ancestry.com Operations Inc., 2007), Ancestry.com. [Source citation includes media item(s)]
Coffin, Mary Frances
Birth: 25 Oct 1842 in Salem, Washington, Indiana, USA
Name: Coffin, Mary Frances
Res: 1885 in Jasper, Iowa
Age: 40
Marital Status: Married

Citation: Ancestry.com, Iowa, State Census Collection, 1836-1925 (Provo, UT, USA, Ancestry.com Operations Inc., 2007), Ancestry.com. [Source citation includes media item(s)]
Coffin, Charles Thompson
Birth: 25 Sep 1850 in Salem, Washington, Indiana, USA
Name: Coffin, Charles Thompson
Res: 1856 in Jasper, Iowa
Age: 4

Citation: Ancestry.com, Iowa, State Census Collection, 1836-1925 (Provo, UT, USA,
             Ancestry.com Operations Inc., 2007), Ancestry.com. [Source citation includes media
             item(s)]
             Coffin, Matthew Starbuck
             Birth: 30 Mar 1853 in Salem, Washington, Indiana, USA
             Name: Coffin, Matthew Starbuck
             Res: 1856 in Jasper, Iowa
             Age: 3

Citation: Ancestry.com, Iowa, State Census Collection, 1836-1925 (Provo, UT, USA,
             Ancestry.com Operations Inc., 2007), Ancestry.com. [Source citation includes media
             item(s)]
             Skiff, Frank Vernon
             Birth: 03 Jul 1869 in Newton, Jasper, Iowa, USA
             Name: Skiff, Frank Vernon
             Res: 1885 in Jasper, Iowa
             Age: 15

Source Title: Iowa, State Census, 1895
Repository: Ancestry.com

Citation: Ancestry.com, Iowa, State Census, 1895 (Provo, UT, USA, Ancestry.com Operations
             Inc., 2003), Ancestry.com.
             Skiff, Blanche Alice
             Birth: Abt. 1873 in Newton, Jasper, Iowa, USA
             Name: Skiff, Blanche Alice
             Res: 1895 in First Ward, Jasper, Iowa
             Age: 22

Citation: Ancestry.com, Iowa, State Census, 1895 (Provo, UT, USA, Ancestry.com Operations
             Inc., 2003), Ancestry.com.
             Skiff, Frank Vernon
             Birth: 03 Jul 1869 in Newton, Jasper, Iowa, USA
             Name: Skiff, Frank Vernon
             Res: 1895 in First Ward, Jasper, Iowa

Citation: Age: 25
             Ancestry.com, Iowa, State Census, 1895 (Provo, UT, USA, Ancestry.com Operations
             Inc., 2003), Ancestry.com.
             Skiff, Vernon William
             Birth: 23 Jan 1841 in Hume, Allegany, New York, USA
             Name: Skiff, Vernon William
             Res: 1895 in First Ward, Jasper, Iowa
             Age: 54

Citation: Ancestry.com, Iowa, State Census, 1895 (Provo, UT, USA, Ancestry.com Operations
             Inc., 2003), Ancestry.com.
             Coffin, Mary Frances
             Birth: 25 Oct 1842 in Salem, Washington, Indiana, USA
             Name: Coffin, Mary Frances
             Res: 1895 in First Ward, Jasper, Iowa
             Age: 52

Source Title: **Kansas State Census Collection, 1855-1925**
Repository: **Ancestry.com**

Citation: Ancestry.com., Kansas State Census Collection, 1855-1925 (Provo, UT, USA, Ancestry.com Operations Inc., 2009), Ancestry.com. [Source citation includes media item(s)]
Marcks, Lillie Belle
Birth: 07 Jul 1862 in Ohio
Name: Marcks, Lillie Belle
Res: 01 Mar 1875 in Sherman, Leavenworth, Kansas
Age: 12

Citation: Ancestry.com., Kansas State Census Collection, 1855-1925 (Provo, UT, USA, Ancestry.com Operations Inc., 2009), Ancestry.com. [Source citation includes media item(s)]
Coffin, Frances
Birth: 31 May 1882 in Kansas, United States
Name: Coffin, Frances
Res: 01 Mar 1895 in Topeka Ward 2, Shawnee, Kansas
Age: 13

Source Title: **Massachusetts, Town and Vital Records, 1620-1988**
Repository: **Ancestry.com**

Citation: Ancestry.com, Massachusetts, Town and Vital Records, 1620-1988 (Provo, UT, USA, Ancestry.com Operations, Inc., 2011), Ancestry.com. [Source citation includes media item(s)]
Starbuck, Sarah Sally
Birth: 26 Jun 1788 in Nantucket Island, Nantucket, Massachusetts, United States
Age: 0
Name: Starbuck, Sarah Sally

Source Title: **Millennium File**
Repository: **Ancestry.com**

Citation: Heritage Consulting, Millennium File (Provo, UT, USA, Ancestry.com Operations Inc., 2003), Ancestry.com.
Coffin, James
Birth: 22 Jun 1783 in New Garden, Guilford, North Carolina, United States
Death: 29 Mar 1838 in Blue River,Indiana
Age: 54
Name: Coffin, James
Marr: 10 Oct 1805 in Deep River, Guilford, North Carolina, United States
Starbuck, Sarah Sally
Marr: 10 Oct 1805 in Deep River, Guilford, North Carolina, United States

Citation: Heritage Consulting, Millennium File (Provo, UT, USA, Ancestry.com Operations Inc., 2003), Ancestry.com.
Coffin, James
Marr: 10 Oct 1805 in Deep River, Guilford, North Carolina, United States
Starbuck, Sarah Sally
Death: 23 Aug 1822 in Blue River, Washington, Indiana, United States
Age: 34
Birth: 26 Jun 1788 in Nantucket Island, Nantucket, Massachusetts, United States
Age: 0
Name: Starbuck, Sarah Sally
Marr: 10 Oct 1805 in Deep River, Guilford, North Carolina, United States

Source Title: New York, Passenger Lists, 1820-1957
Repository: Ancestry.com

Citation: Ancestry.com, New York, Passenger Lists, 1820-1957 (Provo, UT, USA, Ancestry.com Operations, Inc., 2010), Ancestry.com, Year: 1921. [Source citation includes media item(s)]
Skiff, Frank Vernon
Birth: 03 Jul 1869 in Newton, Jasper, Iowa, USA Name: Skiff, Frank Vernon
Depart: Southampton
Arrive: 09 Sep 1921 in New York, New York
Age: 51

Citation: Ancestry.com, New York, Passenger Lists, 1820-1957 (Provo, UT, USA, Ancestry.com Operations, Inc., 2010), Ancestry.com, Year: 1922. [Source citation includes media item(s)]
Skiff, Stella
Birth: 29 Oct 1867 in Newton, Jasper, Iowa, USA Name: Skiff, Stella
Depart: Liverpool, England
Arrive: 22 Oct 1922 in New York, New York
Age: 54 Years 5 Months

Citation: Ancestry.com, New York, Passenger Lists, 1820-1957 (Provo, UT, USA, Ancestry.com Operations, Inc., 2010), Ancestry.com, Year: 1926. [Source citation includes media item(s)]
Skiff, Blanche Alice
Birth: Abt. 1873 in Newton, Jasper, Iowa, USA Name: Skiff, Blanche Alice
Depart: Southampton, England
Arrive: 10 Apr 1926 in New York, New York
Age: 53

Citation: Ancestry.com, New York, Passenger Lists, 1820-1957 (Provo, UT, USA, Ancestry.com Operations, Inc., 2010), Ancestry.com, Year: 1926. [Source citation includes media item(s)]
Ross, Franklin Pierce
Birth: 22 Jul 1869 in Wind Ridge, Greene, Pennsylvania, USA Name: Ross, Franklin Pierce

Citation: Ancestry.com, New York, Passenger Lists, 1820-1957 (Provo, UT, USA, Ancestry.com Operations, Inc., 2010), Ancestry.com, Year: 1926. [Source citation includes media item(s)]
Ross, Franklin Pierce
Depart: Southampton, England
Arrive: 10 Apr 1926 in New York, New York
Age: 56

Citation: Ancestry.com, New York, Passenger Lists, 1820-1957 (Provo, UT, USA, Ancestry.com Operations, Inc., 2010), Ancestry.com, Year: 1927. [Source citation includes media item(s)]
Skiff, Stella
Birth: 29 Oct 1867 in Newton, Jasper, Iowa, USA
Name: Skiff, Stella
Arrive: 10 May 1927 in New York, New York
Age: 59
Depart: London, England

Citation: Ancestry.com, New York, Passenger Lists, 1820-1957 (Provo, UT, USA, Ancestry.com Operations, Inc., 2010), Ancestry.com, Year: 1935. [Source citation includes media item(s)]
Ida C
Birth: Abt. 1871 in Pennsylvania
Depart: Cherbourg, France
Arrive: 16 Sep 1935 in New York, New York
Age: 64
Name: Ida C

Source Title: **Selected U.S. Headstone Photos**
Repository: **Ancestry.com**

Citation: Ancestry.com, Selected U.S. Headstone Photos (Provo, UT, USA, Ancestry.com Operations Inc., 2005), Ancestry.com. [Source citation includes media item(s)]
Coffin, Frances
Birth: 31 May 1882 in Kansas, United States
Death: 17 May 1974 in United States
Age at Death: 92
Name: Coffin, Frances

Source Title: **Texas Death Certificates at Fold3**
Repository: **www.fold3.com**

Citation: Texas Death Certificates at Fold3, www.fold3.com, Boaz, Cyrus Tucker - Texas Death Certificates. http://www.fold3.com/image/91199083/.
Boaz, Cyrus Tucker
Name: Boaz, Cyrus Tucker

Source Title: **The Ogden Standard-Examiner at Newspapers.com**
Repository: **www.newspapers.com**

Citation: The Ogden Standard-Examiner at Newspapers.com, www.newspapers.com, Page 1 - The Ogden Standard-Examiner. http://www.newspapers.com/image/#27140585.
Skiff, Frank Vernon
Name: Skiff, Frank Vernon

Source Title: **U.S. City Directories, 1821-1989**
Repository: **Ancestry.com**

Citation: Ancestry.com, U.S. City Directories, 1821-1989 (Provo, UT, USA, Ancestry.com Operations, Inc., 2011), Ancestry.com. [Source citation includes media item(s)]
Coffin, Charles Thompson
Name: Coffin, Charles Thompson
Res: 1902 in Emporia, Kansas, USA

Citation: Ancestry.com, U.S. City Directories, 1821-1989 (Provo, UT, USA, Ancestry.com Operations, Inc., 2011), Ancestry.com. [Source citation includes media item(s)]
Marcks, Lillie Belle
Name: Marcks, Lillie Belle
Res: 1902 in Emporia, Kansas, USA

Citation: Ancestry.com, U.S. City Directories, 1821-1989 (Provo, UT, USA, Ancestry.com
               Operations, Inc., 2011), Ancestry.com. [Source citation includes media item(s)]
               Jannotta, Alfredo A
               Name: Jannotta, Alfredo A
               Res: 1910 in Oak Park, Cook, Illinois, USA
               Age: 66
               Marital Status: Married
               Relation to Head of House: Head

Citation: Ancestry.com, U.S. City Directories, 1821-1989 (Provo, UT, USA, Ancestry.com
               Operations, Inc., 2011), Ancestry.com. [Source citation includes media item(s)]
               Skiff, Stella
               Name: Skiff, Stella
               Res: 1910 in Oak Park, Cook, Illinois, USA
               Age: 42
               Marital Status: Married
               Relation to Head of House: Wife

Citation: Ancestry.com, U.S. City Directories, 1821-1989 (Provo, UT, USA, Ancestry.com
               Operations, Inc., 2011), Ancestry.com. [Source citation includes media item(s)]
               Ida C
               Name: Ida C.
               Res: 1929 in West Palm Beach, Florida, USA

Citation: Ancestry.com, U.S. City Directories, 1821-1989 (Provo, UT, USA, Ancestry.com
               Operations, Inc., 2011), Ancestry.com. [Source citation includes media item(s)]
               Ida C
               Name: Ida C.
               Res: 1950 in West Palm Beach, Florida, USA

Citation: Ancestry.com, U.S. City Directories, 1821-1989 (Provo, UT, USA, Ancestry.com
               Operations, Inc., 2011), Ancestry.com. [Source citation includes media item(s)]
               Skiff, Frank Vernon
               Name: Skiff, Frank Vernon
               Res: 1929 in West Palm Beach, Florida, USA

Source Title: U.S. Naturalization Record Indexes, 1791-1992 (Indexed in World Archives Project)
Repository: Ancestry.com

Citation: Ancestry.com, U.S. Naturalization Record Indexes, 1791-1992 (Indexed in World
               Archives Project) (Provo, UT, USA, Ancestry.com Operations, Inc., 2010), Ancestry.com
               National Archives and Records Administration (NARA); Washington, D.C.; Soundex
               Index to Naturalization Petitions for the United States District and Circuit Courts, Northern
               District of Illinois and Immigration and Naturalization Service District 9, 1840-19. [Source
               citation includes media item(s)]
               Jannotta, Alfredo A
               Birth: 20 Dec 1843 in Capua, Caserta, Campania, Italy
               Name: Jannotta, Alfredo A
               Res: Illinois, Indiana, Wisconsin, Iowa
               Res: Illinois
               Arrive: 1865
               Age: 22
               Civil: 22 Oct 1903
               Age: 59

Source Title: **U.S. Passport Applications, 1795-1925**
Repository: **Ancestry.com**

Citation: Ancestry.com, U.S. Passport Applications, 1795-1925 (Provo, UT, USA, Ancestry.com Operations, Inc., 2007), Ancestry.com, National Archives and Records Administration (NARA); Washington D.C.; Passport Applications, January 2, 1906 - March 31, 1925; Collection Number: ARC Identifier 583830 / MLR Number A1 534; NARA Series: M1490; Roll #: 1526. [Source citation includes media item(s)]
Skiff, Frank Vernon
Birth: 03 Jul 1869 in Newton, Jasper, Iowa, USA
Name: Skiff, Frank Vernon
Civil: 15 Mar 1921
Age: 51
Res: Millburn, New Jersey

Citation: Ancestry.com, U.S. Passport Applications, 1795-1925 (Provo, UT, USA, Ancestry.com Operations, Inc., 2007), Ancestry.com, National Archives and Records Administration (NARA); Washington D.C.; Passport Applications, January 2, 1906 - March 31, 1925; Collection Number: ARC Identifier 583830 / MLR Number A1 534; NARA Series: M1490; Roll #: 1838. [Source citation includes media item(s)]
Skiff, Stella
Birth: 29 Oct 1867 in Newton, Jasper, Iowa, USA
Name: Skiff, Stella
Res: Wheaton, Illinois
Civil: 24 Feb 1922
Age: 54

Citation: Ancestry.com, U.S. Passport Applications, 1795-1925 (Provo, UT, USA, Ancestry.com Operations, Inc., 2007), Ancestry.com, National Archives and Records Administration (NARA); Washington D.C.; Passport Applications, January 2, 1906 - March 31, 1925; Collection Number: ARC Identifier 583830 / MLR Number A1 534; NARA Series: M1490; Roll #: 2512. [Source citation includes media item(s)]
Ross, Franklin Pierce
Birth: 22 Jul 1869 in Wind Ridge, Greene, Pennsylvania, USA
Name: Ross, Franklin Pierce
Civil: 13 May 1924
Age: 54
Res: Oak Park, Illinois

Source Title: **U.S., Civil War Soldier Records and Profiles, 1861-1865**
Repository: **Ancestry.com**

Citation: Historical Data Systems, comp, U.S., Civil War Soldier Records and Profiles, 1861-1865 (Provo, UT, USA, Ancestry.com Operations Inc., 2009), Ancestry.com.
Skiff, Vernon William
Death: 29 Apr 1926 in Oak Park, , Illinois, USA
Age: 85
Name: Skiff, Vernon William
Miltry: Iowa

Source Title: U.S., Social Security Death Index, 1935-Current
Repository: Ancestry.com

Citation: Ancestry.com, U.S., Social Security Death Index, 1935-Current (Provo, UT, USA, Ancestry.com Operations Inc., 2011), Ancestry.com, Number: 460-86-7764; Issue State: Texas; Issue Date: 1965.
Coffin, Frances
Birth: 31 May 1882 in Kansas, United States Death: 17 May 1974 in United States
Age at Death: 92
Name: Coffin, Frances
Civil: Texas

Source Title: Web: Boyd County, Kentucky, Ashland Daily Independent Obituary Index, 1922-1945, 1970-1973, 1998-2010
Repository: Ancestry.com

Citation: Ancestry.com, Web: Boyd County, Kentucky, Ashland Daily Independent Obituary Index, 1922-1945, 1970-1973, 1998-2010 (Provo, UT, USA, Ancestry.com Operations, Inc., 2011), Ancestry.com.
Skiff, Frank Vernon
Death: 03 Jun 1933 in New York City, New York, New York, USA
Name: Skiff, Frank Vernon

Source Title: Web: Indiana, Find A Grave Index, 1800-2012
Repository: Ancestry.com

Citation: Ancestry.com, Web: Indiana, Find A Grave Index, 1800-2012 (Provo, UT, USA, Ancestry.com Operations, Inc., 2012), Ancestry.com.
Coffin, James
Birth: 22 Jun 1783 in New Garden, Guilford, North Carolina, United States
Death: 29 Mar 1838 in Blue River,Indiana
Age: 54
Burial: Salem (Washington County), Washington County, Indiana, USA
Name: Coffin, James

Source Title: Web: Iowa, Find A Grave Index, 1800-2012
Repository: Ancestry.com

Citation: Ancestry.com, Web: Iowa, Find A Grave Index, 1800-2012 (Provo, UT, USA, Ancestry.com Operations, Inc., 2012), Ancestry.com.
Marcks, Lillie Belle
Death: 14 Feb 1937 in , , , USA
Age: 74
Birth: 07 Jul 1862 in Ohio
Name: Marcks, Lillie Belle
Burial: Newton, Jasper County, Iowa, USA

Citation: Ancestry.com, Web: Iowa, Find A Grave Index, 1800-2012 (Provo, UT, USA, Ancestry.com Operations, Inc., 2012), Ancestry.com.
Coffin, Matthew Starbuck
Death: 16 Apr 1873 in Newton, Jasper, Iowa, United States
Age: 20
Birth: 30 Mar 1853 in Salem, Washington, Indiana, USA
Name: Coffin, Matthew Starbuck
Burial: Newton, Jasper County, Iowa, USA

Citation: Ancestry.com, Web: Iowa, Find A Grave Index, 1800-2012 (Provo, UT, USA, Ancestry.com Operations, Inc., 2012), Ancestry.com.
Coffin, Alice Virginia
Birth: 29 Mar 1848 in Louisville, Kentucky
Death: 28 Jul 1888 in Newton, Jasper, Iowa
Age: 40
Name: Coffin, Alice Virginia
Burial: Newton, Jasper County, Iowa, USA

Citation: Ancestry.com, Web: Iowa, Find A Grave Index, 1800-2012 (Provo, UT, USA, Ancestry.com Operations, Inc., 2012), Ancestry.com.
Skiff, Vernon William
Birth: 23 Jan 1841 in Hume, Allegany, New York, USA
Death: 29 Apr 1926 in Oak Park, , Illinois, USA
Age: 85
Name: Skiff, Vernon William
Burial: 30 Apr 1926 in Newton, Iowa
Age: 85

Citation: Ancestry.com, Web: Iowa, Find A Grave Index, 1800-2012 (Provo, UT, USA, Ancestry.com Operations, Inc., 2012), Ancestry.com.
Thompson, Martha Ellen
Birth: 20 May 1819 in Charleston, Clark, IN
Death: 30 Jul 1857 in ,Washington, Indiana, USA
Age: 38

Citation: Ancestry.com, Web: Iowa, Find A Grave Index, 1800-2012 (Provo, UT, USA, Ancestry.com Operations, Inc., 2012), Ancestry.com.
Thompson, Martha Ellen
Name: Thompson, Martha Ellen
Burial: Newton, Jasper County, Iowa, USA

Citation: Ancestry.com, Web: Iowa, Find A Grave Index, 1800-2012 (Provo, UT, USA, Ancestry.com Operations, Inc., 2012), Ancestry.com.
Coffin, Mary Frances
Death: 30 Dec 1918 in Oak Park, , Illinois, USA
Age: 76
Birth: 25 Oct 1842 in Salem, Washington, Indiana, USA
Name: Coffin, Mary Frances
Burial: 01 Jan 1919 in Newton, Jasper County, Iowa, USA
Age: 76

Citation: Ancestry.com, Web: Iowa, Find A Grave Index, 1800-2012 (Provo, UT, USA, Ancestry.com Operations, Inc., 2012), Ancestry.com.
Coffin, Charles Thompson
Birth: 25 Sep 1850 in Salem, Washington, Indiana, USA
Name: Coffin, Charles Thompson
Death: 31 May 1928 in United States
Age: 77
Burial: Newton, Jasper County, Iowa, USA

Citation: Ancestry.com, Web: Iowa, Find A Grave Index, 1800-2012 (Provo, UT, USA, Ancestry.com Operations, Inc., 2012), Ancestry.com.
Coffin, Matthew Starbuck
Death: 10 Mar 1884 in Newton, Jasper, IA
Age: 72
Birth: 25 Mar 1811 in Deep River, Guilford, NC
Name: Coffin, Matthew Starbuck
Burial: Newton, Jasper County, Iowa, USA

Source Title: **Web: Texas, Find A Grave Index, 1761-2012**
Repository: **Ancestry.com**

Citation: Ancestry.com, Web: Texas, Find A Grave Index, 1761-2012 (Provo, UT, USA, Ancestry.com Operations, Inc., 2012), Ancestry.com.
Coffin, Frances
Birth: 31 May 1882 in Kansas, United States
Death: 17 May 1974 in United States
Age at Death: 92
Name: Coffin, Frances
Burial: Fort Worth, Tarrant County, Texas, USA

Chapter 5: Marie Suela Pearson

Marie Suela Pearson

Marie Suela Pearson, or Suela as she was known to her P.E.O. sisters, was the daughter of a homeopathic physician, Dr. Clement Pearson and Eleanor McKinley Rose Pearson.

Opening his medical practice a mere 16 months before Suela was born; Dr. Pearson was one of the founding members of the International Hahnemannian Association. This Association was dedicated to the task of preserving the tenets of Hahnemann's homoeopathy, and existed from its founding 1880 until 1959.

We find Clement via the 1850 Census living in Wellsville, Ohio with wife Ellen, and sons Horace and William. However, in 1860, the family is located in Mount Pleasant, Iowa and consists of Clement, Ellen, William and Suela. Somewhere between 1850 and 1860, Suela's brother Horace probably died. It is unknown at the time of this writing if Horace died before or after Suela's birth in 1851.

Suela was a second cousin to the 25th President of the United States, William McKinley, Jr. who served as President from March 1897 to September 1901. Interestingly, the McKinley and Rose family inter-married a number of times. In fact, Suela's grandparents, James Rose and Martha McKinley Rose, and William McKinley Jr.'s grandparents, James McKinley and Mary Rose McKinley were each siblings. Suela shared great-grandparents, David and Sarah McKinley, with President William McKinley. Newspaper reports indicated Suela's family were "frequent visitors" to the White House.

Both Suela and her mother, Eleanor, became members of the Daughters of the American Revolution ("DAR") as well as the Daughters of 1812, linking their heritage to patriots who fought in those wars. Per the Lineage book, *National Society of the Daughters of the American Revolution,* published in 1908, Suela's DAR membership is tied to David McKinley (1755-1840),"who enlisted in the Flying Camp, 1776. His company was detailed at Fort Washington and all but he were captured. He served in the defense of Paulus Hook. He applied for a pension, 1832, and it was allowed for twenty-one months' actual service as private in the Pennsylvania Line."

As evidenced by Dr. Pearson's signature on a Civil War Veterans pensioner's claim record on May 13, 1857, the Pearson family appears to have settled in Mount Pleasant, Iowa by 1857. In 1866, at the age of 15, Suela entered Iowa Wesleyan as a freshman. Her decision to pursue the comprehensive classical course at Iowa Wesleyan resulted in her being a student for five years and graduating with her A.B. degree at the age of 19, in 1871.

William, Suela's brother also graduates from Iowa Wesleyan, with an A.B. degree in 1868. He then graduates with a Doctor of Judicial Science degree from Harvard University in 1871. In 1876 he marries Grace Darling Spaulding; there is no evidence of their having had any children.

Suela married Frank Harral Penfield on 2 September 1874. She and Frank have two children, Rose Marie, in July 1875, when Suela was 23 and two years later, Francis Pearson, in July of 1877.

We find the Penfield family living in Cleveland, Ohio on Euclid Avenue in the 1880 Census. The family listed includes Suela's mother, Eleanor (Ellen), who may have been visiting, or perhaps living with the family permanently, at the time of the Census. It has been reported that Mrs. John D. Rockefeller, wife of the president of Standard Oil, was not only godmother to Rose Penfield, but took Suela under her wing within the social community of Cleveland. Historical records indicate that Frank and John Rockefeller had some business dealings. During this period of her life, Suela became known for her singing, her charm and her elegant entertainments.

Further investigation suggests Suela may have had fostered social connections through her uncle, William G. Rose, who was Mayor of Cleveland from 1877 to 1878 and again from 1891 to 1892.

On a side note, it's interesting to note that history does often repeat itself…as reflected by William Rose's statement during his Mayoral inaugural address, which occurred in the aftermath the financial panic of 1873: "The enormous amount of municipal debt, the present low rate of wages, the vast number of men and women out of employment, and the difficult experienced by many of our most substantial citizens in meeting their tax obligations and providing the comforts and even the necessaries of life, all combine to impress upon those in authority the necessity of scrupulous care and fidelity in the economic management of every department of our municipal government." This sounds similar to what happened to our country's economy in the 1930's and again to what has been experienced since 2008.

Suela is 35 when her father dies in January of 1886. From that point forward, it appears that Eleanor and Suela live in the same household.

According to the *Out of the Heart, A Century of P.E.O. History*, by Stella Clapp, Suela was contacted, perhaps in 1890, by her classmate Ella Kilpatrick Dunwiddie, wife to the then commandant of the Iowa Wesleyan University Cadet Corp. Mrs. Dinwiddie desired Suela to send something that might be presented to the best drill cadet corps of the year. Suela responded with a gold badge. This badge was designed especially for the University Cadet Corps. At the top of the badge were the stylized letters "P.E.O." This badge now has a home in the P.E.O. Memorial Room at Iowa Wesleyan.

Sometime between 1891 and 1895, when Suela was between the ages of 40 & 44, she and Frank divorce, for in June of 1895 records indicate Frank married Josephine Blood Voak.

Frank goes on to live in Ohio with Josephine as evidenced in the 1910 Census. However, by 1920 he is recorded living with his step-son, Asa Volk's family. He is again found as living with Asa's family in 1930. Documentation indicates Frank died on 17 November 1931.

Suela, however, lives a very different life after her divorce.

In December of 1900 a news article appears in the New York Times about a process server's attempt to deliver papers to Rose Penfield, who was living with her mother and grandmother in New York City. Apparently, the process server was undaunted by the attempts to turn him away claiming that Rose had smallpox. He marches into the house and upstairs to deliver the papers despite the warnings.

In September of 1901, her mother's first cousin, and her second cousin, President William McKinley,Jr., was assassinated.

A separate newspaper article, which appears in 1911, alludes to a report that in June of 1901 Suela had appeared in court for bankruptcy proceedings.

In October of 1901, Suela's son, Frank Pearson Penfield, then a student at Yale University, dies in at the age of 24 after undergoing surgery.

During her life, Suela, known for her signing abilities, must have kept up her interest in music, as a copy of a piece of sheet music, *Faithful*, dated 1902 was discovered in February 2014 for sale on eBay. The sheet music indicates the music was written by Alfred Solman, the words by Marie Suela Penfield and was produced by W.H. Anstead. Of particular note is that the piece was "Respectfully dedicated to Mr. F. Freeman Proctor, Jr."

Records indicate that F. Freeman Proctor, Jr., born in 1880, was the son of Frederick Freeman Proctor (F.F. Proctor), a successful theater and vaudeville circuit manager. It's is unknown if the dedication came from Mr. Solman, Belle H. Anstead (doing business as W.H. Anstead), or Suela. However, it can be noted that F. Freeman Proctor's mother, Mary Ann Proctor and Suela's son, Frank both died in the fall of 1901, shortly before this song was published.

By July of 1911 we find the newspaper headline: "*Mrs. Penfield Now Penniless She is Divorced Wife of Cleveland Oil Millionaire Fought Against Poverty Woman Who Once Spent $25,000 a Year Was Forced to Borrow Car Fare From Friends*" (Note that $25,000 in 1911 is equivalent to just under $610,000 in today's dollars.) The article relates how Suela, her mother and her daughter reportedly felt forced to leave their home due to financial hardships.

While Suela's life may not have seemed to be the one she imagined who can say? Perhaps, she ultimately lived exactly as she wanted. The music lyrics written by Suela for the 1902 song "Faithful," may have been a realization of a "dream come true" for her.

Whatever else one can say about Suela, she appeared to have had an inner pioneering spirit to keep going, even as life through her curve balls.

The Cleveland Ohio City Directory for 1914 Suela is listed as the "widow" of Frank Penfield., living at 1789 E. 65th NE, in Cleveland. Although, other records suggest that he lived well beyond 1914 until 1931.

For many years, Suela and her daughter Rose cared for Suela's mother, Ellen, until her death in 1917.

Suela herself died on 22 September 1920. Her daughter Marie Rose, a member of P.E.O. Chapter AH, Ohio, never married and died in 1962. Of note is that the birth year engraved on Marie Rose's memorial stone, appears to be incorrectly engraved as 1877 rather than 1875. Rose is buried next to Suela at Lakewood Cemetery in Cleveland, Ohio. The Cleveland Reciprocity Bureau of P.E.O. organized a "Special Visit to Suela" as a way of honoring Suela just prior to the opening of the 2011 Ohio State Convention.

Marie Suela Pearson Penfield – Life Events

DATE	EVENT	AGE
24 August 1851	Born: Salem, Columbiana, Ohio	
June 1860	Residence: Mount Pleasant, Henry, Iowa	9
September 1866	Entered Iowa Wesleyan	15
21 January 1869	P.E.O. Founded	17
July 1870	Residence: Mount Pleasant, Henry, Iowa	18
June 1871	Graduated Iowa Wesleyan A.B. degree	19
About 1871-1873	Moved with family to Washington, D.C.	19-20
1874	Honorary A.M. degree awarded	22
2 September 1874	Married Frank Harral Penfield	23
24 July 1875	Daughter: Rose Marie Penfield born	23
July 1877	Son: Francis Pearson Penfield born	25
4 June 1880	Residence: Cleveland, Cuyahoga, Ohio	28
About 1891-1895	Divorced Frank H. Penfield	40-44
12 June 1895	Frank Penfield married Josephine Blood Voak	45
June 1900	Residence: New York, New York	49
23 October 1901	Son: Francis Pearson Penfield dies after surgery while student at Yale	50
1905	Residence: New York, New York	54
April 1910	Residence: New York, New York	59
22 September 1920	Died: Cleveland, Cuyahoga, Ohio Buried Lake View Cemetery, Cleveland, Cuyahoga, Ohio	69

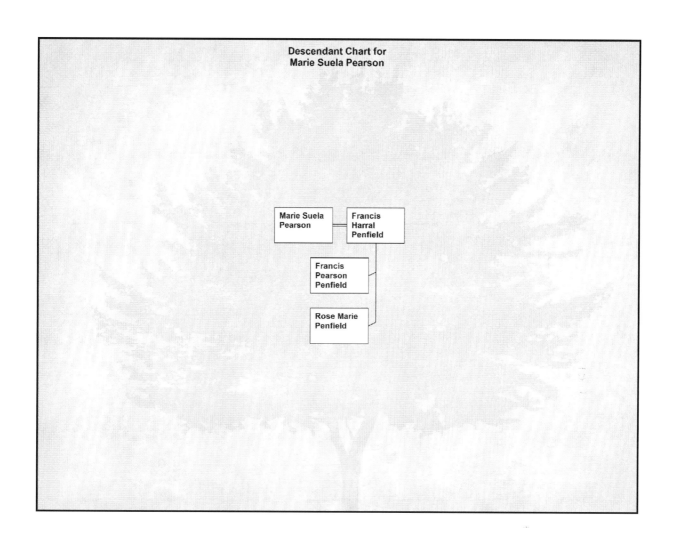

Descendant Chart for
Marie Suela Pearson

Marie Suela Pearson — Francis Harral Penfield

Francis Pearson Penfield

Rose Marie Penfield

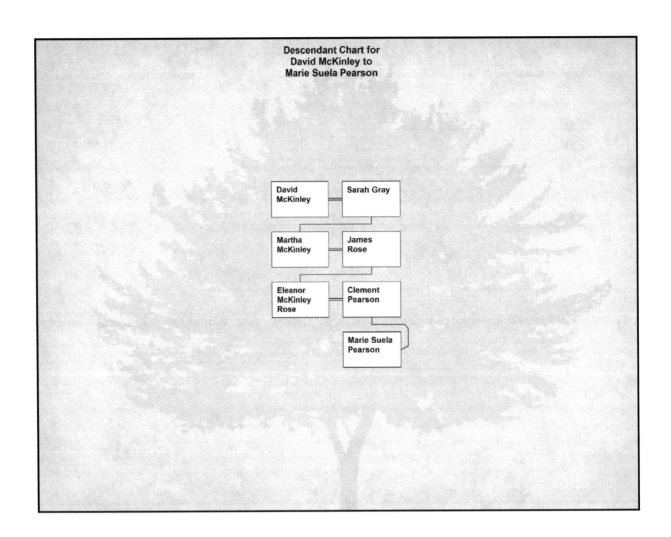

Descendant Chart for
David McKinley to
Marie Suela Pearson

David McKinley — Sarah Gray

Martha McKinley — James Rose

Eleanor McKinley Rose — Clement Pearson

Marie Suela Pearson

Descendant Chart for David McKinley to President William McKinley, Jr.

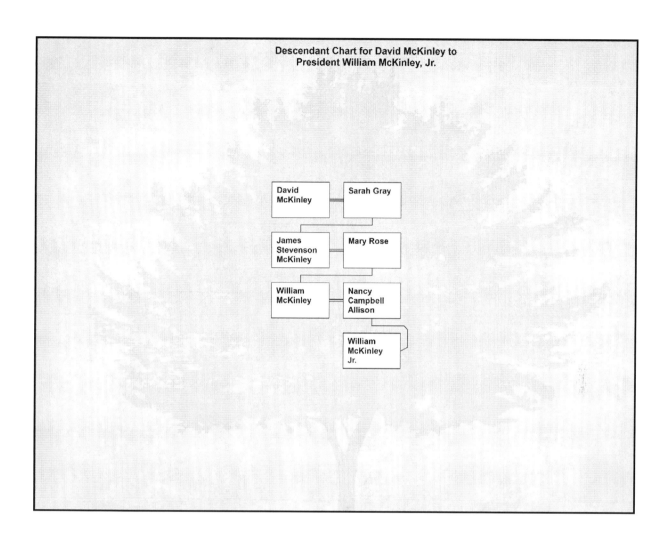

| David McKinley | Sarah Gray |

| James Stevenson McKinley | Mary Rose |

| William McKinley | Nancy Campbell Allison |

| William McKinley Jr. |

refused.

A PROCESS SERVER'S NERVE.

Report that Person He Was Looking for Had Smallpox Did Not Frighten Him.

There is one young process server in New York who is not afraid of smallpox. The story of his experience with that disease is told in the papers on file in the City Court, in which Dr. Wellslake D. Morse sues Miss Marie Rose Penfield, said to be a relative of President McKinley, for a dental bill amounting to $197.85. The dentist obtained judgment by default.

The dentist placed the case in the hands of Lawyer B. W. B. Brown, and he started an action in the Municipal Court. Miss Penfield is the daughter of Frank H. Penfield of Cleveland, Ohio, who is said to be wealthy. She has been living in this city with her grandmother, Mrs. M. Penfield Pierson, at 123 West Eighty-ninth Street. The lawyer could not get service on her in the action in the Municipal Court, so he started a new action in the City Court. All efforts failed as far as serving her with the summons and complaints were concerned. Finally Mr. Brown engaged Meyer Phillips, a young process server. In his affidavit Phillips says that the fourth time he went to the house a servant reported that Miss Penfield was ill.

"I must see her," replied Phillips.

"Well, she has the smallpox, and if you want to take the chance of getting the disease you can go to her room," said the servant.

"All right," said Phillips, and up stairs he went. He found Miss Penfield in her room, and served the papers. As yet he has not shown any signs of having smallpox, and the case of Miss Penfield has not been reported to the Health Department.

256

Transcription from: www.newspapers.com
New York Times, New York, New York, December 21, 1900

A Process Server's Nerve

There is one young process server in New York who is not afraid of smallpox. The story of his experience with that disease is told in the papers on file in the City Court, in which Dr. Wellslake D. Morse sues Miss Marie Rose Penfield, said to be a relative of President McKinley, for a dental bill amounting to $197.85. The dentist obtained judgment by default.

The dentist placed the case in the hands of Lawyer B.W.B. Brown, and he started an action in the Municipal Court. Miss Penfield is the daughter of Frank H. Penfield of Cleveland, Ohio, who is said to be wealthy. She has been living in this city with her grandmother, Mrs. M. Penfield Pierson, at 123 West Eighty-ninth Street. The lawyer could not get service on her in the action in the Municipal Court, so he started a new action in the City Court. All efforts failed as far as serving her with the summons and complaints were concerned. Finally Mr. Brown engaged Meyer Phillips, a young process server. In his affidavit Phillips says that the fourth time he went to the house a servant reported that Miss Penfield was ill.

"I must see her,' replied Phillips.

"Well, she has the smallpox, and if you want to take the chance of getting the disease you can go to her room," said the servant.

"All right," said Phillips, and upstairs he went. He found Miss Penfield in her room, and served the papers. As yet he has not shown any signs of having smallpox, and the case of Miss Penfield has not been reported to the Health Department.

DEATH LIST OF A DAY.

Pearson Penfield.

The funeral of Pearson Penfield, who died while undergoing a surgical operation, will take place this afternoon at 123 East Eighty-ninth Street. The body will be taken to Cleveland, the home of the family, for burial.

Mr. Penfield was related to President McKinley and had frequently been a guest at the White House. For three years he had suffered as a result of an injury which caused a growth on his neck, which the operation was intended to remove. A hemorrhage unexpectedly developed while the surgeons were at work on Wednesday and death followed.

Mr. Penfield was twenty-three years old. He was much interested in athletics, and had hoped to attain a place on the 'Varsity eleven or the boat crew of Yale, for which university he had passed most of his examinations when his affliction developed.

Transcription from: www.newspapers.com
New York Times, New York, New York, October 27, 1901

Death List of A Day – Pearson Penfield

The funeral of Pearson Penfield, who died while undergoing a surgical operation, will take place this afternoon at 123 East Eighty-ninth Street. The body will be taken to Cleveland, the home of the family, for burial.

Mr. Penfield was related to President McKinley and had frequently been a guest at the White House. For three years he had suffered as a result of an injury which caused a growth on his neck, which the operation was intended to remove. A hemorrhage unexpectedly developed while the surgeons were at work on Wednesday and death followed.

Mr. Penfield was twenty-three years old. He was much interested in athletics, and had hoped to attain a place on the Varsity eleven of the boat crew of Yale, for which university he had passed most of his examinations when his affliction developed.

Goes Into Bankruptcy.

Mt. Pleasant, July 8.—Mrs. Luela Pearsons Penfield, a graduate of the Iowa Wesleyan university, has gone bankrupt in the New York courts. She secured a divorce from her husband in Cleveland, O., receiving $50,000 as alimony about five years ago. She was one of the seven young ladies who founded the P. E. O. society here at the college in 1869, and a few years ago gave the college cadet corps a handsome diamond medal. She claims some relationship with President McKinley.

Clipped By:

ssatkins
Sun, Jan 5, 2014

Transcription from: www.newspapers.com
Davenport Daily Republican, Davenport, Iowa, July 9, 1901, page 2

Goes Into Bankruptcy

Mt. Pleasant, July 8 – Mrs. Luela (sic) Pearson Penfield, a graduate of the Iowa Wesleyan university, has gone bankrupt in the New York courts. She secured a divorce from her husband in Cleveland, O., receiving $50,000 as alimony about five years ago. She was one of the seven young ladies who founded the P.E.O. society here at the college in 1869, and a few years ago gave the college cadet corps a handsome diamond medal. She claims some relationship with President McKinley.

Penfield, Marie Suela. *Faithful*. Music by Alfred Solman. W.H. Anstead, 1902.

Faithful

Words by Marie Suela Penfield
Music by Alfred Solman
Copyright, MCMII, by W.H. Anstead 1439 Broadway, N.Y.

I watch the stars that gleam above amid the shades of night,
And harken to the brooklet's gentle flow,
The birds are dreaming in their nest, beneath the silv'ry light,
And all sweet nature faithful seem,
While zephyrs gently blow,
But no, the glitt'ring stars at dawn will fade, will fade away;
And e'en the brook flows to the sea, is lost in ocean spray,
The birdlings, too, soon leave their mates, when flowers fade and die;
But we shall ever faithful be, my love, my love and I!

REFRAIN

Faithful, faithful ever faithful!
Stars may fade and roses die!
Faithless never, faithful ever!
True earth's eternal sky!
Faithful, faithful, ever faithful,
As the seasons wander by!
Faithless never, faithful ever!
Down life's stream together you and I!

I mark the leaves in summer pride that murmur in the tree,
They glad the meadows verdant fresh and fair,
The sunbeams in their golden light are whispering soft to me,
"We're faithful, faithful to the earth, It's love we proudly share,"
But no, the leaves of emerald green will soon be dead and sere;
And sunbeams bright will fade away, when stormy clouds appear!
But hearts that love like yours and mine shall live, sweet heart, alway,
Ah! Faithful ever, constant, true, till life's eternal day!

REFRAIN

Faithful, faithful ever faithful!
Stars may fade and roses die!
Faithless never, faithful ever!
True earth's eternal sky!
Faithful, faithful, ever faithful,
As the seasons wonder by!
Faithless never, faithful ever!
Down life's stream together you and I!

MADE POOR BY GIVING, WOMAN GIVES UP HOME

MYSTERY ABOUT RICHES OF MRS. SUELA P. PENFIELD.

HER CHARITY IN NEW YORK

NEW YORK, July 7.—There was sorrow in the neighborhood of Lexington avenue and Eighty-ninth street when a "To Let" sign was put in the window of a brownstone house, for it meant that Mrs. Suela P. Penfield, who for ten years befriended the poor of the district and made herself loved by many acts of charity, will not return. Mrs. Penfield, who is said to be the wife of a millionaire of Cleveland, impoverished herself by giving to others, and it was her excessive generosity that compelled her to vacate the house in which she lived for more than ten years with her daughter Rose, and her mother, Mrs. Pearson, who is reported to have been related to President McKinley.

To the neighborhood Mrs. Penfield is a woman of mystery, for she disliked to discuss her past, and she resented inquiries concerning her family, but she told a part of her history to Mrs. H. Carpenter, janitor of an apartment house next door to where she lived, who had helped in Mrs. Penfield's charitable work. Mrs. Carpenter said she thought the woman had gone to Cleveland to obtain money due her from a trust fund provided by her husband. Mrs. Carpenter asserted Mrs. Penfield said her husband is Frank Penfield, a friend and neighbor of John D. Rockefeller, and worth $15,000,000.

Transcription from: www.newspapers.com
Indianapolis News, Indianapolis, Indiana, July 7, 1911, page 17

MADE POOR BY GIVING, WOMAN GIVES UP HOME

Mystery About Riches of Mrs. Suela F. Penfield.

New York - There was sorrow in the neighborhood of Lexington Avenue and Eighty-Ninth Street, when a "To Let" sign was put in the window of a brownstone house, for it meant that Mrs. Suela P. Penfield, who for ten years befriended the poor of the district and made herself loved by many acts of charily, will not return. Mrs. Penfield, who is said is the wife of a millionaire of Cleveland, impoverished herself by giving to others, and it was her excessive generosity that compelled her to vacate the house in which she lived for more than ten years with her daughter Rose, and her mother, Mrs. Pearson, who is reported to have been related to President McKinley.

To the neighborhood Mrs. Penfield is a women of mystery; for she disliked to discuss her past, and she resented inquiries concerning her family; but she told a part of her history to Mrs. H. Carpenter, janitor of an apartment house next door to where she lived, who had helped in Mrs. Penfield's charitable work. Mrs. Carpenter said she thought the woman had gone to Cleveland to obtain money due her from a trust fund provided by her husband, Mrs. Carpenter asserted Mrs. Penfield said her husband is Frank Penfield, friend and neighbor of John D. Rockefeller, and worth $20,000,000.

Transcription from: www.fultonhistory.com
Waterville Times, Waterville, New York, July 6, 1911, page 24

Mrs. Penfield Now Penniless

She is Divorced Wife of Cleveland Oil Millionaire

Fought Against Poverty

Woman Who Once Spent $25,000 a Year Was Forced to Borrow Car Fare From Friends – Husband Known as Only Man Who Ever Bested John D. Rockefeller.

New York, July 6 - From affluence of $25,000 a year it has become known that Mrs. Marie Suela Pearson Penfield, the divorced wife of Frank H. Penfield, a Cleveland oil millionaire, once widely known" as the only man who bested Rockefeller," had been for the past two years fighting poverty in the handsome residence here where she had lived for many years - - ever since, in fact, the separation from her husband. She abandoned her residence last Sunday. So great was her financial stress that she had to leave a month's rent unpaid, and friends further declare that she had to borrow the money with which to take herself, her daughter and her mother back to Cleveland, where she once reigned as a society leader and lived as the next door neighbor of Mrs. John D. Rockefeller in Euclid avenue.

The declaration is made by a few to whom Mrs. Penfield gave her confidences that she has gone to Cleveland to begin a legal battle to get funds, held in trust for herself and her daughter, which are now said to be withheld. She has suffered poverty, these friends say, while there are many thousands of dollars strangely kept back from her use and enjoyment.

However this may be the change that came over the manner of living of Mrs. Penfield and her family in the handsome residence was most complete. The carriage with the liveried coachman and footman passed from the door never to return; the brilliant dinner and luncheons were discontinued; so were the regular Easter, Thanksgiving and Christmas feast that she used to give in her own home to the children of the tenements, and the elegance of her gowns held their fine lines, but become old fashioned and from that passed to shabbiness.

The members of the household had first been Mrs. Penfield, her aged mother, Mrs. Pearson, wife of a once famous Washington physician; Miss Marie Rose Penfield, a daughter and Pearson Penfield, her son. The latter was a Yale student. He figured in the football history of the college, but a few years ago, at the age of twenty-five, he died. There were a butler, several women servants and the carriage men in the service of the establishment. One by one all of these servants disappeared.

Marie Suela Pearson was only about fifteen years old when she married Penfield. He was forty and a millionaire. He later became ten times a millionaire. Undeniably she had a place of first rank in Washington society; her father was a distinguished surgeon, and the family was related by blood ties to William McKinley.

The separation of the oil millionaire and his much younger wife dates back many years. He made her a cash settlement of $50,000 and agreed to pay her $400 a month, besides making a liberal allowance for the education of the children. Mrs. Penfield, who had been welcomed with open arms by Cleveland society and, in fact, became a protégée of Mrs. John D. Rockefeller, despite the commercial tilts of Penfield and the oil magnate, decided to move east.

It appears that after a year of living under the separation agreement Penfield repented of his bargain. He went into court, declaring that his wife's extravagance was intolerable. He said that despite liberal provisions she had mortgaged real estate, gone $9000 into debt and required $20,000 to live on. He asked that if the court would not set aside the articles of separation such action should be taken as would prevent her mortgaging real estate further, but compel her to hold it intact for their children.

In June, 1901, Mrs. Penfield appeared in bankruptcy proceedings in which she confessed to $9,000 of debts. She smilingly testified to having spent $45,000 in two years. But nevertheless, after this, for years she went on living as one possessed of a large income.

But last Sunday Mrs. Penfield, her aged mother and her daughter and the maid got into the taxicab and did not return. And the next day there came big moving vans, and the house was stripped of its luxurious furnishings. The once affluent woman was mysteriously gone from the neighborhood.

81-105

STATE OF OHIO
BUREAU OF VITAL STATISTICS
CERTIFICATE OF DEATH

1 PLACE OF DEATH
County *Cuyahoga* — Registration District No. — File No. *57826*
Township — Primary Registration District No. — Registered No. *8177*
or Village — No. *Overland State Hospital* St., *15* Ward
or City of *Cleveland* — (If death occured in a hospital or institution, give its NAME instead of street and number)

2 FULL NAME *Mary L Penfield Marie Suela Pearson*
(a) Residence. No. *Royal Apts.* St., *C* & *Crawford Penfield* Ward
(Usual place of abode) — (If nonresident give city or town and State)
Length of residence in city or town where death occurred — yrs. — mos. — ds. How long in U.S., if of foreign birth? — yrs. — mos. — ds.

PERSONAL AND STATISTICAL PARTICULARS	MEDICAL CERTIFICATE OF DEATH
3 SEX *Female* **4 COLOR OR RACE** *White* **5 Single, Married, Widowed or Divorced** (write the word) *Divorced*	**16 DATE OF DEATH** (month, day and year) *9-22-19 20*
5a If married, widowed or divorced HUSBAND of (or) WIFE of *Frank H. Penfield*	**17** I HEREBY CERTIFY, That I attended deceased from *5-14-19 20*, to *9-22-19 20* that I last saw her alive on *9-22-19 20* and that death occurred, on the date stated above, at *8* m. The CAUSE OF DEATH was as follows:
6 DATE OF BIRTH (month, day, and year) *Aug 24" 1853*	*Artero-sclerosis*
7 AGE Years *67* Months *—* Days *28* If LESS than 1 day hrs. or min.	(duration) — yrs. — mos. — ds.
8 OCCUPATION OF DECEASED (a) Trade, profession, or particular kind of work *none* (b) General nature of Industry, business, or establishment in which employed (or) (c) Name of employer	CONTRIBUTORY SECONDARY *Hypostatic Pneumonia* *Leo-colitis* (duration) — yrs. — mos. — ds.
9 BIRTHPLACE (city or town) *Salem* (State or country) *Ohio*	**18** Where was disease contracted if not at place of death? Did an operation precede death? Date of Was there an autopsy? What test confirmed diagnosis?
10 NAME OF FATHER *Clement Pearson*	(Signed) *Katharine R Moses* M. D.
11 BIRTHPLACE OF FATHER (city or town) (State or country) *Pennsylvania*	*9-22*, 1920 (Address) *C S H*
12 MAIDEN NAME OF MOTHER *Marie Suela Pea*	*State the DISEASE CAUSING DEATH, or in deaths from VIOLENT CAUSES, state (1) MEANS AND NATURE OF INJURY, and (2) whether ACCIDENTAL, SUICIDAL or HOMICIDAL. (See reverse side for additional space.)*
13 BIRTHPLACE OF MOTHER (city or town) *Salem* (State or country) *Ohio*	
14 Informant *Geo Sharr* (Address) *7436 Prospect Av*	**19 PLACE OF BURIAL, CREMATION, OR REMOVAL** *Lake View Cemetery* **DATE OF BURIAL** *Sep 25 1920*
15 Fil *SEP 24 1920* REGISTRAR	**20 UNDERTAKER,** License No. *310 a* *Geo Sharr Son* **ADDRESS** *7436 Prospect av*

(left margin, vertical) PHYSICIANS should state CAUSE OF DEATH in plain terms, so that it may be properly classified. See instructions on back of certificate. AGE should be carefully supplied. Exact statement of information is very important.

STATE OF OHIO
DEPARTMENT OF HEALTH
DIVISION OF VITAL STATISTICS
CERTIFICATE OF DEATH

Certificate of Death for Frank K. Penfield, Cleveland, Cuyahoga County, Ohio, 17 November 1931. Reference number 64622.

"Ohio, Deaths, 1908-1953," index and images, *FamilySearch* (https://familysearch.org/pal:/MM9.1.1/X6DH-MJ2: accessed 11 Jan 2014), Frank K Penfield, 17 Nov 1931; citing Cleveland, Cuyahoga, Ohio, reference fn 64622; FHL microfilm 1992477.

PHOTOTEQUE HOMEOPATHIQUE

Presentee par Homeopathe International

Dr. Clement PEARSON (1819-1886)

Biography by Sylvain Cazalet

PEARSON, CLEMENT, M.D., of Mount Pleasant, Iowa, was born in Mercer County, Pa., December 19th 1819. His father, a native of Chester County, was of English descent, and traced his line through a long ancestry of Quaker blood. His mother, four years younger, was born in Philadelphia. His early education was received in an academy at New Wilmington, Pa. On leaving there, he was engaged for a number of years as a teacher. While thus employed, he gave himself to the study and thorough comprehension of the different schools of Medicine; examining the several theories, and noticing carefully their results. He pursued this study with indefatigable industry, but without the slightest thought of becoming a practitioner of either system. His fondness for the study alone induced his long and earnest labor over it, and it was not until 1847, that his attention was drawn to the expediency of making choice of medicine as a profession. For this, he is indebted to Dr. S. Searles, of Newcastle, Pa., from whom, and his partner, Dr. Porter, he received all necessary books and instruction in homoeopathy. He prosecuted his studies with great care for two years. In the winter of 1849, he formed the acquaintance of Curt Pretsch, M.D., who had but recently arrived in this country from Leipzig; and in April, 1850, they opened an office in Wellsville, Ohio, for the practice of homeopathy. The year following, he attended lectures at the Homeopathic Medical college of Pennsylvania, in Philadelphia, and then removed to Salem, Ohio, where, for five years, he engaged in active and very successful practice. In the winter of 1856-'57, wishing still farther to improve himself in study, he attended lectures in the Homoeopathic College at Cleveland, Ohio, graduating in March, 1857. In April of the same year, he located in Mount Pleasant, Iowa, where he is now actively engaged in a large and valuable practice. His patient and laborious investigation of the several theories of medical practice, though, probably, he little thought of the result, was a most important link in the chain of causation, which led him to choose the profession of medicine, and ultimately to decide upon homoeopathy as the system which combined most of reasonableness with the least of suffering to the afflicted.

On the 17th of June, 1858, he delivered an address before the public, entitled, "Is there a System of Medicine?" This address was induced by the Proceedings of the Iowa State Medical society, and is a reply to them. It is a very able lecture, in which comparing the allopathic and homoeopathic treatments, he presents an array of proof in favor of the latter, which it is impossible to controvert. It excited considerable discussion, and brought out Dr. Sumner Stebbinsa as an allopathic opponent. The discussion both oral and written was one of great ability, and both parties gained renown from it. The lecture was subsequently reviewed at some length by Dr. Marcy in the *North American Journal of Homeopathy.* To this journal he has contributed sundry papers of great value; and to the *United States Journal of Homoeopathy*; to the *Hahnemann Monthly*; to the *Homoeopathic Independent*; to the *Medical and Surgical Reporter*, and to the *United States Medical Surgical Journal.* In addition to these, he has been a frequent contributor to the *Medical Investigator*, of Chicago, for the past fifteen years. He has also prepared a chapter for a work on Materia Medica, which has not yet been published, prepared under the editorship of Dr. Gilchrist. In addition to these literary contributions to the cause of homoeopathy, he has delivered annually addresses (by request) to the teachers of, the country, since the organization of their institute, now over twelve years. Some of these lectures, and one also before the State Medical Association, have been published in the newspapers, and have met with general acceptance.

He is a ready writer and a fluent speaker, an uncompromising friend of temperance, taking the position in numerous addresses he has delivered on this subject that alcohol, through a good vehicle for retaining and preserving medicinal substances, is of itself never necessary either as a medicine or stimulant.

Transcription from:
Avery, Elroy McKendry. *A History of Cleveland and Its Environs - The Heart of New Connecticut.*
Vol. III. New York, New York: Lewis, 1918. 447-48

WILLIAM G. ROSE

William G. Rose was born September 23, 1829, in Mercer County, Pennsylvania. He was one of eleven children of James and Martha Rose. His family was of that celebrated Scotch-Irish stock which has numbered some of the ablest of American statesmen and patriots.

Mr. Rose passed his boyhood in the ordinary routine of labor on the farm and attendance at the district school. At the age of seventeen his attainments were such as to qualify him for the duties of a district school teacher, which occupation, varied with an occasional term at a high school or an academy, he pursued during several years.

At the age of twenty-three Mr. Rose was entered a student at the law office of Honorable William Stewart, of Mercer. Here he remained till 1855, in which year he was admitted to the bar and began practice in his native county. The career of Mr. Rose during the next few years is similar to its main outlines to that of many of our ablest public men. Those were days of passionate discussion of the question of slavery extension. Should the territories be free-soil or slave-soil? Very few young men – least of all young attorneys – of abounding life and energy could long remain neutral with such an issue before them. At this period, accordingly, we find Mr. Rose an associate editor on the staff of the Independent Democrat, the leading newspaper of Mercer County.

From 1857 to 1859 Mr. Rose was a member of the Pennsylvania Legislature, representing in that body the advanced policy of the recently organized Republican party. In 1860 he was chosen a delegate to the National Republican convention which nominated Mr. Lincoln for the Presidency, but was prevented by serious illness from attending.

In 1865 Mr. Rose removed to Cleveland, where he was since resided. His career in this city, in official and in private life, is too familiar among all classes to make necessary a statement in detail. We will mention a few only of the more important events and lines of policy with which his name has been connected.

In 1877 Mr. Rose received the Republican nomination for the mayoralty, and was elected by a large majority over the opposing candidate. His administration fell in perhaps the most critical period of Cleveland's history. Following close upon the financial panic of 1873, the first year of Mr. Rose's administration saw the culmination of the great railway strikes in the memorable riots at Pittsburgh. The Lake Shore & Michigan Southern railway, along which line the force of revolt was most apparent, had its official headquarters in this city; and the great freight yards of the company, the chief point of threatened danger, were but a few miles distant. The course adopted in this emergency reflects great credit upon the good sense and discretion of the official management. At the first suggestion of danger, Mayor Rose took measures for a thorough but secret organization of the police and militia – the result being that a force was soon provided competent for any contingency that might arise.

In his inaugural address before the city council, Mr. Rose sounded the key-note of his entire administration. He said: "The enormous amount of municipal debt, the present low rate of wages…., the vast number of men and women out of employment…, and the difficulty experienced by many of our most substantial citizens in meeting their tax obligations and providing…the comforts and even the necessaries of life, all combine to impress upon those in authority the necessity of scrupulous care and fidelity in the economical management of every department of our municipal government." Retrenchment, where retrenchment was possible, careful attention to every municipal function, and the thorough cooperation of all departments – these were the consistent aims of Mayor Rose's administration. As a worthy and influential citizen, Mr. Rose needs no recognition in this place. During his residence in Cleveland he has gained the respect and confidence of all classes by the faithful performance of the many duties, both public and private, that have devolved upon him.

Photo Album for Marie Suela Pearson

Marie Suela Pearson

Birth:	24 Aug 1851	Father:	Clement Pearson
Death:	22 Sep 1920	Mother:	Eleanor McKinley Rose
Marriage:	02 Sep 1874	Spouse:	Francis Harral Penfield

Marie Suela Pearson

Reproduction of oil portrait by Marion Dunlap Harper, unveiled in P.E.O. Memorial Hall in Mount Pleasant, Iowa, on September 23, 1929.

274

Marie Suela Pearson

Birth:	24 Aug 1851	Father:	Clement Pearson
Death:	22 Sep 1920	Mother:	Eleanor McKinley Rose
Marriage:	02 Sep 1874	Spouse:	Francis Harral Penfield

Marie Suela Pearson

Avery, Elroy McKendry. *A History of Cleveland and Its Environs - The Heart of New Connecticut*. Vol. III. New York, New York: Lewis, 1918. 447.

Marie Suela Pearson

Birth:	24 Aug 1851	Father:	Clement Pearson
Death:	22 Sep 1920	Mother:	Eleanor McKinley Rose
Marriage:	02 Sep 1874	Spouse:	Francis Harral Penfield

Suella Pearson as young woman

Pierson, Merry Anne. The American Descendants of Lawrence Pearson. Kingston Springs, TN: Westview, Inc. 2005.

Photo Album for Clement Pearson

Clement Pearson

Birth:	19 Dec 1819	Father:	Samuel Pearson
Death:	29 Jan 1886	Mother:	Sarah A. Golden
Marriage:		Spouse:	Eleanor McKinley Rose

Dr. Clement Pearson

Reprinted with permission from Sylvain Cazalet,"History of Homeopathy."Pearson, Clement, M.D.

Photo Album for Eleanor McKinley Rose

Eleanor McKinley Rose

Birth:	03 Apr 1824	Father:	James Rose
Death:	08 Jan 1917	Mother:	Martha McKinley
Marriage:		Spouse:	Clement Pearson

Eleanor McKinley Rose

Avery, Elroy McKendry. A History of Cleveland and Its Environs - The Heart of New Connecticut. Vol. III. New York, New York: Lewis, 1918. 447.

Historical Background Sources
for Marie Suela Pearson

1. 1860 United States Federal Census; Census Place: Mount Pleasant, Henry, Iowa; Roll: M653_324; Page: 93; Image: 93; Family History Library Film: 803324.

2. 1870 United States Federal Census; Census Place: Center, Henry, Iowa; Roll: M593_395; page: 194A; Image: 392; Family History Library Film: 545894.

3. 1880 United States Federal Census: Census Place: Cleveland, Cuyahoga, Ohio; Roll: 1004; Family History Library Film: 1255004; Page: 100B; Enumeration District: 004; Image: 0500.

4. 1910 United States Federal Census: Census Place: *Manhattan Ward 12, New York, New York*; Roll: T624_1016; Page 8A; Enumeration District: 0380; FHL microfilm: 1375029.

5. "A Process Server's Nerve." *New York Times* [New York] Dec. 1900: Print.

6. Avery, Elroy McKendry. *A History of Cleveland and Its Environs - The Heart of New Connecticut*. Vol. III. New York, New York: Lewis, 1918. 447-48. Print.

7. Cazalet, Sylvain. "History of Homeopathy." *Pearson, Clement, M.D.- By Sylvain Cazalet*. Web. 21 Nov. 2013. http://www.homeoint.org/history/bio/p/pearsonc.htm.

8. Clapp, Stella. *Out of the Heart A Century of P.E.O. 1869-1969*. Des Moines, Iowa: P.E.O. Sisterhood, 1968.

9. "F.F. Proctor." *Proctors, Schenectady, New York*. 22 February 2014. www.proctors.org/ff-proctor.

10. "Frank Pearson Penfield." *Cleveland Ohio Historical Newspapers* [Cleveland, Ohio] 23 Oct. 1901: Print.

11. "Inflation Calculator." *DaveManuel.com*. Web. 20 Oct. 2013. <http://www.davemanuel.com/inflation-calculator.php>.

12. "International Hahnemann Congress." *International Hahnemann Congress*. Web. 20 Oct. 2013. <http://www.homeopathy-congress.com/en/iha.html>.

13. Johnson, Heidi, ed. "A Society of Our Own." *The P.E.O. Record* (1997).

14. Lee, Emmitt J., Dr., and Walter M. James, Dr."In Memoriam Clement Pearson" *Homeopathic Physician,* VII (1886): 118. Web. 20 Oct. 2013.

15. "Marie Suela Pearson." http://books.google.com/books?id=W24ZAQAAIAAJ&pg=PA139&dq=Eleanor+McKinley+Rose&hl=en&sa=X&ei=0JWOUtzaL4_9iQLEqYH4AQ&ved=0CDMQ6AEwAQ#v=onepage&q=Eleanor%20McKinley%20Rose&f=false p139-140. Web.

16. "Michigan, Marriages, 1822-1995"Index, FamilySearch (https://familysearch.org/pal:/MM9.1.1/FCB6-DRV: accessed 28 August 2013), Frank H. Penfield and Josephine Blood Voak, 12, Jun 1895.

17. "Mrs. Penfield Now Penniless." *Waterville Times* [Waterville, New York] 6 July 1911: Print.

18. National Archives case files Approved Pension Applications of Widows and Other Veterans of the Army and Navy Who Served Mainly in the Civil War, Veteran John Souder, Ohio Infantry, Regiment 3, Company A, Pensioner Mary Chisholm, Application Number WC125289.

19. Penfield, Marie Suela. *Faithful*. Music by Alfred Solman. W.H. Anstead, 1902.

20. Pierson, Merry Anne. *The American Descendants of Lawrence Pearson*. Kingston Springs, TN: Westview, Inc. 2005.

21. "Quinquennial Catalogue of the Officers and Graduates of Harvard University, 1636-1915 (Google EBook)." *Google Books*. p717. Web. 21 Nov. 2013.

22. Robison, W. Scott. *History of the City of Cleveland*. Cleveland, Ohio: Robison & Cockett - The Sunday World, 1887. Web. 20 Oct. 2013.
     http://books.google.com/books?id=yi4VAAAAYAAJ&pg=PA417#v=onepage&q&f=false

23. West, Jill. "Special Visit to Suela." The P.E.O. Record Jan-Feb (2012): 22.

Marie Suela Pearson Descendant Chart
Source Report

Source Title: [no source title]

Citation: Quinquennial Catalogue of the Officers and Graduates of Harvard University ... By Harvard University. http://books.google.com/books?id=JiNOAAAAMAAJ&pg=PA717&dq=%22william+rose+pearson%22&hl=en&sa=X&ei=Xn-OUuOYHcngiAL4s4HIBQ&ved=0CEYQ6AEwAg#v=onepage&q=%22william%20rose%20pearson%22&f=false.

Citation: Pearson, William Rose Sylvain Cazalet, Cleave's Biographical Cyclopaedia, p. 53. http://www.homeoint.org/history/bio/p/pearsonc.htm. [Source citation includes media item(s)] Pearson, Clement

Source Title: 1850 United States Federal Census
Repository: Ancestry.com

Citation: Ancestry.com, 1850 United States Federal Census (Provo, UT, USA, Ancestry.com Operations, Inc., 2009), Ancestry.com, Year: 1850; Census Place: Cleveland Ward 1, Cuyahoga, Ohio; Roll: M432_672; Page: 156B; Image: 141. [Source citation includes media item(s)]

Citation: Penfield, Francis Harral Ancestry.com, 1850 United States Federal Census (Provo, UT, USA, Ancestry.com Operations, Inc., 2009), Ancestry.com, Year: 1850; Census Place: Wellsville, Columbiana, Ohio; Roll: M432_669; Page: 153A; Image: 309. [Source citation includes media item(s)]

Citation: Pearson, Horace Ancestry.com, 1850 United States Federal Census (Provo, UT, USA, Ancestry.com Operations, Inc., 2009), Ancestry.com, Year: 1850; Census Place: Wellsville, Columbiana, Ohio; Roll: M432_669; Page: 153A; Image: 309. [Source citation includes media item(s)]

Citation: Pearson, William Rose Ancestry.com, 1850 United States Federal Census (Provo, UT, USA, Ancestry.com Operations, Inc., 2009), Ancestry.com, Year: 1850; Census Place: Wellsville, Columbiana, Ohio; Roll: M432_669; Page: 153A; Image: 309. [Source citation includes media item(s)]

Citation: Rose, Eleanor McKinley Ancestry.com, 1850 United States Federal Census (Provo, UT, USA, Ancestry.com Operations, Inc., 2009), Ancestry.com, Year: 1850; Census Place: Wellsville, Columbiana, Ohio; Roll: M432_669; Page: 153A; Image: 309. [Source citation includes media item(s)] Pearson, Clement

Source Title: 1860 United States Federal Census
Repository: Ancestry.com

Citation: Ancestry.com, 1860 United States Federal Census (Provo, UT, USA, Ancestry.com Operations, Inc., 2009), Ancestry.com, Year: 1860; Census Place: Cleveland Ward 1, Cuyahoga, Ohio; Roll: M653_953; Page: 627; Image: 67; Family History Library Film: 803953. [Source citation includes media item(s)]

Citation: Penfield, Francis Harral Ancestry.com, 1860 United States Federal Census (Provo, UT, USA, Ancestry.com Operations, Inc., 2009), Ancestry.com, Year: 1860; Census Place: Mount Pleasant, Henry, Iowa; Roll: M653_324; Page: 93; Image: 93; Family History Library Film: 803324. [Source citation includes media item(s)]

Citation: Pearson, Clement Ancestry.com, 1860 United States Federal Census (Provo, UT, USA, Ancestry.com Operations, Inc., 2009), Ancestry.com, Year: 1860; Census Place: Mount Pleasant, Henry, Iowa; Roll: M653_324; Page: 93; Image: 93; Family History Library Film: 803324. [Source citation includes media item(s)]

Citation: Ancestry.com, 1860 United States Federal Census (Provo, UT, USA, Ancestry.com Operations, Inc., 2009), Ancestry.com, Year: 1860; Census Place: Mount Pleasant, Henry, Iowa; Roll: M653_324; Page: 93; Image: 93; Family History Library Film: 803324. [Source citation includes media item(s)] Pearson, Marie Suela

Source Title: 1870 United States Federal Census
Repository: Ancestry.com

Citation: Ancestry.com, 1870 United States Federal Census (Provo, UT, USA, Ancestry.com Operations, Inc., 2009), Ancestry.com, Year: 1870; Census Place: Center, Henry, Iowa; Roll: M593_395; Page: 194A; Image: 392; Family History Library Film: 545894. [Source citation includes media item(s)] Rose, Eleanor McKinley

Citation: Ancestry.com, 1870 United States Federal Census (Provo, UT, USA, Ancestry.com Operations, Inc., 2009), Ancestry.com, Year: 1870; Census Place: Center, Henry, Iowa; Roll: M593_395; Page: 194A; Image: 392; Family History Library Film: 545894. [Source citation includes media item(s)]Pearson, Clement

Citation: Ancestry.com, 1870 United States Federal Census (Provo, UT, USA, Ancestry.com Operations, Inc., 2009), Ancestry.com, Year: 1870; Census Place: Center, Henry, Iowa; Roll: M593_395; Page: 194A; Image: 392; Family History Library Film: 545894. [Source citation includes media item(s)]
Pearson, Marie Suela

Citation: Ancestry.com, 1870 United States Federal Census (Provo, UT, USA, Ancestry.com Operations, Inc., 2009), Ancestry.com, Year: 1870; Census Place: Center, Henry, Iowa; Roll: M593_395; Page: 194A; Image: 392; Family History Library Film: 545894. [Source citation includes media item(s)] Pearson, William Rose

Source Title: 1880 United States Federal Census
Repository: Ancestry.com

Citation: Ancestry.com and The Church of Jesus Christ of Latter-day Saints, 1880 United States Federal Census (Provo, UT, USA, Ancestry.com Operations Inc., 2010), Ancestry.com, Year: 1880; Census Place: Cleveland, Cuyahoga, Ohio; Roll: 1004; Family History Film: 1255004; Page: 100B; Enumeration District: 004; Image: 0500. [Source citation includes media item(s)] Rose, Eleanor McKinley

Citation: Ancestry.com and The Church of Jesus Christ of Latter-day Saints, 1880 United States Federal Census (Provo, UT, USA, Ancestry.com Operations Inc., 2010), Ancestry.com, Year: 1880; Census Place: Cleveland, Cuyahoga, Ohio; Roll: 1004; Family History Film: 1255004; Page: 100B; Enumeration District: 004; Image: 0500. [Source citation includes media item(s)] Pearson, Marie Suela

Citation: Ancestry.com and The Church of Jesus Christ of Latter-day Saints, 1880 United States Federal Census (Provo, UT, USA, Ancestry.com Operations Inc., 2010), Ancestry.com, Year: 1880; Census Place: Cleveland, Cuyahoga, Ohio; Roll: 1004; Family History Film: 1255004; Page: 100B; Enumeration District: 004; Image: 0500. [Source citation includes media item(s)] Penfield, Francis Harral

Citation: Ancestry.com and The Church of Jesus Christ of Latter-day Saints, 1880 United States Federal Census (Provo, UT, USA, Ancestry.com Operations Inc., 2010), Ancestry.com, Year: 1880; Census Place: Cleveland, Cuyahoga, Ohio; Roll: 1004; Family History Film: 1255004; Page: 100B; Enumeration District: 004; Image: 0500. [Source citation includes media item(s)] Penfield, Francis Pearson

Citation: Ancestry.com and The Church of Jesus Christ of Latter-day Saints, 1880 United States Federal Census (Provo, UT, USA, Ancestry.com Operations Inc., 2010), Ancestry.com, Year: 1880; Census Place: Cleveland, Cuyahoga, Ohio; Roll: 1004; Family History Film: 1255004; Page: 100B; Enumeration District: 004; Image: 0500. [Source citation includes media item(s)] Penfield, Rose Marie

Citation: Ancestry.com and The Church of Jesus Christ of Latter-day Saints, 1880 United States Federal Census (Provo, UT, USA, Ancestry.com Operations Inc., 2010), Ancestry.com, Year: 1880; Census Place: Cleveland, Cuyahoga, Ohio; Roll: 1006; Family History Film: 1255006; Page: 138D; Enumeration District: 021; Image: 0282. [Source citation includes media item(s)] Pearson, William Rose

Source Title: **1900 United States Federal Census**
Repository: **Ancestry.com**

Citation: Ancestry.com, 1900 United States Federal Census (Provo, UT, USA, Ancestry.com Operations Inc., 2004), Ancestry.com, Year: 1900; Census Place: Manhattan, New York, New York; Roll: 1116; Page: 5B; Enumeration District: 0798; FHL microfilm: 1241116. [Source citation includes media item(s)] Pearson, Marie Suela

Citation: Ancestry.com, 1900 United States Federal Census (Provo, UT, USA, Ancestry.com Operations Inc., 2004), Ancestry.com, Year: 1900; Census Place: Manhattan, New York, New York; Roll: 1116; Page: 5B; Enumeration District: 0798; FHL microfilm: 1241116. [Source citation includes media item(s)] Penfield, Francis Pearson

Citation: Ancestry.com, 1900 United States Federal Census (Provo, UT, USA, Ancestry.com Operations Inc., 2004), Ancestry.com, Year: 1900; Census Place: Manhattan, New York, New York; Roll: 1116; Page: 5B; Enumeration District: 0798; FHL microfilm: 1241116. [Source citation includes media item(s)] Penfield, Rose Marie

Source Title: **1910 United States Federal Census**
Repository: **Ancestry.com**

Citation: Ancestry.com, 1910 United States Federal Census (Provo, UT, USA, Ancestry.com Operations Inc., 2006), Ancestry.com, Year: 1910; Census Place: Cleveland Ward 14, Cuyahoga, Ohio; Roll: T624_1170; Page: 14B; Enumeration District: 0217; FHL microfilm: 1375183. [Source citation includes media item(s)] Penfield, Francis Harral

Citation: Ancestry.com, 1910 United States Federal Census (Provo, UT, USA, Ancestry.com Operations Inc., 2006), Ancestry.com, Year: 1910; Census Place: Cleveland Ward 25, Cuyahoga, Ohio; Roll: T624_1176; Page: 9B; Enumeration District: 0385; FHL microfilm: 1375189. [Source citation includes media item(s)] Pearson, William Rose

Citation: Ancestry.com, 1910 United States Federal Census (Provo, UT, USA, Ancestry.com Operations Inc., 2006), Ancestry.com, Year: 1910; Census Place: Manhattan Ward 12, New York, New York; Roll: T624_1016; Page: 8A; Enumeration District: 0380; FHL microfilm: 1375029. [Source citation includes media item(s)] Rose, Eleanor McKinley

Citation: Ancestry.com, 1910 United States Federal Census (Provo, UT, USA, Ancestry.com Operations Inc., 2006), Ancestry.com, Year: 1910; Census Place: Manhattan Ward 12, New York, New York; Roll: T624_1016; Page: 8A; Enumeration District: 0380; FHL microfilm: 1375029. [Source citation includes media item(s)] Pearson, Marie Suela

Citation: Ancestry.com, 1910 United States Federal Census (Provo, UT, USA, Ancestry.com Operations Inc., 2006), Ancestry.com, Year: 1910; Census Place: Manhattan Ward 12, New York, New York; Roll: T624_1016; Page: 8A; Enumeration District: 0380; FHL microfilm: 1375029. [Source citation includes media item(s)] Penfield, Rose Marie

Source Title: **1920 United States Federal Census**
Repository: **Ancestry.com**

Citation: Ancestry.com, 1920 United States Federal Census (Provo, UT, USA, Ancestry.com Operations Inc., 2010), Ancestry.com, Year: 1920; Census Place: Lakewood Ward 2, Cuyahoga, Ohio; Roll: T625_1375; Page: 9B; Enumeration District: 580; Image: 1071. [Source citation includes media item(s)]
Penfield, Francis Harral

Citation: Ancestry.com, 1920 United States Federal Census (Provo, UT, USA, Ancestry.com Operations Inc., 2010), Ancestry.com, Year: 1920; Census Place: Manhattan Assembly District 11, New York, New York; Roll: T625_1205; Page: 3B; Enumeration District: 846; Image: 1100. [Source citation includes media item(s)] Pearson, William Rose

Source Title: **1930 United States Federal Census**
Repository: **Ancestry.com**

Citation: Ancestry.com, 1930 United States Federal Census (Provo, UT, USA, Ancestry.com Operations Inc., 2002), Ancestry.com, Year: 1930; Census Place: Lakewood, Cuyahoga, Ohio; Roll: 1786; Page: 2B; Enumeration District: 0638; Image: 444.0; FHL microfilm: 2341520. [Source citation includes media item(s)] Penfield, Francis Harral

Source Title: **Ancestry Family Trees**
Repository: **Ancestry.com**

Citation: Ancestry Family Trees (Online publication - Provo, UT, USA: Ancestry.com. Original data: Family Tree files submitted by Ancestry members.), Ancestry.com, Ancestry Family Tree. Rose, Eleanor McKinley

Citation: Ancestry Family Trees (Online publication - Provo, UT, USA: Ancestry.com. Original data: Family Tree files submitted by Ancestry members.), Ancestry.com, Ancestry Family Tree. Pearson, Clement

Citation: Ancestry Family Trees (Online publication - Provo, UT, USA: Ancestry.com. Original data: Family Tree files submitted by Ancestry members.), Ancestry.com, Ancestry Family Tree. Pearson, Marie Suela

Citation: Ancestry Family Trees (Online publication - Provo, UT, USA: Ancestry.com. Original data: Family Tree files submitted by Ancestry members.), Ancestry.com, Ancestry Family Tree. Penfield, Francis Harral

Citation: Ancestry Family Trees (Online publication - Provo, UT, USA: Ancestry.com. Original data: Family Tree files submitted by Ancestry members.), Ancestry.com, Ancestry Family Tree. Pearson, William Rose

Citation: Ancestry Family Trees (Online publication - Provo, UT, USA: Ancestry.com. Original data: Family Tree files submitted by Ancestry members.), Ancestry.com, Ancestry Family Tree. Penfield, Francis Pearson

Citation: Ancestry Family Trees (Online publication - Provo, UT, USA: Ancestry.com. Original data: Family Tree files submitted by Ancestry members.), Ancestry.com, Ancestry Family Tree. Penfield, Rose Marie

Source Title: **Cuyahoga County, Ohio, Marriage Records and Indexes, 1810-1973**
Repository: **Ancestry.com**

Citation: Ancestry.com, Cuyahoga County, Ohio, Marriage Records and Indexes, 1810-1973 (Provo, UT, USA, Ancestry.com Operations, Inc., 2010), Ancestry.com, Cuyahoga County Archive; Cleveland, Ohio; Cuyahoga County, Ohio, Marriage Records, 1810-1973; Volume: Vol 17-18; Page: 168; Year Range: 1872 Jul - 1876 Dec. [Source citation includes media item(s)] Pearson, Marie Suela Penfield, Francis Harral

Citation: Ancestry.com, Cuyahoga County, Ohio, Marriage Records and Indexes, 1810-1973 (Provo, UT, USA, Ancestry.com Operations, Inc., 2010), Ancestry.com, Cuyahoga County Archive; Cleveland, Ohio; Cuyahoga County, Ohio, Marriage Records, 1810-1973; Volume: Vol 17-18; Page: 168; Year Range: 1872 Jul - 1876 Dec. [Source citation includes media item(s)] Pearson, Marie Suela Penfield, Francis Harral

Source Title: Davenport Daily Republican at Newspapers.com
Repository: www.newspapers.com

Citation: Davenport Daily Republican at Newspapers.com, www.newspapers.com, : Found in Davenport Daily Republican. http://www.newspapers.com/clip/193426/davenport_daily_republican/. Pearson, Marie Suela

Source Title: New York City, Deaths, 1892-1902
Repository: Ancestry.com

Citation: Ancestry.com, New York City, Deaths, 1892-1902 (Provo, UT, USA, Ancestry.com Operations Inc., 2003), Ancestry.com, New York City Deaths, 1892-1902; Deaths Reported in 1901 (M-Z). Borough of Manhattan; Certificate #: 32097. Penfield, Francis Pearson

Source Title: Ohio, Births and Christenings Index, 1800-1962
Repository: Ancestry.com

Citation: Ancestry.com, Ohio, Births and Christenings Index, 1800-1962 (Provo, UT, USA, Ancestry.com Operations, Inc., 2011), Ancestry.com. Penfield, Rose Marie

Source Title: Ohio, Deaths, 1908-1932, 1938-2007
Repository: Ancestry.com

Citation: Ancestry.com and Ohio Department of Health, Ohio, Deaths, 1908-1932, 1938-2007 (Provo, UT, USA, Ancestry.com Operations Inc., 2010), Ancestry.com, Certificate: 17446; Volume: 16828. Penfield, Rose Marie

Citation: Ancestry.com and Ohio Department of Health, Ohio, Deaths, 1908-1932, 1938-2007 (Provo, UT, USA, Ancestry.com Operations Inc., 2010), Ancestry.com. [Source citation includes media item(s)] Rose, Eleanor McKinley

Citation: Ancestry.com and Ohio Department of Health, Ohio, Deaths, 1908-1932, 1938-2007 (Provo, UT, USA, Ancestry.com Operations Inc., 2010), Ancestry.com. [Source citation includes media item(s)]

Citation: Ancestry.com and Ohio Department of Health, Ohio, Deaths, 1908-1932, 1938-2007 (Provo, UT, USA, Ancestry.com Operations Inc., 2010), Ancestry.com. [Source citation includes media item(s)] Pearson, Marie Suela

Citation: Ancestry.com and Ohio Department of Health, Ohio, Deaths, 1908-1932, 1938-2007 (Provo, UT, USA, Ancestry.com Operations Inc., 2010), Ancestry.com. [Source citation includes media item(s)] Penfield, Francis Harral

Source Title: The Indianapolis News at Newspapers.com
Repository: www.newspapers.com

Citation: The Indianapolis News at Newspapers.com, www.newspapers.com, : Found in The Indianapolis News.. http://www.newspapers.com/clip/193436/the_indianapolis_news/. Pearson, Marie Suela

Source Title: **The Times at Newspapers.com**
Repository: **www.newspapers.com**

Citation: The Times at Newspapers.com, www.newspapers.com, : Found in The Times.. http://www.newspapers.com/clip/191877/the_times/. Pearson, Clement

Source Title: **Web: BillionGraves.com Burial Index**
Repository: **Ancestry.com**

Citation: Ancestry.com, Web: BillionGraves.com Burial Index (Provo, UT, USA, Ancestry.com Operations, Inc., 2013), Ancestry.com. Rose, Eleanor McKinley

Citation: Ancestry.com, Web: BillionGraves.com Burial Index (Provo, UT, USA, Ancestry.com Operations, Inc., 2013), Ancestry.com. Penfield, Rose Marie

Source Title: **Web: Ohio, Find A Grave Index, 1787-2012**
Repository: **Ancestry.com**

Citation: Ancestry.com, Web: Ohio, Find A Grave Index, 1787-2012 (Provo, UT, USA, Ancestry.com Operations, Inc., 2012), Ancestry.com.

Citation: Ancestry.com, Web: Ohio, Find A Grave Index, 1787-2012 (Provo, UT, USA, Ancestry.com Operations, Inc., 2012), Ancestry.com. Pearson, Clement

Citation: Ancestry.com, Web: Ohio, Find A Grave Index, 1787-2012 (Provo, UT, USA, Ancestry.com Operations, Inc., 2012), Ancestry.com. Penfield, Francis Harral

Citation: Ancestry.com, Web: Ohio, Find A Grave Index, 1787-2012 (Provo, UT, USA, Ancestry.com Operations, Inc., 2012), Ancestry.com. Pearson, Marie Suela

Citation: Ancestry.com, Web: Ohio, Find A Grave Index, 1787-2012 (Provo, UT, USA, Ancestry.com Operations, Inc., 2012), Ancestry.com. Pearson, William Rose

Citation: Ancestry.com, Web: Ohio, Find A Grave Index, 1787-2012 (Provo, UT, USA, Ancestry.com Operations, Inc., 2012), Ancestry.com. Penfield, Francis Pearson

Citation: Ancestry.com, Web: Ohio, Find A Grave Index, 1787-2012 (Provo, UT, USA, Ancestry.com Operations, Inc., 2012), Ancestry.com. Penfield, Rose Marie

Chapter 6: Frances Elizabeth Roads

Frances Elizabeth Roads

Franc Roads, the youngest of the seven founders, was born 10 February 1852 to Addison and Nancy McClure Roads.

Her parents, Addison and Nancy, were married 7 March 1849. On both the 1850 United States Census of Liberty, Indiana and the 1856 Iowa State Census, Addison's occupation is listed as a "blacksmith."

Sometime in 1851, the family moves to Iowa where Frances (Franc) is born in Marshall, Iowa. And, by 1856 the family is found in Center, Iowa and in 1860 they reside in Mt. Pleasant. By this time, Addison's occupation is identified as "grocer." Franc's younger brother, Charles, came along in 1859.

Records reflect that Addison and Nancy Roads raise a third child, Leona Potts. Leona appears to have joined the family between 1860 and 1870. It is interesting to note that every document and record which refers to Leona after the 1870 Census lists her as "Leona Roads," even her marriage record in 1866 to Henry Bowman. Several historical accounts refer to Leona as Franc's "sister." However, research reveals that Leona was in reality the child of Nancy's sister, Katherine McClure Potts.

Concurrently, Simon Elliott, Franc's future husband, located with his family in Mt. Pleasant, Iowa as Simon's father, Rev. Dr. Charles Elliott, became president of Iowa Wesleyan University from 1857 to 1861. Dr. Elliott was in his mid-sixties at the time of his first tenure. He had been born in Ireland in 1792, and due to his religious affiliation with the Irish Wesleyan Society was unable to study at the University of Dublin. Thus, he studied independently and arrived in Ohio in 1814 where he was accepted into the traveling circuit of the Methodist Episcopal Church. Dr. Elliott would again be president of the Iowa Wesleyan 1862-1866. In between his presidencies, Dr. Elliott was editor of the Central Christian Advocate and earned himself the name of "War Editor."

Dr. Charles Elliott was approximately 49 when his son Simon was born. He was a well-known Methodist Episcopal minister and an educator who prior to being invited to Iowa Wesleyan had co-founded Ohio Wesleyan University in 1841, along with Rev. William P. Strickland, and Rev. Joseph M. Trimble. Additionally, Dr. Elliott founded the Biblical Department at Ohio Wesleyan University. He was known as a great thinker as well as a bold, aggressive writer with good executive ability.

It was during Dr. Elliott's second Presidential tenure that the first woman, Lucy W. Killpatrick would graduate from Iowa Wesleyan. And, upon his resignation from Iowa Wesleyan, the trustees honored him by establishing the first female college in Christendom. Thus, without Franc's father-in-law, perhaps not only she, but the seven founders may not have received a college education; nor would they have met to even conceive the idea of P.E.O.

During September of 1866 Franc, at the age of 14, enrolled at Iowa Wesleyan.

Simon was 11 years older than Franc and during the Civil War; he enlisted in Company A, 45th Regiment of the Iowa Volunteer Infantry. Company A was made up of soldiers from Henry County. The Regiment was formed during the summer of 1864 as part of the scores of regiments known as "Hundred Days Men." This was an effort by the Union to augment manpower in a push to end the war within 100 days. Their assigned duty was guarding the Memphis camp and the Charleston Railroad. The men mustered in on May 25 and mustered out on Sept 15th, six and half months before Lee surrendered at Appomattox.

During the three years Franc was a student at Iowa Wesleyan, and for some of the three years following her graduation, and before their marriage in June of 1872, Simon Elliott was her consistent escort.

Rev. Dr. Charles Elliott dies at the age of 77 in January 1869, just 15 days before Franc and the other seven founded the P.E.O. Sisterhood. His son Simon was 27, but Franc was just a month shy of 17.

For a period of time Simon was living in Lincoln, Nebraska as we find him on the 1870 Census, listing his occupation as a drug merchant.

By the time of the 1880 Census, Simon and Franc Elliott were married and living in Lincoln, Nebraska with two children, Charles Addison Elliott aged 7 and Stella Roads Elliott, age 3. Simon lists his occupation as owner of a china store. With Franc's interest in art, it is believed that she mastered the art of china painting along with her other art projects.

Franc is chosen to represent Nebraska as the Assistant Commissioner of Art at the New Orleans Exhibit of 1884. This appointment was most unusual for a woman during that timeframe.

The economic "Panic of 1893" led to changes within the Elliott family. Franc made the decision to teach art in order to be able to keep their son, Charles in medical school. We find several newspaper articles dated between January 1899 and December 1904, when Franc would have been between the ages of 46 and 52, referencing her as teaching art in the Salt Lake City school system. These reports reveal that she developed a remarkable reputation as not only an excellent teacher of art, but as a speaker.

The news article of January 16th 1899, written by Franc, entitled "The Function of Art in the Development of the Individual," reflects upon the fact that ten years prior, the very idea of including art along with other studies, would have been considered "ridiculous." She contended that a child should be able to express and create what they see and that a child's mind is weakened by all school processes that increase the store of knowledge without at the same time, and by the same processes, increase the tendency to express and use that knowledge. She further expounds upon how the practice of art encourages observation.

Later that year, in August of 1899, Franc attends her daughter, Stella and James Canfield's wedding in Jamestown, New York. James was the son of another educator, James Hulme Canfield, the fourth president of Ohio State University (July 1, 1895 – June 30, 1899).

Stella's husband, James was also the brother of Dorothy Canfield Fisher, a strong supporter of women's rights and lifelong education. Dorothy is well known for bringing the Montessori Method of teaching to America by translating Montessori's book into English. She was also a best-selling author. And, she was named by Eleanor Roosevelt as one of the ten most influential women of her time in the United States.

According to the account of the Canfield-Elliott wedding written in the Jamestown Evening Journal, the bride's brother, Dr. Charles Elliott, gave his sister Stella away in the "unavoidable absence" of her father. The absence of Simon may be explained by a note from one of Franc's descendants, Stella Canfield Fisher when she writes, "Neither financial reverses nor the care of an invalid husband quenched her (Franc's) enthusiasm for life." The conjecture that Simon was an invalid is further supported by the evidence of the record found in the Civil War Pension Index reflecting an "invalid" status for Simon awarded in October 1898.

Franc's daughter Stella and James ultimately had two sons, Charles Elliott and Robert Elliot Canfield.

The year 1900 brings further changes and recognition in Franc's life. Although she is listed in the Census as a part of her son's household in Chicago, she is also definitely still teaching in Salt Lake City schools. The year 1900 was an active one for Franc for in February we read Franc is recognized as a "Notable Utah Woman;" in April it is reported she speaks before the Utah county teachers on "Art;" in November her first grandchild, Charles Elliott Canfield is born and in December, she is reported to have presented a speech, "Art as a Factor in Public Education" at the State Teacher Association meeting.

During the turn of the century and the early years of the 20th Century, Franc continues to teach and promote art as an important part of a child's education. She is also active in Women's Clubs and the National Federation of Women's Clubs. She is listed in the 1900 program for the General Federation of Women's Clubs (GFWC) as a representative of Utah and she presented a report on the State Federation's Art Department on 8 June. It was during 1901 that the GFWC received its charter from the United States Congress.

Later in 1903, on October 13, Franc and Simon's second grandson, Robert Elliott Canfield joins the family.

Towards the end of 1904, when she was 52, Franc was "released" from her duties as a supervisor of drawing in the Salt Lake City School system. A job she had for at least eight years. She apparently got caught in the middle of a "political" struggle for control of the Salt Lake City School system by the Mormon Church. According to the December 4th edition of The Salt Lake Tribune, Franc, although considered a teacher of "unusual ability," was a Gentile and she was replaced by a Mormon teacher, D.W. Parratt. Dr. Parratt is described by the author of the news article, as only being able to demonstrate his drawing abilities by being able to "draw a larger salary."

During the time of the 1910 Census while we find Franc living in Chicago with her son, Dr. Charles Elliott; Simon is living with his sister Phebe, next door to his daughter and son-in-law, the Canfields. Phebe was older than Simon, and was 71 at the time. Perhaps Phebe is helping to care for Simon? Of note is that they all live in a town in New York, known as.... Mt. Pleasant.

Franc and Simon's son, Charles, marries Genevieve Cole in December of 1911. Genevieve and Charles may have known each other through their parents, as Genevieve's grandfather, Rev. William R. Cole, was a preacher in Mt. Pleasant, Iowa during the same years that Simon and Franc lived in Mt. Pleasant with their families. Charles would spend his career as a professor of medicine at Northwestern University and become a well-known diagnostician.

Genevieve and Charles have three children: two sons, Frank Roads Elliott, born in 1913 and Ernest Charles Elliott born in 1920. They also have a daughter, Margaret C. Elliott, born November 1914. According to the P.E.O. history book, by Stella Clapp "Out of the Heart," two of these children, Frank and Margaret, also become M.D.'s.

In May of 1915, Simon Elliott dies and does not live to see the last of his grandchildren, Ernest, born (1920).

According to his US Passport Application, as well as to the Rockefeller Foundations annual report for 1918, Charles is appointed in 1918 by the Rockefeller Foundation's International Health Board to membership on a five man Commission which was sent to Guayaquil, Ecuador, to investigate the presence of yellow fever and "allied diseases."

An epidemic of yellow fever had made an appearance there in June of 1918. At the time, the Surgeons General of the United States Army and United States Public Health Service regarded the presence of this uncontrolled epidemic so near our southern border as to warrant "energetic measures." The Foundation's board offered its services to the President of the Republic of Guatemala and the Government of Ecuador.

From this expedition, the commission implemented epidemic control measures and the foundation ultimately developed the first vaccine to prevent yellow fever. This version of a yellow fever vaccine was used until 1926, when it would quietly be discontinued, with no alternative offered.

What a legacy and impact on the world Franc, her pioneering spirit and her family and her descendants accomplished!

Franc spends her last nine years living in Chicago with her son and his family, until she dies in August of 1924.

Frances Elizabeth Roads Elliott – Life Events

DATE	EVENT	AGE
10 February 1852	Born: Marshall County, Iowa	
1856	Residence: Center, Henry, Iowa	4
1857-1861	Simon Elliott's father, Rev. Charles Elliott President Iowa Wesleyan	5-9
June 1860	Residence: Mount Pleasant, Henry, Iowa	8
1864-1866	Simon Elliott's father, Rev. Charles Elliott President Iowa Wesleyan (second time)	12-14
21 January 1869	P. E.O. Founded	16
June 1869	Graduated from Iowa Wesleyan with B.S. degree	17
1869	Taught school	17
June 1870	Residence: Center, Henry, Iowa	18
6 June 1872	Married: Simon Charles Elliott	20
June 1872	Honorary M.S. degree awarded	20
6 March 1873	Son: Charles Addison Elliott born	21
31 October 1876	Daughter: Stella M. Elliott born	24
June 1880	Residence: Lincoln, Lancaster, Nebraska	28
1884	Assistant Commissioner of Art at New Orleans Exhibition	32
1893	Enters workforce due to Economic Panic of 1893 Taught school in Aurora, Illinois	41
1899	Supervisor of Drawing Salt Lake City schools	46
16 January 1899	Speech: "The Function of Art in the Development of the Individual"	46
August 1899	Daughter Stella married to James Canfield	47
29 December 1899	Led discussion at State Teachers' Institute, Salt Lake City	47
24 February 1900	Recognized as a "Notable Utah Woman"	48
14 April 1900	Spoke before Utah County teachers re: Art	48
June 1900	Residence: Chicago, Cook, Illinois	48
3 November 1900	Grandson, Charles Elliott Canfield born	48
19 December 1900	Speaker at State Teacher Association: "Art as a Factor in Public Education"	48
1901	Retained as Drawing teacher	49
1902	Active in Women's Club and National Federation of clubs	50
13 October 1903	Grandson Robert Elliott Canfield born	51
December 1904	Released from teaching position in Salt Lake City	52

DATE	EVENT	AGE
April 1910	Residence: Chicago, Cook, Illinois	58
13 December 1911	Son Charles Elliott married Genevieve Comstock Cole	59
1 February 1913	Grandson Frank Roads Elliott born	60
1 November 1914	Granddaughter Margaret C. Elliott born	62
9 May 1915	Simon Charles Elliott died	63
June 1915	Residence: Mt. Pleasant, Westchester, New York	63
January 1920	Residence: Chicago, Cook, Illinois	67
15 April 1920	Grandson Ernest Charles Elliott born	68
9 August 1924	Died: Chicago, Cook, Illinois Buried: Forest Home Cemetery, Mount Pleasant, Iowa	72

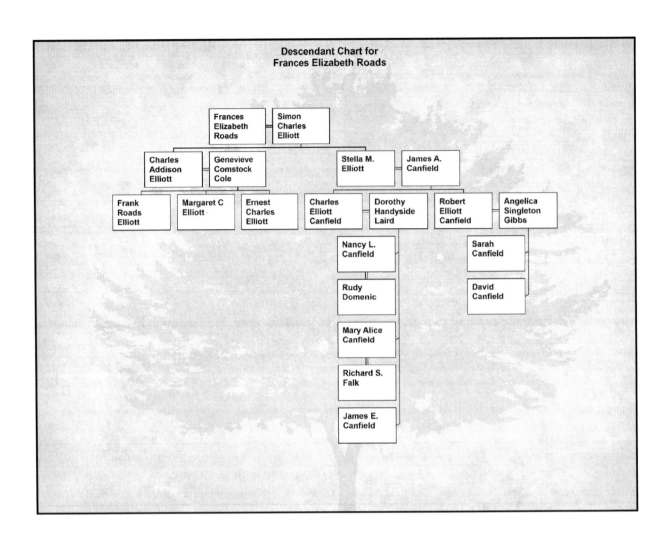

**Descendant Chart for
Frances Elizabeth Roads**

Frances Elizabeth Roads	Simon Charles Elliott

Charles Addison Elliott	Genevieve Comstock Cole

Stella M. Elliott	James A. Canfield

Frank Roads Elliott

Margaret C Elliott

Ernest Charles Elliott

Charles Elliott Canfield

Dorothy Handyside Laird

Robert Elliott Canfield

Angelica Singleton Gibbs

Nancy L. Canfield

Rudy Domenic

Mary Alice Canfield

Richard S. Falk

James E. Canfield

Sarah Canfield

David Canfield

294

were Capt. and Mrs. J. C. Ayres, Miss Rodman, Miss Nash, Miss McKenna, Miss Wakeley, Capt. Crowder, Major McElderry, Lieut. A. G. C. Quay, Mr. Doane and Mr. Charles H. Wilson.

Mr. Hardy has arranged with Professor Fossler to deliver a course of lectures on Roman history at the Crete Chautauqua assembly.

Hon. G. M. Lambertson will be the orator at the old settler's picnic to be held Thursday at Burlington beach.

Mrs. D. L. Brace gave a charming musicale yesterday afternoon for her sister Mrs. Cropsey, of Cheyenne. Mrs. Cropsey and Mrs. Lippincott sang, and a very enjoyable program was rendered.

Mrs. C. E. Yates and Willard Yates left for the east yesterday.

Dr. White, of the State university, left yesterday for Baltimore. He will spend his vacation at the seaside and other resorts in the east and will not return till fall.

Mrs. M. H. Tilton and Miss Baird were Omaha visitors Wednesday.

Mrs. Harris, Miss Harris, Mrs. Clark and Miss Clark spent yesterday in Omaha.

Mrs. John B. Wright received a few friends Thursday afternoon in honor of her sister, Mrs. Weaver.

Mrs. Cropsey, of Cheyenne, whose singing has been so thoroughly enjoyed the last few weeks, will sing in the Congregational church tomorrow.

Miss Maggie Hallett left Wednesday afternoon for a short visit with friends at Hiawatha, Kansas.

"The Chimes of Normandy," presented by a talented local company under the direction of M. J. W. Seamark, for the benefit of Holy Trinity, drew the usual large and enthusiastic audience that assembles to do honor to home talent, at the Lansing theatre Wednesday evening. Mr. Seamark had drilled his company very carefully, and the performance was really meritorious in more ways than one. In the familiar role of *Serpolette* Miss Minnie Gaylord appeared to decided advantage, her singing and acting both calling for warm praise. Her rendition was very clever. Miss Jennie Hoffman made a pleasing impression as *Germaine*. She has the dramatic instinct and her stage presence is unusually good. Mr. Seamark, one of the most popular singers in the city, had a fine opportunity in *Henri* to bring out the best qualities in his voice, and he achieved much success. Dr. Eddy as *Grenicheux* was enjoyable as Dr. Eddy's vocal efforts always are. Mr. Kellum and Mr. Harry Shears contributed the comedy element, and they acquitted themselves with much credit. Mr. Keens also succeeded in interpreting his part to the satisfaction of the audience. The chorus was strong and well disciplined and the Lansing theatre orchestra under the direction of Mrs. P. V. M. Raymond did excellent work. It is said that the success of the performance of "The Chimes of Normandy" foreshadows the formation of an operatic society in this city under the leadership of Mr. Seamark.

The annual promenade by the senior class of the state university was given in Representative hall at the capitol last evening. It was one of the gayest and most enjoyable dancing events that have occured in Lincoln in a long time. The members of the senior class were particularly anxious that the promenade should be distinctively a university affair, and invitations were bestowed accordingly; but there was a fair representation of local society people. It was altogether a very brilliant gathering. Tonight the exercises incidental to the commencement season will be continued by a meeting of the literary societies of the university in the chapel. A joint program will be rendered. The annual sermon will be delivered Sunday afternoon in the chapel by the Rev. Henry Hopkins, D. D; of Kansas City. Sunday evening the Rev. Frank Crane, of Omaha, will deliver the baccalaureate sermon. There will be music by the university

chorus and glee club. Monday evening at the Lansing theatre will occur the annual contest by the musical department. Monday morning the senior class day exercises will be held at the Lansing. A feature of the program will be a German play. Tuesday evening at 7:30 the glee club and cadet band will give an open air concert on the steps of the chemical building. On Wednesday at 10 o'clock in the Lansing, the regular commencement exercises will be held. Prof. George D. Herron, of Iowa college, will deliver the oration. His subject will be "A New Political Vision." There will be a reunion of the alumni Wednesday at Burlington beach, from 5 till 9 o'clock.

The following graduated from the high school Thursday night: Miss Nellie Cochrane, Miss Stella Elliott, Miss Bessie Crawford, Miss Olive Graham, Miss Flora Hartley, Miss Edith Parrish, Miss Myrtle Russell, Miss Emma Sherwood, Miss Isabel Upton and Miss Clara Watkins.

IN OMAHA.

On Tuesday evening the Carlton Opera company gave their last performance for this season at Boyd's theatre. "The Chimes of Normandy" was sung to a well filled and very enthusiastic house. Mr. Carlton himself did not sing, and I fear was little missed by the audience, his part being so well rendered by Mr. Taylor. Mr. Rickets responded to a well deserved curtain call. Miss Vincent and Miss Aell both sang and acted well, Miss Vincent showing much more vivacity than is usual with her.

Apropos of Mr. Carlton's visit to Omaha, I was the witness of a very disgraceful scene enacted at Dohany's opera house in Council Bluffs last Friday evening. It seems that Miss Vincent on the plea of illness was released from singing in Omaha that night and when Mr. Carlton called upon her at her hotel to offer his sympathies, he was informed that she had recovered sufficiently not only to dine out with Omaha's lady-like society reporter, but also to accompany him across the river to see Mr. Frohman's company's presentation of "Lady Windemere's Fan." To say that Mr. Carlton was provoked at thus finding himself duped is putting it very mildly. After imbibing copiously there was blood on the face of the moon when he boarded the express for Council Bluffs. Upon his arrival at the theater he beheld in the proscenium box his beautiful and commanding prima donna with her little boy companion. During the first entre act without any announcement Mr. Carlton entered the box and after a short and very much to the point conversation, which was distinctly heard by the entire audience, planted his good sized English fist on our would-be gay Lothario's neck and then jumped behind the portiers to await developments. After a short absence during which time the onlookers as well as the pugilistic baritone waited with bated breath, Miss Vincent's gallant escort came up from the carpet smiling still, but a trifle white about the gills. Upon seeing that no active steps were being taken on the part of his adversary Mr. Carlton deemed it safe to return to the box where he continued to disturb the audience until the party was finally ejected by the attaches of the theatre. Mr. Carlton, being too much under the influence of liquor to realize his position, Miss Vincent dignified and very much embarrassed, her escort, still without his usual ruddy complexion, and longing for the bosom of his family, beat a hasty retreat.

A wedding that is of deep interest to Omaha society by reason of the great popularity of the bride and that is to take place on Tuesday, June 26th, will be that of Miss Clara Brown, daughter of Mr. and Mrs. J. J. Brown, to Mr. Henry Wyman. Miss Hoagland Miss Chandler, Miss Margaret Brown, Miss Nash, Miss Chambers, Miss Pratt and Miss Bessie Yates will be the attendants at the ceremony, which comes off at the family residence.

Mr. and Mrs. H. Klingenfeld (nee Ljams) of New York, are expected early next week on a visit to Mr. and Mrs. Dan S. Lander.

Miss Balcombe will leave Omaha tomorrow for New York, from whence she will sail on the 13th for Antwerp. During her absence, which will be until September, she will visit France, Italy, Switzerland and England.

Mrs. Brooke left on Wednesday for Concord where she will pass the month of June, the general joining her about the 20th.

Transcription from:
The Courier, Lincoln, Nebraska, June 9, 1894, page 8

The following graduated from the high school Thursday night Miss Nellie Cochrane, Miss Stella Elliott, Miss Bessie Crawford, Miss Olive Graham, Miss Flora Hartley, Miss Edith Parrish, Miss Myrtle Russell, Miss Emma Sherwood, Miss Isabel Upton and Miss Clara Watkins

The Salt Lake Herald, Salt Lake City, Utah, January 16, 1899, page 3
www.chroniclingamerica.loc.gov

Transcription from:
The Salt Lake Herald, Monday, 16 January 1899, page 3

TALKS BY UTAH EDUCATORS

Number 8

"The Function of Art in the Development of the Individual"

By Mrs. Franc R. Elliott, Supervisor of Drawing in Salt Lake City Schools

There is simple proof that we are not a fallen but an ever rising race in the fact that an educational club is willing to discuss the proposition that beauty has a place in educating the human being. Ten years ago the proposal that art should be given a place along with the time-honored studies that minister directly to the intellect, would have been considered to say the least ridiculous; but thanks to a growing comprehension as to the part of every liberated man and women who has the welfare of the community at heart, that the true heads for deciding whether any subject shall have a place on the school programme is that the subject must be educational, not economic; that in the culture of so definitely interdependent a unity as the human mind the attempt to train only certain powers and omit the training of others, must inevitably result in the partial development even of those powers whose training is attempted. That the established school course of the past has been one-sided, and the result a warped training, educationists are ready to admit. There has been much preaching on the training of the will, though the formal intellectual studies that have claimed most of the attention of the schools, such as mental exercise in number, the technicalities of grammar, and the study of language, but after all the results have been disappointing. And has the will been trained to the extent that warrants the effort? To the student of sociology the conclusion is inevitable that the present education is not a guarantee against selfishness, and does not direct to the best well-being of the whole community. Children's eyes and ears and hearts have a hunger that the mastery of the three Rs by the old time process cannot feed. "Through my heart I am what I am," exclaimed the great Pestalozzi. The thirst of the imagination must be satisfied in the school room or materialism will leave its blight on our people. The state does not do its duty to the individual or the community, if it fails to develop the best in each child. The progressive and harmonious growth of the universal community depends on the complete development of the individuals of which it is composed. The highest test of any educational system is its influence on the expansion and strengthening of the spiritual nature. In the old Greek world they knew better than we. There the true nature of the individual was recognized, and those students which brought culture to the soul, as well as the body and intellect, were fostered. Because of this the Greeks were the most harmoniously developed of any people, and we hold as a result of their rich legacy in art, literature and mathematics. The pressing demand that the social order be spiritualized can be accomplished through the only available avenue, the public schools. The conditions of life in large centers are such that from ethical and social reasons the demand must be granted. Today the anxiety on the part of those who form the plan of study for the schools is how education may spiritualize itself. Education has come to

298

mean the development of the whole man; the physical, intellectual and aesthetic or spiritual. It must help the individual to understand himself to justly value his kind, put himself in harmony with his surroundings, and show him how to better social conditions.

The social idea is the center of all the teachings of Froebel. If we go right to the heart of things we will find that the clay modeling, the drawing, the mat weaving, the song and the game exist primarily to relate the child to his world, for the promotion of altruism between him and his teachers, his companions and his studies. It is through this relating of things to each other and through their application in life, that the soul gains its intelligence, not through the producing of a result. Drawing in the schools has come to its present importance because preeminently it mediates, relates and unifies other studies to each other. In its several forms when rightly taught it is more altruistic than any other study. It transports and connects imagination and intellect, the actual and ideal, the objective and subjective worlds. It lends itself out to all other recognized studies, while in itself it is a thought study, generating in the mind an activity, a quality of feeling and synthetic grasp of ideas not to be attained through the most faithful devotion to literature of mathematics. The instinctive love for beauty is innate with every human and with it its natural outgrowth, expression. Side by side with this instinctive love of beauty in childhood we find the other instinctive desire of productions – the desire to create, to put outside of himself in some form the loved idea. In the crudest drawing or rudest, most absurd clay figures, seemingly lacking in every element of beauty, we must assure ourselves we see the testimony of the divine creative power. As I note this universal love for beauty and the desire to create in my continual contact with children, I am convinced that the potential artist, poet, or seer is within every child, and that the world has been made the poorer, because through our clumsy educational processes we have stifled the best until the stupid, average, or commonplace citizen is the result. The difference between the artist or poet and the rest of the world, is simply that on the one hand the mind has been trained to give attention to the things about him, until he sees in the most common things beauties of which the other never dreamed. In his immortal confession Wordsworth tells of this highly trained soul-sense when he says that the meanest thing that grows gave him thoughts too deep for tears. We wonder sometimes that men follow so meekly the leadership of demagogues. We should not wonder when the training in the schools has been so much that which makes copyists of them, too often the most successful teacher has been the one who could soonest destroy individuality. The mind is weakened by all school processes that increase the store of knowledge without, at the same time, and by the same processes, increasing the tendency to express and use the knowledge gained. It is a law that the one who never has learned to exercise self-expression forever remains a material being, always influenced from the without and subject to the will of others. Unexpressed feeling or thought is accompanied by gradual loss of mental power. The possibility of mind growth is evidenced by increasing the power of expression. No thought can be thoroughly wrought into selfhood until it has been expressed, and each new form of expression strengthens, purifies or enables selfhood – the individual. Drawing, which is one form of art, affords one of the best opportunities for self-expression, for this reason, I would make a large place for it in the schools.

Drawing trains the observation. Seeing is really an act of the mind; thousands of pictures form themselves in the eye daily that are not seen. We see only those things to which we give attention. Culture in seeing means culture of the mind, not of the eye. The power to see accurately and fully depends on the power of giving intelligent attention. No two men see exactly the same picture in the same landscape; ten men will see then different pictures from the same point of view. Each sees the picture most in harmony with his main center of interest. No finite mind can see them all; the power to see increases as the finite mind grows consciously toward the infinite. The true work of education promotes a growth of the finite toward the infinite. All true art training increases the ability to see size, color, form and relationship in the child's environment. Children do not reason very much, but they observe a great deal. The greater part of the study of drawing should be in observation, simple and direct from objects, simple, free and un-initiative work. I would lay more stress on that part of drawing that trains the eye to see and the hand to test the position and relation of actually observed objects, and less on that which makes smooth, finished, false drawings that please pupils and parents, and too often teachers. We do not write words for mere show; we want the idea, the thought, back of the expression. Drawing is nothing if it is not putting things in their right place; of what use is a line if it is not in the right place, if it means nothing, expresses nothing?

The practice of art trains the judgment – to judge, to judge vertically, to judge horizontally, to judge height and width; the greatest height and the greatest width, and every height and every width; to block in and leave blocked in; to simplify and see that there is beauty in simplicity, and that such a thing as imitation is false. Accurate observation leads to correct judgment, and comprehensive observation leads to broader thinking in regard to a greater variety of individual things and their true relationship to each other. A great portion of human thought depends on conceptions of size, form, color and relationships. Art training cultivates new and exact perceptive centers of size, form, color and relationships, and defines judgment.

One of the most important advantages of an art training comes from its usefulness in revealing the child to himself. It is an important epoch in the life of a child when it gains the consciousness of original power. While any form of self-expressions may be made the means of self-revelation, no other form exceeds this for making clear to the child the transforming truth that it was intended to be more than an imitator and follower. The highest school processes are those that do most to develop the child's originality and apply it to lines of utility and aesthetic culture. There should be no barren lives. No man accomplishes his true destiny who fails to put forth some thought or product that will make it easier for his fellow man to be happy and to attain a more complete development. Art develops originality and helps men to aid in the increase of human wisdom and power by the production of new thought, of new power and new appliances.

No teacher should ever be satisfied unless the thought implanted in the mind of the child comes forth in improved form, charged with new life and dynamic power through the child's individuality. Mistakes have been made in teaching drawing. I do not speak of it in the old sense of copying from the flat, making lines and reciting definitions. This had little or nothing in it that developed selfhood. In music, the instruments, the hand, the voice and the ear have been trained, but the soul that should originate the music has been left to chance development. Even the art of oral expression has been made a process of imitation. It is doubtful whether it is possible to cultivate the habit of repeating the thoughts of others in the exact language of others without weakening selfhood and the powers of self-expression. There is no doubt whatever that we may be trained to express most admirably the thoughts of others, in the language of other, without having our powers of self-expression improved by the process. Oft-repeated drill, as mere drill, has been too much practiced as a means of defining and establishing certain powers of the mind and hand. Drill divorced from self-expression cannot retain interest, and without interest there can be no lasting benefit to the child. All true growth is from within outward. All drill for drill's sake attempts the unnatural to produce growth from without inward.

Imagination is the foundation for all the constructive arts, the builder machinist. The inventor, as well as the artist and poet, lives in the imagination. Wherever inert wood, heavy stone, dull, cold iron and steel have been made to come into life and join hands to produce a bridge, an engine, a dwelling house, a printing press, there you find human imagination at the heart of it; positive, clear and creative. Cultivating the aesthetic nature kindles the imagination and quickens the conscience. Through the imagination we put ourselves in the place of another; without imagination there can be no sympathy for others. The imaginative man is indignant at the perpetration of a wrong and feels for the time that he is the victim of the wrong. Through imagination we become cosmopolitan; cultivating the aesthetic creates an atmosphere in which the proprieties, the amenities and virtues unconsciously grow. The latest testimony of the scientist is that the study of the harmonious and beautiful builds cell tissues in the brain that makes for the harmonious in all relations of life. One high in authority, the director of Smithsonian Institute, recently declared that if all the people could study the beautiful in color and form, prisons and police courts would soon be eliminated.

Art should form a part of the education of every child, so that he may enjoy the productions of the human mind and the beauty and uplifting suggestiveness of nature. The poet and artist interpret for us every point; Robert Browning shows us this when he make Fra, Lippo Lippo, a middle century artist monk, say:

"For don't you mark, we're made so that we love
First when we see them painted, things we have passed
Perhaps a hundred times, nor cared to see.
And so they are better painted; better to us,
Which is the same thing. Art was given for that
God uses us to help each other, so
Lending our minds out."

Pictures are the most subtle and far reaching of any influence. I would rather put before the children impure books than a picture in which there is false teaching. Because of this subtlety of art, reproductions of the very best examples from world-famed artists, in pictures and casts, should find a place on the walls of every school room. What could be more powerful or far-reaching in its influence upon the future citizens of this beautiful city than to have the daily influence of the best art upon the children of the schools during the most impressionable period of their lives? School rooms should be the most beautiful places on earth, far more so than churches, which are closed six days out of the seven; but, instead, the vision of the typical school room, bare as factory walls, aside from a few maps, perhaps, haunts me.

Taste is something that grows; it is not innate. To create taste requires an atmosphere of beauty. If we are to have national art; if we are to bring the beautiful into the lives of the American people, the public schools, where the children pass so much of their time, is the place to begin. One of the most practical ways in which ministers, artists, cultured fathers and mothers, women's and men's clubs, can co-operate with teachers, is the organization of art leagues for the purpose of raising money to purchase carefully selected pictures for the schools. Nothing will bring the homes and schools, which have been too long divorced, together sooner than an effort of this kind. Here in Salt Lake City, where we are so far from art centers, is this sort of effort most desirable. The children, too, should be interested and help in such a movement. The wholesome, social influence of having a hand in working together toward a beautiful object fosters a community spirit which the children cannot afford to lose.

With a word form John La Farge, in a recent address, in which he pleads for what he calls the habit of art, and I will close. He says, "From the point of view of making more money, from the point of view of the employer and the wealth of the state, the education of children in art has been thoroughly examined, but I do not know that its general advantage to the whole state, to the protection of wealth, to the orderly arrangement of life has been sufficiently recognized. I allude to place and order, which the habit of art seems to encourage, because I care more for that side of the question. Such forms of culture help in good citizenship and in making men bear more easily with one another."

was unable to be present and named Mrs. L. W. Huntington as her substitute. In the absence of Capt. Mailly Captain Herpolsheimer responded.

Miss Ella Robertson, president of the young ladies auxiliary, being ill, Miss Nina Prey, vice president, appeared for her. Miss Prey's remarks were very clear, and representative of the public sentiment.

The soldiers having explained that public speaking was not so much in their line as fighting, were not heard by the expectant people, but were promptly and cheerfully forgiven.

The program in full was as follows:

"The Stars and Stripes Forever," Sousa, Hagenow's band.

Invocation, Mrs. Persis Bentley.

"Home, Sweet Home," Miss Pauline Oakley.

Address of welcome on behalf of women's patriotic league, Mrs. W. J. Bryan.

Response, James Medley.

Music—Overture "Stradella," Flotow, Hagenow's band.

Address, Miss Ella Robertson, young ladies' auxiliary.

Address, Mrs. L. C. Pace, Appomattox corps.

Patrol, "The Blue and the Gray," Dalbey, Hagenow's band.

Address, Mrs. Belle C. Bokhaw, Columbia Rebekah Lodge No. 90.

Address, Mrs. O. S. Ward, Farragut corps.

Waltz, "Birds' Voices," Vollstedt, Hagenow's band.

Address, Mrs. Maggie Allen, Chasity lodge No. 2.

Address, Mrs. Marian E. Cramphin, General Custer circle.

Medley, "The Winner," Mackay, Hagenow's band.

Occasional poem, Miss Flora Bullock.

Address, Mrs. L. W. Pomerene, women's bimetallic league.

American Patrol," Meacham, Hagenow's band.

The committee on the program comprised the following: Mrs. L. W Pomerene, Mrs. Mary Heaton, Mrs. Kate Zehrung, Mrs. O. S. Ward, Mrs. Anna Pace, Mrs. Marion Cramphin, Mrs. Maggie Allen, Miss Howland and Miss Ella Robertson.

After the program each soldier was decorated with a gold badge of unique design. After which they with their mothers, wives and sweethearts adjourned to the senate chamber from the second. Miss Zediker, Miss Nabon and Mr. Baker also assisted. A number of photographs and relics were scattered about the parlor. At half past nine the guests gathered on the lawn and listened to addresses of welcome delivered by Mrs. King and Dr. Pole of Raymond. Responses were made by Captain Congrove and the soldiers. Ices were served on the lawn. During the evening more than a hundred friends had the pleasure of meeting the soldiers and congratulating them upon their safe and happy return.

One of the popular union parties which have been social features of late was given on Tuesday evening at the home of Mr. and Mrs. Geo. W. Davenport of 3005 R street. Guests to the number of eighty enjoyed the hospitality of Mr. and Mrs. Davenport. Some were the members of the Welcome Circle of the aid society of Grace M. E. church. The membership is limited to ladies but on this occasion the men so fortunate as to belong to the families of the members were invited to the party. The lawn decorated with lanterns presented attractions not to be resisted and the majority of the guests enjoyed its inviting coolness.

Mr. and Mrs. Willard Kimball, Masters George and Willard and Misses Katherine and Margery Kimball have returned from a delightful summer outing in Colorado, the greater part of which was spent at Pico, a woodsy place which

chosen for the ceremony. The wedding party left the New Sherman home at eleven o'clock and entered the church through the chapel porch at the side. Mr. Canfield was accompanied to the chancel rail by the bride's brother, Dr. Charles A. Elliott, of Mercy hospital, Chicago. The bride followed with her mother, Mrs. Frances R. Elliott, supervisor of drawing to the public schools of Salt Lake City, Utah. Then came Mr. Canfield's only sister, Miss Dorothy Canfield of New York City, who passed to the bride's left at the chancel, and acted as the bridesmaid. Following came Mr. Canfield's mother and father, Dr. James H. Canfield, librarian of Columbia university, New York, and Mrs. James H. Canfield. In the unavoidable absence of the bride's father, her brother gave her away. The beautiful service of the Episcopal church was followed throughout, the organist of St. Luke's maintaining a soft accompaniment. The church was tastefully decorated with potted plants. At the close of the ceremony the bridal party passed to the vestry, where the parish records were duly signed and witnessed. Several photographs of the party were taken by Mrs. James H. Canfield, to be sent to absent relations and friends. The entire party was breakfasted at high noon at the New Sherman by Mrs. Elliott, after which the bridal couple left for Buffalo beyond which point their destination was not revealed. Dr. and Mrs. Canfield and daughter returned to New York on Thursday evening, and Dr. and Mrs. Elliott go back to Chataqua for a few days—then to Chicago and the west.

An interesting reception was that given on Wednesday evening by Mr. and Mrs. H. L. Andrews of No. 1 S street, to their son Howard L. Andrews, a member of the First Nebraska. The parlors were decorated with evergreens and golden rod, and without the house, red, white and blue dominated. Above the entrance were the words "Welcome Home" in the national colors. Lanterns lent an additional touch of gayety, while two large head lights brilliantly lighted the lawn. In the receiving line were Mr. H. L. Andrews, Mr. Harvey, Captain Congrove of Company I, Mr. Stern of the First regiment and Mr. Zediker of

has won the favor of many Lincoln people. Mr. Kimball is very busy looking after the preliminary arrangements for the opening of the University School of Music which takes place Monday next. Mr. Kimball expresses himself as much pleased with the outlook for the year. The house is already filled and preparations are being made for a larger number of students than ever before. Mr. Kimball thinks a larger number of instructors than are now announced will be needed. Miss Florence Worley, well and favorably known in Lincoln, and for the past two years instructor of music at Peru, will arrive soon having accepted a position at the University School of Music.

On Monday evening at half past eight was performed the quiet ceremony which united the lives of Mrs. Emmeline Peckham and Rev. John L. Gregg of Manhattan, Kansas. The wedding occurred at the home of the bride 1117 L street. Only a few friends witnessed the ceremony which was performed by Rev. Dr. Wharton. The invited guests were Dr. and Mrs. F. S. Wharton, Rev. and Mrs. R. T. Chipperfield, Elder and Mrs. T. H. Davis, Mr. and Mrs. Harry Peckham and Mrs. George Root. After the ceremony Mr. and Mrs. Gregg were serenaded by the Epworth League of St. Paul's church of which Mrs. Gregg has long been an honored and efficient member. Mr. and Mrs. Gregg will reside in Kansas.

Miss Maud Shamp entertained the Good Templars at her home at 1636 South seventeenth street on Monday evening. Miss Gulick and Miss Lydia Shamp furnished music and Mr. Sylvester Johnson entertained the guests with a pleasing recitation. The guests enjoying Miss Shamp's hospitality were Messrs Peters, Metzger, Johnson, Lons, Kitt; Misses Manley, Kitt, Malong and Mrs. Winebarger.

Mrs. Geo. Bonnell, Miss Bonnell, Miss Winnie and Mr. Roland Bonnell are home again after a delightful summer spent in the Lake Geneva region. The

cottage occupied by Mrs. Bonnell is situated on Lake Beulah, a small but beautiful lake north of Lake Geneva. Mr. Bonnell joined the family for a few days rest and recreation before their return. The party regret the situation as ideal one for summer vacation, including in the category of its inducements fine scenery, clear waters, which furnish boating, bathing or fishing as optional amusements. Mr. Bonnell has leased the same cottage for next year.

A reception was held at the home of Thomas Darnell at 20th and Y streets, on Monday evening in honor of Miss Jennie Pentzer who left Lincoln this morning for Bestwood where she will fill a position in the public schools. Miss Pentzer is a graduate of the state university, class of '99. The reception was attended by about a hundred of Miss Pentzer's friends. The evening was warm and the young people found the lawn, which was brilliantly lighted by two headlights and many lanterns, an enticing place. Refreshments were served and a pleasant evening passed. Miss Barnaby, Miss Woodly, and Miss Dill furnished some delightful music. The East Lincoln quartette composed of Messrs Van Sickle, Odell, Rheinschild, and Crawley also sang acceptably.

Rev. Manss, pastor of the First Congregational church, returned Wednesday from his vacation trip which included visits to Chadwick, Polo, Ill. Chicago and Sault Ste Marie. Mrs. Manss has not yet returned, remaining for a few days more in Polo, Ill. At present Mr. Manss is immersed in the delights which accompany a change of residence. Mr. and Mrs. Manss will reside at 1523 K street.

Cards are out announcing a postponement of the marriage of Miss Susie Riner to Mr. Fred G. Hurd, announced for Wednesday of this week. Mr. E. B. Riner, father of the bride elect, sailed from Havana last Saturday and expects to reach Lincoln in time for the wedding which is to take place September sixth.

Miss Clara Watkins gave a morning

Transcription from:
The Courier, Lincoln, Nebraska, September 2, 1899
Regarding Stella Elliott and James Canfield Wedding

Jamestown, New York, Evening Journal, August 18th – There was a quiet but interesting wedding in St. Luke's church on Thursday morning, the contracting parties being Mr. James A. Camp Canfield and Miss Stella M. Elliott, both of Columbus, Ohio. Miss Elliott is the assistant director of the gymnasium at the Ohio state university, having entire charge of the work with young women, and has been spending the summer at Chatauqua, taking a course in remedial gymnastics, which has just closed. Mr. Canfield is with the Central Ohio paper company of Columbus. It was more convenient for the families of both parties to meet here, so Jamestown and St. Luke's were chosen for the ceremony. The wedding party left the New Sherman house at eleven o'clock and entered the church through the chapel porch at the side. Mr. Canfield was accompanied to the chancel rail by the bride's brother, Dr. Charles A. Elliott, of Mercy hospital, Chicago. The bride followed with her mother, Mrs. Frances R. Elliott, supervisor of drawing in the public schools of Salt Lake City, Utah. Then came Mr. Canfield's only sister, Miss Dorothy Canfield of New York City, who passed to the bride's left at the chancel, and acted as the bridesmaid. Following came Mr. Canfield's mother and father, Dr. James H. Canfield, librarian of Columbia university, New York, and Mrs. James H. Canfield. In the unavoidable absence of the bride's father, her brother gave her away. The beautiful service of the Episcopal church was followed throughout; the organist of St. Luke's maintaining a soft accompaniment. The church was tastefully decorated with potted plants. At the close of the ceremony the bridal party passed to the vestry, where the parish records were duly signed and witnessed. Several photographs of the party were taken by Mrs. James H. Canfield, to be sent to absent relations and friends. The entire party was breakfasted at high noon at the New Sherman by Mrs. Elliott, after which the bridal couple left for Buffalo beyond which point their destination was not revealed. Dr. and Mrs. Canfield and daughter returned to New York on Thursday evening, and Dr. and Mrs. Elliott go back to Chatauqua for a few days – then to Chicago and the west.

Deseret Evening News, Salt Lake City, Utah, February 24, 1900
www.chroniclingamerica.loc.gov

Transcription from:
Deseret Evening News, Salt Lake City, Utah, February 24, 1900, page 14

NOTABLE UTAH WOMEN

MRS. FRANC R. ELLIOTT

Mrs. Franc R. Elliott, Supervisor of Drawing in the schools of this city has had a broad experience in educational fields. Mrs. Elliott received her university training in the Iowa University, and has taken post graduate work in art, history, pedagogy and archeology. Her art training was received principally in the art schools of Cincinnati and Chicago. Mrs. Elliott was one of the educational commission at the World's Cotton Centennial exposition at New Orleans. Before coming to Salt Lake Mrs. Elliott was supervisor of drawing in the schools of Aurora, Illinois, and through her influence in that city Aurora became ideal in having the best reproductions of world-famed art placed in her school. Mrs. Elliott's influence along these same lines is being felt in Salt Lake.

During the exhibit held by the Utah Art Institute in December the confidence of the Directors in Mrs. Elliott's artistic judgment was evidenced by making her chairman of the committee of Awards in the exhibition prize contests.

Mrs. Elliott's ability has been also recognized by the local woman's club element – a factor which is becoming potent in the line of higher culture and educational progress, she having best chosen to act as chairman of the State Art Committee of the Federation of Women's clubs.

il Chief Knight saved the Dowieites on farther harm.

CHINESE TROOPS BEATEN.

efeated by Allied Villagers Near Pao Ting Fu.

New York, July 11.—A dispatch from ——— says: The Imperial troops under Gen. Lu Pen Yuen have been desired by the allied villagers society at ——, forty miles southeast of —— Ting Fu. The magistrate of the strict has arrived in Pekin and has ——ed Li Hung Chang to dispatch a —— reenforcements under Col. —— from Lechieu Fu, where there —— 2,000 Shan Tung troops waiting the —— of the allies to come to ——.

The French who stopped these troops —— Lechien Fu some weeks ago, have —— agreed that they can enter any of —— districts in the province of Chili.

The Hyde Family Incorporates.

New York, July 11.—The Hyde family —— Plainfield, N. J., has incorporated it—. Hereafter the $2,000,000 estate left —— Charles Hyde will be known as the —— County Investment company, —— its widow, his four sons and his —— at the six stockholders. There —— be a paid up capital of $300,000, the —— owning 505 shares and the five —— 487 shares each, each worth —— par.

Mr. Hyde died on June 12 last. He —— his large estate to his wi——, Elizabeth Keppler Hyde, his four —— Dorsey W. Hyde, Francis De Lacy ——, Lewis K. Hyde and Charles ——, Jr., and his only daughter, Miss —— Hyde.

IGH PRICES FOR PAINTINGS.

American Prosperity Influences Them in London.

New York, July 11.—According to the —— correspondent of the Tribune —— prices obtained at Christies, Lon——, this year, have been higher for —— pictures, paintings, engravings and —— than have ever before been ——, and the results are attributed —— to American prosperity. Deal—— are becoming speculative when mil—— are constantly crossing the —— and picking up everything in ——.

STEEL RAIL POOL.

Formally Agrees Upon $28 a Ton for the Coming Year.

New York, July 11.—The Herald says: —— rail manufacturers forming what —— to the trade as the steel rail —— have formally agreed upon $28 a —— as the price which will be asked for —— coming year. This price is $2 a ton —— than that agreed upon at the —— pool meeting last fall, when —— price was announced. Since —— however, a new schedule went —— effect, and prices were advanced

SCHOOL TEACHERS CHOSEN.

Seventeen Selected by the Committee— Mrs. W. C. Jennings Employed.

At the meeting of the committee on teachers and school work of the board of education held yesterday afternoon seventeen new teachers were employed and George C. Young was retained as supervisor of music and Mrs. Franc E. Elliott of drawing each at $122 a month, the same salary as last year. The committee received the formal resignation of Miss Holton as supervisor of the primary department, but there was no action taken towards choosing her successor.

The new teachers are as follows:

Mrs. A. Robbins, nee Bartholomew, city, $65; A. F. Elgren, city, $90; Beatrice Wilkinson, city, $45; A. J. Neil—, city, $45; Miss Ethla E. Shipp, city, $40; Miss Valentina R. Murphy, city, $45; Miss Rosa E. Thomas, city, $45; Miss Alice Mahoney, city, $40; Miss Hattie Ferron, city, $40; Joseph Hughes, Spanish Fork, $55; Miss Ida Coombs, Payson, $40; Pharos Dunyon, Tooele, $40; Miss Lizzie Barnett, Payson, $40; Miss Ruby Knowlton, Kaysville, $40; G. F. Hickman, Provo, $40; Miss Edith Herman, city, $40; Miss Catherine McDonald, city, $40.

There was a unanimous decision on the part of the committee to employ Mrs. William C. Jennings as teacher of modern languages in the high school and Clarence Crandall of the Ogden high school as teacher of biology in the high school here. The salaries will be fixed later.

Free normal scholarships in the normal department of the University were granted to the following: Jennie Grossbeck, Carrie Dunyon, Hulda Hamlin, Lila Green, Sylvia Pearl McAllister, Francis E. Meier, Emma A. Christensen. There is still one scholarship open.

The committee authorized the purchase of $215 worth of chemicals for the high school laboratory.

MRS. WATSON EVICTED.

Unpleasant Duty Performed by Two Deputy Sheriffs.

To Deputy Sheriffs Cummock and Ed. Naylor fell the unpleasant task of evicting Mrs. Helen Watson from the home at 21 South Fifth West street. Shortly before her death Mrs. Watson's step-father, James Chatfield, deeded the property to the Church, and it is now owned by the Fifteenth Ward Relief society. Mrs. Watson's mother, Chatfield's widow, according to the terms of the deed, was to have a life estate in the property, but when she died some two years ago the daughter continued to live at the old homestead, and last fall suit to recover possession of the premises was brought. Mrs. Watson set up as a defense that undue influence had been brought to bear on

—— still has it tied up in his little grip with a sprig of rosemary—"That's for remembrance."

When the matter was called up for consideration by the league last night, Joseph stated his proposition. In the first place, he refused to assume the indebtedness of the club, as was quite natural; further, he would pay a salary list of $600 a month, no more. He wanted the forfeit money of the club to remain in the league treasury, and to have the paraphernalia of the club turned over to him. Bates got in his clever little talk on all these things. The forfeit money must be cut up among the players, he asserted, and bigger salaries had to be paid. With the franchise locked tight within his breast, Bates held out sturdily against any adjustment of the affairs of the club. The meeting adjourned without anything being done. To all intents and purposes, the club is no better off than it was before.

But all the players who have worn miners' suits this season do not think as does George Bates, and do not sanction the action which he took last night. Bates claims to have authority from the players to hold the franchise until a backer shall have been secured who will pay off all the back salaries. Two or three members of the club asserted that no such authority has ever been given, and there the matter rests.

But there is to be more to it. George Bates intends to make it a continued story. As his wives are now laid, the games which Park City will play from now on will be worse than the hippodrome in the rottenest barn-storming, one-ringed country circus that ever walked from hamlet to hamlet. Kids of tender years and anything but saline propensities will be run in, and everything will be done by George Bates to put baseball as he himself expressed it, "On de bum." After this has been done, George Bates will take Tommy Cope

rounds of the hardest kind of fighting. Those who have seen him fight here know that Lafontie must have simply hammered him all over the ring to get him to quit in twenty rounds.

It is reported that Johnnie Green has been holding clandestine flirtations with the Lagoon aggregation. But he won't play with that bunch if Sharkey Griffin has anything to say about it, and Charley usually does make his side count for something. Money and tick—are lying in Cheyenne waiting for Green and will continue to stay to re—all season unless that flirtatious youth take them out and comes down to play with Salt Lake.

The White Wings and the Maccabees will cross willows tomorrow morning at 11 o'clock on Mr. Walker's pasture. As the day belongs to the Maccabees, there will doubtless be a big crowd out and the White Wings won't be too stringent in the matter of scoring. The lodge men will line up as follows: Wood, first base; Smith, catcher; Fottx, third base; Cutler (captain), second base; Martin, shortstop; Donkin, center field; Gunn, left field; Garland, right field; Papworth, Conklin, pitchers.

OUTSIDE EVENTS.

EASTERN BALL GAMES.

Remarkable Twelve Inning Game on Boston Pasture.

National League.
STANDING OF THE CLUBS.

	P.	W.	L.	P.C.
Pittsburg	....	..	64	31	25	.698
New York	....	..	29	22	36	.551

the China ——
race under ——

The official ——
posed it a few ——
has never an ——
was towed ——
Each ship ye ——
registers 2,90 ——
thirty-six me ——
thirty-three ——

The Retila ——
and made a ——
lofnic. She ——
the Acme, e ——
is fitted to co ——

Tro——

To benefit ——
hour time I ——
leg. I tried ——
benefit, until ——
Salve, which ——
Sores Eruptl ——
Salt Rheum ——
hands have ——
grand block ——
cures thes ——
guaranteed ——
M. I. Drug D ——

Children o ——
but from hu ——
antly. The ——
tion! their fo ——
devoured by ——
WHITE'S C ——
destroy the ——
will begin t ——
25 cents. Z ——

BANK STA——
And printing ——
the Deseret ——
promptly fu ——
specialty.

The Clothing Sa

TOMORROW COMMENCES OUI

AND A CLEAN SWEEP OF ALL SUMMER WEARABLES. WE'LL MAINTAI— MAKING PRICES THAT CANNOT BE RESISTED BY ANY ECONOMICAL BUYER. —TWEEN OUR REGULAR LOW PRICES AND THE SALE OFFERS. BUT IT MEAN— ED IN THIS SALE IS OF A MOST DEPENDABLE MANUFACTURE AND LATEST —NEEDS SUCH ARTICLES.
OF COURSE THE MAJORITY OF PEOPLE HAVE ALREADY PURCHASED M— GET A FEW EXTRA THINGS OR IT WILL EVEN PAY YOU TO LAY IN A SUPL— SO BE HERE ON THE FIRST DAY IF POSSIBLE OR EVERYBODY ELSE WIL—

Transcription from:
Deseret Evening News, Salt Lake City, Utah, July 11, 1901, page 5

SCHOOL TEACHERS CHOSEN
Seventeen Selected by the Committee – Mrs. W.C. Jennings Employed

At the meeting of the committee on teachers and school work of the board of education held yesterday afternoon seventeen new teachers were employed and Gorge C. Young was retained as supervisor of music, and Mrs. Franc R. Elliott of drawing, each at $135 a month, the same salary as last year. The committee received the formal resignation of Miss Holton as supervisor of the primary department, but there was not action taken towards choosing her successor.

The new teachers are as follows:

Mrs. A. Robbins, nee Bartholomew, city, $65; A.R. Elgren, city, $60; Beatrice Wilkinson, city, $45; M.J. Nielsen, city, $65; Miss Ellie B. Shipp, city, $40; Miss Valentina R. Murphy, city $45; Miss Rose K. Thomas, city, $45; Miss Alice Mahoney, city, $40; Miss Hattie Ferson, city, $45; Joseph Hughes, Spanish Fork, $45; Miss Ida Coombs, Payson, $65; Pharos Dunyon, Toole, $65; Miss Lizzie Barnett, Payson, $50; Miss Ruby Knowlton, Kaysville, $60; G.F. Hickman, Provo, $65; Miss Edith Herman, city, $30; Miss Catherine McDonald, city, $30.

There was a unanimous decision on the part of the committee to employ Mrs. William C. Jennings as teacher of modern languages in the high school and Clarence Crandall of the Ogden high school as teach of biology in the high school here. The salaries will be fixed later.

Free normal scholarships in the normal department of the University were granted to the Following: Jennie Grossbeck, Carrie Danyon, Linda Hamlin, Lila Green, Sylvia Pearl McAllister, Francis E. Meler, Emma A. Christensen. There is still one scholarship open.

The committee authorized the purchase of $216 worth of chemicals for the high school laboratory.

Transcription from:
The Salt Lake Tribune, Salt Lake City, Utah, December 4, 1904, page 3

Mormonizing the Schools
Progress Already Made Toward It.

If the Voters like it, They Can Have More of It.

Church Leaders Take Credit for Employing Gentiles When They Have No Alternative.

Returns from the school election next Wednesday will tell the Mormon hierarchy just how far it is safe to go in the demoralization of the public schools. The election of the so-called bi-partisan ticket will be taken as an endorsement (sic) of church rule. With such an endorsement the authorities will have no hesitation in hastening the Mormonization of the schools. The defeat of their ticket will warn them to keep hands off.

The progress already made toward Mormonizing education in Salt Lake is the best indication of what may be expected if the voters express a desire for more of it.

We have seen the founder of the present school system, Superintendent Millspaugh, harassed by a Mormon minority on the School board until he gave up his work. We remember that the board, when it was controlled by broad-minded Americans, searched the United States for the man best qualified to carry on the work begun by Prof. Millspaugh. Such a man was found. Frank B. Cooper, a brilliant and progressive educator, was secured for the place. The church finally gained control. The work of the former board was undone. Mr. Cooper was gotten rid of only to find a better position at a greatly increased salary in Seattle.

With Mr. Cooper went the teachers whom the present Superintendent called "Our best instructors."

Board Went to Payson.

Having accomplished its object, where did the Mormon board go to find a successor for Mr. Cooper? To Payson, Utah! Whom did they find? A missionary returned from Germany. Although he was not a college graduate, the board lost no time in raising his salary to the maximum allowed by law.

It cannot be said that either Millspaugh or Cooper was hostile to the Mormon religion. Neither allowed one thing to be taught that would prejudice a child against the faith of its parents. Their sole endeavor was to develop the children under their care into reasoning, intelligent, self-reliant young Americans. From the efforts that were made to oust them it is plain that this is just what the church hierarchy does not want the children to become.

Following the missionary-Superintendent came a retinue of missionary principals bearing bishops' "recommends" and credentials from Payson and Pleasant Grove. The best schools were reserve for teachers having these peculiar qualifications. Older and more experienced teachers were pushed aside in order that obedient Mormons might be advanced. In some instances, as in the case of W.S. Wallace of the Union School, Independent Mormons were denied deserved promotion because of the stronger claims of subservient church men.

The alleged "non-sectarian" character of the public schools under Mormon control is again exemplified in the career of the supervisors of drawing and manual training.

Gentile and Mormon Supervisor

Mrs. Franc R. Elliott, the Gentile supervisor of drawing, was let out on the plea of economy, although a teacher of unusual ability, D.W. Parratt, a Mormon, who had shown his skill in drawing by drawing a raise of salary from $82 to $122.50 in a few months was put in her place.

Samuel Doxey, a Mormon who failed as a teacher in Ogden and taught in the grades with indifferent success under Cooper, was sent to Chicago by the School Board and educated in manual training at the expense of the taxpayers.

Such is the non-sectarianism which now prevails in the public schools of Salt Lake City.

The same brand of non-sectarianism is to be found in large quantities in the organization of the School Board. Messrs. Newman, Glanque, Branting, Moyle and Thomas, with their ally Byron Cummings from the big six, who dominate all the important committees of the board. Newman, Giauque and Branting are bishops' counselors. Not one of them dares to act without the advice or consent of his bishop.

The Gentiles who have been suffered to sit on the board are absolutely powerless to stem the swelling tide of ecclesiastical domination. They have had nothing to say regarding the employment of principals and teachers. Their protests have been vain. Yet they have never opposed the Mormon faith as such. It is because of their opposition to the deteriorating influence in the schools that they have been bound, gagged and marooned by the triumphant Mormon majority.

Mormon "Disinterestedness."

In the face of Mormon protestations of disinterred love for education it has been show that more than $15,000 is taken annually in the form of tithes from the Superintendent, supervisors, principals, teachers and janitors of the schools. The money is never accounted for and is doubtless used for the financial aggrandizement of the "Trustee in Trust for the Church of Jesus Christ of Latter-day Saints." Some of the money may be paid voluntarily, but whether it is or not, this Mormon teacher's only hope of preferment is in paying the tribute.

Thus the teachers are deprived of means that could be used by them to good advantage in travel and self-improvement. The tithing system wrongs the public wrongs the pupil and most of all, wrongs the faithful and ambitious Mormon teacher.

Does anyone think that the avaricious leaders of any movement will overlook such a simple expedient for increasing their revenue as the employment of more and more teachers – if the voters indorse their pretensions?

Not only is the Mormon teacher expected to give of her money. The insatiable hierarch expects her to keep a watchful eye upon the religious tendencies of the children in her charge and keep them reminded of their duties to the bishop and the church. If she be in a country school she may be required to teach the religion class which is held from two to three times a week in the school-room.

Signs and Wonders

And such stuff as is sometimes taught in these religion classes! Can the Mormon people expect their children to become great thinkers, great discoverers or broad-minded, intelligent men and women when they are taught as youngsters that the great laws which govern the universe have been and may be set aside at the instance of priest or prophet to case the pains or remove the doubts of insignificant, egotistical man?

Although there are not enough Mormon school teachers in the State to fill the vacancies which exist today, the hierarchy claims credit for the fact that 70 percent of the teachers in the Salt Lake schools are Gentiles. Although the best positions have been filled as rapidly as possible with inferior talent for purely religious reasons we are told that the School Board has nothing in view but the betterment of the schools.

When in due season 70 per cent of the teachers and all the principals are Mormons the ecclesiastics will have some new argument to prove that there is no religious preference in the board.

If the evidence already at hand be not enough to show that the hierarch has already begun the conquest and demoralization of the Salt Lake school, what evidence is needed? Must we wait until the ruin is complete? Shall we suffer the process to go on until the evil becomes too firmly rooted to the eradicated?

Transcription from:
Mount Pleasant News, Mount Pleasant, Iowa, September 29, 1952, page 1

Memorial to One of P.E.O. Founders Dedicated

A memorial to one of the founders of the P.E.O. Sisterhood-Franc Roads Elliott – was formally dedicated by national officers of the Sisterhood assembled in Mt. Pleasant Sunday afternoon.

A section of the program was given at the Memorial hall in the P.E.O. Memorial building at Iowa Wesleyan with Mrs. Mabel Scurrah of Victoria, B.C. Supreme Chapter president, giving the address.

Formal dedication then took place in the quiet beauty of Forest Home cemetery where stands a newly erected granite marker to the memory of Mrs. Elliott. There Mrs. Neil Farrell Stevenson, second vice president, Supreme Chapter, of Tulsa, Okla., paid brief tribute to the founder whose memory was honored and spoke the formal words of dedication.

On the memorial stone are engraved these words under the P.E.O. Star:"In memory of Franc Roads Elliott, wife of Simon Elliott, 1852-1924 – a founder of the P.E.O. Sisterhood."

Mrs. Gertrude P. Tomhave, First Vice president, Supreme Chapter, of Montevideo, Minn., presided. At the Memorial Hall, Mrs. Enola Carter, chairman of the committee, presided. Mrs. Bessie R. Raney, Past Supreme President, Chicago, Ill, gave the preliminary history. Dr. J. Raymond Chadwick, president of Iowa Wesleyan, gave the prayers.

Introductions

Introductions of honored guests took place at Memorial Hall and included: Mrs. Scurrah, Mrs. Tomhave, Mrs. Stevenson.

Members of the Memorial Stone committee: Mrs. Raney, Mss. Winona Evans Reeves, Past Supreme and State President, Chicago, Ill., Mrs. Gail Page of Ottumwa.

Trustees of the Supply Department: Mrs. Stella Clapp, Manhattan, Kan. Mrs. Beulah M. Thornton, Chicago, and Mrs. Marian Blaine, Philadelphia, Pa.:

Mrs. Gracia Linder, Committee of Ore. Memorial Hall: Miss Margaret Mohler, Executive Secretary of the P.E.O. Sisterhood, both of Mt. Pleasant:

Mrs. Turner, past state president of Missouri, Mrs. Minear, state president of Illinois; Mrs. Crawford, organizer, Mrs. Durree of Centerville, Mrs. Bernice Olson, president of Original A, and Mrs. J. Raymond Chadwick, Mt. Pleasant.

Tea At Chadwick Home

After the dedicatory service, a tea was given at the home of Dr. and Mrs. Chadwick by Chapter Original A for the visiting officials and others from a distance as well as local residents. Over 200 attended.

Mrs. Harold Garrison was in charge of the table and Mrs. H.G. Leist was in charge of refreshments, with Mrs. Paul Rathff and Mrs. Raymond Kerr assisting. Mrs. Garrison was assisted by Mr. H. F. McLaren and Mrs. Louise Clark, Mrs. Olson and Mrs. Winona Kyle, vice-president of Original A, poured.

Parlor hostesses were: Mrs. Hall Weir, Mrs. A.T. Lanning, Mrs. Richard Hall, Mrs. Dan McAllister, Mrs. Gerald Lange, and Mrs. Olan Ruble.

In the parlor, as many as could, gathered around and heard Mrs. Winona Evans Reeves, Past President, Supreme Chapter. Past President Iowa State Chapter and retired editor of the P.E.O. Record; tell of anecdotes and memories of the girlhood days of Franc Roads Elliott.

Two grandnieces of Franc Roads Elliott were present for the dedication, Dorothy Evans Carrithers of Morning Sun and Anna Evans Walker of Yarmouth.

Towns and cities, or states, represented at the dedication not previously listed, included: Barlington, New London, Brighton, Ottumwa, Washington, Iowa City, Milton, Winfield, Fairfield, Des Moines, Kansas City, Kan., and South Dakota.

The following are excerpts from the address by Mrs. Mabel Scurrah, president of Supreme Chapter, P.E.O., in connection with the dedication of the memorial stone for Franc Roads Elliott, one of the founders of P.E.O.

"It is always a source of great interest to me to come to Mount Pleasant to attend the meetings of the Executive Board of Supreme Chapter but it is an especial privilege this time to be here on the campus of Iowa Wesleyan College, the Mecca for all P.E.O.'s and in the home city of the seven who in their youth gave to us the beginning of a great organization. We are here today to pay honour to all of them, but in a special way to memorialize one of them.

"Today, we are remembering by a very small stone, one who was to us a great woman, who unconsciously to herself and perhaps to us here today set the pattern for P.E.O. philanthropies since here activities were in the field of education and in civic service, particularly in the advancement of women, politically and in her participation in the affairs of the church. She worked and spoke and wrote for the abolition of war as it was then called; now we speak of it as the promotion of peace, but it is one and the same thing...

"The Roads family lived here in Mount Pleasant, members of her family are doubles remembered by some who are here. During her college days, she became engaged to Simon Charles Elliott; son of Dr. Charles Elliott who was twice president is remembered as one of Iowa Wesleyan's most scholarly presidents. It is on Dr. Elliott's family cemetery lot that the Memorial stone is placed. The Roads-Elliott wedding was solemnized in 1872 here in Mount Pleasant. Two children were born to them, Charles A. and Stella. After a few years the young people moved to Lincoln, Neb., where Mr. Elliott was in the mercantile business and Franc, true to her tradition took graduate work. Their son, Dr. Charles Elliott, a widely known physician, was head of the School of Medicine, Northwestern University. Their daughter, Stella, married James Canfield, brother of Dorothy Canfield (Fisher). None of the family are now living. Mrs. Elliott's activities and achievements are a part of P.E.O. history…

"Mrs. Elliott worked for seventeen years to have women admitted to the General Conference of the Methodist Episcopal church, which is the law-making body of that denomination…

"She was the first to suggest and to carry out the plan of a model school room, a room with hard-wood floors, tinted walls, on which were hung beautiful pictures; a room properly lighted and well ventilated…

"She was an art supervisor in the public schools of Lincoln, and was the first instructor of art in the Nebraska State University, where her two children were educated…."

Monday, November 10, 1958

Dorothy Canfield Fisher, 79, Dies

By Associated Press

ARLINGTON, VT., Nov. 9—Dorothy Canfield Fisher, a quiet, motherly looking woman who forged a remarkable career as novelist, scholar, translator and educator, died Sunday amid the Vermont hills she loved. She was 79.

She became famous for the novels she wrote before World War I and in the years shortly after—"The Squirrel Cage," "The Bent Twig" and "The Deepening Stream" were outstanding among them. In recent years she became best known for her articles and nonfiction, and as a judge on the Book-of-the-Month Club selection board.

A NATIVE of Lawrence, Kan., she adopted Vermont as her favorite state and her recent book, "Vermont Tradition," was an eloquent statement of the philosophy and character of the state's ruggedly independent people.

One of her most recent articles told the story of a Vermont town meeting in which the voters, faced with limited local funds, chose to erect a school instead of a much-desired bridge.

THE DAUGHTER of a prominent educator, James Hulme Canfield, and of Flavia (Camp) Canfield, an artist, she had some early schooling in France, spoke French fluently and worked there during and after World War I helping refugee children. She often said she loved Vermont and France best of all places in the world.

After receiving a bachelor's degree from Ohio State University and studying at the Sorbonne in Paris, she received a Ph.D. in French from Columbia University in 1905. She was preparing to be a language teacher when, in 1907, she married James Redwood Fisher.

—Associated Press Wirephoto
Dorothy Canfield Fisher ... Writing career concludes.

ALL STORES OPEN TUES., VETERANS' DAY

CANNERY SALES
GROUND BEEF 100% PURE BEEF lb. 39c

315

Transcription from: www.newspapers.com
The Salt Lake Tribune, Salt Lake City, Utah, November 10, 1958, page 32

Dorothy Canfield Fisher, 79, Dies

By Associated Press

Arlington, VT. Nov 9 – Dorothy Canfield Fisher, a quiet, motherly looking woman who forged a remarkable career as novelist, scholar, translator and educator, died Sunday amid the Vermont hills she loved. She was 79.

She became famous for the novels she wrote before World War I and in the years shortly after –"The Squirrel Cage," "The Bent Twig" and "The Deepening Stream" were outstanding among them. In recent years she became best known for her articles and non-fiction, as a judge on the Book-of-the-Month Club selection board.

A native of Lawrence, Kan., she adopted Vermont as her favorite state and her recent book, "Vermont Tradition," was an eloquent statement of the philosophy and character of the state's ruggedly independent people.

One of her most recent articles told the story of a Vermont town meeting in which the voters, faced with limited local funds, chose to erect a school instead of a much desired bridge.

The daughter of a prominent educator, James Hulme Canfield, and of Flavia (Camp) Canfield, an artist, she had some early schooling in France, spoke French fluently and worked there during and after World War I helping refugee children. She often said she loved Vermont and France best of all places in the world.

After receiving a bachelor's degree from Ohio State University and studying at the Sorbonne in Paris, she received a Ph.D. in French from Columbia University in 1905. She was preparing to be a language teacher when, in 1907, she married James Redwood Fisher.

Transcription from:
Bennington Banner, Bennington, Vermont, May 7, 1973

Charles E. Canfield of Arlington, 72, dies

Charles E. Canfield, 72, of Arlington, husband of Dorothy (Laird) Canfield, died early Sunday morning at Putnam Memorial Hospital after a long illness.

Mr. Canfield, nephew of the late author Dorothy Canfield Fisher, was born in Columbus, Ohio, Nov 3, 1900, son of James A. and Stella (Elliot) Canfield. He moved to Arlington about 20 years ago from Pleasantville, N.Y., after having spent more than 25 years here as a summer resident. He graduated from Dartmouth College in 1922, and during World War II served as a procurement specialist and consultant for the Office of the Quartermaster General.

At the time of his death, Mr. Canfield was chairman of the board of the Canfield Paper Co. of New York City and previously had been president of the company. While living in Pleasantville, he was active on the village and town school boards, and he served the town of Arlington for many years as a member of the Arlington School Board.

He was a member of St. James Episcopal Church in Arlington and also belonged to the Equinox Country Club in Manchester.

Survivors besides his wife are two daughters, Mrs. Rudy (Nancy) Domenic of Atherton, Calif., and Mrs. Richard (Mollie) Falk of Fayetteville, N.Y.; one son James E. Canfield of South Burlington, Vt.; one brother, Robert F. Canfield of Buena Vista, Va.; seven grandchildren, nieces, nephews and cousins.

There will be no calling hours at the Hanson-Walbridge Funeral Home in Arlington.

A memorial service will be held on Wednesday at 2 pm in St. James Episcopal Church, Arlington, with the Rev. Lawrence A. Sherwin, rector, officiating, and following by a committal service in Evergreen Cemetery in Arlington.

The family urgently requests that no flowers be given. If friends desire, memorial contributions may be made to the Arlington Recreation and Park Committee, Arlington, or the St. James Episcopal Church, Arlington, through the office of the Hanson-Walbridge Funeral Home, Arlington, 05250.

Transcription from:
News-Gazette, Lexington, Virginia, March 19, 1980

Robert E. Canfield, 77, of Rt. 1, Buena Vista, a retired official with the paper industry, died Sunday in Stonewall Jackson Hospital.

Mr. and Mrs. Canfield moved here in 1972 from New York city and built their modern house, Lee's View, with a commanding view of the valley and mountains.

Born in Columbus, Ohio, Mr. Canfield grew up in New York, where his father founded the Canfield Paper Co., and graduated from Dartmouth College and Harvard Law School. He was a partner in the New York law firm of Wise, Whitney and Parker and successor firms from 1934 to 1956. From 1957 until his retirement in 1968 he was president of the Printing Paper Manufacturers Association. Since his retirement he had continued to take an interest in the Canfield family property at Arlington, VT.

He is survived by his wife, Althaea Kindlund Canfield; a son; a daughter; and six grandchildren.

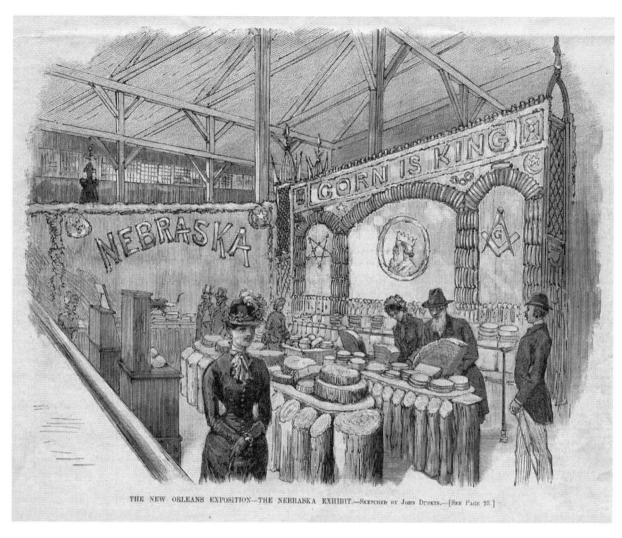

THE NEW ORLEANS EXPOSITION—THE NEBRASKA EXHIBIT.—Sketched by John Durkin.—[See Page 25.]

Reprinted with permission from the collection of Stu Haats,
Antique Engravings, Prints, Maps and Newspapers
Franc was Assistant Commissioner of Art at the New Orleans Exhibit of 1884

			(3-H-8)
NAME OF SOLDIER:	Elliott, Simon L.		

NAME OF DEPENDENT:	*Widow,*	Elliott Franc R.
	Minor,	

SERVICE:	A. 45 La Inf.

DATE OF FILING.	CLASS.	APPLICATION NO.	CERTIFICATE NO.	STATE FROM WHICH FILED.
1898 Oct 17	*Invalid,*	1211007	1073601.	Neb
1915 June 1	*Widow,*	1048.174	797.397	NY
	Minor,			

ATTORNEY:	J. C. Williams
CW? **REMARKS:**	

8–112

National Archives and Records Administration. *U.S. Civil War Pension Index: General Index to Pension Files.* 1861-1934 (database on-line). Provo, UT. USA: Ancestry.com Operations Inc. 2000. Original data: *General Index to Pension Files, 1861-1934.* Washington, D.C.: National Archives and Records Administration. T288, 546 rolls.

Dorothy Canfield Fisher

Dorothy Canfield Fisher (February 17, 1879 – November 9, 1958) was an educational reformer, social activist, and best-selling American author in the early decades of the twentieth century. She strongly supported women's rights, racial equality, and lifelong education. She was named by Eleanor Roosevelt as one of the ten most influential women in the United States. In addition to bringing the Montessori method of child-rearing to the United States, she presided over the country's first adult education program, and shaped literary tastes by serving as a member of the Book-of-the-Month Club selection committee from 1925 to 1951.

Biography

Dorothea Frances Canfield, - named for Dorothea Brook of the novel *Middlemarch* - was born in Lawrence, Kansas on February 17, 1879. Her father was James Hulme Canfield, president of The Ohio State University and librarian at Columbia University: her mother, Flavia Camp, was an artist and writer. Canfield is most closely associated with Vermont, where she spent her adult life, and which served as the setting for many of her books.

In 1899 Dorothy Canfield received a B.A. from The Ohio State University. She was also a member of Kappa Kappa Gamma. She went on to study Romance languages at University of Paris and Columbia University and in 1904 received a doctoral degree from Columbia University; *Corneille and Racine in English* (1904). With G.R. Carpenter from Columbia she co-wrote *English Rhetoric* and Composition (1906). She was the first woman to receive an honorary degree from Dartmouth College, and also received honorary degrees from the University of Nebraska, Middlebury, Swarthmore, Smith, Williams, Ohio State University, and the University of Vermont.

In 1907 she married John Redwood Fisher, and together they had two children, a son and a daughter.

Another concern of Dorothy Canfield was her war work. She followed her husband to France in 1916 during World War I, and while raising her young children in Paris worked to establish a Braille press for blinded veterans. She also established a convalescent home for refugee French children from the invaded areas; continuing her relief work after the war, she earned citations of appreciation from Eleanor Roosevelt, Madame Chiang Kai-shek, and the government of Denmark.

Fisher died at the age of 79, in Arlington, Vermont, in 1958.

Biographies of Canfield Fisher include:

- Elizabeth Yates' *The Lady from Vermont: Dorothy Canfield Fisher's Life and World.* (Brattleboro: Stephen Green Press, 1971) originally published by E.P. Dutton and Co., in 1958 as *Pebble in a Pool.*

- *Dorothy Canfield Fisher – A Biography*, by Professor Ida H. Washington (The New England Press, Inc., Shelburne, Vermont 1982)

May 27, 1918

Bureau of Citizenship
Department of State
Washington, D. C.

Sirs:

This is to certify that Dr Charles Addison Elliott of Chicago, Illinois, has been appointed to membership on a Commission which is being sent to Guayaquil, Ecuador, for the purpose of investigating the presence of yellow fever and allied diseases. Dr Elliott is planning to leave New York on the SS "Carrillo" scheduled to sail on June 12, 1918.

Respectfully

Wickliffe Rose

DESCRIPTION OF APPLICANT.

Age: 45 years.   Mouth: medium
Stature: 5 feet, 8½ inches, Eng. Chin: dimpled
Forehead: high   Hair: gray and Brown
Eyes: gray   Complexion: fair
Nose: straight   Face: full
Distinguishing marks: none

IDENTIFICATION.

X June 1, 1918, 19____

I, Franc R. Elliott, solemnly swear that I am a { native / naturalized } citizen
of the United States; that I reside at Chicago, Illinois; that I have known
the above-named Charles A. Elliott personally for 45 years and
know { him } to be a native citizen of the United States; and that the facts stated in { his } affidavit
are true to the best of my knowledge and belief.

Franc R Elliott

Mother, 7017 Constance Ave.,
(Occupation.)
Chicago,Ill
(Address of witness.)

Sworn to before me this 1st day

[Seal.]   of June, 19 18

Deputy   Clerk of the U.S.Dist. Court at Chicago

Applicant desires passport to be sent to the following address:

Care James A. Canfield,

Pleasantville, Westchester County, New York.

A duplicate of the photograph to be attached here
must be sent to the Department with the application
to be affixed to the passport with an impression of
Department's seal.

Frances Elizabeth Roads

Birth:	10 Feb 1852	Father:	Addison Roads
Death:	09 Aug 1924	Mother:	Nancy McClure
Marriage:	1869	Spouse:	Simon Charles Elliott

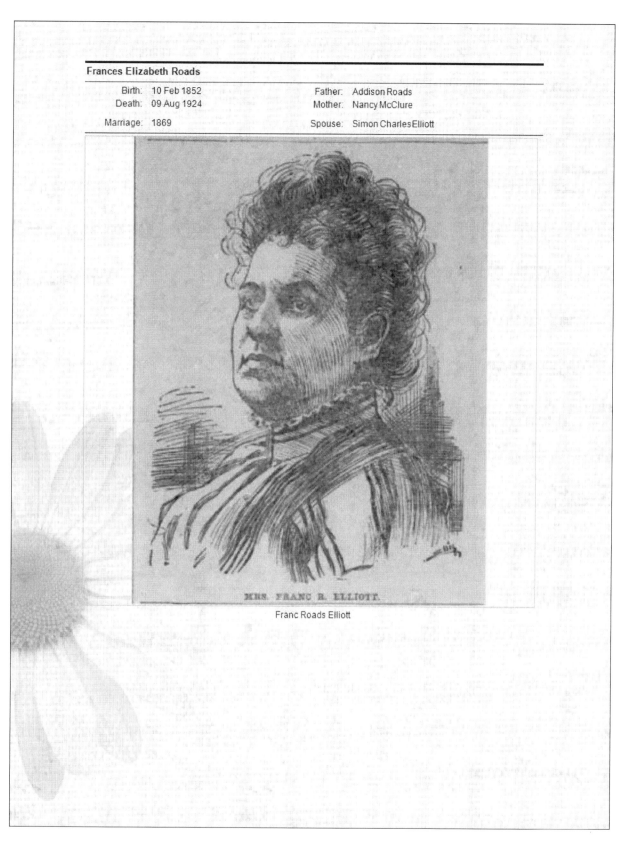

MRS. FRANC R. ELLIOTT.

Franc Roads Elliott

Frances Elizabeth Roads

Birth:	10 Feb 1852	Father:	Addison Roads
Death:	09 Aug 1924	Mother:	Nancy McClure
Marriage:	1869	Spouse:	Simon Charles Elliott

Frances Elizabeth Roads

Reproduction of oil portrait by Marion Dunlap Harper, unveiled in P.E.O. Memorial Hall in Mount Pleasant, Iowa, on September 23, 1929.

Photo Album for Rev. Charles Elliott

Charles Elliott

Birth:	16 May 1792	Father:	
Death:	06 Jan 1869	Mother:	
Marriage:	14 May 1822	Spouse:	Phebe Leech

Rev. Charles Elliott

Photo Album for Dorothy Frances Canfield

Dorothy Frances Canfield

Birth:	17 Feb 1879	Father:	James Hulme Canfield
Death:	09 Nov 1958	Mother:	Flavia Camp
Marriage:	May 1907	Spouse:	John Redwood Fisher

Dorothy Canfield Fisher

Dorothy Canfield Fisher

Dorothy Canfield Fisher

Dorothy Frances Canfield

Dorothy Frances Canfield and John R. Fisher

Passport photo: Ancestry.com. *U.S. Passport Applications, 1795-1925* [database on-line]. Provo, UT, USA: Ancestry.com Operations, Inc., 2007.National Archives and Records Administration (NARA); Washington D.C.; *Emergency Passport Applications, Argentina thru Venezuela, 1906-1925*; Collection Number: *ARC Identifier 1244183 / MLR Number A1 544*; Box #: *4569*; Volume #: *185*. Other photos contributed by robertluther1963 to Ancestry.com 29 September 2011

Photo Album for Charles Elliott Canfield

Charles Elliott Canfield

Birth:	03 Nov 1900	Father:	James A. Canfield
Death:	06 May 1973	Mother:	Stella M. Elliott
Marriage:	28 Apr 1925	Spouse:	Dorothy Handyside Laird

Charles Elliott Canfield

Historical Background Sources
for Francis Elizabeth Roads

1. 1850 United States Federal Census; Census Place: *Liberty, Hendricks, Indiana*; Roll: M432_150; Page 7A; Image 18.

2. 1860 United States Federal Census; Census Place: *Mount Pleasant, Henry, Iowa*; Roll: M653_324; Page: 39; Image: 39; Family History Library Film: 803324.

3. 1870 United States Federal Census; Census Place: *Center, Henry, Iowa*; Roll: M593_395; Page: 158A; Image 320; Family History Library Film 545894.

4. 1880 United States Federal Census; Census Place: *Mt. Pleasant, Henry, Iowa*; Roll: 344; Family History Film: 1254344; Page 312B; Enumeration District: 095; Image: 0187.

5. 1880 United States Federal Census; Census Place: *Lincoln, Lancaster, Nebraska*; Roll: 751; Family History Film; 1254751; Page: 197C; Enumeration District: 231; Image 0579.

6. 1900 United States Federal Census; Census Place: *Center, Henry, Iowa*; Roll: 436; Page: 22A; Enumeration District: 0030; FHL microfilm: 124046.

7. 1900 United States Federal Census; Census Place: *Chicago Ward 34, Cook, Illinois*; Roll; 289; Page:10A; Enumeration District: 1089; FHL microfilm: 1240289.

8. 1910 United States Federal Census: Census Place: *Mt. Pleasant, Westchester, New York*: Roll: T624_1089; Page 7B; Enumeration District: 0050; FHL microfilm: 1375102.

9. 1910 United States Federal Census: Census Place: *Chicago, Ward 2, Cook, Illinois*: Roll: T624-242; page 1B; Enumeration District; 0191; FHL microfilm: 1374255.

10. 1920 United States Federal Census: Census Place: *Chicago Ward 6, Cook (Chicago), Illinois*; Roll: T625_310; Page 4B; Enumeration District: 348; Image: 386.

11. 1930 United States Federal Census; Census Place: *Chicago, Cook, Illinois*, Roll: 422; Page 4B; Enumeration District: 203; Image: 1032.0; FHL microfilm: 2340157.

12. 1940 United States Federal Census; Census Place: *Chicago, Cook, Illinois*; Roll: T627_934; Page: 2A; Enumeration District; 103-436.

13. "American Civil War."*Wikipedia*. Wikimedia Foundation, 24 Oct. 2013. Web. 25 Oct. 2013. <http://en.wikipedia.org/wiki/American_Civil_War>.

14. "Charles Elliott" *RootsWeb Genealogical Data Cooperative*. Web. 25 Oct. 2013. <http://homepages.rootsweb.ancestry.com/~eelliott/Gannon/celliott-minister.html>.

15. Clapp, Stella. *Out of the Heart A Century of P.E.O. 1869-1969*. Des Moines, Iowa: P.E.O. Sisterhood, 1968.

16. "Dorothy Canfield Fisher." *Wikipedia*. Wikimedia Foundation, 13 Oct. 2013. Web. 23 Oct. 2013. <http://en.wikipedia.org/wiki/Dorothy_Canfield_Fisher>.

17. "Educational." *The Salt Lake Herald* [Salt Lake City, Utah] 15 Apr. 1900: 16. Print.

18. Elliott, Franc R. "The Function of Art in the Development of the Individual." The Salt Lake Herald [Salt Lake City, Utah] 16 Jan. 1899: 3. Print.

19. "Free Family History and Genealogy Records — FamilySearch.org."*FamilySearch.org*.: Wiki: 45th Regiment, Iowa Volunteer Infantry. Web. 25 Oct. 2013. <https://familysearch.org/>.

20. "General Federation of Women's Clubs." *Wikipedia*. Wikimedia Foundation, 18 Oct. 2013. Web. 24 Oct. 2013. <http://en.wikipedia.org/wiki/General_Federation_of_Women's_Clubs>.

21. Hendricks County, Indiana: Index to Marriage Record 1823-1920 Inclusive Volume, W.P.S. Indiana Original Record Located: County C; Book: 4; Page: 62.

22.   Iowa, State Census Collection, 1836-1925. Microfilm of *Iowa State Censuses, 1856, 1885, 1895, 1905, 1915, 1925* as well as various special censuses from 1836-1897 obtained from the State Historical Society of Iowa va Heritage Quest.

23.   "Iowa Wesleyan College Historical Sketch." *Iowa Wesleyan College Its History and Its Alumni 1842 - 1917.* Ed. Edwin A. Schell, A. M., Ph. D., D. D. (http://archive.org/stream/historicalsketc0iowa/historicalsketc0iowa_djvu.txt.).

24.   "James A. Camp Canfield and Miss Stella M. Elliott." *Evening Journal* [Jamestown, New York] 18 Aug. 1899:

25.   Johnson, Heidi, ed."A Society of Our Own." *The P.E.O. Record* (1997):

26.   "Memorial to One of the P.E.O. Founders Dedicated." *The Mt. Pleasant News* [Mt. Pleasant, Iowa] 29 Sept. 1952: 1. Print.

27.   "Mormonizing the Schools." *The Salt Lake Tribune* [Salt Lake City, Utah] 4 Dec. 1904: 3. Print.

28.   National Archives and Records Administration. *U.S. Civil War Pension Index: General Index to Pension Files.* 1861-1934 (database on-line). Provo, UT. USA: Ancestry.com Operations Inc. 2000. Original data: *General Index to Pension Files, 1861-1934.* Washington, D.C.: National Archives and Records Administration. T288, 546 rolls.

29.   *NCBI.* U.S. National Library of Medicine, *The Yellow Fever Vaccine: A History,* Web. 25 Nov. 2013.

30.   "NEBRASKA EXHIBIT NEW ORLEANS EXPOSITION, CORN IS KING." *EBay.* Web. 25 Oct. 2013. <http://www.ebay.com/itm/NEBRASKA-EXHIBIT-NEW-ORLEANS-EXPOSITION-CORN-IS-KING-/360245289437?pt=LH_DefaultDomain_0>.

31.   Nebraska State Historical Society; *Nebraska State Census:* Year *1880:* Series/Record Group: *RG207;* County: *Lancaster;* Township; *Capital:* Page; *263.*

32.   "Notable Utah Women Mrs. Franc R. Elliott." *Deseret Evening News* [Salt Lake City, Utah] 24 Feb. 1900: 14. Print.

33.   "Office of the President." *James Hulme Canfield.* Web. 23 Oct. 2013. <http://president.osu.edu/presidents/canfield.html>.

34.   "Office of the President. "*Presidents.* Web. 23 Oct. 2013. <http://president.osu.edu/presidents/>.

35.   "Our Shared History: Delaware, Methodism, and Ohio Wesleyan University." *Our Shared History: Delaware, Methodism, and Ohio Wesleyan University.* Web. 25 Oct. 2013. <http://drc.owu.edu/handle/2374.OWES/3>.

36.   "Pythian Hall Friday Morning. "*Official Proceedings of the Fifth Biennial of the General Federation of Women's Clubs.* Detroit, Michigan: John Bornman & Son, 1900. 30. Print.

37.   "School Teachers Chosen." *Deseret Evening News* [Salt Lake City, Utah] 11 July 1901: 5. Print.

38.   "State Teachers' Association An Exceedingly Interesting Program Is to Be Given." *Deseret Evening News* [Salt Lake City, Utah] 19 Dec. 1900: 5. Print.

39.   "Teachers Choose New Set of Officers." *The Salt Lake Herald* [Salt Lake City, Utah] 29 Dec. 1899: 1. Print.

40.   The Rockefeller Foundation Annual Report 1918 (1918): p79-89. Web. 25 Nov. 2013.

Frances Elizabeth Roads Descendant Chart
Source Report

Source Title: **1850 United States Federal Census**
Repository: **Ancestry.com**

Citation: Ancestry.com, 1850 United States Federal Census (Provo, UT, USA, Ancestry.com Operations, Inc., 2009), Ancestry.com, Year: 1850; Census Place: Liberty, Hendricks, Indiana; Roll: M432_150; Page: 7A; Image: 18. [Source citation includes media item(s)]. McClure, Nancy .

Citation: Ancestry.com, 1850 United States Federal Census (Provo, UT, USA, Ancestry.com Operations, Inc., 2009), Ancestry.com, Year: 1850; Census Place: Liberty, Hendricks, Indiana; Roll: M432_150; Page: 7A; Image: 18. [Source citation includes media item(s)] Roads, Addison

Source Title: **1860 United States Federal Census**
Repository: **Ancestry.com**

Citation: Ancestry.com, 1860 United States Federal Census (Provo, UT, USA, Ancestry.com Operations, Inc., 2009), Ancestry.com, Year: 1860; Census Place: Mount Pleasant, Henry, Iowa; Roll: M653_324; Page: 39; Image: 39; Family History Library Film: 803324. [Source citation includes media item(s)] Roads, Charles A.

Citation: Ancestry.com, 1860 United States Federal Census (Provo, UT, USA, Ancestry.com Operations, Inc., 2009), Ancestry.com, Year: 1860; Census Place: Mount Pleasant, Henry, Iowa; Roll: M653_324; Page: 39; Image: 39; Family History Library Film: 803324. [Source citation includes media item(s)] McClure, Nancy

Citation: Ancestry.com, 1860 United States Federal Census (Provo, UT, USA, Ancestry.com Operations, Inc., 2009), Ancestry.com, Year: 1860; Census Place: Mount Pleasant, Henry, Iowa; Roll: M653_324; Page: 39; Image: 39; Family History Library Film: 803324. [Source citation includes media item(s)] Roads, Addison

Citation: Ancestry.com, 1860 United States Federal Census (Provo, UT, USA, Ancestry.com Operations, Inc., 2009), Ancestry.com, Year: 1860; Census Place: Mount Pleasant, Henry, Iowa; Roll: M653_324; Page: 39; Image: 39; Family History Library Film: 803324. [Source citation includes media item(s)] Roads, Frances Elizabeth

Citation: Ancestry.com, 1860 United States Federal Census (Provo, UT, USA, Ancestry.com Operations, Inc., 2009), Ancestry.com, Year: 1860; Census Place: Mount Pleasant, Henry, Iowa; Roll: M653_324; Page: 42; Image: 42; Family History Library Film: 803324. [Source citation includes media item(s)] Elliott, Simon Charles

Source Title: **1870 United States Federal Census**
Repository: **Ancestry.com**

Citation: Ancestry.com, 1870 United States Federal Census (Provo, UT, USA, Ancestry.com Operations, Inc., 2009), Ancestry.com, Year: 1870; Census Place: Center, Henry, Iowa; Roll: M593_395; Page: 158A; Image: 320; Family History Library Film: 545894. [Source citation includes media item(s)] Roads, Charles A

Citation: Ancestry.com, 1870 United States Federal Census (Provo, UT, USA, Ancestry.com Operations, Inc., 2009), Ancestry.com, Year: 1870; Census Place: Center, Henry, Iowa; Roll: M593_395; Page: 158A; Image: 320; Family History Library Film: 545894. [Source citation includes media item(s)] McClure, Nancy

Citation: Ancestry.com, 1870 United States Federal Census (Provo, UT, USA, Ancestry.com Operations, Inc., 2009), Ancestry.com, Year: 1870; Census Place: Center, Henry, Iowa; Roll: M593_395; Page: 158A; Image: 320; Family History Library Film: 545894. [Source citation includes media item(s)]

Citation: Ancestry.com, 1870 United States Federal Census (Provo, UT, USA, Ancestry.com Operations, Inc., 2009), Ancestry.com, Year: 1870; Census Place: Center, Henry, Iowa; Roll: M593_395; Page: 158A; Image: 320; Family History Library Film: 545894. [Source citation includes media item(s)] Roads, Leona Katherine Potts

Citation: Ancestry.com, 1870 United States Federal Census (Provo, UT, USA, Ancestry.com Operations, Inc., 2009), Ancestry.com, Year: 1870; Census Place: Center, Henry, Iowa; Roll: M593_395; Page: 158A; Image: 320; Family History Library Film: 545894. [Source citation includes media item(s)] Roads, Addison

Citation: Ancestry.com, 1870 United States Federal Census (Provo, UT, USA, Ancestry.com Operations, Inc., 2009), Ancestry.com, Year: 1870; Census Place: Center, Henry, Iowa; Roll: M593_395; Page: 158A; Image: 320; Family History Library Film: 545894. [Source citation includes media item(s)] Roads, Frances Elizabeth

Citation: Ancestry.com, 1870 United States Federal Census (Provo, UT, USA, Ancestry.com Operations, Inc., 2009), Ancestry.com, Year: 1870; Census Place: Lincoln, Lancaster, Nebraska; Roll: M593_830; Page: 115A; Image: 233; Family History Library Film: 552329. [Source citation includes media item(s)] Elliott, Simon Charles

Source Title: **1880 United States Federal Census**
Repository: **Ancestry.com**

Citation: Ancestry.com and The Church of Jesus Christ of Latter-day Saints, 1880 United States Federal Census (Provo, UT, USA, Ancestry.com Operations Inc., 2010), Ancestry.com, Year: 1880; Census Place: Lincoln, Lancaster, Nebraska; Roll: 751; Family History Film: 1254751; Page: 197C; Enumeration District: 231; Image: 0579. [Source citation includes media item(s)] Elliott, Charles Addison

Citation: Ancestry.com and The Church of Jesus Christ of Latter-day Saints, 1880 United States Federal Census (Provo, UT, USA, Ancestry.com Operations Inc., 2010), Ancestry.com, Year: 1880; Census Place: Lincoln, Lancaster, Nebraska; Roll: 751; Family History Film: 1254751; Page: 197C; Enumeration District: 231; Image: 0579. [Source citation includes media item(s)] Elliott, Simon Charles

Citation: Ancestry.com and The Church of Jesus Christ of Latter-day Saints, 1880 United States Federal Census (Provo, UT, USA, Ancestry.com Operations Inc., 2010), Ancestry.com, Year: 1880; Census Place: Lincoln, Lancaster, Nebraska; Roll: 751; Family History Film: 1254751; Page: 197C; Enumeration District: 231; Image: 0579. [Source citation includes media item(s)] Roads, Frances Elizabeth

Citation: Ancestry.com and The Church of Jesus Christ of Latter-day Saints, 1880 United States Federal Census (Provo, UT, USA, Ancestry.com Operations Inc., 2010), Ancestry.com, Year: 1880; Census Place: Lincoln, Lancaster, Nebraska; Roll: 751; Family History Film: 1254751; Page: 197D; Enumeration District: 231; Image: 0580. [Source citation includes media item(s)] Elliott, Stella M.

Citation: Ancestry.com and The Church of Jesus Christ of Latter-day Saints, 1880 United States Federal Census (Provo, UT, USA, Ancestry.com Operations Inc., 2010), Ancestry.com, Year: 1880; Census Place: MT Pleasant, Henry, Iowa; Roll: 344; Family History Film: 1254344; Page: 312B; Enumeration District: 095; Image: 0187. [Source citation includes media item(s)] Roads, Charles A

Citation: Ancestry.com and The Church of Jesus Christ of Latter-day Saints, 1880 United States
               Federal Census (Provo, UT, USA, Ancestry.com Operations Inc., 2010), Ancestry.com,
               Year: 1880; Census Place: MT Pleasant, Henry, Iowa; Roll: 344; Family History Film:
               1254344; Page: 312B; Enumeration District: 095; Image: 0187. [Source citation includes
               media item(s)] McClure, Nancy

Citation: Ancestry.com and The Church of Jesus Christ of Latter-day Saints, 1880 United States
               Federal Census (Provo, UT, USA, Ancestry.com Operations Inc., 2010), Ancestry.com,
               Year: 1880; Census Place: MT Pleasant, Henry, Iowa; Roll: 344; Family History Film:
               1254344; Page: 312B; Enumeration District: 095; Image: 0187. [Source citation includes
               media item(s)] Roads, Leona Katherine Potts

Citation: Ancestry.com and The Church of Jesus Christ of Latter-day Saints, 1880 United States
               Federal Census (Provo, UT, USA, Ancestry.com Operations Inc., 2010), Ancestry.com,
               Year: 1880; Census Place: MT Pleasant, Henry, Iowa; Roll: 344; Family History Film:
               1254344; Page: 312B; Enumeration District: 095; Image: 0187. [Source citation includes
               media item(s)] Roads, Addison

Source Title: **1900 United States Federal Census**
Repository: **Ancestry.com**

Citation: Ancestry.com, 1900 United States Federal Census (Provo, UT, USA, Ancestry.com
               Operations Inc., 2004), Ancestry.com, Year: 1900; Census Place: Center, Henry, Iowa;
               Roll: 436; Page: 22A; Enumeration District: 0030; FHL microfilm: 1240436. [Source
               citation includes media item(s)] McClure, Nancy

Citation: Ancestry.com, 1900 United States Federal Census (Provo, UT, USA, Ancestry.com
               Operations Inc., 2004), Ancestry.com, Year: 1900; Census Place: Center, Henry, Iowa;
               Roll: 436; Page: 22A; Enumeration District: 0030; FHL microfilm: 1240436. [Source
               citation includes media item(s)] McClure, Nancy

Citation: Ancestry.com, 1900 United States Federal Census (Provo, UT, USA, Ancestry.com
               Operations Inc., 2004), Ancestry.com, Year: 1900; Census Place: Center, Henry, Iowa;
               Roll: 436; Page: 8A; Enumeration District: 0030; FHL microfilm: 1240436. [Source citation
               includes media item(s)]

Citation: Ancestry.com, 1900 United States Federal Census (Provo, UT, USA, Ancestry.com
               Operations Inc., 2004), Ancestry.com, Year: 1900; Census Place: Center, Henry, Iowa;
               Roll: 436; Page: 8A; Enumeration District: 0030; FHL microfilm: 1240436. [Source citation
               includes media item(s)]

Citation: Ancestry.com, 1900 United States Federal Census (Provo, UT, USA, Ancestry.com
               Operations Inc., 2004), Ancestry.com, Year: 1900; Census Place: Chicago Ward 34,
               Cook, Illinois; Roll: 289; Page: 10A; Enumeration District: 1089; FHL microfilm: 1240289.
               [Source citation includes media item(s)]

Citation: Ancestry.com, 1900 United States Federal Census (Provo, UT, USA, Ancestry.com
               Operations Inc., 2004), Ancestry.com, Year: 1900; Census Place: Chicago Ward 34,
               Cook, Illinois; Roll: 289; Page: 10A; Enumeration District: 1089; FHL microfilm: 1240289.
               [Source citation includes media item(s)] Elliott, Simon Charles Roads, Frances Elizabeth

Citation: Ancestry.com, 1900 United States Federal Census (Provo, UT, USA, Ancestry.com
               Operations Inc., 2004), Ancestry.com, Year: 1900; Census Place: Chicago Ward 34,
               Cook, Illinois; Roll: 289; Page: 10A; Enumeration District: 1089; FHL microfilm: 1240289.
               [Source citation includes media item(s)] Elliott, Simon Charles

Citation: Ancestry.com, 1900 United States Federal Census (Provo, UT, USA, Ancestry.com
               Operations Inc., 2004), Ancestry.com, Year: 1900; Census Place: Columbus Ward 19,
               Franklin, Ohio; Roll: 1270; Page: 16A; Enumeration District: 0128; FHL microfilm:
               1241270. [Source citation includes media item(s)] Elliott, Stella M.

Citation: Ancestry.com, 1900 United States Federal Census (Provo, UT, USA, Ancestry.com Operations Inc., 2004), Ancestry.com, Year: 1900; Census Place: Columbus Ward 19, Franklin, Ohio; Roll: 1270; Page: 16A; Enumeration District: 0128; FHL microfilm: 1241270. [Source citation includes media item(s)] Elliott, Stella M.

Source Title: **1910 United States Federal Census**
Repository: **Ancestry.com**

Citation: Ancestry.com, 1910 United States Federal Census (Provo, UT, USA, Ancestry.com Operations Inc., 2006), Ancestry.com, Source Citation: Year: 1910; Census Place: MT Pleasant, Westchester, New York; Roll: T624_1089; Page: 7B; Enumeration District: 0050; FHL microfilm: 1375102. Name: Simon C. Elliott residence date: 1910 residence place: MT Pleasant, Westchester, New York, USA birth date: 23 December 1843 birth place: Ohio. http://search.ancestry.com/cgi-bin/sse.dll?db=1910uscenindex&h=138402490&ti=0&indi v=try&gss=pt. [Source citation includes media item(s)] Elliott, Simon Charles

Citation: Ancestry.com, 1910 United States Federal Census (Provo, UT, USA, Ancestry.com Operations Inc., 2006), Ancestry.com, Year: 1910; Census Place: Center, Henry, Iowa; Roll: T624_405; Page: 14A; Enumeration District: 0032; FHL microfilm: 1374418. [Source citation includes media item(s)] Roads, Leona Katherine Potts

Citation: Ancestry.com, 1910 United States Federal Census (Provo, UT, USA, Ancestry.com Operations Inc., 2006), Ancestry.com, Year: 1910; Census Place: Chicago Ward 2, Cook, Illinois; Roll: T624_242; Page: 1B; Enumeration District: 0191; FHL microfilm: 1374255. [Source citation includes media item(s)] Elliott, Charles Addison

Citation: Ancestry.com, 1910 United States Federal Census (Provo, UT, USA, Ancestry.com Operations Inc., 2006), Ancestry.com, Year: 1910; Census Place: Chicago Ward 2, Cook, Illinois; Roll: T624_242; Page: 1B; Enumeration District: 0191; FHL microfilm: 1374255. [Source citation includes media item(s)] Roads, Frances Elizabeth

Citation: Ancestry.com, 1910 United States Federal Census (Provo, UT, USA, Ancestry.com Operations Inc., 2006), Ancestry.com, Year: 1910; Census Place: MT Pleasant, Westchester, New York; Roll: T624_1089; Page: 7B; Enumeration District: 0050; FHL microfilm: 1375102. [Source citation includes media item(s)] Elliott, Stella M.

Source Title: **1920 United States Federal Census**
Repository: **Ancestry.com**

Citation: Ancestry.com, 1920 United States Federal Census (Provo, UT, USA, Ancestry.com Operations Inc., 2010), Ancestry.com, Year: 1920; Census Place: Chicago Ward 6, Cook (Chicago), Illinois; Roll: T625_310; Page: 4B; Enumeration District: 348; Image: 386. [Source citation includes media item(s)]. Elliott, Charles Addison.

Citation: Ancestry.com, 1920 United States Federal Census (Provo, UT, USA, Ancestry.com Operations Inc., 2010), Ancestry.com, Year: 1920; Census Place: Chicago Ward 6, Cook (Chicago), Illinois; Roll: T625_310; Page: 4B; Enumeration District: 348; Image: 386. [Source citation includes media item(s)] Roads, Frances Elizabeth.

Citation: Ancestry.com, 1920 United States Federal Census (Provo, UT, USA, Ancestry.com Operations Inc., 2010), Ancestry.com, Year: 1920; Census Place: Mount Pleasant, Henry, Iowa; Roll: T625_493; Page: 3B; Enumeration District: 37; Image: 672. [Source citation includes media item(s)] Roads, Leona Katherine Potts.

Citation: Ancestry.com, 1920 United States Federal Census (Provo, UT, USA, Ancestry.com Operations Inc., 2010), Ancestry.com, Year: 1920; Census Place: Pleasantville, Westchester, New York; Roll: T625_1276; Page: 7A; Enumeration District: 75; Image: 771. [Source citation includes media item(s)] Elliott, Stella M.

Source Title: **1930 United States Federal Census**
Repository: **Ancestry.com**

Citation: Ancestry.com, 1930 United States Federal Census (Provo, UT, USA, Ancestry.com Operations Inc., 2002), Ancestry.com, Year: 1930; Census Place: Chicago, Cook, Illinois; Roll: 422; Page: 4B; Enumeration District: 0203; Image: 1022.0; FHL microfilm: 2340157. [Source citation includes media item(s)] Elliott, Charles Addison

Source Title: **1940 United States Federal Census**
Repository: **Ancestry.com**

Citation: Ancestry.com, 1940 United States Federal Census (Provo, UT, USA, Ancestry.com Operations, Inc., 2012), Ancestry.com, Year: 1940; Census Place: Miami, Dade, Florida; Roll: T627_632; Page: 4B; Enumeration District: 69-119A. [Source citation includes media item(s)] Elliott, Stella M.

Source Title: **Ancestry Family Trees**
Repository: **Ancestry.com**

Citation: Ancestry Family Trees (Online publication - Provo, UT, USA: Ancestry.com. Original data: Family Tree files submitted by Ancestry members.), Ancestry.com, Ancestry Family Tree.

Citation: Ancestry Family Trees (Online publication - Provo, UT, USA: Ancestry.com. Original data: Family Tree files submitted by Ancestry members.), Ancestry.com, Ancestry Family Tree. Elliott, Charles Addison.

Citation: Ancestry Family Trees (Online publication - Provo, UT, USA: Ancestry.com. Original data: Family Tree files submitted by Ancestry members.), Ancestry.com, Ancestry Family Tree. Elliott, Simon Charles .

Citation: Ancestry Family Trees (Online publication - Provo, UT, USA: Ancestry.com. Original data: Family Tree files submitted by Ancestry members.), Ancestry.com, Ancestry Family Tree. McClure, Nancy. Roads, Charles A.

Citation: Ancestry Family Trees (Online publication - Provo, UT, USA: Ancestry.com. Original data: Family Tree files submitted by Ancestry members.), Ancestry.com, Ancestry Family Tree. Roads, Leona Katherine Potts.

Citation: Ancestry Family Trees (Online publication - Provo, UT, USA: Ancestry.com. Original data: Family Tree files submitted by Ancestry members.), Ancestry.com, Ancestry Family Tree.

Citation: Roads, Addison Ancestry Family Trees (Online publication - Provo, UT, USA: Ancestry.com. Original data: Family Tree files submitted by Ancestry members.), Ancestry.com, Ancestry Family Tree. Roads, Frances .

Citation: Elizabeth Ancestry Family Trees (Online publication - Provo, UT, USA: Ancestry.com. Original data: Family Tree files submitted by Ancestry members.), Ancestry.com, Ancestry Family Tree. Elliott, Stella M.

Source Title: **Border Crossings: From Canada to U.S., 1895-1956**
Repository: **Ancestry.com**

Citation: Ancestry.com, Border Crossings: From Canada to U.S., 1895-1956 (Provo, UT, USA, Ancestry.com Operations, Inc., 2010), Ancestry.com, National Archives and Records Administration; Washington, D.C.; Manifests of Passengers Arriving at St. Albans, VT, District through Canadian Pacific and Atlantic Ports, 1895-1954; National Archives Microfilm Publication: M1464; Record Group Title: Records. [Source citation includes media item(s)] Elliott, Charles Addison

Source Title: **California, Passenger and Crew Lists, 1882-1957**
Repository: **Ancestry.com**

Citation: Ancestry.com, California, Passenger and Crew Lists, 1882-1957 (Provo, UT, USA, Ancestry.com Operations Inc., 2008), Ancestry.com. [Source citation includes media item(s)] Elliott, Charles Addison

Source Title: **Civil War Service Index - Union - Iowa at Fold3**
Repository: **www.fold3.com**

Citation: Civil War Service Index - Union - Iowa at Fold3, www.fold3.com, Page 1 - Civil War Service Index - Union - Iowa. http://www.fold3.com/image/298827719/. Elliott, Simon Charles

Source Title: **Cook County, Illinois Death Index, 1908-1988**
Repository: **Ancestry.com**

Citation: Ancestry.com, Cook County, Illinois Death Index, 1908-1988 (Provo, UT, USA, Ancestry.com Operations Inc., 2008), Ancestry.com. Elliott, Charles Addison

Source Title: **Cook County, Illinois, Deaths Index, 1878-1922**
Repository: **Ancestry.com**

Citation: Ancestry.com, Cook County, Illinois, Deaths Index, 1878-1922 (Provo, UT, USA, Ancestry.com Operations, Inc., 2011), Ancestry.com. Roads, Addison

Source Title: **Cook County, Illinois, Marriages Index, 1871-1920**
Repository: **Ancestry.com**

Citation: Ancestry.com, Cook County, Illinois, Marriages Index, 1871-1920 (Provo, UT, USA, Ancestry.com Operations, Inc., 2011), Ancestry.com. Elliott, Charles Addison

Citation: Ancestry.com, Cook County, Illinois, Marriages Index, 1871-1920 (Provo, UT, USA, Ancestry.com Operations, Inc., 2011), Ancestry.com. Elliott, Charles Addison

Source Title: **Illinois, Deaths and Stillbirths Index, 1916-1947**
Repository: **Ancestry.com**

Citation: Ancestry.com, Illinois, Deaths and Stillbirths Index, 1916-1947 (Provo, UT, USA, Ancestry.com Operations, Inc., 2011), Ancestry.com. Elliott, Charles

Citation: Addison Ancestry.com, Illinois, Deaths and Stillbirths Index, 1916-1947 (Provo, UT, USA, Ancestry.com Operations, Inc., 2011), Ancestry.com. Roads, Leona Katherine Potts

Citation: Ancestry.com, Illinois, Deaths and Stillbirths Index, 1916-1947 (Provo, UT, USA, Ancestry.com Operations, Inc., 2011), Ancestry.com. Roads, Frances Elizabeth

Source Title: **Iowa, State Census Collection, 1836-1925**
Repository: **Ancestry.com**

Citation: Ancestry.com, Iowa, State Census Collection, 1836-1925 (Provo, UT, USA, Ancestry.com Operations Inc., 2007), Ancestry.com. [Source citation includes media item(s)] McClure, Nancy

Citation: Ancestry.com, Iowa, State Census Collection, 1836-1925 (Provo, UT, USA, Ancestry.com Operations Inc., 2007), Ancestry.com. [Source citation includes media item(s)] McClure, Nancy

Citation: Ancestry.com, Iowa, State Census Collection, 1836-1925 (Provo, UT, USA, Ancestry.com Operations Inc., 2007), Ancestry.com. [Source citation includes media item(s)] Roads, Leona Katherine Potts

Citation: Ancestry.com, Iowa, State Census Collection, 1836-1925 (Provo, UT, USA, Ancestry.com Operations Inc., 2007), Ancestry.com. [Source citation includes media item(s)] Roads, Leona Katherine Potts

Citation: Ancestry.com, Iowa, State Census Collection, 1836-1925 (Provo, UT, USA, Ancestry.com Operations Inc., 2007), Ancestry.com. [Source citation includes media item(s)] Roads, Addison

Citation: Ancestry.com, Iowa, State Census Collection, 1836-1925 (Provo, UT, USA, Ancestry.com Operations Inc., 2007), Ancestry.com. [Source citation includes media item(s)] Roads, Addison

Citation: Ancestry.com, Iowa, State Census Collection, 1836-1925 (Provo, UT, USA, Ancestry.com Operations Inc., 2007), Ancestry.com. [Source citation includes media item(s)] Roads, Frances Elizabeth

Citation: Ancestry.com, Iowa, State Census Collection, 1836-1925 (Provo, UT, USA, Ancestry.com Operations Inc., 2007), Ancestry.com. [Source citation includes media item(s)] Elliott, Stella M.

Source Title: **Nebraska, State Census Collection, 1860-1885**
Repository: **Ancestry.com**

Citation: Ancestry.com, Nebraska, State Census Collection, 1860-1885 (Provo, UT, USA, Ancestry.com Operations, Inc., 2009), Ancestry.com, Nebraska State Historical Society; Nebraska State Census; Year: 1880; Series/Record Group: RG207; County: Lancaster; Township: Capital; Page: 263. [Source citation includes media item(s)] Elliott, Charles

Citation: Addison Ancestry.com, Nebraska, State Census Collection, 1860-1885 (Provo, UT, USA, Ancestry.com Operations, Inc., 2009), Ancestry.com, Nebraska State Historical Society; Nebraska State Census; Year: 1880; Series/Record Group: RG207; County: Lancaster; Township: Capital; Page: 263. [Source citation includes media item(s)] Elliott, Simon Charles

Citation: Ancestry.com, Nebraska, State Census Collection, 1860-1885 (Provo, UT, USA, Ancestry.com Operations, Inc., 2009), Ancestry.com, Nebraska State Historical Society; Nebraska State Census; Year: 1880; Series/Record Group: RG207; County: Lancaster; Township: Capital; Page: 263. [Source citation includes media item(s)] Elliott, Stella M.

Citation: Ancestry.com, Nebraska, State Census Collection, 1860-1885 (Provo, UT, USA, Ancestry.com Operations, Inc., 2009), Ancestry.com, Nebraska State Historical Society; Nebraska State Census; Year: 1880; Series/Record Group: RG207; County: Lancaster; Township: Capital; Page: 263. [Source citation includes media item(s)] Roads, Frances Elizabeth

Source Title: **New York, Passenger Lists, 1820-1957**
Repository: **Ancestry.com**

Citation: Ancestry.com, New York, Passenger Lists, 1820-1957 (Provo, UT, USA, Ancestry.com Operations, Inc., 2010), Ancestry.com, Year: 1931. [Source citation includes media item(s)] Elliott, Stella M.

Source Title: **New York, State Census, 1915**
Repository: **Ancestry.com**

Citation: Ancestry.com, New York, State Census, 1915 (Provo, UT, USA, Ancestry.com Operations, Inc., 2012), Ancestry.com, New York State Archives; Albany, New York; State Population Census Schedules, 1915; Election District: 10; Assembly District: 03; City: Mount Pleasant; County: Westchester; Page: 09. [Source citation includes media item(s)].Elliott, Stella M.

Citation:	Ancestry.com, New York, State Census, 1915 (Provo, UT, USA, Ancestry.com Operations, Inc., 2012), Ancestry.com, New York State Archives; Albany, New York; State Population Census Schedules, 1915; Election District: 10; Assembly District: 03; City: Mount Pleasant; County: Westchester; Page: 09. [Source citation includes media item(s)] Roads, Frances Elizabeth
Source Title:	**U.S. Passport Applications, 1795-1925**
Repository:	**Ancestry.com**
Citation:	Ancestry.com, U.S. Passport Applications, 1795-1925 (Provo, UT, USA, Ancestry.com Operations, Inc., 2007), Ancestry.com, National Archives and Records Administration (NARA); Washington D.C.; Passport Applications, January 2, 1906 - March 31, 1925; Collection Number: ARC Identifier 583830 / MLR Number A1 534; NARA Series: M1490; Roll #: 533. [Source citation includes media item(s)] Elliott, Charles Addison
Source Title:	**U.S., World War I Draft Registration Cards, 1917-1918**
Repository:	**Ancestry.com**
Citation:	Ancestry.com, U.S., World War I Draft Registration Cards, 1917-1918 (Provo, UT, USA, Ancestry.com Operations Inc., 2005), Ancestry.com, Registration State: Illinois; Registration County: Cook; Roll: 1493511; Draft Board: 18. [Source citation includes media item(s)] Elliott, Charles Addison
Source Title:	**Web: Boyd County, Kentucky, Ashland Daily Independent Obituary Index, 1922- 1945, 1970-1973, 1998-2010**
Repository:	**Ancestry.com**
Citation:	Ancestry.com, Web: Boyd County, Kentucky, Ashland Daily Independent Obituary Index, 1922-1945, 1970-1973, 1998-2010 (Provo, UT, USA, Ancestry.com Operations, Inc., 2011), Ancestry.com. Elliott, Charles Addison
Source Title:	**Web: Illinois, Find A Grave Index, 1809-2012**
Repository:	**Ancestry.com**
Citation:	Ancestry.com, Web: Illinois, Find A Grave Index, 1809-2012 (Provo, UT, USA, Ancestry.com Operations, Inc., 2012), Ancestry.com. Elliott, Charles Addison
Source Title:	**Web: Iowa, Find A Grave Index, 1800-2012**
Repository:	**Ancestry.com**
Citation:	Ancestry.com, Web: Iowa, Find A Grave Index, 1800-2012 (Provo, UT, USA, Ancestry.com Operations, Inc., 2012), Ancestry.com, burial place: Mount Pleasant, Henry County, Iowa, USA birth date: 23 December 1843 birth place: Ohio death date: 1915 death place: New York, New York, New York, United States Name: Simon C. Elliott. http://search.ancestry.com/cgi-bin/sse.dll?db=websearch-3903&h=2717703&ti=0&indiv=try&gss=pt. Elliott, Simon Charles
Citation:	Ancestry.com, Web: Iowa, Find A Grave Index, 1800-2012 (Provo, UT, USA, Ancestry.com Operations, Inc., 2012), Ancestry.com. Roads, Addison.

Chapter 7: Ella Lovenia Stewart

Ella Lovenia Stewart

Ella Lovenia Stewart was born in Pittsburgh, Iowa in 1848 as the second child born to Reverend Isaac Ingersoll Stewart and Mary Robinson Stewart. Civil War military pension records, signed and certified as accurate by Mary R. Stewart, refer to Ella's middle name being spelled as "Lovenia" rather than Lovina, as previously referred to in P.E.O. historical documents. Additionally, the military records reflect a birthdate of 8 October 1848, rather than the May date previously reported in P.E.O. historical accounts.

It is known that Mary Robinson was born in Ireland, but unknown when or how she made her way to Iowa. However, documentation of the marriage of Isaac and Mary refers to Mary as "of the house of Richard Robinson," and it is believed her father was Richard Robinson of Des Moines County, Iowa Territory.

Before marrying Mary, Rev. Stewart, who had started his life in New Jersey as the son of Scoby Stewart and Jane Ingersol, had already lost two wives and four children. In the early years of their marriage, Rev. Stewart's daughter, Emily, only 11 years younger than Mary, is found with the family.

In March of 1829, Ella's grandfather, Scoby Stewart, provided the financing required for the establishment of the Wabash County Courthouse in Mt. Carmel, Illinois. This courthouse remained until it was destroyed by fire in 1857.

When Reverend Isaac I. Stewart was appointed financial agent of the Mt. Pleasant Collegiate Institute in 1852, Ella's family moved to Mt. Pleasant to live in a building called Pioneer Hall. Reverend Stewart was instrumental in the development of the school. In the summer of 1853 Rev. Stewart and James Harlan (who would later become a U.S. Senator and Secretary of the Interior under Andrew Jackson) went door to door for donations to construct what is now the Old Main Building on campus.

Mt. Pleasant Collegiate Institute was initially chartered by an act of the legislature of the Territory of Iowa, on March 15, 1844; just less than two years before Iowa became a state. The articles of association provided for its patronage and supervision under the Methodist Episcopal Church. However, by August of 1844, the trustees of the Institute sought to have the new Iowa Conference of the Methodist Episcopal Church accept responsibilities for the school. At a session of the Iowa Conference in August of 1849, Isaac Stewart, Alcinous Young, Joseph McDowell, Erastus Lathrop, and D. N. Smith were appointed a committee to negotiate with the trustees of the Institute to become the Iowa Conference University. On September 11th the agreement was made; "That the Mt. Pleasant Collegiate Institute shall be recognized as our Conference University, and that we, as a Conference will give the above-named Institute our perpetual patronage." This action was ratified at the next session of the Iowa Conference, on 7 August 1850. Thus, Mt. Pleasant Collegiate Institute changed its name to the Iowa Conference University.

In 1854, Iowa Conference University became Iowa Wesleyan University. And, in 1912, it became Iowa Wesleyan College, as it is known today.

After the funds for the building were assured, the Stewarts, including Ella, lived in parsonages in various southeast and central Iowa locations. Census records from 1860 show the family living in Oskaloosa, Iowa.

Ella's father, Reverend Stewart, died in August of 1864 in Keokuk, Iowa. Pension records found in the National Archives Records for civil war pensions and U.S. Headstone Applications for military veterans, indicate that Reverend Stewart mustered into the Union Army in January of 1863 and was serving as a hospital Chaplin at the Keokuk Iowa Army Post at the time of his death. When he was serving as Chaplin there were five Army hospitals in the area to help care for the sick and wounded soldiers. Further, military pension records contain a letter from a Dr. Taylor, Surgeon U.S. Volunteers, relating his personal knowledge of the facts surrounding the when, where and circumstances of Rev. Stewart's death. According to Dr. Taylor's letter, Rev. Stewart became ill, but did not consult with any medical officer connected with the hospitals where he was serving as Chaplin. Dr. Taylor further stated he was informed that Rev. Stewart "totally ignored the government official and employed a homoeopathist." One might wonder if that homoeopathist was Suela's father, Dr. Clement Pearson, who by that time was living in Mt. Pleasant and at the forefront of homoeopathic medicine.

After the Reverend's death, Mary, Ella's mother, moved Ella, age 16, and her four living siblings, William, Anna, Charles and John Franklin back to Mt. Pleasant. A fifth sibling, Isaac Ingersoll Stewart was born shortly thereafter. Throughout his life, Ella's brother Isaac would be referred to as Harry.

Ella entered Iowa Wesleyan a year later in 1865. While a student at Iowa Wesleyan, Ella wore the Beta pin of her class mate, Dillon Payne. Dillon, a biographer's name you may recognize, is often quoted in "Out of the Heart" the book by Stella Clapp honoring the first hundred years of P.E.O. But, their relationship went no further.

The 1870 Census reflects Ella living with her mother in Mt. Pleasant. It is believed that she is teaching music, specifically offering piano lessons to local students.

It was in 1870, Reverend Thomas E. Corkhill, of Mount Pleasant, Iowa became a member of the Iowa Industrial School Board. The school had initially been established by an act of the Iowa legislature in March of 1868 and was known as the Reform School. It was he who recommended to Ella that she teach at the school. Rev. Corkhill eventually became president of the Industrial School Board in July 1894, five months before Ella's death.

In 1872 the school moved to the Eldora location and admitted boys between the ages seven and 16. They were usually kept until they reached the age of 21. And, in 1880 it became known as the Industrial School for Boys. According to the report written in 1911

"Past and Present of Hardin County, Iowa" and edited by William J. Moir, the Industrial School was "not a prison, but a compulsory educational institution."

The Iowa State Census puts Ella living in Hardin County, Iowa in 1885. Hardin is the County where Eldora, the home of the Iowa Industrial School, is located.

Ella's health deteriorated after she returned in 1891 to help care for her mother. And, in December of 1894 Ella died. Ella Stewart's funeral was held in the old Asbury Church in Mt. Pleasant and was conducted by Mary Allen Stafford's husband, Dr. C.L. Stafford. The funeral procession was made up of many P.E.O.'s from Mt. Pleasant, former school, music and Sunday school students, and many friends.

Years later, a P.E.O. Sister, Lucille M. Boyce Myers (1908-2002), of Eldora, Iowa, suggested naming one of the dormitories after Ella at the Industrial School, now known as the Iowa State Training School for Boys. Thus, Ella Stewart Hall came into being and still exists at the school. This is truly a lasting tribute to the accomplishments of Ella and her pioneering spirit.

Ella's picture was initially hung in the foyer of Ella Stewart Hall. According to Mark Day, superintendent of ISTS, this picture is now on loan to the International Headquarters office of P.E.O. in Des Moines, Iowa.

Mary Stewart, Ella's mother, lived out her life in Mt. Pleasant until her death in 1909 at the age of 87. If we trace the lives of Ella's siblings, we find that only 3 were still living by 1900, Charles, John Franklin and Harry (Isaac I). Charles appears to be the only sibling of Ella's to marry. He and his wife Ella Harding Stewart married in 1879. Thus far four children, thirteen grandchildren and 5 great-grandchildren have been identified as their descendants.

John Franklin makes his way to Douglas, in the Arizona Territory where he works for the Copper Queen Smelter; one of two smelters in the area. Douglas was a town founded in January of 1901 by the International Land & Improvement Company, and named after a Doctor Douglas, the father of the developer, James S. Douglas. Since the Copper Queen smelter did not really begin until March 1904, it's assumed that John found his way to Douglas sometime between 1904 and 1910 as he is found living and working for the smelter by the 1910 Census. Data from 1906 indicates between the two smelters in Douglas at the time, upwards of 1000 men were employed. John dies in Douglas in July 1926. His death certificate indicates he was a foreman for the Copper Queen smelter and was to be buried in El Paso, Texas. Information on this certificate was provided by his brother, Harry Stewart.

In 1900 we find Harry working as a saw mill laborer in Big Eddy, Idaho. Ten years later in 1910, Harry has moved 110 miles south to Culdesac, Idaho, where he is a farmer. However by 1925 Harry has relocated to El Paso, where we find him living up until the time of the 1940 Census.

Ella Lovenia Stewart – Life Events

DATE	EVENT	AGE
8 May 1848	Born Mount Pleasant, Henry, Iowa	
August 1850	Residence: New London, Henry, Iowa	2
1856	Residence: Oskaloosa, Mahaska, Iowa	8
July 1860	Residence: Oskaloosa, Mahaska, Iowa	12
15 August 1864	Father Rev. Isaac I. Stewart died in Keokuk, Iowa	16
September 1865	Entered Iowa Wesleyan	17
21 January 1869	P.E.O. Founded	20
July 1870	Residence: Center, Henry, Iowa	22
July 1880	Residence: Mount Pleasant, Henry, Iowa	32
1884-1892	Taught at Iowa Industrial School in Eldora, Illinois	36-44
1885	Residence: Mount Pleasant, Henry, Iowa	37
1891 or 1892	Returned to Mount Pleasant, Iowa for health reasons	44
12 December 1894	Died Mount Pleasant, Henry, Iowa (lung disorder) Buried: Old Cemetery, Mount Pleasant, Henry, Iowa	46

Descendant Chart for
Stewart Family

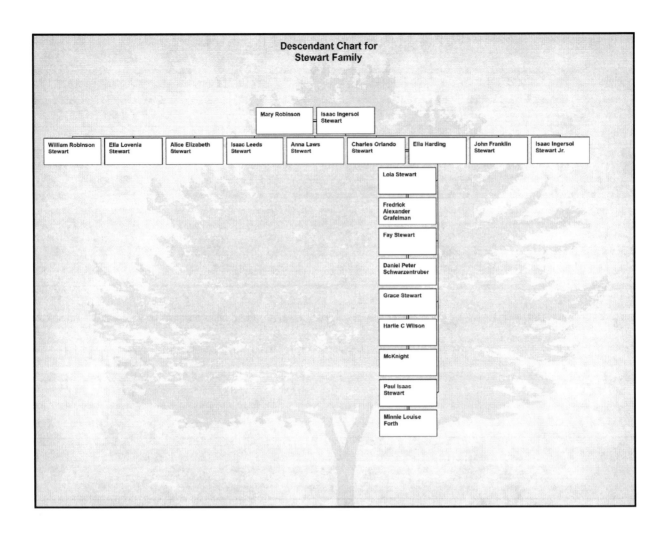

Mary Robinson — Isaac Ingersol Stewart

William Robinson Stewart | Ella Lovenia Stewart | Alice Elizabeth Stewart | Isaac Leeds Stewart | Anna Laws Stewart | Charles Orlando Stewart | Ella Harding | John Franklin Stewart | Isaac Ingersol Stewart Jr.

Lola Stewart

Fredrick Alexander Grafelman

Fay Stewart

Daniel Peter Schwarzentruber

Grace Stewart

Harlie C Wilson

McKnight

Paul Isaac Stewart

Minnie Louise Forth

Combined History of Edwards, Lawrence and Wabash Counties, Illinois. Philadelphia, Pennsylvania: J.L. McDonough &, 1883. Page 121.

William Robinson Stewart, Dubuque,
I. T. December 3, 1845

Ella Lavinia Stewart, Pittsburgh, Iowa.
October 5th 1848.

Alice Elizabeth Stewart, New London, Iowa,
Feby 2, 1851

Isaac Leeds Stewart, Mt Pleasant, Feb. 12, 1853

Annie Laws Stewart, Oskaloosa, April
10, 1855,

Charles Orlando Stewart, Oskaloosa, 14th
November, 1857

John Franklin Stewart, February 1st Oskaloosa, 1860,

Isaac Ingersoll Stewart, Jr Oct. 21st Mt
Pleasant, 1862,

State of Iowa
Henry County ss't Mary R. Stewart
on her oath says that she is the widow
of Isaac I. Stewart, who was Chaplain
of the Military Hospital at Keokuk

National Archives Case Files of approved Pension Applications of Widows and Other Dependents of Civil War Veterans, ca 1861- ca 1910. National Archives Catalog ID 300020, Record Group 15, Fold3 Publication 2008, US Vols., Application Number WC70918, Veteran: Isaac I Stewart, Pensioner: Mary Robinson.

State of Iowa
County of Henry ss. Mary B Stewart on her
oath says that she is unable, as she verily
believes to procure the affidavit of Dr. Coolidge
who professionally attended her at the birth of
her children Anna Laws Stewart, Charles
Claude Stewart, and John Franklin Stewart,
that she caused an affidavit to be sent to said
Dr Coolidge at Stillwater Minn, his post office address,
but the same was returned with an endorsement
thereon that the Dr. was on a visit in Europe.
She has therefore presented affidavits of credible
persons who were present at or near said births.

Mary B. Stewart

Subscribed & sworn to before me by said
Mary B Stewart, at Mt Pleasant Iowa, this
1893.
As witness my hand and
Notarial Seal.

M.R. J. Babb
Notary Public

certificate of
Notarial qualification
on file

National Archives Case Files of approved Pension Applications of Widows and Other Dependents of Civil War Veterans, ca 1861- ca 1910. National Archives Catalog ID 300020, Record Group 15, Fold3 Publication 2008, US Vols., Application Number WC70918, Veteran: Isaac I Stewart, Pensioner: Mary Robinson.

Transcription from military pension application:
National Archives Case Files of approved Pension Applications of Widows and Other Dependents of Civil War Veterans, ca 1861- ca 1910. National Archives Catalog ID 300020, Record Group 15, Fold3 Publication 2008, US Vols., Application Number WC70918, Veteran: Isaac I Stewart, Pensioner: Mary Robinson

William Robinson Stewart, Dubuque, I.T. December 2, 1845

Ella Loveina Stewart, Pittsburgh, Iowa October 8, 1848

Alice Elizabeth Stewart, New London, Iowa Feby 2, 1851

Isaac Leeds Stewart, Mt. Pleasant, Feby 12, 1853

Annie Laws Stewart, Oskaloosa, April 10, 1855

Charles Orlando Stewart, Oskaloosa, 14th November 1857

John Franklin Stewart, February 8th, Oskaloosa, 1860

Isaac Ingersol Stewart Jr. Oct. 28th, Mt. Pleasant, 1864

State of Iowa

Henry County

Mary R. Stewart on her oath says that she is the widow of Isaac I. Stewart who was Chaplain of the Military Hospital at Keokuk

Transcription from military pension records:
National Archives Case Files of approved Pension Applications of Widows and Other Dependents of Civil War Veterans, ca 1861- ca 1910. National Archives Catalog ID 300020, Record Group 15, Fold3 Publication 2008, US Vols., Application Number WC70918, Veteran: Isaac I Stewart, Pensioner: Mary Robinson

State of Iowa,

County of Henry

Mary R. Stewart on her oath says that she is unable, as she verily believes to procure the affidavit of Dr. Coolidge who professionally attended her at the birth of her children Anna Laws Stewart, Charles Orlando Stewart, and John Franklin Stewart; that she caused an affidavit to be such to said Dr. Coolidge at Oskaloosa Iowa, his post office address but the same was returned with an endorsement therein that the Dr. was on a visit in Europe. She has therefore presented affidavits of credible persons who were present at or near said births.

Mary R. Stewart

Subscribed and sworn to before me by said Mary R. Stewart, at Mt. Pleasant, Iowa, this 1873.

As witness my hand and notarial seal

W.I. Babb Notary Public

Certificate of Notarial qualification on file.

ARIZONA STATE BOARD OF HEALTH

STANDARD CERTIFICATE OF DEATH

State File No. _36_

1. PLACE OF DEATH

County _Cochise_ State _____ Registered No. _____

District or Township _Douglas_ or Village _____ or

City _Douglas_ No. _____ St. _____ Ward

(If death occurred in a hospital or institution, give its NAME instead of street and number).

2. FULL NAME _John F. Stewart_

(a) Residence No. _875 12th Douglas_ St. _____ Ward _____

(Usual place of abode) (If non-resident, give city or town and State)

Length of residence in city or town where death occurred _____ yrs. _____ mos. _____ ds. How long in U. S. if of foreign birth? _____ yrs. _____ mos. _____ ds.

PERSONAL AND STATISTICAL PARTICULARS	MEDICAL CERTIFICATE OF DEATH

3. SEX _Male_ **4. COLOR or RACE** _White_ **5. SINGLE, MARRIED, WIDOWED or DIVORCED.** (Write the word) _Single_

5a. If married, widowed, or divorced HUSBAND of (or) WIFE of _____

6. DATE OF BIRTH (month, day and year) _____

7. AGE Years _65_ Months _____ Days _____ IF LESS than 1 day _____ hrs. or _____ min.

8. OCCUPATION OF DECEASED

(a) Trade, profession, or particular kind of work _Foreman_

(b) General nature of industry, business or establishment in which employed (or employer) _Copper Queen_

(c) Name of employer _Smelter_

9. BIRTHPLACE (city or town) (State or country) _Iowa_

10. NAME OF FATHER _Isaac I Stewart_

11. BIRTHPLACE OF FATHER (city or town) (State or country) _Scotland_

12. MAIDEN NAME OF MOTHER _Mary Robinson_

13. BIRTHPLACE OF MOTHER (city or town) (State or country) _Ireland_

14. Informant (Address) _Harry J Stewart_ _Mohler Idaho_

15. Filed _7-16_ 19_25_ _B Causey_ Registrar.

16. DATE OF DEATH (month, day, and year) _July 15th 1925_

17. I HEREBY CERTIFY, That I attended deceased from _July 13_ 1925 to _July 15_ 1925 that I last saw h__ alive on _July 15_ 1925 and that death occurred, on the date stated above, at _8_ P. m.

The CAUSE OF DEATH was as follows:

Cardio Renal disease

(duration) _____ yrs. _____ mos. _____ ds.

CONTRIBUTORY (Secondary) _____

(duration) _____ yrs. _____ mos. _____ ds.

18. Where was disease contracted if not at place of death? _____

Did an operation precede death? _no_ Date of _____

Was there an autopsy? _no_

What test confirmed diagnosis? _Clinical_

(Signed) _B Lowry_ M. D.

_7-18_ 19_25_ (Address) _Douglas, Ariz_

State the Disease Causing Death, or in deaths from Violent Causes, state (1) Means and Nature of Injury, and (2) whether Accidental, Suicidal, or Homicidal. (See reverse side for additional space.)

19. PLACE OF BURIAL, CREMATION OR REMOVAL _El Paso Texas_ **DATE OF BURIAL** _7/20/25_

20. UNDERTAKER _Poate & Ivee_ **ADDRESS** _Douglas Ariz_

"Genealogy.az.gov-Arizona Genealogy Birth and Death Certificates." *Genealogy.az.gov-Arizona Genealogy Birth and Death Certificates.* Web. 19 Jan 2014

Photo Album for Ella Lovenia Stewart

Ella Lovenia Stewart

Birth:	08 Oct 1848	Father:	Isaac Ingersol Stewart
Death:	12 Dec 1894	Mother:	Mary Robinson
Marriage:		Spouse:	

Ella Lovenia Stewart

Reproduction of oil portrait by Marion Dunlap Harper, unveiled in P.E.O. Memorial Hall in Mount Pleasant, Iowa, on September 23, 1929.

Ella Lovenia Stewart

Birth:	08 Oct 1848	Father:	Isaac Ingersol Stewart
Death:	12 Dec 1894	Mother:	Mary Robinson
Marriage:		Spouse:	

Ella Lovenia Stewart

Printed with permission from Evan Jones.

Historical Background Sources
for Ella Lovenia Stewart

1.   1850 United States Federal Census: Census Place: *New London, Henry, Iowa*: Roll: M432_184; Page 164A; Image 71.

2.   1860 United States Federal Census: Census Place: *Oskaloosa, Mahaska, Iowa*; Roll; m563_334: Page 148: Image: 268; Family History Library Film: 803334.

3.   1870 United States Federal Census: Census Place; *Center, Henry, Iowa*; Roll: M593_395; Page: 184B; Image: 373; Family History Library Film: 545894.

4.   1880 United States Federal Census: Census Place: *Mt. Pleasant, Henry, Iowa*; Roll; 344; Family history Film: 1254344; Page: 326A; Enumeration District: 095; Image 0214.

5.   1895 *Iowa, State Census* (database on-line). Provo, UT, USA: Ancestry.com Operations Inc. 2003. Original data: Iowa: *1895 Iowa State Census*, Des Moines, Iowa: State Historical Society of Iowa.

6.   Ancestry.com, *Iowa State Census Collection*. 1836-1925 (database on-line). Provo, UT, USA; Ancestry.com Operations Inc. 2007 Original data: Microfilm of Iowa State Censuses, 1856, 1885, 1895, 1905, 1915, 1925 as well various special censuses from 1836-1897 obtained from the State Historical Society of Iowa via Heritage Quest.

7.   Case Files of Approved Pension Applications of Widows and Other Dependents of Civil War Veterans, ca 1861-1910, Isaac I. Stewart, National Archives Records, www.fold3.com.

8.   Clapp, Stella. *Out of the Heart A Century of P.E.O. 1869-1969*. Des Moines, Iowa: P.E.O. Sisterhood, 1968.

9.   *Combined History of Edwards, Lawrence and Wabash Counties, Illinois*. Philadelphia, Pennsylvania: J.L. McDonough &, 1883. 120-21.

10. Garrels, Elizabeth E. *A Dream Come True*. Rep. Print. P.E.O. Conference 1996.

11. "Genealogy.az.gov-Arizona Genealogy Birth and Death Certificates."*Genealogy.az.gov-Arizona Genealogy Birth and Death Certificates*. Web. 19 Jan 2014.

12. Hull, Druscilla J., ed. *Iowa Wesleyan College, Old Main Building*. Rep. Washington, DC: National Parks Service, Print.

13. Hayostek, Cindy. *Images of America Douglas*. San Francisco, CA: Arcadia, 2009.

14. James, Henry Lee. *History of the Stewart or Stuart Family*. New York, New York: R.L. Polk and Company, Inc. 1920. p94.

15. Johnson, Heidi, ed. "A Society of Our Own." *The P.E.O. Record* (1997):

16. "List of Officers of the Army of the United States from 1779 to 1900, Embracing a Register of All Appointments by the President of the United States in the Volunteer Service During the Civil War, and of Volunteer Officers in the Service of the United States: June 1, 1900 (Google EBook)."*Google Books*. 30 Nov. 2013.

17. Moir, William J."Past and Present of Hardin County Iowa."(1911).

18. "P.E.O. Sisterhood in Convention." *The Oelwein Daily Register* [Oelwein, Iowa] 14 May 1925: p6.

19. Wood, James, I.N. Kinsey, F.B. Dorr, and A.A. Cohn. "Douglas, Arizona, The Smelter City of the Southwest." *The National Magazine* XXII (1905): 572-77.

Stewart Family Descendant Chart
Source Report

Source Title: **1850 United States Federal Census**
Repository: **Ancestry.com**

Citation: Ancestry.com, 1850 United States Federal Census (Provo, UT, USA, Ancestry.com Operations, Inc., 2009), Ancestry.com, Year: 1850; Census Place: New London, Henry, Iowa; Roll: M432_184; Page: 164A; Image: 71. [Source citation includes media item(s)] Stewart, Ella Lovenia

Source Title: **1850 United States Federal Census**
Repository: **Ancestry.com**

Citation: Ancestry.com, 1850 United States Federal Census (Provo, UT, USA, Ancestry.com Operations, Inc., 2009), Ancestry.com, Year: 1850; Census Place: New London, Henry, Iowa; Roll: M432_184; Page: 164A; Image: 71. [Source citation includes media item(s)] Stewart, William Robinson

Citation: Ancestry.com, 1850 United States Federal Census (Provo, UT, USA, Ancestry.com Operations, Inc., 2009), Ancestry.com, Year: 1850; Census Place: New London, Henry, Iowa; Roll: M432_184; Page: 164A; Image: 71. [Source citation includes media item(s)] Robinson, Mary

Citation: Ancestry.com, 1850 United States Federal Census (Provo, UT, USA, Ancestry.com Operations, Inc., 2009), Ancestry.com, Year: 1850; Census Place: New London, Henry, Iowa; Roll: M432_184; Page: 164A; Image: 71. [Source citation includes media item(s)] Stewart, Isaac Ingersol

Source Title: **1860 United States Federal Census**
Repository: **Ancestry.com**

Citation: Ancestry.com, 1860 United States Federal Census (Provo, UT, USA, Ancestry.com Operations, Inc., 2009), Ancestry.com, Year: 1860; Census Place: Oskaloosa, Mahaska, Iowa; Roll: M653_334; Page: 148; Image: 268; Family History Library Film: 803334. [Source citation includes media item(s)] Stewart, William Robinson

Citation: Ancestry.com, 1860 United States Federal Census (Provo, UT, USA, Ancestry.com Operations, Inc., 2009), Ancestry.com, Year: 1860; Census Place: Oskaloosa, Mahaska, Iowa; Roll: M653_334; Page: 148; Image: 268; Family History Library Film: 803334. [Source citation includes media item(s)] Stewart, John Franklin

Citation: Ancestry.com, 1860 United States Federal Census (Provo, UT, USA, Ancestry.com Operations, Inc., 2009), Ancestry.com, Year: 1860; Census Place: Oskaloosa, Mahaska, Iowa; Roll: M653_334; Page: 148; Image: 268; Family History Library Film: 803334. [Source citation includes media item(s)] Stewart, Charles Orlando

Citation: Ancestry.com, 1860 United States Federal Census (Provo, UT, USA, Ancestry.com Operations, Inc., 2009), Ancestry.com, Year: 1860; Census Place: Oskaloosa, Mahaska, Iowa; Roll: M653_334; Page: 148; Image: 268; Family History Library Film: 803334. [Source citation includes media item(s)] Stewart, Anna Laws

Citation: Ancestry.com, 1860 United States Federal Census (Provo, UT, USA, Ancestry.com Operations, Inc., 2009), Ancestry.com, Year: 1860; Census Place: Oskaloosa, Mahaska, Iowa; Roll: M653_334; Page: 148; Image: 268; Family History Library Film: 803334. [Source citation includes media item(s)] Robinson, Mary

Citation: Ancestry.com, 1860 United States Federal Census (Provo, UT, USA, Ancestry.com Operations, Inc., 2009), Ancestry.com, Year: 1860; Census Place: Oskaloosa, Mahaska, Iowa; Roll: M653_334; Page: 148; Image: 268; Family History Library Film: 803334. [Source citation includes media item(s)] Stewart, Isaac Ingersol

Citation: Ancestry.com, 1860 United States Federal Census (Provo, UT, USA, Ancestry.com Operations, Inc., 2009), Ancestry.com, Year: 1860; Census Place: Oskaloosa, Mahaska, Iowa; Roll: M653_334; Page: 148; Image: 268; Family History Library Film: 803334. [Source citation includes media item(s)] Stewart, Ella Lovenia

Source Title: **1870 United States Federal Census**
Repository: **Ancestry.com**

Citation: Ancestry.com, 1870 United States Federal Census (Provo, UT, USA, Ancestry.com Operations, Inc., 2009), Ancestry.com, Year: 1870; Census Place: Center, Henry, Iowa; Roll: M593_395; Page: 184B; Image: 373; Family History Library Film: 545894. [Source citation includes media item(s)] Stewart, Isaac Ingersol Jr.

Citation: Ancestry.com, 1870 United States Federal Census (Provo, UT, USA, Ancestry.com Operations, Inc., 2009), Ancestry.com, Year: 1870; Census Place: Center, Henry, Iowa; Roll: M593_395; Page: 184B; Image: 373; Family History Library Film: 545894. [Source citation includes media item(s)] Stewart, John Franklin

Citation: Ancestry.com, 1870 United States Federal Census (Provo, UT, USA, Ancestry.com Operations, Inc., 2009), Ancestry.com, Year: 1870; Census Place: Center, Henry, Iowa; Roll: M593_395; Page: 184B; Image: 373; Family History Library Film: 545894. [Source citation includes media item(s)] Stewart, Charles Orlando

Citation: Ancestry.com, 1870 United States Federal Census (Provo, UT, USA, Ancestry.com Operations, Inc., 2009), Ancestry.com, Year: 1870; Census Place: Center, Henry, Iowa; Roll: M593_395; Page: 184B; Image: 373; Family History Library Film: 545894. [Source citation includes media item(s)] Stewart, Anna Laws

Citation: Ancestry.com, 1870 United States Federal Census (Provo, UT, USA, Ancestry.com Operations, Inc., 2009), Ancestry.com, Year: 1870; Census Place: Center, Henry, Iowa; Roll: M593_395; Page: 184B; Image: 373; Family History Library Film: 545894. [Source citation includes media item(s)] Robinson, Mary

Source Title: **1870 United States Federal Census**
Repository: **Ancestry.com**

Citation: Ancestry.com, 1870 United States Federal Census (Provo, UT, USA, Ancestry.com Operations, Inc., 2009), Ancestry.com, Year: 1870; Census Place: Center, Henry, Iowa; Roll: M593_395; Page: 184B; Image: 373; Family History Library Film: 545894. [Source citation includes media item(s)] Stewart, Ella Lovenia

Source Title: **1880 United States Federal Census**
Repository: **Ancestry.com**

Citation: Ancestry.com and The Church of Jesus Christ of Latter-day Saints, 1880 United States Federal Census (Provo, UT, USA, Ancestry.com Operations Inc., 2010), Ancestry.com, Year: 1880; Census Place: MT Pleasant, Henry, Iowa; Roll: 344; Family History Film: 1254344; Page: 326A; Enumeration District: 095; Image: 0214. [Source citation includes media item(s)] Robinson, Mary Stewart, Ella Lovenia Stewart, Isaac Ingersol

Citation: Ancestry.com and The Church of Jesus Christ of Latter-day Saints, 1880 United States Federal Census (Provo, UT, USA, Ancestry.com Operations Inc., 2010), Ancestry.com, Year: 1880; Census Place: MT Pleasant, Henry, Iowa; Roll: 344; Family History Film: 1254344; Page: 326A; Enumeration District: 095; Image: 0214. Record for Ella L. Stewart. [Source citation includes media item(s)] Stewart, Ella Lovenia

Citation: Ancestry.com and The Church of Jesus Christ of Latter-day Saints, 1880 United States Federal Census (Provo, UT, USA, Ancestry.com Operations Inc., 2010), Ancestry.com, Year: 1880; Census Place: MT Pleasant, Henry, Iowa; Roll: 344; Family History Film: 1254344; Page: 326A; Enumeration District: 095; Image: 0214. Record for Ella L. Stewart. [Source citation includes media item(s)] Robinson, Mary

Citation: Ancestry.com and The Church of Jesus Christ of Latter-day Saints, 1880 United States Federal Census (Provo, UT, USA, Ancestry.com Operations Inc., 2010), Ancestry.com, Year: 1880; Census Place: MT Pleasant, Henry, Iowa; Roll: 344; Family History Film: 1254344; Page: 326A; Enumeration District: 095; Image: 0214. [Source citation includes media item(s)] Stewart, Isaac Ingersol Jr.

Citation: Ancestry.com and The Church of Jesus Christ of Latter-day Saints, 1880 United States Federal Census (Provo, UT, USA, Ancestry.com Operations Inc., 2010), Ancestry.com, Year: 1880; Census Place: MT Pleasant, Henry, Iowa; Roll: 344; Family History Film: 1254344; Page: 326A; Enumeration District: 095; Image: 0214. [Source citation includes media item(s)] Stewart, Anna Laws

Citation: Ancestry.com and The Church of Jesus Christ of Latter-day Saints, 1880 United States Federal Census (Provo, UT, USA, Ancestry.com Operations Inc., 2010), Ancestry.com, Year: 1880; Census Place: MT Pleasant, Henry, Iowa; Roll: 344; Family History Film: 1254344; Page: 339C; Enumeration District: 096; Image: 0240. [Source citation includes media item(s)] Stewart, Charles Orlando

Source Title: 1900 United States Federal Census
Repository: Ancestry.com

Citation: Ancestry.com, 1900 United States Federal Census (Provo, UT, USA, Ancestry.com Operations Inc., 2004), Ancestry.com, Year: 1900; Census Place: Big Eddy, Nez Perce, Idaho; Roll: 234; Page: 24B; Enumeration District: 0083; FHL microfilm: 1240234. [Source citation includes media item(s)] Stewart, Isaac Ingersol Jr.

Citation: Ancestry.com, 1900 United States Federal Census (Provo, UT, USA, Ancestry.com Operations Inc., 2004), Ancestry.com, Year: 1900; Census Place: Center, Henry, Iowa; Roll: 436; Page: 6B; Enumeration District: 0030; FHL microfilm: 1240436. [Source citation includes media item(s)] Robinson, Mary

Citation: Ancestry.com, 1900 United States Federal Census (Provo, UT, USA, Ancestry.com Operations Inc., 2004), Ancestry.com, Year: 1900; Census Place: Charleston, Lee, Iowa; Roll: 442; Page: 2B; Enumeration District: 0056; FHL microfilm: 1240442. [Source citation includes media item(s)] Stewart, Charles Orlando

Citation: Ancestry.com, 1900 United States Federal Census (Provo, UT, USA, Ancestry.com Operations Inc., 2004), Ancestry.com, Year: 1900; Census Place: Charleston, Lee, Iowa; Roll: 442; Page: 2B; Enumeration District: 0056; FHL microfilm: 1240442. [Source citation includes media item(s)]

Citation: Ancestry.com, 1900 United States Federal Census (Provo, UT, USA, Ancestry.com Operations Inc., 2004), Ancestry.com, Year: 1900; Census Place: Charleston, Lee, Iowa; Roll: 442; Page: 2B; Enumeration District: 0056; FHL microfilm: 1240442. [Source citation includes media item(s)] Stewart, Charles Orlando

Source Title: 1910 United States Federal Census
Repository: Ancestry.com

Citation: Ancestry.com, 1910 United States Federal Census (Provo, UT, USA, Ancestry.com Operations Inc., 2006), Ancestry.com, Year: 1910; Census Place: Aurora Ward 7, Kane, Illinois; Roll: T624_296; Page: 1B; Enumeration District: 0041; FHL microfilm: 1374309. [Source citation includes media item(s)] Stewart, Charles Orlando

Citation: Ancestry.com, 1910 United States Federal Census (Provo, UT, USA, Ancestry.com Operations Inc., 2006), Ancestry.com, Year: 1910; Census Place: Culdesac, Nez Perce, Idaho; Roll: T624_226; Page: 12A; Enumeration District: 0215; FHL microfilm: 1374239. [Source citation includes media item(s)] Stewart, Isaac Ingersol Jr.

Citation: Ancestry.com, 1910 United States Federal Census (Provo, UT, USA, Ancestry.com Operations Inc., 2006), Ancestry.com, Year: 1910; Census Place: Douglas Ward 1, Cochise, Arizona; Roll: T624_38; Page: 8B; Enumeration District: 0018; FHL microfilm: 1374051. [Source citation includes media item(s)] Stewart, John Franklin

Source Title: **1920 United States Federal Census**
Repository: **Ancestry.com**

Citation: Ancestry.com, 1920 United States Federal Census (Provo, UT, USA, Ancestry.com Operations Inc., 2010), Ancestry.com, Year: 1920; Census Place: Douglas Ward 5, Cochise, Arizona; Roll: T625_47; Page: 12A; Enumeration District: 24; Image: 153. [Source citation includes media item(s)] Stewart, John Franklin

Source Title: **1930 United States Federal Census**
Repository: **Ancestry.com**

Citation: Ancestry.com, 1930 United States Federal Census (Provo, UT, USA, Ancestry.com Operations Inc., 2002), Ancestry.com, Year: 1930; Census Place: El Paso, El Paso, Texas; Roll: 2329; Page: 7A; Enumeration District: 0064; Image: 284.0; FHL microfilm: 2342063. [Source citation includes media item(s)] Stewart, Isaac Ingersol Jr.

Source Title: **1940 United States Federal Census**
Repository: **Ancestry.com**

Citation: Ancestry.com, 1940 United States Federal Census (Provo, UT, USA, Ancestry.com Operations, Inc., 2012), Ancestry.com, Year: 1940; Census Place: El Paso, El Paso, Texas; Roll: T627_4181; Page: 88A; Enumeration District: 256-28. [Source citation includes media item(s)] Stewart, Isaac Ingersol Jr.

Source Title: **Ancestry Family Trees**
Repository: **Ancestry.com**

Citation: Ancestry Family Trees (Online publication - Provo, UT, USA: Ancestry.com. Original data: Family Tree files submitted by Ancestry members.), Ancestry.com, Ancestry Family Tree. Stewart, William Robinson

Citation: Ancestry Family Trees (Online publication - Provo, UT, USA: Ancestry.com. Original data: Family Tree files submitted by Ancestry members.), Ancestry.com, Ancestry Family Tree. Stewart, Charles Orlando

Citation: Ancestry Family Trees (Online publication - Provo, UT, USA: Ancestry.com. Original data: Family Tree files submitted by Ancestry members.), Ancestry.com, Ancestry Family Tree. Stewart, Anna Laws

Citation: Ancestry Family Trees (Online publication - Provo, UT, USA: Ancestry.com. Original data: Family Tree files submitted by Ancestry members.), Ancestry.com, Ancestry Family Tree. Stewart, Ella Lovenia

Citation: Ancestry Family Trees (Online publication - Provo, UT, USA: Ancestry.com. Original data: Family Tree files submitted by Ancestry members.), Ancestry.com, Ancestry Family Tree. Robinson, Mary

Citation: Ancestry Family Trees (Online publication - Provo, UT, USA: Ancestry.com. Original data: Family Tree files submitted by Ancestry members.), Ancestry.com, Ancestry Family Tree. Stewart, Isaac Ingersol

Citation:	Ancestry Family Trees (Online publication - Provo, UT, USA: Ancestry.com. Original data: Family Tree files submitted by Ancestry members.), Ancestry.com, Ancestry Family Tree. Stewart, Isaac Ingersol Jr.
Citation:	Ancestry Family Trees (Online publication - Provo, UT, USA: Ancestry.com. Original data: Family Tree files submitted by Ancestry members.), Ancestry.com, Ancestry Family Tree. Stewart, John Franklin

Source Title: Civil War
Repository: www.fold3.com

Citation:	Civil War, www.fold3.com, Page 2 - Civil War. http://www.fold3.com/image/271231527/. Stewart, Isaac Ingersol
Citation:	Civil War, www.fold3.com, Page 26 - Civil War. http://www.fold3.com/image/271231826/. Stewart, Isaac Ingersol
Citation:	Civil War, www.fold3.com, Page 27 - Civil War. http://www.fold3.com/image/271231832/. Stewart, Isaac Ingersol
Citation:	Civil War, www.fold3.com, Page 29 - Civil War. http://www.fold3.com/image/271231844/. Robinson, Mary
Citation:	Civil War, www.fold3.com, Page 38 - Civil War. http://www.fold3.com/image/271231872/. Stewart, Charles Orlando
Citation:	Civil War, www.fold3.com, Page 44 - Civil War. http://www.fold3.com/image/271231891/. Robinson, Mary
Citation:	Civil War, www.fold3.com, Page 49 - Civil War. http://www.fold3.com/image/271231910/. Stewart, Charles Orlando
Citation:	Civil War, www.fold3.com, Page 49 - Civil War. http://www.fold3.com/image/271231910/. Stewart, Anna Laws
Citation:	Civil War, www.fold3.com, Page 6 - Civil War. http://www.fold3.com/image/271231542/. Stewart, Isaac Ingersol
Citation:	Civil War, www.fold3.com, Page 7 - Civil War. http://www.fold3.com/image/271231545/. Robinson, Mary
Citation:	Civil War, www.fold3.com, Page 7 - Civil War. http://www.fold3.com/image/271231545/. Stewart, Isaac Ingersol
Citation:	Civil War, www.fold3.com, Page 9 - Civil War. http://www.fold3.com/image/271231555/. Robinson, Mary

Source Title: Civil War and Later Veterans Pension Index at Fold3
Repository: www.fold3.com

Citation:	Civil War and Later Veterans Pension Index at Fold3, www.fold3.com, Stewart, Isaac I. - Civil War and Later Veterans Pension Index. http://www.fold3.com/image/24263829/. Stewart, Isaac Ingersol

Source Title: Iowa, State Census Collection, 1836-1925
Repository: Ancestry.com

Citation:	Ancestry.com, Iowa, State Census Collection, 1836-1925 (Provo, UT, USA, Ancestry.com Operations Inc., 2007), Ancestry.com. [Source citation includes media item(s)] Stewart, William Robinson

Citation: Ancestry.com, Iowa, State Census Collection, 1836-1925 (Provo, UT, USA, Ancestry.com Operations Inc., 2007), Ancestry.com. [Source citation includes media item(s)] Stewart, Isaac Ingersol Jr.

Citation: Ancestry.com, Iowa, State Census Collection, 1836-1925 (Provo, UT, USA, Ancestry.com Operations Inc., 2007), Ancestry.com. [Source citation includes media item(s)] Stewart, Anna Laws

Citation: Ancestry.com, Iowa, State Census Collection, 1836-1925 (Provo, UT, USA, Ancestry.com Operations Inc., 2007), Ancestry.com. [Source citation includes media item(s)] Stewart, Anna Laws

Citation: Ancestry.com, Iowa, State Census Collection, 1836-1925 (Provo, UT, USA, Ancestry.com Operations Inc., 2007), Ancestry.com. [Source citation includes media item(s)] Robinson, Mary

Citation: Ancestry.com, Iowa, State Census Collection, 1836-1925 (Provo, UT, USA, Ancestry.com Operations Inc., 2007), Ancestry.com. [Source citation includes media item(s)] Robinson, Mary

Citation: Ancestry.com, Iowa, State Census Collection, 1836-1925 (Provo, UT, USA, Ancestry.com Operations Inc., 2007), Ancestry.com. [Source citation includes media item(s)] Stewart, Isaac Ingersol

Source Title: Iowa, State Census Collection, 1836-1925
Repository: Ancestry.com

Citation: Ancestry.com, Iowa, State Census Collection, 1836-1925 (Provo, UT, USA, Ancestry.com Operations Inc., 2007), Ancestry.com. [Source citation includes media item(s)] Robinson, Mary

Citation: Ancestry.com, Iowa, State Census Collection, 1836-1925 (Provo, UT, USA, Ancestry.com Operations Inc., 2007), Ancestry.com. [Source citation includes media item(s)] Stewart, Ella Lovenia

Source Title: Iowa, State Census, 1895
Repository: Ancestry.com

Citation: Ancestry.com, Iowa, State Census, 1895 (Provo, UT, USA, Ancestry.com Operations Inc., 2003), Ancestry.com. Stewart, Ella Lovenia

Source Title: New Orleans, Passenger Lists, 1813-1945
Repository: Ancestry.com

Citation: Ancestry.com, New Orleans, Passenger Lists, 1813-1945 (Provo, UT, USA, Ancestry.com Operations, Inc., 2006), Ancestry.com, Passenger Lists of Vessels Arriving at New Orleans, Louisiana, 1903-1945; Series: T905; Roll #: 175. [Source citation includes media item(s)] Stewart, Isaac Ingersol Jr.

Source Title: U.S., Headstone Applications for Military Veterans, 1925-1963
Repository: Ancestry.com

Citation: Ancestry.com, U.S., Headstone Applications for Military Veterans, 1925-1963 (Provo, UT, USA, Ancestry.com Operations, Inc., 2012), Ancestry.com. [Source citation includes media item(s)] Stewart, Isaac Ingersol

Source Title: Web: Iowa, Find A Grave Index, 1800-2012
Repository: Ancestry.com

Citation: Ancestry.com, Web: Iowa, Find A Grave Index, 1800-2012 (Provo, UT, USA, Ancestry.com Operations, Inc., 2012), Ancestry.com. Stewart, Anna Laws

Citation: Ancestry.com, Web: Iowa, Find A Grave Index, 1800-2012 (Provo, UT, USA, Ancestry.com Operations, Inc., 2012), Ancestry.com. Stewart, Isaac Ingersol

Source Title: Web: Iowa, Find A Grave Index, 1800-2012
Repository: Ancestry.com

Citation: Ancestry.com, Web: Iowa, Find A Grave Index, 1800-2012 (Provo, UT, USA, Ancestry.com Operations, Inc., 2012), Ancestry.com. Stewart, Ella Lovenia

Made in the USA
San Bernardino, CA
21 January 2017